Nall's G

East Anglian Dialect

Reprinted from the second volume of 'Chapters on the East Anglian Coast', first published in 1866,

by

John Greaves Nall

'History and the aspect of the country show Eastern Norfolk to have been a well cultivated and enclosed district from a very early period. Isolated on three sides by wide heaths, marshes, and the sea, it was almost severed from its neighbours. Peopled by a primitive race of small farmers, many of whom cultivated their own lands, it possessed the conditions most favourable for the perpetuation of localized speech and usages.'

Larks Press

Published by the Larks Press
Ordnance Farmhouse, Guist Bottom, Dereham,
Norfolk NR20 5PF
01328 829207
Larks.Press@btinternet.com
Website: www.booksatlarkspress.co.uk

Printed by the Lanceni Press,
Garrood Drive, Fakenham, Norfolk

November 2006

Nall's *Chapters on the East Anglian Coast* in two volumes was first published in 1866 by Longmans, Green, Reader and Dyer.

British Library Cataloguing–in-Publication Data
A catalogue record for this book is available
from the British Library

ISBN 1 904006 34 5

Editors' Introduction

Preliminary investigations had revealed practically no information about John Greaves Nall other than his birth in 1826 and death in June 1876 when, thanks to the efforts of the staff of the Heriatge Centre in Norwich, the following article was uncovered, written 22 years after his death by James Hooper.

Eastern Daily Press Tuesday, 14 June, 1898

In the year 1866 was published one of the fullest, one of the most learned, one of the most interesting works which ever dealt with East Anglian matters, with the history, topography, and language of any part of Eastern England. A book of 728 closely printed pages, of which every page is interesting, yet I doubt if there are half-a-dozen men living who know even the barest outlines of the author's life, such is the swift forgetfulness, such the cold neglect which effaces the memory of a laborious worker, who did immense service as a local historian and as a local glossarist for Suffolk and Norfolk. The title of the work deserves to be given in full, for its promise is amply fulfilled:–"Great Yarmouth and Lowestoft. A handbook for visitors and residents; with chapters on the Archaeology, Natural History, &c., of the District; a history, with statistics, of the East Coast Herring Fishery, and an Etymological and Comparative Glossary of the Dialect of East Anglia."

This comprehensive work is divided into two parts, the second part, of over 320 pages, containing a very elaborate disquisition on East Anglian Dialect and Provincialisms, together with a glossary which has by no means been superseded by any subsequent work, indeed no one should affect to discuss any East Anglian words or phrases without consulting Nall. He may, and of course does, sometimes err, but he always says something worth saying, and worth considering, about every locution with which he deals. So full of learning is he that he seems to find it difficult to exhaust his stores of information. His chapters on the fisheries, and especially on the herring, teem with out-of-the-way lore. Herring cookery, herring heraldry, herring proverbs, there seems no end to the divagations of the author's versatile and facile pen. Dainty recipes from France jostle pawky songs from over the border, and we have no sooner ceased laughing at a jingling Macaronic Latin verse in praise of King Herring, than we are plunged into a series of herring remedies culled from recondite works by erudite Teutonic and mediæval Sangrados. Here, for instance, is a charming prescription from Dr Solas Dodd, 1753:– "Take the oile pressed out of fresh herrings, a pint, a boar's gall, juices of henbane, hemlock, arsel, lettuce and wild catmint, each six ounces; mix, boil well, and put into a glass vessel, stoppered. Take three spoonsfuls and put into a quart of warm ale, and let the person to undergo any operation, drink of this by an ounce at a time, till he falls asleep, which sleep will continue the space of three or four hours, and all that time he will be unsensible of anything done to him." We can well believe it! Most people we fancy would rather undergo any operation in full consciousness than imbibe so horrible a drench.

Our Norfolk Archbishop Herring carried herrings in his *armes pailantes* to the primatial See of Canterbury, and the Cobbs of Sandringham, bore little herrings, known as *cobs*, on their blazon.

In his glossary Nall sometimes has quite a considerable article on a single word, with abundant illustrations and arguments; thus treating of the word *pheesy*, irritable, &c., he devoted five pages of small print to its elucidation.

But what of the man himself? John Greaves Nall was born at Bakewell on the Wye, in Derbyshire, in the year 1826. His mother, a devout Churchwoman, and a woman of cultivated mind and refined tastes, died young, leaving six children, but had always expressed a desire that John should be trained for the Church. To fulfil her wishes he was sent to King William College, Isle of Man, preparatory to entering one of the Universities. At this school he displayed exceptional ability, worked very hard, and was remarkable for his retentive memory. Unfortunately, through the stoppage of a bank, his father suffered heavy losses, so that John had to be apprenticed to a business. When 20 years old he went to London as an assistant to the well-known publisher, H.G.Bohn, in York Street, Covent Garden, where he remained until Dickens started *Household Words*, when he joined the publishing staff of the great novelist. In 1850 Nall started business for himself in Bedford as printer and bookseller, and frequently gave lectures in the Town Hall there, chiefly historical and descriptive sketches of the old masters and their works. He also formed a fine collection of valuable engravings and of old china. It was during his residence at Bedford that Nall wrote his great work, for such in truth it is. His custom was to spend many of his holidays in Norfolk and Suffolk, when he visited churches and any other ancient buildings, taking careful notes from tombstones and other available records. He ransacked old curiosity shops (more remunerative then than now), talked with farmers, fishermen, and people of all sorts, delighting to stroll through the markets to take notes of character and dialect, besides most industriously searching through libraries for information likely to serve his turn.

In 1864 he left Bedford and bought a printing business in Mark Lane, which turned out a sad failure, though he manfully tried to turn it to good account. All his endeavours proving vain he gave it up in 1867, or thereabouts, and went to Rotterdam with his wife and children, but within a year moved to Frankfort on the Maine, where he left his family and went on a protracted tour through Belgium, Holland, Norway, Sweden, Russia,

Austria, Hungary, and Italy. There is a long letter of his extant, dated 4th October, 1868, in which he gives a vivid description of the chief places he visited, and the characteristics of the people. In 1869 he returned to Frankfort, but only to set out almost immediately on a journey through Northern Germany.

On the outbreak of the Franco-Prussian war he acted as a correspondent for the *Times* and the *Graphic*, and, while thus occupied, was on one occasion arrested as a spy together with a Frenchman; the two suspects were bundled into a wretched cell, where Nall was detained three days until a telegram from the British Consul at Frankfort procured his release. His less fortunate companion was incontinently shot.

A few months after peace was proclaimed, he returned with his family to England, but shortly after started off to South America. On December 4th, 1871, he wrote:– "I have been in Rio Janeiro six weeks, and in a day or two intend to leave for the River Plate. Beautiful as the scenery here is I do not like this climate, it is too hot." Next, in 1873, we still find him globe-trotting, this time to North America, the East Indies, China, and Japan, after which extended journeying he returned to England, but only for a few months' rest. In the winter of 1875 he left England for the last time, and went again to South America. His last letter to his wife was from Monte Video, and in it he complained of "very indifferent health," but hoped the rest on the steamer to Valparaiso would benefit him. The next news was of his death in Valparaiso, at the comparatively early age of 51.

John Greaves Nall was a good linguist, speaking and writing fluently in French, German, and Dutch, and able to converse in Spanish and Italian.

Few people who consult the familiar squat thick volume written by him have any idea what a varied and adventurous life he led. Probably most of his readers would be prone to assume that he was a native, or at least a resident, of Yarmouth, but he tells us in his interesting *Introduction*:– "Preceding notices of the town have been written by its natives or residents. In this, drawn up by a stranger, an attempt is made to present the aspect of the town as it may appear to the eye of any visitor who explores it properly, and feels his interest in it sufficiently roused to induce him to make himself acquainted with its past history." The industry of this "stranger" must have been simply prodigious, and the merest dip into his pages will demonstrate that his literary outfit was of no common order. To conclude, I do not hesitate to say that any person taking the least interest in the history of Norfolk, much more every person interested in Yarmouth, owes a debt of deep gratitude to the wandering scholar who made so substantial a contribution to the annals of the county, and to the intimate history of Great Yarmouth. Lastly, amateur word-hunters and would-be students of East Anglian language will deserve to go astray so long as they remain ignorant of the glossary of John Greaves Nall.

This glossary is here reprinted. The remainder of Nall's great work, including the 'very elaborate disquisition on East Anglian Dialect and Provincialisms', remains to be rescued from obscurity. The glossary quickly impresses on the reader the great weight of learning of this man. He had studied local dialects in Britain from Land's End to John o' Groats and ancient and modern languages from Icelandic to Arabic. He made use of every previous dialect work that was available, including those of Tusser, Skelton, Major Moor from Suffolk and Forby from Norfolk. The list of his sources at the end of this volume runs to eight pages.

The original edition was full of type-setting errors, littorals, mispunctuation and mistakes in alphabetization. We have attempted to correct all errors of this kind and to introduce some consistency into the presentation of the information, but 'attempted' is the right word, for complete consistency has proved elusive.

The words listed under 'Additions and Corrections' at the end of Nall's work have here been incorporated into the full glossary.

We have shared the work of editing, but the major labour of typing the original on to disc was completed by Thomas Yaxley over a period of fifteen months.

David, Susan & Thomas Yaxley

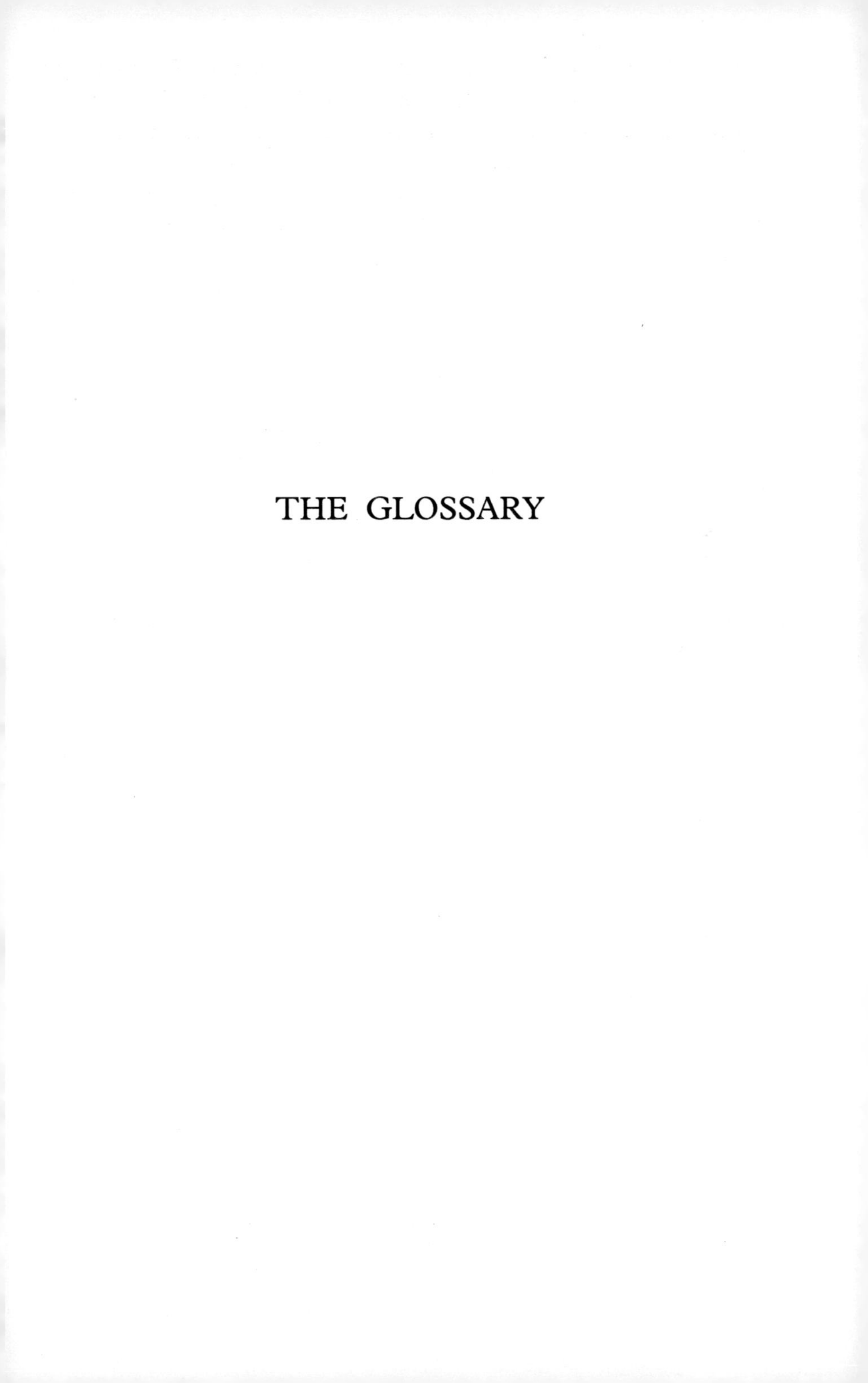

THE GLOSSARY

Nall's list of Abbreviations

A.S.	Anglo-Saxon
Ar.	Arabic
C.Brit.	Cambro-British
C. Bret.	Celto-Breton
Cotgr.	Cotgrave's Fr.-Eng. Dict.
Fl.	Flemish
Fr.	French
Fris.	Frisic
Fries.	Friesic
Gael.	Gaelic
Gr.	Greek
Ger.	German
Id.	Idem
Ir.	Irish
Isl.	Icelandic
It.	Italian
Lang.	Languedoc
Lin.	Linnæus
L. Ger.	Low German or Platt Dutsch
Med. Lat.	Mediæval Latin
O. Fr.	Old French
O.H.G.	Old High German
O. N.	Old Norse
Palsg.	Palsgrave's Fr.-Eng. Dict.
Per.	Persian
Pl.Dut.	Platt Dutch
P.	Portuguese
Pr. C.	Pricke of Conscience
Pr. Pv.	Promptorium Parvulorum
Prov.	Provencal
Sc.	Scotch
Sp.	Spanish
Sw.	Swedish
U.S.	United States
Wal.	Walloon
Wel.	Welsh

A

A. Used as an abbreviation for ***he, or, our, if, on, at, have, of***

Ex. from *Moor: **he***: 'there a go', for there he goes; ***or:*** 'Wutha 'a wool 'a nae'; ***at*** or ***our***: ' 'a'l go out of 'as farm next a-Lady'; ***if:*** 'I'll gi ye a dunt i' the hid 'a ye dew so no more'; ***on:*** 'We'll go 'a Sunday'; ***in:*** ' 'a live a hin house'; ***have***: 'you mought as well 'a dunt as nut'; ***of***: ' 'a'v a touch a the Sheers in um.'

ABOUT. Near to. Ex. 'Is the horse worth forty pounds?' 'Nothing ***about*** it.'

ADDLE, AADLE. To thrive or flourish: applied to crops. 'Ta don't fare to ***aadle,'*** implies the reverse.

'Where ivy embraceth the tree very sore
Kill ivy, else tree will ***addle*** no more.' *Tusser.*

Latham, in his *New Eng. Dict.*, calls it obsolete. Its occurrence in our early literature in this sense seems to be very rare. In Scotland, to ***addle*** is to moisten the roots of plants. The Gael has ***adhart***, progress, advance; ***adhalrach,*** a nourisher. Wel., ***adlar***, to spring up after cutting; ***adlonair***, refreshened.

Also, to earn. The sense in which it is used out of East Anglia. A.S. ***edleanian***, to reward. In Lanc., ***addle;*** in Staff., ***adle;*** Chesh., ***yeddle***.

To the conjectural Keltic etym. already given, may be added the A.S. ***œthel***, growing fast or quick. Der. from the Su.-Goth., ***adel*** (Isl., ***adall***), of noble blood or high qualities, and applied also (see examples in *Ihre's Lex.*) to vigorous growth and vegetation.

ACRE-SPIRE. The sprouting of barley. Also, Scot., ***Acre-sprit***, the sprouting or shooting of potatoes.

A.S., ***œccr;*** Isl., ***akur***, corn, Dan., ***spire***, to sprout.

AFEARD. Afraid, Scot., ***afferd,*** from A.S. ***ferght***, fright; whilst afraid is from Fr., ***effrayer***. Frequently used by Shakspeare.

'The Lordes were ***aferd*** of swech maner puple.'*Capgrave,* 1464.

AFTERMATH. The feed left on meadows after having been mown. The second crop.

After. A.S., ***œfter***, afterwards, again; Goth., ***aftaro***. ***Math***. A.S., ***maweth,*** 3rd per. sing. ind. of ***maw-an***, to mow.

'The first mowing thereof for the king's use, is wont to be sooner than the common ***mathe.'*** *Bp. Hall's Hard Texts. – Amos, c. 7.*

Garnett, *Phil. Essays*, p. 32, has '***average***, or ***averish***, after-grass stubble; a sense confined to the Anglian and Northumbrian Counties, – the Icelandic ***afrett;*** Dan., ***afred*** – primarily an inclosure, also pasturage, after-grass.'

AGUE. Swelling and inflammation from taking cold. An ***ague*** in the face (pronounced agah) is a common consequence of facing a Norfolk north-easter. ***Agarified***, having the ague. Suff.

Fr. ***aigu,*** sharp. The Wel. has ***agawr***, to expand; Gael., ***ag***., swelling. If derived from the tremor attending *ague*, the Gael has ***lagaich***, to quiver; Goth. ***agis,*** trembling; Wel., ***acreth***, quaking, ague, A.S. ***hrithian***. Robert de Brunne writes ***hage.***

AHUH. ALL OF A HUGH. Awry, aslant. A.S., ***awoh***.

ALLEN. Grass land, newly broken up. ***Ald-land;*** A.S., ***ald***, old. In Suffolk the term is ***olland***, or ***allens***.

AINT, AAINT. To anoint. Used to denote a drubbing. 'I'll ***aaint*** yar hide for ye.' In Cheshire, ***'noint***.

ALP or **OLP**. The Bullfinch. Also ***Blood-alp***.

AMPER. An inflamed swelling, pustules. A.S., ***ampre***.

ANINND. On end. 'Rise the ladder up ***aninnd.***' 'Go ***aninnd,***' go forward. Also, upright, rearing.

In the *Two Gentlemen of Verona*, Proteus angrily calls Launce 'A slave, that, still, ***an end*** turns me to shame.' Collier and Singer accept Gifford's and Monk Mason's remarks that 'still an end,' was an old colloquialism for commonly, generally. Surely, a much stronger force is conveyed in the passage — that implied by 'without end, perpetually.'

ANTRUMS. Affected airs, insolences, whims, maggots. ' 'As in 'as ***antrums*** this morning' said alike of a rude person, or skittish horse.

More common as *tantrums*, the North country term. In Chesh., ***antrums;*** Lanc., 'a terrible ***tanterum,***' a fit of passionate excitement. The Rev. J. Davies, *Phil. Trans.,* 1855, derives it from ***tant***, Welsh, a gust of passion, or whim.

APPLE-JOHN, or **FLAP-JACK**. Sugared apples, baked in a square thin paste, the two opposite corners flapped, or turn'd over.

'Thou shalt go home with me, and we'll have flesh for holidays, fish for fasting-days, and, moreover, puddings and ***Flap-Jacks,*** and thou shalt be welcome.' *Pericles, Prince of Tyre.*

Collier's and Singer's Notes thereon, say 'pancakes.' Major Moor remarks, 'In Suffolk, we should deem him but a "pudden-hiddid" fellow, who did not know a Flap-Jack from a pancake.'

ARSLE. To move backward, to fidget. Also, Lowland Scottish. Fris., ***aarselen,*** to go backward.

A baker's oven pole is called an ***arseling***, or ***wrastling*** pole. ***Arselens***, backwards. Flem., ***aerselincks***.

ASOSH, ASHOSH. Awry, aslant.

ATTER, pus, morbid matter.

Gael., ***Athar***; Arabic, ***aghbar***, dregs of a disease. A.S., ***atter,*** poison; Fris. and Dut. ***etter***, pus. Yorks., ***atteril,*** 'matter of a sore'; a tongue furred with fever is said there to have 'a dry white ***atter***.' *Pr. Pv.* ***attyr***, fylthe.

ATHWART. Across. Of common occurrence on the coast, pronounced ***athart,*** and ***athowt***. In Dorset, ***athirt***.

An Ordnance surveyor visiting Winterton lighthouses, whose lights intercross, they were described to him on the spot as '***thowt*** lighthouses,' and appeared on the map, soon after, as 'the Thought Lighthouse.' ***Thowt*** pegs are the pins between which the oars of a boat are confined – the oars by their means can also be laid ***athwart*** the boat. A.S., ***thweorian***, to traverse, cross, hence to ***thwart.***

AUGHT. Owed.

AUSIER. Osier.

AVEL. The beard or awns of barley. The corn is said to be ***avely*** if, when dressed for market, the awns adhere to the grains.

Essex, ***ails;*** Scot., ***awns; avvermeyl.*** oat-meal; Fris. and Yorks., ***Haver,*** oats.,

Dut. and Old Scot.. Isl., ***ogn;*** Dan., ***avne,*** chaff.

AVELLONG WORK. Mowing or reaping lying out of the perpendicular at the sides of fields is ***avolling***. A.S. ***awoh***; Wel., ***havyn,*** an extending out. *Pr. Pv.* '***auelonge***, oblongus.' Leeds and Craven, oblong.

AVISED. Advised.

AWK, AUK. Inverted or confused. Bells are rung ***awk*** to give alarm of fire. Used by Fairfax, L'Estrange, and other old writers of East Anglia, in the sense of confusedness.

'Whose wild and mad brain humour nothing fitteth so just, as the stalest dudgen or absurdest balductum, that they or their mates can invent in odd and ***awk*** speeches, disguisedly shapen after the antic fashion, and monstrously shorn, like old Captain Lister's spaniel.' *Gabriel Harvey's Pierce's Supererogation,* 1593.

'I know a camel passeth in the Latine proverb either for gibbous and distorted, or for one that undertaketh a thing ***awkely***, or ungeenly.' *Fuller's Worthies,—Cambridgeshire,* 1662.

'A Fool's heart is at his left hand, he is left-handed in his work; he doth it ***aukedly,*** untowardly.' *Rogers' Rich Fool,* 1662.

'What we have hitherto spoken, will seem to have less of ***auk*** in it, if we do but pattern our leasting of body with a now of time.' *Fairfax's Bulk and Selvedge,* 1674.

Pr. Pv. ***awke,*** or angry, ***awkly*** or wrongly. Dan., ***avel,*** crooked; Flem. ***auwiis,*** foolish; Prov. Ger., ***awechi,*** gawky; Fr. ***gauche***, Sc., ***gowk***, fool, are cognate.

'How often have we heard as arrant jangling in the pulpits as ever we did in the steeples, and professors ringing as *awk* as the bells, to give notice of the conflagration which they themselves were raising.' *L'Estrange's Æsop.*

AX. To ask. A.S., ***acsian.*** The common form in old English, and still prevalent in East Anglia and the United States.

B

BABBING. A mode of fishing without rod or hooks for eels in the fens, and for crabs on the coast, by letting down a line baited. Elsewhere known as ***bobbing***.

BADGET. A badger.

BACKSTRIKING. A mode of ploughing, in which the earth having been previously turned, is turned again.

BADLY. In ill health. Sometimes ***sadly-badly***, and ***sad-bad.***

BAFFLED. I. Standing corn, or grass, beat about by the wind or stray cattle, are said to be ***baffled about*** or ***buffled***. Nickled, snaffled, and walted, are other terms applied to standing corn beat about by wind or rain.

II. Said of children capriciously and irregularly brought up. Ex., 'He was sadly ***baffled*** in his bringing up.'

III. To ill-use and beat about. To foil, disgrace, deceive. Of a man knocking another about the head, it would be said, ' 'a ***baffled*** 'em about the hid.'

> 'He by the heels him hung upon a tree,
> And ***bafful'd*** so, that all which passed by,
> The picture of his punishment might see.' *Spenser's Faerie Queen*

'Our names would be ***baffuld*** on euerie booke-sellers stall, and not a chandler's mustard pot, but would wipe his mouth with our waste paper.' *Nash's Pierce Penilesse*, 1592.

It., ***beffare***, Fr., ***beffler***, to deceive, mock; Fr., ***baffoner***, to disgrace, revile; Dut. ***baffen***, to bark at: ***verblaffen***, to put out of countenance.

BAIL. The handle of a pail or bucket. Hence the sailor's term 'to ***bale*** out.' Also the bow of a scythe. Gael, ***speal***.

Gael., ***ballan***; Bret., ***bal***; Du., ***baalie***; Dan., ***balle***; Sw., ***balga***, a pail, or tub. Hence Du., ***baalien***, to empty out water with a bowl or pail.

BAHANGS. Hanging down untidily, said of clothes. 'Frisic ***bengelen***,' Hettema.

BAHD. A bird: ***'bahd's-neezen,'*** bird's-nesting.

BAIN. Pliant, limber. Chesh., near, convenient. North., near, ready, easy; Dan., ***bane***, to level, smooth; Isl., ***bein***. Apparently synonymous with ***gain***, which see.

BALDERDASH. The local meaning attached to it by Forby is filthy, obscene talk. **BALDER,** to use coarse language. The common meaning is idle, senseless talk.

Wel., ***baldorz***, prating, babbling talk; ***baldorzi,*** to speak foolishly, from ***bal,*** what jets out, and ***tordd***, din, tumult. Gael., ***ballartaich,*** a loud noise, shouting; Isl., ***buldra***, to blether; Dan. ***buldre***; Fris., ***bolderen***. Balderdash is also used to signify washy drink.

BALK, BAUK. A ridge of land left unploughed as a boundary; a ridge left at intervals in balk-ploughing. Hence, to pass over in ploughing, to skip.

'But so well halt no man the plow
That it ne ***balketh*** other while.' *Gower*, 1325.*

Sw. G., ***balka***, a ridge between two furrows; Isl., ***baulkur***; a partition between the stalls of a cow-house; Isl., ***balkr***.

Also, a beam, or squared timber. Hence haylofts and hen roosts (Fris. ***hanebalken***) are termed ***balks***, as situate among the rafters. Straight young trees when felled are termed elm ***bawks***, oak ***bawks***, &c. When standing, ***stands.*** Fir ***bawks***, ***Spurshers***, and ***Yofers***, are nearly the same.

Also an East Anglian contrivance in the ***Nettuses*** or milking houses, for confining the cow's head whilst being milked, by a beam or ***balk.*** Swed., ***balk***; Dan., ***biælke***; Picard, ***bauque***.

Bulkar as a great beam is used also in Lincolnshire, where the front of a butcher's shop is still called a ***bulkar***. Fris., ***balk.***

'Nor that they set debate betwene their lords,
By earing up the ***balks*** that part their bounds.' *Gascoigne's Steele Glas*.

BAMBLE. To shamble, move awkwardly, walk unsteadily.

The Sc. has a ***bambling*** child, clumsily made. Sp., ***bambolcar***, to swing; Norm., ***bamboler***; Walloon, ***bambi***, to waver; Burg., ***rambe***, the swing of a bell; Gr., ***bambalo***, to stammer, hence It., ***bambolo***, ***bambo***, a child. *Diez*. ***Bancale***, said of one with crooked legs. Walloon.

*John Gower, the senior of Chaucer, his friend and brother poet, possessed the manor of Multon, in Suffolk.

BANDY. A hare, from the curvature of her legs. Fr., ***bandé,*** bent. A curved stick, used for ball-striking in sundry games.

BANDY-HOSHOE. A game at ball played by two parties or sides, striking the ball into their opponent's goal.

BANDY-WICKET. The game of Cricket.

Wedgewood derives ***bandy*** from the Sp., ***banda,*** a party, side, or faction.

> '...Mercutio, the Prince expressly hath
> Forbidden ***bandying*** in Verona streets.'

Fr., ***bander,*** to drive the ball in Tennis from side to side.

BANG. Suffolk cheese, made of milk several times skimmed. ***Trip, wonmil,*** and Suffolk ***thump,*** are other local names for it.

> 'Unrivall'd stands thy county cheese, O Giles!
> Whose very name alone engenders smiles;
> Whose fame abroad by every tongue is spoke,
> The well-known butt of many a flinty joke,
> Its name derision and reproach pursue,
> And strangers tell of "three times skimm'd skye-blue" '. *Bloomfield.*

Its toughness has given rise to a number of local illustrations. In one, the cheese exclaims

> Those that made me were uncivil,
> For they made me harder than the d—l;
> Knives won't cut me; fire won't sweat me;
> Dogs bark at me, but can't eat me.

'Hunger will break through stone walls, or anything except Suffolk cheese,' is a proverb from Ray. Mowbray says 'it is only fit to be cut up into gate latches, a use to which it is often applied.' Other writers represent it as most suitable for making wheels for wheelbarrows.

Trip and ***wonmil*** appear to be corruptions of ***strip,*** and ***milk*** of ***one*** milking.

BANGE. Light rain. ***Bangy, bengy,*** dull, gloomy. Essex.

Gael., ***boinne,*** rain drops; Dut., ***beneveld,*** misty, drizzly. ***Bange*** in Dut. and Dan. has a sense of stifling in relation to weather.

BANGING. Great, large. Also common in the United States. In Suffolk and Essex ***Bonnka*** is large, strapping, applied to young persons, especially girls. Ex., 'What a ***Bonnka*** that there ***Mawtha*** dew grow.'

BANGLED. Applied to young shoots and broad-leaved plants, when they droop under heavy rain, or sunshine. Fris. ***bengelen***.

Fl., ***bangheyd,*** stifling; L. Ger., ***banglen,*** to languish. Su.-Goth., ***bængel***; Ger., ***bengel,*** a cudgel, club.

BANK. 'Generally used for ***beach.'*** Miss Gurney.

Isl. ***bakki,*** a shore; Ger. and Dut. ***bank,*** used in a similar sense. A.S., ***bænce.***

BARGAIN. A waggon load. Ex., 'I'd three ***bargains*** off 'a that there small filld.' An indefinite quantity. Ex., 'I've a fairish ***bargain*** a' lambs ta year.' 'Two good tidy ***bargains*** of hay from an acre.' 'A poor ***bargain*** of wool.' 'A sad bargain of lazy chaps.'

BARGOOD. Yeast; corrupted also into ***burgood*** and ***bulgood.***

Possibly from the Wel., ***bragawd,*** a sprouting up; also, a liquor of the wort of ale and mead fermented. ***Bragiaw***, to swell out; ***bragu***, to malt.

BARK. 'Between the bark and the wood,' a well-adjusted bargain, where neither party has the advantage.

BARK and TREE. 'Let none of them ***come between barke and tree***, to defeat your faith and conversion.' *D. Rogers' Naaman.*

'If every poor soule should thus goe ***between barke and tree***, and cavill, who should ever come to believe?' *D. Rogers' Naaman, p. 122.*

BARKSELE or **BARSELE**. The season of stripping bark. A.S., ***Sæl,*** season.

BARLEY BIRD. The nightingale.

BARLEY-MUNG. Barley meal mixed with water to fatten poultry.
Dut. ***mengen***; Fris. ***amenge***, to mix.

BARNABEE. The golden-bug of Suffolk, or lady-bird. Also ***Bishop-barney***.

'One settling on a child is always sent away with this sad valediction –

'Gowden-bug, Gowden-bug, fly awah home,
Yar house is bahnt deown an yar children all gone.'

It is sure to fly off on the third repetition.' *Moor.*

BARROW, or **BARRA PIG**. The smallest and shrillest grunter of the litter; the ***pitman***, Mr. Forby says is the more general term. A.S., ***berga***, a pig. In Kent, Anthony pig.

'Barra, or ***barrow***, a hog, is a very familiar word to all New Englandmen.' *Elwyn.* It is also an Exmoor word. Portg. ***bacoro,*** a one-year old pig. Arab., ***bakr***, the first born.

BARLEY-SELE. The barley sowing season.

BARRATOR. An inciter to lawsuits. O. Fr., ***bareter***, to deceive, cheat, whence ***barter***.

A term of opprobrium formerly often levelled at East Anglians, especially against the men of Norfolk, by their neighbours, from their litigious propensities.

The fullest notices of the word occur under many articles in *Ducange's Med. Lat. Gloss.*, folio ed., 1733. ***Barare***, to deceive, ***baratare***, to change about, ***baratum***, cheating (It., ***barattare***, to coney-catch, chop and change), ***barataria***, fraud, false dealing in bargains and sales (It., ***barratteria***, any trucking, chaffering, cogging, foisting, cozening, false dealing in hugger mugger, simony, indirect dealing in law, bribe taking, corrupt conscience), ***baraterii***, brawlers, wranglers, ***à barris***, the courts of law where they stir up litigation, impede settlement of causes, mix up fraud and falsehood in their hearing, and are corruptors of just judgement by bribes; ***baraterii***, notione nonnihil diversa, vagabonds, mendicants, paupers, ***baratator***, impostor, swindler, ***barra***, the judgement bench, ***barrare***, to debate, contest, litigate; O. Fr., ***barroyer***, to use delays in law.

Barrator, was the angry term hurled at Abbot Samson of Bury by his outwitted monks, on finding the quiet demure brother they had promoted as their head suddenly transformed into the vigorous reformer of their sloth and self-indulgence.

The Island of Barataria is immortalised as the scene of Sancho Panza's famous government, a locale which, strange enough, bewildered so acute and critical an editor of *Don Quixote* as Lockhart. Spanish editors seem to have equally lost their way to it, Lockhart writes. Pellicer is at great pains to find out the true etymon of the word, which is without doubt given by Cervantes himself, ***barato***, meaning in Spanish cheap. In old Spanish dictionaries ***barqto, barateria***, etc., have precisely the Ital. and Med. Lat. senses given above. The idea intended by Cervantes might possibly be akin to that of a Chateau en Espagne, or a sense which may be implied from one of the meanings of the O. It., ***baratto***, deception, transformation; ***barattare***, cambiar una cosa ad un altra.

BARTH. A shelter for cattle; ***Barsh***, shelter, *Kennett.* Ray and Pegge explain it 'a warm place, or pasture for calves and lambs.' *Richards Wel. Dict.* has ***bar***, a bush, its probable derivation. In the South it signifies a warm shelter. ***Bartheless***, houseless. Devon dialect.

'Young broom, or good pasture thy ewes do require,
Warm ***barth***, and in safety their lambs do desire.' *Tusser.*

Owen's Welsh Dict. has ***barth,*** a ground floor. Forby says from ***bar,*** enclosure. Wedgewood includes it under ***berth***, the seaman's term for snug anchorage for themselves or vessels. Both are pronounced alike in East Anglia. Wedgewood conjectures that a ***berth*** in the sense of a place boarded off in a ship may be derived from the Isl., ***byrda***, a large place or chest of wood, or from ***bord***, a board.

The **BARF HOUSE** is the Yarmouth term for the shed or ground floor open at the side, where the first stage in curing herrings takes place.

BASK. To buffet, baste; Su.-Goth., ***bösta***; Isl., ***beysta***; O. Fr., ***bastre***; Goth., ***busa***, to beat, thresh; Su.-Goth., ***basa***; Bret., ***bazata***; Dan., ***baske***, to slap, thwack, flap.

'Many things befall one in such an estate, which buffet and ***baske*** it shrewdly.' *D. Rogers' Naaman.*

'Under an handsome gale we put to sea, * * * but it failed us, and soon proved worse than so, fresh and contrary, which forced us to be ***basking*** in those narrow seas.' *North's Lives, ii., 341.*

'After three or four days ***basking*** thus in the Archipelago, with contrary winds, * * * with wind and current in our teeth.' *Id., ii., 34.*

BASKING. I. A drenching in a heavy shower. II. A sound drubbing. Dan., ***bask***, to slap, thwack.

BASTING. Also, a sound drubbing. Isl., ***beysta***, to strike. A.S., ***baist***, to beat. Sc., ***baistin.***

BATLINS. The loppings or ***stowin*** of trees. ***Battens***, rails used for fencing.
A.S, ***bat***, a staff or stick; ***bat-en.*** made of bats, as wood-en, made of wood.

BATTRY. A tea kettle, Suffolk. *Halliwell.*

BAVENS, BAVINS. Light, loose faggots.

Baven, the smaller trees whose sole use is for the fire. *Skinner.* Richardson conjectures from Dut., ***bauwen***, to build. Old Fr., ***baffe***, a fagot, *Wedgewood.* A more probable derivation seems to be the Gael., ***badan***, a little grove, a tuft, cluster, or bunch, ***bad-aidh***, to make into tufts. See *Highl Soc. Gael. Dict.*

'In stacking of ***bavin*** and piling of logs
Make under thy ***bavin*** a hovel for hogs.' *Tusser.*

In Dorset, a ***baven*** is a faggot of long untrimmed wood.

'Men think that women (seeing them so sumptuously pearled and bespangled) cannot choose but offer to tender their tender souls at their feet. The women, they think, that (having naturally clear beauty, scorchingly blazing, which enkindles any soul that comes near it, and adding more ***bavins*** unto it of lascivious embolsterings,) men should even flash their hearts at first sight into purified flames of their fair faces.' *Nash's Christ's Tears,* 1613.

BAVISH. To drive away; cor. of banish.

BAWDA. To abuse grossly. A Suffolk man complains whiningly of having been '***bawder'd*** and ragg'd in a shameful waah.' *Moor.*

From Welsh, ***baw.***, dirty, filthy; Scot., ***bourd,*** to mock, to jest; Isl., ***baga.***
Fr., ***bourder,*** to mock, jest, gibe at; Gael. ***bûrd***, a gibe; O. Fr., ***behourdir***, to joust with lances, make a blustering noise.

BAWND. Swollen. One of Sir T. Browne's collection, now obsolete. Dan., ***bulne***; Isl., ***bolgna***, swollen.

BAY. A squirrel's nest. Elsewhere called ***dray***. Sp. ***arda***, a squirrel.

'Climb'd, like a squirrel to his ***dray***,
And bore the worthless prize away.' *Cowper.*

BAY-DUCK. The shell-duck; from its bright bay colour, the shade between red and brown.

Lat., ***badius***; It., ***bajo***; Fr., ***bai***; Span., ***bayo***; also ***bazo***, chestnut, yellowish brown. *Diez.*

BEANS. *Moor* writes 'three blue beans in a blue bladder, rattle bladder, rattle,' is as old a frolicksome sort of Suffolk shibboleth as I can recollect, and is still frequently heard.'

A very old saw. See *Nares' Glossary.* Prior has it in his *Alma* –
'They say

That putting all his words together,
'Tis three blue beans in one blue bladder.'

BEARN. A barn, the exact A.S., ***bœrn***.

BEATH or **BATH.** To place green wood by the fire, to set or straiten it by heat. A.S., ***bethian***.

BEAT-OUT. Puzzled.

BEATWORLD. Beyond control.

BEAU-TRAPS. Loose pavements in the footway, under which dirt and water collects, liable to splash any one that treads on them. *Halliwell.*

BEAVER. O. Fr., ***beweter***, to drink, sup; ***beuveur***, a tosse pot. *Cotgr.* Lat., ***bibere.***

BECK. A brook or rivulet. A.S., ***becc***; Isl., ***bekkr***; Dut., ***beek***; Fr., ***bec***; Su.G., ***baeck***; Teut., ***beke***; common to all the Northern dialects.

Cognate derivatives possibly exist in the Wel. ***bac***, little, crooked, having many windings; Gael., ***bac***; in the North Highlands, gurges limosus, a muddy torrent. Also, ***bac,*** a bending ground or hill. See *High Sy. Gael. Dicty.*

Wedgewood supposes that ***beck***, a brook, may be fundamentally the same as Isl., ***bakki***, a bank. A beck is not a river where the water first catches the eye, but a brook, where at a little distance the broken banks are the conspicuous object, while the water is often not seen at all.

BECKET. A spade used in cutting turf. A.S., ***beceorfan***, to cut, pare away.

BECOMES. One's best clothes.

BEDREPES. Days of harvesting, formerly performed by customary tenants, at the bidding of their lords. See *Cullum's Hawsted*, 1784, p. 189.

BEDSETTLE. A bedstead. A.S. ***setl,*** a seat. Essex.

BEEIN. A home, a place to ***be in.*** 'If I could but git a ***beein,*** I can fisherate for myself.' *Moor.*

Clearly, Mr. Dickens made use of '*Moor's Suffolk Words*,' for the dialect introduced into David Copperfield, – 'Theerfur 'tan't my intentions to moor Missis Gummidge 'long with them, but to find a ***Beein*** fur her, wheer she can fisherate for herself.' ***Fisherate*** is not in *Forby*.

BEET, BET UP. To mend nets. Beetster, a net mender. A.S., ***betan***; Dut. ***beteren***; to make better, repair. Fris., ***beta.***

'Pipen he coude, and fishe, and nettes ***bete.***' *Chaucer's Reve's Tale.*

In the East Coast Herring, and the Cornish Pilchard Fisheries, used to denote mending nets. In Lancashire, ***'beet t'foire,'*** means either to kindle or mend it. '***Böten füer***,' mend the fire, is a very common Low-German phrase.

BEETLE. A large heavy wooden hammer, its head hooped with iron, and studded all over with nails, used for riving wood: a heavy mallet.

> 'A plough-beetle, plough-staff, to farther the plough,
> Great clod to asunder that breaketh so rough.' *Tusser.*
> 'If I do, fillip me with a three-man ***beetle.***' *Hen. IV., P. 2., I 2.*

A.S., ***bytel***, a mallet, Plat. Deut., ***betel***, from Su.-Goth. root, ***beta***, to strike.

'If they get thee within their reach, thou must come to knokham fair, and what between the block and the ***beetle***, be thumpd like a stock fish.' *Nashe's Plaine Percevall.*

BEEZLINS. Milk of the third or fourth milking after calving.

The first milking is called ***beestings***, or ***beastlings***. A.S., ***beost***, ***byst***; G., ***biest milch***; Frisic, ***byst***; Dut., ***biest***.

BED-FAGGOT. A contemptuous name for bed-fellow.

BEGGAR'S VELVET. The lightest particles of down shaken from a feather bed, left by sluttish housemaids to collect under the bed. *Forby.* ***Beggary,*** full of weeds.

BEGONE. Worn, aged, decayed. Ex., 'The thatch is lamentably ***begone***.'

BEING, part. Because. Used somewhat like the abl. abs. in Latin. Ex., 'I could not meet you yesterday, ***being*** I was ill in bed.' Employed by Bp. Pearson, a Norfolk man. In Dorset, ***beëns***.

Much in use in the Middle States of America, and among the illiterate in New England. *Bartlett.*

'I'll let you have her for eight hundred dollars, ***being*** as you're a minister.' *Mrs. Stowe's Dred.*

BELKING. Lounging at full length. A.S., ***belicgan***, to lie along.

BELLIBORION. A variety of apple; cor. of Fr., ***belle et bonne***.

BELSIZE. Bulky, of goodly size.

BELL-SOLLER. The loft on which ringers stand. See **Soller**.

BEN. A figure set on the top of the last harvest load, dressed up with ribbons.

BEN JOLTRAM. Brown bread soaked in skimm'd milk, the ploughboy's usual breakfast.

BENT, BENTEN, BENTLES. Coarse reedy grass. Under the name are comprised *arundo arenaria, agrostis vulgaris,* the *triticum junceum* &c., pasturage rejected by cattle.

Ger., ***bissen***, rushes. In Wessex, ***bennets.*** A Suffolk saw, is —

'The dow she dew no sorrow know
Until she dew a ***benten*** go.

i.e., when other food failing, she is forced to betake herself to the seeding ***Bentles***, where she finds but scurvy fare.' *Moor.*

By 15 and 16 Geo. II., c. 33, plucking up and carrying away ***Starr*** or ***Bent*** within five miles of the Lancashire coast 'sand hills,' was punishable by fine, imprisonment and whipping.

'***Benting-time***, when pigeons feed on ***Bents***, before pease are ripe.' *Walker.*

In the North, ***bents*** are called ***wringle-streas*** and ***windle-straws***.

Dr. R. C. Prior, Pop. Names of Brit. Plants, has '***Bent Grass***, any wiry grass, such as usually grows upon a ***bent,*** – a common, or other neglected ground.' The term is frequent in Old English and Scottish poetry.

BESTOW. I. To lay up, to put out of the way, as in the seaman's phrase, 'to stow away.' 'Where did you ***bestow*** that there hahm?' A.S., ***stow***, a place.

II. To put a woman to bed. 'She was ***bestowed*** last week.'

BETTY-TIT. The titmouse. Suf.

BEVER. The afternoon snack of harvest men and out-door workers.

'A mid-daies meale; an undermeale; a boire or ***beaver***; a refreshing betwixt meales.' *Nomenclator,* 1585.

'The afternoon and evening compotations in *Academiarum, jurisque collegis* are called ***bevers***.' *Spellman.* Beverage was a drink given as a reward for labour, and expected. In Devon, a mixture of cider, water, and and spice is called beverage. '***Beverage***, drink money, demanded on the first appearance of a new suit of clothes. In Scotland, a kiss given to a female on her first wearing a new dress.' A Suffolk workman's *extra* meals, as looked for at gentlemen's houses, are descanted on with considerable humour by *Moor.* They consist of ***leveners, noonins,*** or ***nunshens, bevers,*** and ***foorzes***, exclusive of sundry little interjectional stimuli and interpolations under the head of ***whets, baits, snaps, snacks,*** and ***snatches***, relieved by ***lowans*** of beer.

'In Dorset, the agricultural labourers were accustomed some years since to say that in harvest time they required seven meals in the day – ***dewbit, breakfast, nuncheon, cruncheon, nammet, crammet*** and ***supper***.' *Barnes.*

In Cheshire and Lancashire, ***bagging-time*** is the time for afternoon luncheon.

BEZZLE. I. To tipple, debauch, drink greedily. Probably imitative, like guzzle, of the sounds made in greedy eating and drinking.

'Oh me! what odds there seemeth 'twixt their cheer,
And the swoln bezzle at an alehouse fire.' *Hall's Satires.*

Possibly from the It., ***bezza***, merrymaking, mirth, or feasting. The date of the word's introduction into our language appears to be coincident with the dawn of the Italianising influences which characterised the literature of the Tudor epoch.

II. A tool when blunted or turned in whetting or grinding is said to be ***bezzled***. Also, used as a corruption of ***bevel,*** to slope.

Bizeau, a ***bezle, bezeling,*** or scuing; such a slopefulness as is in the point of a chizle, &c. *Cotgr. Fr. Dict.*, 1632; Leeds dial., ***bezzle***; Cumb., ***belving***.

BIBBLE. To eat like a duck gathering its food from water. To tipple. Lat., ***bibere.***

'I perceive you are no great ***bybler*** (reader of the Bible) Pasiphilo?

Pas. Yes, Sir, an excellent good ***bibbiler***, 'specially in a bottle.' *Gascoigne.*

'Soft, quod one hyght sybbyll,
And let me wyth you ***bybyll.***' *Skelton.*

BIESTS. The wen-like protuberances on growing trees. An excrescence. Possibly from Ger. ***beissen***, to scar. Dut., ***biezen***, to be inflamed; Wel., ***pws***, that which is expelled. Or probably from the Prov. Ger., ***bieze***, bubbies.

BIFFIN. An apple peculiar to Norfolk, also called ***beau-fin***.

Its name is popularly said to be ***beefin***, from its resemblance to a piece of raw beef.

BIGG. A species of barley, called also ***barley bigg, hordeum hexastichon***, *Lin. Forby* states it is much cultivated in the fens of Norfolk and Ely. It yields and grinds well, but will not malt. Isl., ***bygg***. Dan., ***byge***.

'For to say truth, the ***big*** (viz., a four-rowed barley) is seldom ripe, and the oats which they call yeats are commonly first covered with snow.' *North's Lives, i., 289.*

BIGGE. A pap or teat. Essex.

Appears in *Bailey's Dict.,* 1735, as an Essex word. Wright, *Prov. D.* says 'usually applied to a cow.' Gifford, a native of Essex, introduces the word in his *Dialogue on Witches.* 1603. A.S. ***bige.*** a bosom; Gael., ***balg***, a bag; Dan. ***bugne***, to bulge; ***bigne,*** a bump, knob. *Cotgr. Fr. Dict.*, 1632.

BIGHES. Jewels, female ornaments, used figuratively. Ex., 'She's all in her ***bighes*** to day,' i.e. best graces. Vulg. of Fr. ***bijoux***.

Bijou, a jewel, from a compound ***bisjocare, bijouer***, something doubly sparkling. Perhaps from the Celtic (O. Cornish) ***bisou,*** 'anulus.' Bret. ***bizou***; Wel., ***byson***; from ***bys***, a finger. *Diez.* A cognate is ***bizarre.*** Dut. ***bagge,*** an ear jewel; Fries., ***baech.***

In his Gloss. to *Pricke of Conscience,* Mr. Morris derives ***bigg***, rich, well-furnished from Isl., ***bolga***, a swelling.

'Now er we ***bigg***, now er we bare,
Now er we hale, now seke and sare.' *Pr. C.*

BILLY-WIX. An owl.

BING. A bin for corn, flour, wine, &c. Dan., ***bing***; Sw., ***binge***; a division in a granary, or bin.

BINK. A bench, series of shelves, raised sea-banks. Isl., ***bingr***, a heap, hillock.

BINNE-BINNE, bye and bye.

BIRD OF THE EYE. The pupil, or rather the little reflected image on the retina.

'Babies in the eyes,' is a phrase occurring in our Elizabethan poets.

BISHOP. To confirm. A.S., ***biscoped,*** confirmed.

'Itm in reward to my son Nicholas mayde, when the child was ***bushopped***, xij*d.*' *L'Estrange, Household Accounts.*

BITTOUR, see ***Bottle-bump*** – 'The ***botoorc*** that etith the greet eel.' – *Lydgate.*

'The ***bytter*** sayd boldly that they were to blame;

The feldfare wolde have fydled, and it wolde not frame.' *Skelton.*

'It., a ***buttour*** kylled wt ye crosbowe.' *L'Estrange Household Accounts.*

BLACK-SAP. An advanced stage of jaundice.

BLAR, BLARE, BLORE. Calves, sheep, asses, and children, are all said to ***blare***. 'What a ***blaren*** you dew keep,' is said to a noisy child. *Moor.*

Dut., ***blaaren***, to bellow; Gael., ***blaor***, a cry; Wel., ***blaw***. Early North Ang. ***blere,*** to mock. ***Blerynge***, wythe mowe makynge. *Pr. Pv.*

BLAUTHY. Bloated. Dut., ***blaet,*** ventosus.

BLEE. General resemblance, not 'colour and complexion,' the ordinary meaning attached to it. Ex., 'That boy has a strong ***blee*** of his father.' A.S., ***bleo***. Fries., ***bläy***, colour; Wel., ***blaidd***, look, appearance.

Nares declares the word obsolete in Queen Elizabeth's time. It appears in *Kemp's Nine Daies Wonder in a Daunce to Norwich,* 1600.

'A country Lass, brown as a berry,
Blith of *blee*, in heart as merry,
Checkes well-fed and sides well larded,
Every bone with fat flesh guarded.'

BLEEK. Pale, sickly, also sheepish. To bleach. Dut., ***bleek***, pale; A.S., ***blæcan,*** to bleach; Isl., ***bleikja;*** Dan., ***bleg***, to grow pale.

BLEFF. Turbulent, noisy. Wel., ***blwth***, a blast, stir. Wel., ***bloedd*** (th), noisy, also a shout or outcry.

BLIND. Said of infertile blossoms, and of an empty nut, elsewhere called deaf. A.S., ***blind-netel***, a dead nettle which does not sting.

BLINKED BEER. Said not of sour beer, but beer with an ill flavour from too long delay in fermentation, is said to be ***blinked,*** before it turns sour.

'***Blink***, to become a little sour. Su. G., ***blaenka***; Germ. ***blinken***, to lighten, which has the effect of making liquids sour.' *Jamieson's Scot. Dict.*

BLOATERS. Lightly cured herrings, intended for speedy consumption.

BLOOD-OLPH or **ALP**. The bull-finch. ***Green-olph***, the green-finch.

BLOOD-FALLEN. Chill-blained.

BLOSSOMED. Said of cream whilst churning becoming full of air, rendering the task of churning butter tedious.

BLOTE. To swell. Also to set a smoaking or drying by the fire. *Bailey.*

Mr. Wedgewood writes (*Trans. Phil. Soc.*, 1855),– 'I do not believe that to puff out, to swell, is the primary meaning of this word; nor yet to smoke, as it is often explained. The fact is that there are two ways of preserving herrings; one intended to last for a comparatively short time, when the juices of the animal are allowed to remain; and it is subjected to a single smoking only; the other, when the process of drying is thoroughly carried out, and the smoking process is repeated three times. Fish prepared in the former way are properly called bloaters or blote-herrings, while those that have undergone the more complete process are the true red-herring. *Derivation.* Isl., ***blautr***, soft, soaked; Sw., ***blot***; Dan., ***blödagtig***, blod fisk, fresh undried fish, as opposed to ***tor fisk***, cured fish.'

'I have four dozen of fine firebrands in my belly, I have more smoke in my mouth than would ***blote*** a hundred herrings.' *Beaumont and Fletcher.*

'Why you stink like so many ***blote-herrings***, newly taken out of the chimney.' *Ben*

Jonson.

'Lay you an old courtier on the coals like a sausage or a ***bloat-herring***.' *Idem.*

'Make a meal of a ***bloat-herring***, water it with four shillings beer, and then swear we have dined as well as my Lord Mayor.' *Match at Midnight. – Old Play – from Nares.*

'Let the ***bloat*** king tempt you again to bed.' *Hamlet.*

By some writers a smoke-dried, and therefore shrivelled sense was attached to the word, thus –

'And dry them like herrings with this smoak;
For herrings in the sea are large and full,
But shrink in ***bloating***, and together pull.' *Sylvester's Tobacco batt.*

Bloaters are also called on the East Coast ***blown*** herrings, ***bawen*** herrings, ***bone*** herrings. Also ***tow-bowen*** herrings, and, adds *Forby*, ***bloaters***, but we do not acknowledge the word!

BLOUZE. I. A woman with loose and disordered hair or head dress, decorated with vulgar finery.

Its primary sense is to exhibit bright colours, to glow. Dut., ***bloeden, blose,*** redness of the cheeks. 'A girl whose face looks red by running abroad in the wind and weather is called a ***blowze***.' *Kennet.* Dut., ***blossaerd,*** a red-cheeked person. Dan., ***blusse***, to blush.

'Out trudgeth Hew Make-shift, with hook and with line;
Whiles Gillet, his *blouse*, is a milking thy cow.' *Tusser.*
'To paint some ***Blowesse*** with a borrowed grace.' *Hall's Satires.*

II. Also a woman's bonnet, of the sort called a ***slouch***.

BLOW. Blossoms. Ex., 'There is a fine ***blow*** of apples this year.' 'Six pound of ***blows*** to ten gallons of water,' is a receipt for cowslip or peagle wine.

BLUNK. Squally, tempestuous. Wel., ***blwng,*** ruffled, turbulent.

BLUSTER WOOD. Shoots of fruit trees or shrubs that require pruning.

BLUTHER. I. To blot in writing. II. Daub the face with crying, both also Scot., see *Jam.* III. Blubber, a ***bubble***.

Su. Goth. ***Plutra,*** to write badly. Mœs. Goth., ***blothjan***, irritum reddere. Hence also ***blubber***, to bubble up (to weep till the tears stand in bubbles, *Baker's N. Gl.*), ***blober***, I wepe, *Palsgrave,* 1530. *Pr. Pv.* ***Blobure***, burbulium. ***Blubber***, a bubble, or ***blob*** or blister, is common to the Anglian dialects. '***Bluthers*** an' roars like a barn.' ***Leeds Dial.***

'Her swollen eyes were much disfigured,
And her fair face with tears was foully ***blubbered.***' *Fairy Queen.*

BOB. To cheat. Also A smart movement, jerk, blow, or trick. Gael., ***bog***, to bob, move, agitate. ***Bobbish,*** well, hearty, brusk, ***bobbery***, a row, a disturbance; O. It., ***boare***, to bellow; O. Fr., ***baube***, a jangler, babbler; ***bobbishly,*** cleverly, ***bob***, a joke, a pleasantry, also a blow.

'O painfull time, for every crime!
What tonged ears, like baited bears'
What ***bobbed*** lips, what jerks, what nips! *Tusser.*

Pr. Pv. ***bobet***. – 'a ***coup de poing***.' *Palsg.*

'For Lucius thinking to become a foule
Became a fool, yea, more than that, an asse,

A ***bobbing*** block, a beating stocke, an owle.' *G. Gascoigne.*
'And laymen very lobbs, beating them with ***bobbes***.' *Skelton.*

'Madam, I am even with you for your London tricks, I have given you such a ***bob***.' *Shadwell's Epsom Wells.*

BODE. To board. Ex., 'He ***bodes*** and lodges there.' A.S. ***beod,*** Fris., ***boed.*** Platt. Deut., ***boord***; Norse, ***brod. Bode cloth***, a table cloth.

BODGE. To patch clumsily; to bungle. 'Dew it kiender tidily now, an dont make a ***bodge*** ont.' *Moor.* Isl., ***bagi***, damage, detriment, ***baga***, awkward, preposterous, wrong. To ***boggle***, to fail.

'***Bodge*** differs from botch in that while the latter implies more of awkwardness, the former has more of the ludicrous.' *Leeds Dial.*

'If you coyne words, as Chankerburie, Canterburines, &c., while I know a foole that shall so inkhornize you with straunge phrases, that you shall blush at your own ***bodges***.' *Nashe's Pap with a Hatchet,* 1589.

BOGG. Sturdy, self-sufficient, petulant. Wel., ***bob***, a swelling, ***bogwyn***, might. *Ray* in his *South and East country words* has ***bogge***, bold, forward, sawcy. So we say a very ***bog*** fellow. Isl., ***bogna***; Wel., ***bog***, to swell out; Gael., ***bòchd***, proud, puffed out.

'The thought of this should cause the jollity of thy spirit to quail, and thy *bog* and bold heart to be abashed.' *D. Rogers' Naaman.*

BOIST. A swelling. ***Boistous*** is used by Wycliffe and Chaucer in the modern sense of ***boisterous***.

Boystows, rudis. *Pr.Pv.* Wel., ***bwystus***, wild, ferocious; Dut., *byster*, troubled, violent.

'Inflamed also with anger, they ***boysteously*** entered among the people.' *Bale, Image, pt. ii.*

BOKE, bulk, swelling out. Ex., 'There is more ***boke*** than corn in that grass.' 'Ta rise well, according to the ***boke***.' ***Boke load***, a bulky load, also to swell. Scot., ***bouk***.

BOKE. To nauseate, to vomit. A.S., ***bealcan***, to belch.

'Me thoughȝe of wordes that he had a full poke;
His stomak stuffed ofte tymes dyde ***reboke***.' *Skelton.*

BOKE-OUT. To swell out, to gain prominence. Isl., ***bulka.***

'So, 'tis hard to think there should be a whereness so unlike to ours, as we are creatures with body, as not to be ***boakt*** out after the way that we are.' *Fairfax.*

BOMBAZE. To confound, bewilder, perplex. Ex., 'I am right on ***bombazed***,' dazzled, overcome.

It., ***bombanza***, rejoicing, riot. O. Fr., ***bombance,*** saucy boasting, immoderate display.

BONE-CART. To carry on the shoulder. Ex., 'I couldn't av a horse, so I was fohst to ***bone-cart*** 'em.'

BONE-DRY. Bone-lazy, bone-tired, bone-sore, perfectly so.

BONNKA. Strapping, bouncing – applied to young girls.

Gael., ***bonnanta***, strong, stout, having a good bottom, well set; ***bonn-***

chas, strong-legg'd.

BONNY. Brisk, cheerful, in good health and spirits, good looking.

'Their goynge out of Britayne was to become honest Christen menuys wyves, and not to go on pylgrymage to Rome, and so become byshoppes ***bonilasses*** or prestes playeferes.' *Bale's Votaries.*

BONX. To beat batter for puddings, Essex. Dut., ***bonzen.***

BOOBY-HUTCH. A clumsy covered carriage or seat.

'A carriage-body put on runners and used as a sleigh, was called in New England a ***booby-hut.***' *Elwyn.*

BOODLE. The corn marygold, *Chrysanthemum segetum.* A great plague to farmers. A.S. ***bothen.*** In Dorset ***botherum.***

'The brake and the cockle, be noisome too much,
Yet like unto ***boodle***, no weed there is such.' *Tusser.*

BOPP. To dip or duck suddenly. 'I sah Gran-paa! did yeow see that there guse ***bop*** under the gate wah?' 'Aah, Jim baw.'

Dut., ***doppen, duypen,*** to duck the head; Sc., ***doup.***

BORH, BOR. One of the most characteristic of colloquial *Norfolcisms*, applied indiscriminately to persons of both sexes and all ages – one of which it has been wittily observed, that in Norfolk, 'together' is its plural.

Its most probable derivation appears to be neigh-bour. A.S., ***neah***, near. ***Neah-bur***; ***ge-bure***, a countryman; Ger., ***nach-bar***; Dan., ***na-bo***; bo, a dwelling; ***boe***, to reside; Ger., ***bauen***, to build, cultivate. Dut., ***buur***, our ***boor.***

'Our Saxons otherwile did term them, like the Dutchmen, ***boors***, that is such as live by tilth or grasing, and by works of husbandry.' *Spelman.*

If this explanation be admitted, one old woman may, without absurdity, say to another (as often happens), 'Co' ***bor***, let's go a sticking in the squire's plantations.' And the other may answer, 'Aye, ***bor***, so we will.'

'Physiologically speaking, I should say that the phonetic corruptions are always the result of muscular effeminacy, * * * produced by slurring over.' *M. Muller on Language, Second Series.*

As an expletive of incessant use, neighbour would soon be shorn of its first syllable, as *Horne Tooke*, in his *Diversions of Purley*, remarks, 'Letters, like soldiers, being very apt to desert and drop off in a long march. When a boy answers a lady in the words 'yes'm,' he is not aware that his 'm is a fragment of the five syllables mea domina (madonna, madame, madam, ma'am, 'm).

Bor and ***together*** seem to play that indispensable part in Norfolk dialect which ***gaily, likely, belike, whereby, however, you know, you see, just so*** and similar expletives serve in other rural districts in filling up the gaps and rounding off the abrupt edges of colloquial utterance. Almost every one of us has an unconscious trick of this kind.

De Quincey, in his *Essay on Style*, denounces these dialectic forms as debasing the Greek prose style, and as a badge of garrulity from which it never cleansed itself. 'The colloquial expletives so profusely employed by Plato, more than anybody, the forms of his sentences, his transitions, and other intense peculiarities of the chattering man, as opposed to the meditating man, have crept over the face of Greek literature, and though some people think everything holy which is printed in Greek characters, we must be allowed to rank these forms of expression as mere vulgarities. Sometimes in Westmoreland, if you chance to meet an ancient father of his valley, one who is thoroughly vernacular in his talk, being unsinged by the modern furnace of revolution, you may have a fancy for asking him how far it is to the next town. In which case you will receive for answer pretty nearly the following words: "Why like, it's gaily nigh like to four mile like." Now if the pruriency of your curiosity should carry you to torment and vex this aged man, by pressing a special investigation into this word ***like***, the only result is likely to be that you will kill him, and do yourself no good. Call it an expletive indeed! a filling up! Why to him it is the only indispensable part of the sentence; the sole fixture. It is the balustrade which enables him to descend the stairs of conversation without falling overboard; and if the word were proscribed by Parliament, he would have no resource but in everlasting silence. Now the expletives of Plato are as gross, and must have been to the Athenian as unintelligible as those of the Westmoreland peasant. It is true, the value, the effect to the feelings, was secured by daily use and by the position in the sentence. But so it is to the English peasant. ***Like*** in his use is a modifying, a restraining particle, which forbids you to understand anything in a dangerous unconditional sense. But then again the Greek particle of transition, that eternal ***de*** strictly equivalent to the ***whereby*** of a sailor; "whereby I went to London; whereby I was robbed; whereby I found the man that robbed me." All relations, all modes of succession or transition, are indicated by one and the same particle. This could arise, even as license, only in laxity of conversation.'

BOSH. To cut a ***bosh*** is a stronger expression than to cut a dash, more showy and expansive.

Wedgewood ascribes its introduction to our modern intercourse with Turkey; ***bosh,*** Tur., is empty, vain. We had the word centuries before in the Wel. ***bost,*** a boasting or bragging; Gael., ***bosd.***

BOSKY. Tipsy. Wel., ***brwysgaw,*** drunk. Also Devonsh.

BOSS. A mortar hod carried on the shoulders like a hump. Dut., ***boss,*** a knob; Fr., ***bosse,*** a hump.

BOSSOCH. To toss and tumble clumsily; to throw the limbs as it were in a heap.

Gael., ***bosag***, a handfull, bunch; Dut., ***bos***.

BOTCHER. A bungler. To mend by clumsy patching. Var. of ***bodge***; Dut., ***boetxen***, to mend. Swiss, ***batschen-patschen***, to ***botch*** or ***patch***. *Stalder.*

'They sweat, they blunder, they bounce and plunge in the pulpit; but all is voice, but no substance; they deaf men's ears, but not edify. Scripture, peradventure, they come off thick and threefold with: but it is so ugly daubed, plastered, and patched on, so peevishly specked and applied, as if a ***botcher***, with a number of sattin and velvet shreds, should clout and mend leather-doublets and cloth breeches.' *Nash's Christ's Tears.*

BOTTLE OF HAY. Not 'a truss,' *Nares,* nor 'a quantity of hay or grass bundled up,' *Johnson,* but such a moderate bundle as may serve for one feed, twisted somewhat in the shape of a bottle. ***Barley-bottles***, little bundles of barley in the straw were formerly given to farm horses in East Anglia. The dug of a cow is called her ***bottle,*** as well as her ***bag***.

Cotgrove's Fr. Dict., 1629, has ***boteau***, a bundle or bottle, as of hay, &c.; ***boteler***, to make into botles or bundles. Wel., ***bothel***, a rotundity, from ***bol***, belly; Gael.,

boiteil a bundle of hay or straw; Lat., ***botulus***, a sausage. ***Bottleman*** occurs as an ostler. 'Botelle of hey, fenifascis.' *Pr. Pv.*

'For he shall tell a tale by my fey,
Altho' it be not worth a ***botel*** hey.' *Chaucer.*
'How! hosteler, fetche my hors a ***botell*** of hay!' *Skelton.*

'Lawiers are troubled with the Heat of the Liver, which makes the Palms of their hands so hot, that they cannot be coold, vnlesse they be rub'd with the Oile of Angels; but the poore Man, that giueves but his bare Fee, or, perhaps, pleads *in forma pauperis*, he hunteth for hares with a Taber, and gropeth in the Darke to find a Needle in a ***Botle*** of Hay.' *Green's Quip for an Vpstart Courtier, 1592.*

'Methinks I have a great desire to a ***bottle of hay***; good hay, sweet hay, hath no fellow.' *Bottom, in Mids. N. D., iv., 1.*

'This I am sure, a needle may be sooner found in a ***bottle*** of hay, than the arms of some sheriffs of counties to be found in the herald's visitation of the said counties.' *Fuller's Worthies.*

BOTTLE-BIRD. An apple rolled up and baked in a crust.

BOTTLE-BUMP. The Bittern, anciently called ***bittour*** or ***buttour***, of which the first part of the East Anglian term is a corruption. The last syllable is derived from its dull hollow note.

Wel., ***bwmp***, a hollow sound, ***bwmp y gors***, the bittern; Dut., ***butoor;*** Sw., ***rördrum.***

'And as a ***bitour bumbleth*** in the mire.' *Chaucer,*

paraphrased by Dryden,

'And as a ***bittour bumps*** within a reed.'

'That a ***bittor*** maketh that mugient noyse, or as we term it ***bumping,*** by putting its bill into a reed, as most believe, or as Bellonius and Aldrovandus conceive by putting the same in water or mud, and after a while retayning the Ayr, by suddenly excluding it again, is not so easily made out.' *Sir T. Browne's Vulgar Errors, B. III.*

BOTTLE-NOSE. The common porpoise. So called by the coast fishermen.

BOTTY. Proud; Wel., ***balcez***, pride; and ***poten***, to swell out, pout; Gael., ***boiteal,*** pride; It., ***boria***, pride; Dut., ***bout,*** bold.

BOUGE. I. To make a bouge, to commit a gross blunder, to get a heavy fall by taking an awkward false step. II. To bulge or swell out, to bilge.

A ship is said to ***bilge***, when striking on a rock; opening its ***bulge*** or belly.
Gael., ***bolg***; Isl., ***bolga. Bouge***, to swell out, is still used in New England.

'For feare, lest therevpon
Our shippe should ***bowge***, then callde we fast for fire.' *Gascoigne.*

BOUT. A furrow. 'Four ***bouts*** to a yard,' means that the plough turns over nine inches of soil in each ***bout.*** It., ***botta***.

Hartshorne, in his *Salop Ant.,* describes ***bout*** as two furrows, one up, one down the ridge.

BOUT-HAMMER. A blacksmith's heavy two-handed hammer.

BOWDER. Suff., the side table at which the servants take their meals in gentlemen's houses. Dut. and Fl., ***die booden***, the domestic servants.

BOWDS. Weevils, maltworms, ***circulio granarius***. *Lin.* An insect that injures grain, flour, and malt in mills and granaries. Gael., ***boiteag***, maggot. May der. from the Su.-Goth., ***bod***, granary.

'But foisty the bread corn and ***bowd-eaten*** malt.' *Tusser.*
'Long kept in ill soller (loft) undoubted thou shalt
Through ***bowds*** without number lose quickly thy malt.' *Id.*

Ray gives the word as local to East Anglia. *Pr. Pv.* ***bowde***, malte worme.

BOYSTOUS. '***Boystous*** bochers al bespreynt with bloode.' *Lydgate.* See ***Boist***

BRABBLE. 'A ***brabbly*** sea,' a short swell, little waves in quick succession. Dut., ***brabbelen***, to rattle, mingle confusedly.

BRACK. 'The brightest day is not withoute his cloude, the finest lawne not without its ***bracke***, nor the purest gold without some drosse.' *Rogers' Lost Groat.*

BRACKLE, BRACKLY, BRICKLE. Brittle. Applied here particularly to standing corn so quickly ripened as to snap short off. ***Bruckle***, not coherent.– Somerset. ***Bracks***, minute brittle particles, as straw, dust, &c.

'Cleavesomeness we know is the great hanger on to body; but yet the least ***brack*** of body cannot be broken a pieces, because 'tis already the least; yet 'tis as really body as that piece which can, and no whit nearer ghost than it was when knit to more.' *Fairfax.*

'God then being as Almighty in the least ***brack*** of the world, as in the whole world.' *Fairfax.*

The Lanc. and Scot. form of brittle; also brackle; Gael., ***brisg***: Mœso Goth., ***brickan***; A.S., ***brecan***; Dut., ***brokel; breke-lick***. Fris., ***brackle***. In Old Eng., ***brecca*** is a breach; ***breck***, a bruise, a hedge gap.

BRADCOCKS. Young turbots. Sw., ***butta***; O. Eng., ***bret, brut***, or ***burt***; Norm., ***bertonneau.*** Der. probably from its shape. A.S., ***bryt*** and ***bred***; Sw. and Dan., ***bred***; Su.-Goth., ***braedd***, broad. The A.S. has also ***bryt***, spotted; Wel., ***brith***.

BRAIDING. Applied on the East Coast to net making. A.S., ***bredan***; Dut., ***breyden***, to knit, weave; Wel., ***brwyd; Ic brade me max,*** I ***braid*** myself nets. *Col. Monast Elf.* To net or wash out lightly. *Leeds Dial.*

'The single twyned cordes may no such stresse endure,
As cables ***brayded*** thre-fould may, together wreathed sure.' *Surrey.*
'But curle their locks with bodkins and with ***braids***.' *Gascoigne.*
'Dian rose with all her maids,
Blushing thus at love's ***braids***.' *Greene's Radagon in Dianam.*

Perhaps crafts, deceits, comments the Rev. A. Dyce. This would be the A.S., ***bræd***, deceit, craft, ***brædan***, to pretend.

'Since Frenchmen are so ***braid,***
Marry that will, I live and die a maid.' *All's Well that Ends Well.*

BRAMISH. To boast, assume affected airs. Ger. ***bramar***, to brag.

BRAME-BERRIES. Blackberries or bramble-berries. Flem., ***braam***, a blackberry.

BRAND OR BRANDED. Smutty corn. Frisic, ***brand,*** the smut in wheat. Dan., ***brand***; Flem., ***braon***; Ger., ***brandig***.

Branded, Sc. having a reddish brown colour, as if singed by fire; a ***branded*** cow, almost entirely brown. Goth., ***braun***; Isl., ***brun***, the colour of things burnt; G.

brennen, to burn; ***brand corn***, blighted corn. East Anglicisms and New Englandisms are ***brand-new, brand-fire-new; brandon***, a wisp of straw.

BRANDY BOTTLES. The yellow water lilies. *Nuphar Luteum* from the shape of the seed vessel.

BRANK. Buck-wheat. *Polygonum fagopyrum*. Lat., ***brance.***

'Galliœ quoque suum genus farris dedere, quod illic ***brance*** vocant, apud nos sandalam, nitidissimi grani.' *Pliny Hist. Nat., xviii., c. 7.*

Brance, bearded red wheat. *Cotgrave, 1632.* ***Brank***, a sort of grain called Buck wheat. *Bailey*. In some counties called crap.

BRASH. An acid watery rising from the stomach to the mouth, as in the heartburn.

Occurs, also, in the North, in Warwicksh., and the Scot. dialects with the same meaning. Gael, ***braise,*** sickness; ***brághaid,*** heartburn from acrid humour.

BRASH. Refuse boughs, clippings of hedges, twigs, &c.

Brash, rubbish, fuel gathered by the poor from 'the ***brash*** sand,' the beach within Whitby harbour, a mixture of coal dust, chips and twigs deposited by the river in its tidal flow. *Whitby Gloss.* Refuse – Teesdale; cut brushwood – Her. and Glouc. ***Brawche***, rakings of straw to kindle fires. *Grose*. Ger., ***bros***; Cornish, ***brau***; O. Ger., ***broosch***, frail, brittle.

BRASHY. Applied to land overgrown with rushes, twigs, &c.

Wel., ***brwyn***, abounding with rushes. 'Land light and brittle, full of small stones and gravel, is said in Gloucestershire to be ***brashie***.' *Wright.* ***Brashy,*** small, rubbishing, also of delicate constitution. *North.*

In New York it is often heard in the markets applied to vegetables, ex., 'these radishes are ***brash***, i.e. brittle.' *Bartlett's Americanisms.*

The O. Fr. has ***brassique***, sea cole-wort, mistaken for sea bind-weed, or Scot. scurvie grass. *Cotgr.* The root may be the Gael., ***ras***, a shrub, twig; ***rasach***, full of twigs; ***rasan***, brushwood. ***Raüs***, Goth., is a rush, in Sc., a ***rash***. The Ger. has ***bruchig***, full of holes, boggy, marshy, brittle, fragile. Fr., ***buschailles***, small twigs.

BRATTLINGS. Loppings from felled trees. ***Brawtch***, or ***broachwood,*** the twisted hazel, willow, &c. used to peg down straw or reed by thatchers. In Chesh. called Thatch pricks.

Su.-Goth., ***bräte, brutta***, applied to heaps of strippings from felled trees; from ***bryta*** (Isl., ***hryta***), to break off, pluck away. (A.S., ***Brittan***; Eng., ***brittle***); Ger., ***bruchig***, fragile; L. Ger., ***britte***; Fries., ***brutte,*** cœspes (lit. the cut thing) turf, a clump of plants, etc.

'For after the full nice ***brattling*** out of reality, into muchnesses and littlenesses, there falls to the share of this, as little as may be, to keep it from dwindling into an altogether nothing, or a middlekin between something and nothing, that is neither of them.' *Fairfax.*

BRECK. I. A fracture, a breach. A.S., ***brecan***; L. Ger., ***breken***; Fris., ***brekke***; Isl., ***breki***; Fr., ***breche***. II. Also a picce of unenclosed arable land, a sheepwalk, if in grass. A.S. and Fris., ***brec***, use, occupation of lands, fruit or profit from, etc. A.S., ***breck***, a gap.

> 'St. Michel doth bid thee amend the marsh wall,
> The ***breck*** and the crab-hole, the foreland and all.' *Tusser.*

BRED. A board to press curd for cheese, less in circumference than the vat into which it is pressed. A.S., ***bredan***, to gripe.

BRED-SORE, BREEDER. A whitlow, or any sore without visible cause. Wel., ***briwdon***, a broken surface, a sore.

BREEDER. A fine day.

BREER. A dyke bank. A.S., ***brerd***, brim, or the Fris., ***broer***, marsh, fen.

BREIT, BRETTCOCKE, a turbot. N. Ang. ***bratt***.

'Itm pd to John Syff for a ***brettcocke***, viij*d*.' *L'Estrange, Household Accounts.*

'Itm in reward to the parson's servant of Burnham Debdale, for bryngyng of a ***brett***, ij*d*.' *Id.*

'***Bret, bretcock***, and ***skulls***, comparable in taste and delicacy to the sole.' *Sir T. Browne.*

BREW. The field side of a ditch, its brim, brow, or berm. A.S., ***brerd***, margin. Isl., ***barmr***, edge.

Brim is used in Yorks. in the sense of exposed. 'The house is ***brimmer*** than any in the neighbourhood.' *Hamilton's Yorks. Dial.*

BRINK-WARE. Small faggots to repair the banks of rivers. Usually of white thorn. ***Brincke***, brim. *Sherwood's Eng. Dict.*, 1632.

BROACHES. Rods of sallow, hazel, or other pliant wood sharpened at each end, and bent in the middle like a hair pin. Used by thatchers to pierce and fix their work. Fr., ***broche***; It., ***broco***. '***Broche*** for a thackstare.' *Pr. Pv.*

BROAD. A lake formed by the expansion of a river in a flat country. Numerous in East Anglia, as Oulton, Fritton, Braydon, &c. A.S., ***Brædan***, to broaden.

BROAK, BROCK. To belch. Gael., ***bruchd;*** Fris. and Dut., ***brake.***

BROGUES. Breeches, Suff.; Dut., ***broek***. Used in U.S.

BROOK. To digest, stomach. A.S., ***brwan,*** to enjoy, profit.

'I remember yat water of mynte, or water of millefole, were good for my cosyn Bernay to drynke, for to make hym to browke.' *Paston Letters.*

BROOM-FIELD. To inherit the entire property, make a clean sweep of it.

BRUCKLED, BRUCKET. Grimy, speckled with dirt. Ex., 'That child's hands are all over ***bruckled***.' A ***brucket*** complexion, a dirty one. Gael., ***brucach***; Wel., ***bryceulyd,*** full of spots, freckled. Prov., ***brac***, mud; Walloon, ***briac***, North, ***brucke,*** to make dirty.

BRUFF. Hearty, well. Ex., 'How are you?' 'Oh, pretty ***bruff***!' Possibly a corruption of ***brave***, or of ***brusk***, brisk. Full featured, fresh looking. *Leeds Dial.* Proud, elated. *Craven.* Gael., ***brisg;*** Wel., ***brysg***; or Gael., ***brigh,*** strength; Gr. ***briao***, to make strong. In West Dorset, ***bruff*** is brittle.

BRUMBLE-GELDER. A farmer. *Pr. Pv.*, ***brymbyll***.

BRUMBLES. Brambles.

BRUMP. One who lops or ***stoughs*** trees in the night. ***Brumps,*** faggots, the produce of such roguery.

BRUN. Bran. Wel., ***bran***, the husk of corn, Bret., ***breun.***

BRUSH. To cut down with an old scythe or bill, nettles, bracken, weeds in fences, or fog in meadows.

'A ***brush***-scythe and grass scythe.' *Tusser.*

'Bruschalle,... ramalia, arbustum.' *Pr. Pv.* Sp., ***broza***, fallen leaves; Fr., ***brosse,*** small bushes, ***broussailles***, brushwood; A.S., ***brustian,*** to sprout; Bret., ***broust***, a bramble-***bush***. *Diez.* ***Broust, brouze***-wood. *Cotgr.*

BUCK. The body or belly of a cart. 'Full up to the ***bucks.***'

A.S., ***buce***; Sw., ***buk***; Dut., ***buyck***; the belly, trunk.

BUCK. To spring or bound. A skittish horse is said to ***buck***. 'Th'owd mare ***buck'd*** like a cowt.' 'He's a ***bucker***, een't a?' 'A ***buck*** tew much for me.' *Moor.* A.S., ***bucca***, a goat, male deer. Wel., ***bwch***; Gael., ***boc.***

BUCKER. I. A horse's hind leg. II. A bent piece of wood (A.S., ***bugan***, to arch, to bend,) by which slaughtered cattle are hung up and extended before cutting out. See *Gambrel.* ***Bucker-ham*** is the hock joint of a horse.

BUCK-HEAD, BUCK-STALL. To cut down quickset hedges to a height of two or three feet.

BUD. A yearling calf, when the horns begin to shoot.

BUFFLE. I. To handle clumsily, as if the fingers were stuffed or blown up. II. To speak thick and inarticulate, as if the mouth were stuffed. Ger., ***buffel,*** blockhead; ***buffeln,*** to drudge.

Buffalo, 'as we say a gull or loggar-head.' *Florio's World of Words*, 1598.

Buffle head, a dull sot, an ignoramus. *Bailey.*

'You know nothing, you ***buffle-headed***, stupid creature you.' *Wycherley's Plain Dealer.*

It may be derived from Fr. ***bouffer,*** to puff, swell out. Hareng ***bouffi***, a full-roed herring. *Cotgr.*, 1632. In Scotland, ***buffed*** herrings are salt ones steeped in water, swollen out.

'If the bones of a good skeleton weigh little more than twenty pounds, his inwards and the flesh remaining could make no ***bouffage***, but a light bit for the grave.' *Sir T. Browne's Letters.* Common in Shropshire.

BULKING. A throbbing in the flesh. In Suffolk, ***bullock*** or ***boolk***, where ***galva*** or ***galver*** (qy. ***gather,*** i.e. inflame) and ***pritch,*** also prevail. Gael. ***bolg,*** to blister, swell; Isl., ***bulka.*** Su.-Goth., ***bulgja***, to swell; ***bolde***, an ulcer; ***bula***, a tumour.

'The following is a genuine speech of an old lady: "I ha got sitch a lamentable push, an ta ***boolk*** sadly, an at night ta itch and ta ***pritch*** an ta ***gaa-alva***." This, as delivered with the true Suffolk intonation, may be set to music.' *Moor.*

BULL-FIEST. The common puff-ball. *Lycoperdon bovista. Lin.* Lat., ***bovista***, of which it is a corrupt translation.

Called elsewhere, puck-fiest, frog-ball, mully puff, frog cheese. In Scotland, blindman's ball, Devil's snuff box.

BULLOCK. To bully. Isl., ***bulla***, to abuse, to bellow vociferously. Ex. 'sobbing and ***bullocking***.'

BULL'S NOON. Midnight.

'For the propriety of the term, the inhabitants of dairy counties can vouch feelingly. Their repose is often broken in the dead of the night by the loud bellowing of the lord of the herd, who rising vigorous from his evening rumination, rushes forth on his adventures, and ***blores*** with rage and disappointment when he comes to a fence which he cannot break through.' *Forby.*

BULLIMONG. A mixture of oats, peas, and vetches, or buckwheat.

'But rather sow oats or else ***bullimong*** there,
Grey peason, or runcivals, fitches or tare.' *Tusser.*

Possibly a corruption of the Lat., ***pulmentum***. The Old Fr. has ***boulimie,*** extreme hunger; It., ***bullimo***; Gr., ***boulimos***; The Dut., ***bymengen***, to intermix.

BULLY-RAG. To revile in opprobrious terms.

Isl., ***bulla***, to abuse; ***ragma***, to imprecate. Gael., ***bagarach,*** threatening.

BULVER. To increase in bulk by being rolled over and over like snow. Applied to hay or corn collecting into increasing heaps. Fr., ***bouleverser.***

BUMBASTE, BUMBRUSH. To beat severely. Isl., ***beysta***; Dan., ***baste***.

BUMBLE. To muffle. 'The bells were ***bumbled*** at his funeral.' Dut., ***bommen;*** Ger., ***bummeln.***

BUMBLES. Coverings for horses' eyes more effectual than blinkers.

BUMBLE-BEE. The East Anglian name of the bee. Dut., ***bommell bee***; Lat., ***bombilare***. Common in the United States.

'At first I thought he was mad; but the truth flashed upon me that he had buttoned up a ***bumble bee*** in his pantaloons.' *Peter Parley's Reminiscences.*

BUMBLE-FOOTED. Having a thick lumpish foot. Wel., ***pwmplaw***.

BUMBY. A quag, quagmire. Wet, unsolid land will be thus described 'ta quail like a ***bumby***.' 'A ***bumby***, a deep place of mire and dung, a filthy puddle.' *Ray's Eastern Words.*

Possibly an onomatopœia, from its quaking sucking sound, like the Romagnol ***bombare***, to suck. Hence through the Romanic dialect comes ***pump***, to suck up. The It. has ***bomba***, a steeping in water; ***bombilare***, to lay in soak; ***bomletto***, a sucking bottle.

BUMP. A punishment used amongst school boys, in which the seat of honour is brought into rough contact with a post or tree. Isl., ***bompa***, a stroke against any object; Wel., ***pwmp***, a round mass.

Formerly, in perambulating bounds it was customary to ***bump*** the juniors in the procession against the boundary stones, to impress their localities more forcibly on their memories.

BUNCH, to thump, bang. '***Dunchyn*** or ***bunchyn***, tundo,' *Pr. Pv.* L. Ger., ***bunsen***, to knock, punch; ***bons***, a thump. Bret., ***bunta***, to knock, to thump.

Bunch was also applied to beating hemp in Bridewell with a beetle called a dolly (***dolle***, Ger., is a dent, vide the Su.-Goth., ***dolja***, and Isl., ***dolgur***, a piercing or stabbing thing; Gr., ***dolo*** ingens contus cum ferro brevissimo, according to Varro. The L. Ger. has ***tillen***, to lift, take up, move about; the Wel. ***dilin***, that is acted upon, worked, or wrought, beaten, made fine. Compare with above, the O. Eng. ***dolly-tub***.)

'As it is said of Peter, that the angell gave him a ***bunch*** on the to-side, and then his chaines fell off.' *D. Rogers' Naaman.*

BUND-WEEDS. Wild centaureæ, particularly the *nigra*, *Lin.*, much infesting grass land. A.S., ***bune***.

BUNGAY-PLAY. Leading in whist all winning cards in succession, without any finesse.

BUNKAS. A crowd collected together confusedly. 'Kinder! what a ***bunkas*** on 'em.' *Moor.* Isl., ***bunki***; Dan., ***bunke***, a heap.

BUNKS, also **BUNNY**. A rabbit.

'The origin is in the idea of striking. Bret., ***bunta***; Eng., to ***bunt***. Manx ***bun***, butt-end; Gael., ***bun***; Prov. Eng. ***bun***, the tail of a rabbit, hence ***bunny***, rabbit. *Diez.*

Gael., ***bun-fean***, a bobtail. ***Bunt***, to run like a rabbit. Northern dialects.

BUNKS. The wild succory, *Chicoreum intybus*, *Lin.*

BUNNY. A swelling caused by a fall or blow. O. Fr., ***bugne***, a bump; It., ***bugno***, a boil. In Essex called 'a ***boine*** on the head.'

BUNT. To butt with the head, to gore. 'Take care, yinder old cow ***bunts***.' Bret., ***bunta***, to knock, push.

BUNTING, BUNTY. Miserably mean, shabby. A wanton. Bristol.

BURBLES. Small pimples, such as those caused by sting of nettles.

'***Burble*** in the water, ***bubette***. To boyl up or ***burbyll*** up, as a water dothe in a spring, ***bouillonner***'. *Palsg. Fr.-Eng. Dict.*, 1530. Sp., ***burbuja***; Portg., ***borhulla***, a bubble, knob.

BURGAD. Yeast. Wel., ***bragawd***, a fermenting.

BURR. A mistiness over and around the moon. Fr., ***brouée***, mist; ***bruff***, a halo, Whitby, dial. Mist, Ger., ***brodem***; Gael., ***braon***.

'A far-off ***brugh*** tells of a near-hand storm.' Cumb. Saw. 'We'll hev change seúnn, theer a ***bur*** aboot meúnn.' *Id.*

BURTHEN. To charge closely and pressingly. Ex., 'I ***burthened*** him with it as strong as I could, but he would not confess.' *Forby.*

BUSK. To bask, applied to poultry, game, &c. A flock of sheep.

Applied, says Forby, to fowls basking in the sun on a hot day in the most dusty place they can find, and scratching up the dust among their feathers, to rid themselves, it is said, of the vermin with which they are infested. Traces are left where a covey of partridges have been ***busking***.

> 'No fowler that had wylie witte But will forsee such hap,
> That birds will always ***buske*** and bate And scape the fowler's trap.'
>
> *Tuberville. – Of the Divers Passions.*

> 'Now to continue what my tale begun,
> Lay Madam Partlet ***basking*** in the sun,
> Breast high in sand; her sisters in a row
> Enjoyed the beams above, the warmth below.' *Dryden.*

Probably from the ***basking*** or baking in the sun's warmth. Isl., ***baka***; Lap., ***pakestet***.

BUSK also occurs in East Ang. literature, with meanings clearly derived from It., ***buscare***, to catch. 'To proul or shift by craft, and diligently search, to scamble for, to go a free-booting.' *Florio.* O.F. ***busquer***, to prowle, catch by hooke or crooke. *Cotgr.* O. Sp., ***boscar***, to track; ***busca***, a hunting dog.

'Their trade is running up and down and through the city, like so many of Job's devils, perpetually ***busking*** after one thing or other, according as they are employed.' *North's Lives, ii., 54.*

'The grocers declared they would throw up, and not deal in those commodities; insomuch that my Lord Rochester was frighted, and was inclined to fall from this, and to ***busk*** for some other way to raise the supply.' *North's Lives, ii., 122.*

'And so, sometimes a-try and sometimes a-hull, we ***busked*** it out, rain and snow continually falling.' *Id., ii., 316.*

'He was here at hand to ***busk*** for some other employment, as his friends or fortune might lift him into.' *Id., ii., 363.*

BUSK. I. A kiss. Su.-Goth., ***puss***; Pers., ***bus***. II. A flock of sheep. Gael., ***buachaille***, a keeper of sheep; Sc., ***buse-airn***, an iron for marking sheep; ***bust***, tar mark on sheep; A.S., ***bosg***, a cattle enclosure, or may der. from the Lat. and It. ***pascere***.

BUSS. A kiss. Lat., ***basium***; Wel., ***bus***, the human lip.

BUSS. A fishing boat. O. Norse, ***bûssa***; Dut., ***buyse***; A.S., ***butse-carlas***, shipmen.

'Herfor King Richard wrathes him and sais,
Dight us thider ward our ***busses*** and galais.'*Robert de Brunne.*
'A grete ***busse***, and gay, full hie of saile was he.' *Id.*

BUSSEN-BELLY. Ruptured. '***Brostyn***, or ***broke.***' *Pr. Pv.* ***Brustenkited***. Whitby. A.S., ***borsten***, to rupture; Cornish, ***bors***, hernia; Wel., ***bol***, belly.

BUTT. A flounder, so called at Yarmouth, remarks Yarrell, in his *Brit. Fishes.* Dut., ***bot***. Sw., ***butta***, a turbot.

'Item spent in playce, xd, and in ***butt***, vj.' *L'Estrange Household Accounts.*

BUTTER-TEETH. Broad and yellow teeth. The two incisors in front of the upper jaw. Dut., ***botertanden***.

BYLDERS. A kind of watercress. See *Way's Pr. Pv. and Prior's Plants.*

'In a meadow I use in Norwich beset with willows and sallows, I have observed these plants to grow upon their heads, ***bylders***, currants, &c.' *Sir T. Browne on Grafting.*

C

CABOBBLED. Confused, puzzled. Ex., 'Why you 'olly ***cabobble*** me.' Fr., ***accabler***, to confound, overwhelm.

CADE of herrings. An old measure, disused. Gr., ***kados***; Lat., ***cadus***.

'A barrel of herryng sholde contene 1000, and a cade of herryng six hundreth, six score to the hundreth.' *Accounts of the Cellarist of Berking Abbey.* ***Cade*** of heryinge; ***cada, lacista, ligatura***.. *Pr. Pv.*

CADDOW, CADDAW. A Jackdaw. Dut., ***kaauw***; Gael., ***cadhagh, cadha***, a jackdaw; Wel., ***caw-ci***; A.S., ***ceo***; Swed., ***kaja***; Dan., ***kaa***; Norse, ***kaga***.

Chowchetto and ***chouette***, a Chough. ***Cadesse,*** Daw, Jackdaw. *Cotgr. Fr. Dicty.*, 1632. *Randle Holmes' Acad. of Armory*, 1688, has 'Jackdaw. In some places called a ***cadasse***, or choff'. ***Caddow.*** A jackdaw or ***chough,*** Norf., *Bailey.*

'And as a falcon frays,
A flock of stares or ***caddesses*** such fear brought his assays.'
Chapman's Iliad, xvi.

'Kill crow, pie and ***cadow***, rook, buzzard and raven.' *Tusser.*

CAIL or **CALE.** To throw. Ex., 'A ***cail'd*** a stone right at my hid.'— to throw weakly: a boy throws a stone, a mauther ***cails*** it. To move with wavering gait. A colt gambolling and throwing out its heels is 'kicking and ***cailing***.' In the West Counties cock shying is called cock-***squailing***.

I have failed in meeting with any quite satisfactory derivation. *Forby* has Fr., ***caillou***, flint, a common missile. There is the Gael. ***cail***, a spear, ***sgaoil***, to throw, scatter by hand. To this I incline. In the North a ***cale*** or ***kale*** is a turn, chance at various games, particularly at ball, in which 'its my ***cale*** now'; 'give me a ***cale***,' are common phrases. *Wilbraham, Chesh. Glos.,* gives the Flem. ***kavel***, lot, as the derivation. Casting ***cavels***, casting lots. North. Wel., ***coel***, a lot; Norm. French, ***cule***, time, season.

CALIMANCO-CAT. A glossy-skinn'd, tortoise-shell tabby. Derived from the old Norwich worsted manufacture of ***calimanco***, which shone like satin. ***Calliminky***, a kind of cotton. –Teesdale; woollen, – Cumb.

CALLOW, CALLA, or **CALLER**. The surface of the land removed to dig for gravel, &c. ***Uncallow***, to remove this. A.S., ***calo, caluw***, bald. Gael., ***sgailceach, sgallach***, bald. Dut., ***kaluwe***.

CALM, KAMMY. The settlement or scum of bottled liquors. Said also to be ***mothery*** in this state, and the scum called the ***mother***. In Craven, ***caind***; Wel., ***cann***, white; Dut., ***kaam***, mothery.

Var. of ***scum***; Fr., ***escúme***. The Ger. has ***klamm***, viscous. ***Mother,*** Prov. Ger., ***muth***, froth, scum; Dan., ***mudder***.

CALYON and mortar. The ordinary flint and boulder walls of the Suffolk churches. Fr., ***caillou***, flint; ***callierd***, a hard stone. – North. *Pr. Pv.*, '***calyon***, rounde stone.'

CAMBUCK, KEX and **KISK**. The dry stalks of hemlock and other dead ditch plants. Ex., 'As dry as a ***cambuck***.' Of legs lacking a goodly calf it is said, 'His legs are like ***cambucks***.'

> 'But nettles, ***kix*** and all the weedy nation,
> With empty elders grow, sad signs of desolation.' *Giles Fletcher.*

A.S., ***cammoc***, rest harrow, bog fennel; Gael., ***canach***, moss crops, ***catstail***, &c. Until lately much used in E.A. to light pipes with.

CAMPING. An athletic game, fought out by two sides, usually of twelve each, and resembling foot ball, but much rougher. Once popular in the district it has fallen into disuse.

We abridge Major Moor's animated description of the game: 'Goals were pitched 150 or 200 yards apart, formed of the thrown off clothes of the competitors. Each party has two goals 10 or 15 yards apart. The parties 10 to 15 aside, stand in line, facing their own goals and each other, at 10 yards distance, mid-way between the goals and nearest that of their adversaries. An indifferent spectator throws up the ball – the size of a cricket ball – midway between the confronted players, whose object is to seize and convey it between their own goals. The shock of the first onset to catch the falling ball is very great, and the player who seizes it speeds home pursued by his opponents, through whom he has to make his way aided by the jostlings of his own sidesmen. If caught and held, or in imminent danger of it, he *throws* the ball – but must in no case give it – to a comrade who, if it be not arrested in its course, or be jostled away by his eager foes, catches it, and hurries home, winning the notch or ***snotch*** if he contrive to carry – not throw – it between the goals. A holder of the ball caught with it in possession loses a snotch. At the loss of each of these the game recommences after a breathing time. Seven or nine snotches are the game, and these it will sometimes take two or three hours to win.

It is a noble and manly sport. The eagerness and emulation excited in the competitors and townsmen are surprising. Indeed, it is very animating to see twenty or thirty youths stripped to their skin, and displaying the various energies that the game admits of; rushing with uplifted eye, breast to breast, to catch the descending ball, and all at once, running full *ding* to gain a point, and when nearly gained, half falling over the stumbling object of pursuit (for the game is always played where the grass is short and slippery) and after much scuffling to see the ball again in the air, thrown to a wily distant sidesman – and seized and carried in the contrary direction – backwards and forwards, perhaps half a score times, and the shouting and roaring of half the population of the contiguous villages. Sometimes a large football was used, and the game was then called "kicking camp," and if played with the shoes on "savage camp."

Windham, the statesman, greatly encouraged it, and got up many matches at Felbrigg. He was wont to say it combined all athletic excellencies, a successful combatant requiring to be a good boxer, runner and wrestler. It appears to have escaped the attention of the Young Englandism and Muscular Christianity of our day. Ray says, in his time it prevailed most in Norfolk, Suffolk and Essex. It was new to Sir T. Browne on his settling in Norfolk.' Strutt, an East Anglian, omits it from his *Sports and Pastimes of the English People.* A.S. ***camp***, a combat; Ger., ***kempf***; Isl., ***kempa***, a champion; Wel., ***camp***, a feat, game; ***champ***, a scuffle; Eng. dialects, ***cample***, to argue, to reply pertly.– Cumb.; able to do.– North. ***Campar***, or ***pleyar*** at foot balle; ***campyon***, or ***champyon***.*Pr. Pv.*

Mr. Spurdens, in his *Supplement to Forby's Vocabulary*, remarks, 'The contests were not unfrequently fatal to many of the combatants. I have heard old persons speak of a celebrated *camping*, Norfolk against Suffolk, on Diss common, with 300 on each side. Before the ball was thrown up the Norfolk men enquired tauntingly of the Suffolk men if they had brought their coffins! The Suffolk men after fourteen hours were the victors. Nine deaths were the result of the contest within a fortnight. These were called ***fighting camps***, for much boxing was practised in them.' Teut., ***kemp-fight***.

> 'This fair floure of womanheed
> Hath too pappys also smalle,
> Bolsteryd out of lenghth and breed,
> Lyche a large ***campyng*** balle.' *Lydgate.*

CAMPING LAND was a piece of ground set apart for the game. A field abutting on the churchyard at Swaffham was willed for the purpose by the Rector in 1472. At East Bilney is a small strip or ***spong*** near the church called the ***camping land***. At Stow Market is a large pasture still called the ***camping land.*** Sir John Cullum, in his *History of Hawstead, Suffolk*, describes the ***Camping-pightle*** as mentioned, A.D. 1466.

> 'In meadow or pasture (to grow the more fine)
> Let campers be camping in any of thine;
> Which if you do suffer when low is the spring,

You gain to yourself a commodious thing.' *Tusser.*

'Get campers a ball
To camp therewithall.' *Id.*

Lydgate, the Monk of Bury, compares the breast of a woman to a large campyng balle.

The game died away in Suffolk in consequence of two men having been killed at Easton, in their struggles at a grand match, about the close of the last century.

CANCH, [?CAUCH]. A lot of corn in the straw, put in a corner of the barn; a short turn or spell at anything; a trench, cut sloping; a breadth of digging land. *Halliwell.*

Su.-Goth., ***kant***; Gr., ***kanthos***; Wel., ***cant***; Ger., ***kante***, edge, border, rim, limit, corner, etc. (whence a ***Canton***); Ger. and Fl., ***kanten***, to give an edge or slant to.

CANK. Calcareous earth, any sort of limestone. ***Calc, caulk chalk***, is the substratum of a wide extent of Norfolk. Fris., ***calke.***

CANKER. The common red field poppy. Otherwise called ***copper-rose***, and ***head ache. Cankers***, caterpillars.

A copper saucepan requiring tinning, is said to have the ***canker fret; canker weed,*** the *Senecio jacobæa Lin.*, with other kindred species, as *tennifolius* and *sylvaticus*, were formerly so rife on the commons and waste lands of Suffolk as to be gathered and burnt for potash.

CANSEY. A raised footpath or causeway, numerous in the fens and marshlands. Dut., ***kantsige***; Gael., ***cabhsair;*** Wel., ***cam***, a step.

CANT. To set up on edge (so used also in the U.S.); to throw upwards with a jerk edgeways; a jerk edgewise.

Isl., ***kantr***, a side border; Dan. ***kant***, edge; Wel., ***cantel,*** a rim; ***ergo***, the part easiest broken off. Picard, ***canteau***, a piece broken off the corner. In Welsh ***cant*** has also the meaning of a circle, hoop.

'And yet she brought her fees – a ***cantle*** of Essex cheese
Was well a fote thick – full of maggottes quicke.' *Skelton.*

Cant rail, a triangular rail, of which two are cut from a square piece of timber sawn diagonally. ***Cant***, a corner of a field. – Sussex.

CAP. To challenge. 'I'll set yeow a ***cap***.' Capping texts or verses. To cover the object of rivalry by its equal or superior; to come up to, or outdo.

From a root in many diverse languages signifying to cover. A.S., ***cæppe***, cap. Sp., ***capa***, a cloak; Sc., ***hap***, to cover; Turk., ***kaput***, a cloak; ***kepi***, a cap; Lat., ***caput***; Fr., ***chapeau***; Wel., ***capan***; Gael., ***capa. Capt***, crowned; beat in argument, Whitby; puzzled,Cumb., surprised, Leeds.

CAPPER. The hard, wrinkled, crackly crust formed on newly harrowed land by a fall of heavy rain quickly absorbed and evaporated. To chap the hands.

CAPPERED CREAM. Cream coagulated by heat, by an impure receptacle, or by exposure to a brisk current of air.

Both appear derived from the Gael., ***criopag***, a rimple, wrinkle***; kippered*** (salmon), a word which the compilers of the Scot. and Gaelic dictionaries appear unable to make anything of, would seem to be from the same root. Dan., ***kippre***, to rib; Isl., ***kypringr***, to crimp, to shrink together. Pigeons ***cappé,*** ruffed pigeons;

cappéer, to go very near the wind. *Cotgr.*,1632. ***Kipper*** nuts, chestnuts. *Sherwood's Dicty.*, 1632.

CARR. A wood or grove on a swampy soil, generally of alders.

Probably from Gael., ***garan***, a thicket, also underwood. Wel., ***carz***, a thicket, a brake.

CAST. I. Warped. II. Yield, produce. Ex., 'How did your wheat ***cast***?' – a Norfolk phrase. III. Cast, vomit. Common to Suffolk. 'A ***cast*** 'as stomach an' 'as butta.' Fris., ***kotsen***.

CASUALTY. The flesh of an animal that dies by chance. Ex., 'Gipsies feed on ***casualties***.' 'This mutton is so pale and flabby it looks like a ***casualty***.' 'He gave a bullock to the poor at Christmas little better than a ***casualty***.' It should be pronounced cazzlety. *Forby*. Lat., ***casus***, accident.

Casardly, unlucky, North dialects; ***caselings***, skins of beasts that die by accident, Chesh. ***Cazelty*** weather in Dorset, – stormy.

CAT. I. A ferret. 'A cop'd cat;' a muzzled ferret. A.S., ***cops***, a fetter. II. A lump of meal, clay, &c., mixed with a quantity of salt placed in dovecots to allure or retain them.

'In Hants and elsewhere, a ***salt-cat*** is a kind of cake to entice pigeons.' *Barnes' Dorset Dial.* Wel., ***cat***, a piece, fragment. O.E. ***cates***, provisions.

CATCH-LAND. Border debateable land. ***Catch-rogue***, a constable, or bum-bailiff.

CAVE IN. To give way at the edge. To fall into a hollow below; an accident to which any stratum incautiously excavated is liable. Fr., ***cave***, a cellar; Lat., ***cavare***, to dig out; ***cavus***, hollow, Corn. and Breton, ***cau.***

Pronounced ***keeve*** in Suffolk, where Moor says the idea of an avalanche is conveyed by the word. In Chesh. to ***keeve*** is to overturn or to lift up a cart so as to unload it all at once. *Wilbraham*.

This old East Anglicism, reintroduced amongst us as one of the most popular and expressive of Yankeeisms, bids fair to supersede 'collapse.' American glossaries have a number of illustrations, all forcible.

'A very hungry traveller made a very expressive application of the word, by saying his stomach was so empty that he thought he should ***cave in***.' *Elwyn*.

'At the late dinner Mr. W— arose to make a speech, but soon ***caved in***.' *Washington Paper. Bartlett*.

Cavey, a corruption of 'peccavi': 'a begun to cry ***cavey***;' he began to knock under.

CAVING. Refuse unthreshed ears of corn thrown to poultry. A.S., *ceaf.* Gael., ***catha,*** husks, ***caruinnean*** refuse ears.

CAWF, CORF. A floating cage for keeping alive till wanted lobsters and Nancies. An Aldboro' word. An eel box.

Dut., ***korf***; Ger., ***korb***; Wel., ***caw***, a hamper, basket. The stout travelling basket used in mines is called a ***corf*** or ***corve***. Lat., ***cophinus***.

In N. Britain a temporary building or shed is called a ***corf*** or ***corf*** house, a hole or hiding place, remarks Jamieson. Isl., ***korbae***, a little hut. Compare with ***Barfe,*** which see.

CHADS. Husky fragments amongst food. In Low. Sc. and N. Ang. small gravelly stones in river beds. From the L. Ger., ***kade***, a beach, says

Jamieson. It., ***ciotto***, any pebble stone or potsherd.

Wel., ***Cib*** (ch) a husk. Gael., ***cath.***

Chaddy is applied to bread made of meal not properly sifted.

CHALDER. To crumble and fall away as the surface of cawk, gravel, &c. by the action of air. Also called ***cholder*** and ***cholter.***

Lat., ***calx***; Fr., ***chaulx***, lime, ***calciner***, to powder; Ger., ***schalbar***, that may be peeled; Dan., ***skaldes***, to become bald, to peel off.

CHALM. To chew or nibble into small pieces.

Books and papers are said to be ***chalmed*** by mice. The l is dropped in pronunciation.

CHAMBLE. To chew minutely. In Bucks, ***chimble***. Cumb., ***cheg***.

Wedgewood remarks ***chamm, champ***, to chew, so as to make the snapping of the jaws be heard. Hung., ***tsammogui***, to make a noise with the teeth in chewing. Isl., ***kampa***, to chew; ***kiammi***, a jaw. Gael., ***cnamh***, to ruminate.

An onomatopœia; the most expressive form in which the word occurs is in Golding's old black letter translation of Ovid, 1587.

> 'When seeking long for Famine, she the gap-toothed elf did spy,
> Amid a barren stony field, a ramping up the grass,
> And ***chanking*** it.'

This word seems overlooked by all our glossarists. In our Southern dialects ***chanks*** is the underpart of a pig's head; the ***chaule*** of the North.

CHAP. An idle fellow. Used in a disparaging sense. Ex., 'A lolloppen chap.'

> 'Give servants no dainties, but give him enough,
> Too many ***chaps*** walking do beggar the plough.' *Tusser.*

Forby derives from Sui.-Goth., ***kaeps***, one of servile condition. More probably an abridgment of ***chapman***. A.S., ***ceapman***; Dut., ***keopman***; one who traffics, bargains.

CHATE, CHOAT. A feast, treat, rustic merry-making, jolly frolic. Essex. Gael., ***taite***, pleasure, delight.

CHATTS, CHATES. Broken victuals, refuse food.

Turnip ***chaits*** are the remains left by fattening sheep, and to which leaner stock are turned in 'to pick up the ***chaits*** or orts.'

'***Chat***-wood, little sticks fit for fuel.' *Bailey*. ***Chat,*** a twig. Yorks. Black thorn. ***Chats***, fircones. Whitby. Seedling ash, the keys or capsules of ash, sycamore, &c. small branches of oak, stripling boys, Cumb; ***chaity,*** careful,. Somerset; ***chats,*** dead sticks, Heref.; small twigs, Derb.; ***chattocks***, refuse wood, Glouc.; small fagots, Salop.

Chats, the young shoots or suckers, cut and faggotted. *Forby*. Wel., ***cedys,*** faggots. To ***chit***, to germinate, sprout. Ger., ***katze***, a bunch, the keys of a tree.

CHAW, CHAW UP. To chew. 'You don't half ***chaw*** yar wittuls.'

> 'The trampling steed with gold and purple trapt,
> ***Chawing*** the foamie bit, there fiercely stood.' *Surrey's Æneid.*

A.S., ***ceowan***; Dut., ***kawwen***; Wel., ***cerniaw***, to grind with the ***chaw*** or jaw.

'I heerd Tom Jones swar he'd ***chaw*** me ***up***, if an inch big of me was found in them diggins in the mornin.' *Robb, Squatter Life.*

'So doth the Devil, as that excellent and holy Martyr, Mr. Bradford, in his Sermon of Repentance saith; He will spit you, and broach you, after he hath well fed you;

roast you, and eat you; champ you, and ***chaw*** you, and make a full meal of you, even of you that lead a voluptuous life.' *Rogers' Rich Fool.*

CHECK. To taunt, reproach. Ex., 'He ***checked*** him by the favours he had done him.' *Forby.* ***Checked***, chapped, Suff.

'That weake treachery was worthy of a ***checke***, not a desertion.' *Bp. Hall.*

CHICE. A small portion, Essex. ***Chife***, a fragment, Suff. Fr., ***chiche,*** niggard, sparing. *Cotgr.* A.S., ***cicel,*** a morsel.

CHICK. I. A flaw, as in earthenware. II. To crack, chap, chop, as the skin in frosty weather. III. To germinate, as seeds or leaves in bud. Gael., ***cinnich***, to sprout; Wel., ***cyndwv***.

A.S., ***cinan***, to chink, open, gape. Loosening earth in East Anglia is called ***chinking*** it. A sprain in the back implying a slight separation of the vertebræ is called to ***chink*** it. A frequent corrupt pronunciation is ***jink. Cherts*** of grass, the first blades of spring. Cumb.; ***chark***, a crack; ***charkt*** hands, chapped, *Craven.*

CHILL. To warm anything; to take off extreme coldness by heating. 'Do you like your beer chilled?' Now an Americanism.

CHIMDY, CHIMBLY, CHIMLEY. Local corruptions of chimney.

CHINE. The part of a cask into which the head is fixed. Dut., ***kim***, the barrel brim. ***Chim-hoop***, the extreme iron hoop which binds the staves together.

'***Chimb*** is the English for the end of a barrel.' *Barnes' Dorset Dialect.*

Chine, is the swell in the middle of a cask. Var. Dial.

CHINGLE, CHINGLY. A local form for shingle, loose gravel, pebbly beach, &c. Also Scot. Lat., ***scendere***, to split.

CHINK. To loosen earth for planting. To cut small.

CHIP-UP. To recover from a state of weakness or depression.

Probably from ***cheep-up, chirrup*** up, as young birds. An imitative word. Scot. ***cheiper***, a cricket.

CHITTERLINGS. A pig's small entrails, which fried, and eaten with sugar, mustard and vinegar, used to be reckoned a good dish.

The frill of a shirt not crimped or gathered into close plaits, but ironed flat, somewhat resembles it, and is called a ***chitterlin***. When ***crimped*** the shirt frill is said to be ***gofered***. Ger., ***kutteln***, intestines; in Dorset, ***chetléns***; Belg., ***schyterlingh***. *Blount.*

'We make of a French ruff an English ***chitterling***.' *Gascoigne.*

CHIZZLY. Harsh and dry under the teeth. Ger., ***kieselig***, flinty, pebbly; Dut., ***keyzel***; A.S. ***ceosel***; the deriv. of ***Chesil Bank***, Dorset. Gael., ***clachag***. ***Chysel***, or gravel. *Pr. Pv.* ***Chizzle,*** wheat-bran, Teesdale. ***Chizzel***, bran, Sussex.

CHOAT. A merry-making. Possibly from the O. Fr. ***jouant, jouëts***, sports, pastimes.

CHOBBINS, CHOBS. Unripened grain, adhering to the husks under the flail. Wel., ***cib,*** a husk; ***cobyn***, a tuft, bunch; Ger., ***schob***, a bundle of straw.

CHOP. To flog. Prov. Ger., ***kappen***, to strike, quarrel, fight.

CHOP-LOGGER-HEAD. An intense blockhead. ***Chop***, to flog, Essex.

CHOVY. A small beetle, swarming like a plague of locusts in gardens and orchards in hot summers, in the sandy districts. It is common there to drive ducks and swine into the orchards and shake the insects from the trees to be devoured. Wel., ***chwilen***, a beetle, chafer. ***Chwyvaw***, to move, flit about, waver.

A Norfolk term for the insect. Moor says he never heard of it. Sir J. Cullum notes it in his *History of Hawstead, Suffolk.*

CHUBBY. Angry, threatening, surly. Wel., has ***chwibl***, sour, sharp.

CHUFFY. 'In our usage,' writes Forby, 'has no reference to clownishness or surliness which is given to it in all the Dictionaries. It merely means fat and fleshy, particularly in the cheeks.' In Kent, ***choaty***. *Grose.*

If Forby be correct, ***chuffy*** retains its original meaning in East Anglia, that which now a days we attach to chubby. ***Jaffu, chuffy***, fat-cheeked *Cotgr. Fr. Dict.*, 1632. A.S., ***ceaflas***, the chaps; Fr., ***gifle,*** a cheek; Fl., ***chiffe***, cheek; Dan., ***kiæft***. ***Chuff*** is, however, applied to surly, miserly persons. Ger., ***schuft***, a shabby fellow.

'At length (as Fortune servde) I lighted vppon an old straddling usurer, clad in a damaske cassocke, edgde with fox-furre: a pair of trunke slops sagging down like a shoemaker's wallet, and a short thrid-bare gown on his backe fac't with moath-eaten budge: vpon his head he wore a filthy coarse biggin, and next it a garnish of nightcaps, with a sage butten cap of the forme of a cow sheard, overspread verie orderly: a fat ***chuffe*** it was (I remember), with a grey beard cut short to the stumps, as though it were grymde, and a huge, worm-eaten nose, like a cluster of grapes hanging downwards.' *Nash's Pierce Penilesse.*

In the Lanc. and Yorks. dialects, ***chuff*** is pleasurably excited, full of.

CHUMP, CHUNK. A small log of wood, root end. *Ray* gives as a Suff. word, ***chuck,*** a great chip. ***Chumpy,*** small, stunted, Linc. Isl., ***kumbr***, a stump, log.

'Provincial in England, colloquial in the U.S. To ***chunk***, to throw sticks or chips at one. ***Chunked,*** said of any one impudent or bold. ***Chunky,*** short and thick.' *Bartlett's Americanisms.*

CLACK-BOX. The mouth containing a nimble tongue. Teut., ***klack.***

CLAGGY. Clogged with moisture, sticky. A.S., ***clæg,*** clay.

Claggum, treacle made hard by boiling. North Anglian Dialects.

CLAM. I. Clamminess. Ex., 'The meat has been kept too long, and has got a ***clam***,' begins to decay. A.S., ***clam***; Dut., ***klam***. II. A slut so excessively dirty that her skin looks ***clammy***. *Forby.*

CLAMBER-SCULL. Very strong ale.

CLAMM. To starve with hunger. Ex., 'I'm ***clamm'd*** ta dead amost.' Suff. To clog up, Heref. To stick, adhere, Glouc.

More common in the North. From A.S., ***ge-liman***, to glue together. Dut., ***klemmen***; Ger., ***klamm***, to pinch together. '***Clem'd*** or ***clam'd***, starved, because by famine the bowels are, as it were, ***clam'd*** or stuck together.' *Ray.*

The A.S. has also ***clæmian***, to clam, to smear. 'A child ***clames*** the newly whitewashed wall with dirty fingers. A bill sticker ***clames*** up his bills.' Yorks.

'In the conclusion, the sprigs were all daub'd with lime, and the poor wretches ***clamm'd*** and taken.' *L'Estrange's Æsop.*

CLAMP. A potato pit or hog, a rude brickhill. A.S., ***clam***.

CLAMPER, CLUMPER. To make a noisy trampling in walking. ***Clumpers***, very thick and heavy shoes, pattens. Fl., and Dut., ***klempens;*** Isl., ***kumbr***, a lump; Dan., ***klump-fodet***, club footed. Applied also to a ***clump*** of wood, of trees, &c.

In Lanc., wooden clogs are called ***clumpers***; and in the U.S. thick-soled shoes. 'The meaning of the word will be gathered from a short conversation which a minister in this county once overheard between a poor man on his death bed, and a farmer's wife who had come to visit him. "Well," she said, "when yo getten theer, yo'll mayhappen see eawr Tummus, and yo'll tell 'im we'n had th' shandry mended, un a new pig-stoye built, un at we dun pratty weel beawt him." "Beli, me, Meary!" he answered, "dost think at aw's ha nowt for t'do, bo go ***clumpin'*** up un deawn t'skoies a seechin' yore Tummus?' *Gaskell's Lanc. Dial.* ***Clomperton***, one who walks heavily. *Craven.*

CLART. To daub with syrup, juice of fruit, or the like. See ***Slar.***

A Scot. and North country word, adhesive dirt, to smear, &c. Perthshire, ***clort***; Gael., ***clodach***; Dan., ***klatte***; Fris., ***kladdig***; Dut., ***klad-den***, to blot, spirt. '***Clarty-paps***, a dirty sloven of a wife.' *Halliwell.* ***Clarts***, snow flakes, mud. In Linc., ***clatty,*** dirty. Fl., ***kladdegat***, a nasty girl, a slut.

CLAUMB. To clamber in a heavy manner.

CLAUNCH. To lumber along, as if the feet were dragged through the dust to save the trouble of lifting. Ex., 'yinder go black Betty, ***claunching*** along in her creepers.' North Ang., ***cluntering***. Dan., ***kluntet***, awkward, lumbering.

CLEAD. To clothe, ***cleading***, clothing. Ger., ***kleid***; A.S., ***claded.***

CLEAS, CLEYES. Claws, of a lobster, &c. Ex., 'Crack the ***cleas*** in the hinge of the door.' A.S., ***clea***, common to English dialects.

CLEAT. A thin metallic plate. Shoe heels are ***cleated*** with iron. A race horse's light shoe is a ***clate***. A.S., ***cleot***; Wel., ***clwt***.

CLEAT. Strong axle-treed cart that is ***clouted*** and shod. *Tusser.*

CLEPE. To call. The A.S., ***cleopan***, still in use in East Anglia.

At play in the Eastern Counties boys ***clape*** sides at a game.

CLEVER. Handsome, good looking, healthy, tall, dexterous, adroit, applied without reference to talent or intellect.

'This is a low word, scarcely ever used but in burlesque or conversation, and applied to anything a man likes, without any settled meaning.' *Johnson's Dict.*

Clever is an instance of a dialectic colloquialism rising into our literature. Sir T. Browne, a master of the written language of his age, noted it as an East Anglian provincialism. It was used by our humourists in the seventeenth century, Butler, L'Estrange, South. Ray terms it a provincialism, and derives from O. Fr. ***legier***, light, speedy. It can no longer be called so. In the eighteenth century it appears in our classic writers. Dexterous, skilful (*Addison*); just, fit, commodious (*Pope*); well shap'd, handsome (*Arbuthnot*). A.S., ***geleffæst***, lively, nimble. In Scot. and the North ***deliver*** is used in the sense of active. Wedgewood states the provincial Danish has ***klöver, klever*** in the same sense as ours. ***Det er en klöver kerl***, that's a clever fellow! Wel., ***clin***, clever, compact; Sc., ***cleik, clewch***, quick fingered, Old Eng., ***cliver***, a claw; Dan., ***klavre***, to scramble; Dut., ***kleveren***. In short, ***clever***

appears to retain its primary sense of quick movement; a quality which has risen in estimation in these days of competition, implying those shewy, ***catching***, outside qualities which our generation approves. A ***clever*** horse, a ***clever*** girl, a ***clever*** performance.

In America it is applied, write Elwyn and Bartlett, exclusively to moral qualities, as good natured, mild, well disposed, '***clever*** but not ***smart***'; and the definitious English clever and Yankee clever are used to indicate the precise meaning implied – English clever more faithfully reflecting the Yankee 'smart.'

Clever, lusty, very well, Lanc., – affable; South, – ***clever through***, clean through straight along; Leic., ***clever-clumsy, clever-boots***, used ironically in the North. '***Clever*** and silly are not intellectual phenomena. "How are you?" "***Cleverer*** than I was." "I am getting quite ***clever***." "Is your wife better?" "I think she is sillier than she was." "She is very silly." These are points of health.'. *Hamilton's Yorks. Dial.*

CLEVERS. Tussocks or tufts of coarse grass or rushes turned up by the plough on recent grass lands, pronounced ***cluovas***.

A.S., ***cleofa***, that which is cleft.

CLICKET. To chatter incessantly; Dut., ***klicken***. O. Fr. ***cliquette***.

'With her that will ***clicket*** make danger to cope.' *Tusser.*

'Dan'l my good man,' said she, 'you must eat and drink, and keep up your strength, for without it you'll do nowt. Try, that's a dear soul! And if I disturb you with my ***clicketten***, tell me so, Dan'l, and I won't.' *David Copperfield.*

CLIMP. To touch a polished surface with greasy fingers. Isl., ***klina***, to smear. Also to steal.

CLINK and **CLIP**. A smart blow; both imitative sounds, the former more resonant. Dut., ***klincke*** and ***klippen***. Isl., ***klingja, klippa***.

CLINKERS. Small hard paving bricks, set on edge, when thrown together they do not rattle like bricks, but make a ***clinking,*** like metallic substances. Frisic, ***klinkerts***; Dut., ***klinkerds***, the common paving brick of Holland.

CLIVER. A chopping knife. A.S., ***clifian***, to cleave.

CLOD. To clothe; ***clodden***, clothed; ***clodding***, clothing, see ***Clead***.

CLODGER. A book cover. '***Closere*** of bokys or other lyke.' *Pr. Pv.*, 1498. Fr., ***clausure***.

CLODGE. To clog. Used by Bp. Hall. ***Cledgy***, stiff, Kent. A.S. ***clæg***, clay.

CLOGSOME. Heavy roads are so termed.

CLOG-WHEAT. A bearded species, called in Mark Lane, rivets. *Forby.*

CLOTCH. To tread heavily, move awkwardly. Ger., ***klotsig***.

CLOUT. A heavy cuff. Dut., ***klotsen***, to strike. A ***cleat***, which see.

CLOW. A slice of bread, cheese, &c. *Moor.* L. Ger., ***kloue***, a slice, cut, section.

CLUNCH. A name given to the lower and harder beds of the cretaceous (chalky) rocks. It has been largely used in the interior work of East Anglian Church architecture; soft when quarried, it hardens with exposure.

Also applied in E. Ang. to chalk. Ger., ***tünchen***; Dan., ***klunt***, a block, mass; Su.-Goth., ***klaus***, massa quavis conglomerata; L. Ger., ***klunte***; Prov. Ger., ***klunch***.

CLUNCHY. Short, thick and clumsy. Dut., ***kluntet.***

CLUNG. Shrunk, dried, shrivelled, juiceless, from evaporation. Said of apples, turnips, carrots, &c. A.S., ***clingan,*** to wither. ***Clungy***, sticky. Leeds.

'Who would have thought to have found the wit of Pierce so starved and ***clunged***.' *Gab. Harvey's Pierce's Supererogation*, 1593.

'***Clings*** not his guts with niggish fare, to heap his chest withal.' *Surrey's Ecclesiastes, v. 18.*

CLUTCH. A brood of chickens, a covey of partridges. In Lanc., ***clatch***. Dan., ***klekke,*** to hatch. Isl., ***klekka***. North Ang., ***cletch.***

CLUTTER. Confusion, disorder, not used in the sense of noise or bustle as in clatter. Wel., ***cludwair***, a heap. An Americanism.

In Lanc., when things are heaped higgledy piggledy, 'They're aw in a ***clutter***.' Yorks., ***cluther***. ***Clutter-up***, to crowd together in disorder.

'And foully wallowing in ***clutter'd*** blood.' *Phineas Fletcher's Purple Island.*

'I have observed that if there were a crowd or a ***clutter*** in the street to which most people go to see what is the matter, they always draw off.' *North's Lives, iii, 206.*

COACH-HORSE. A dragon fly.

COARSE. Opposed to fine, as applied to weather. Ex., 'It is a very ***coarse*** morning.' One of the most characteristic East Anglicisms, specially met with on the sea coast.

Formerly written ***course***, ordinary; Lat., ***cursus***, in the usual common way. Both words have depreciated; thus, very ordinary, is now very common, plain.

COATHY. Surly, easily provoked. Var. of ***cothy.***

Cothish, morose, Norf. *Bp. Kennett's Gloss. Coll., Lands. M.S.*

COB. I. A sea-gull. II. A young herring. III. Clover head, containing the seed: separating these from the straw or ***stuvva*** is called ***cobbing***. IV. A seed ***cob*** or ***lib*** is a wicker basket used in sowing. V. A small, compact, punchy, powerful little horse.

All these, with the exception of the last, are local, differing from the multiplicity of dialectic meanings attached to this word. No. I. is the Frisic ***kob, zeekob***. III. From the A.S., ***cop,*** top, tuft; Wel., ***cob***. IV. ***Cob,*** a basket, is from the Lat., ***corbis***; A.S. ***cyp***, a measure; ***cypa***, a basket. V. ***Cob*** may be from the Wel., ***cwb***, compact, a small mass. ***Cob*** also was used for a rich, miserly person, ex.:–

'And of them, all ***cobbing*** country chuffes, which make their bellies and their bagges theyr gods, are called rich ***cobbes.***' *Nash's Lenten Stuff.* Wel., ***cybyz***, covetous, grasping.

'Many sorts of lari, sea-mews, and ***cobs***.' *Sir T. Browne.*

COBBLES. I. Round paving stones, any small pebbly substance. II. Fruit stones.

Wedgewood derives from the sound of pebbles rolling on a beach, as pebble, from Dan. ***pible***, to purl; Dut., ***kabbelen***, to beat, as water against a bank or shore. Is not ***cobble*** rather a diminutive of ***cob***, a lump, round mass; Wel., ***co***, a rounding; ***cobyn***, a small bundle, mass? In Cornwall, the girls who break the tin ore into small pieces are called ***cobbers***; Wel., ***cob***, a thump, whence the game of cob-nut.

COB-IRONS. The andirons on which wood was burnt in large grateless fireplaces. Also called ***Dogs***.

Ray says ***cob-iron*** is an Essex and Lanc. word.

COBLE. A fishing boat, sharp in the brow, with square stern and flat bottom. A.S., ***cuople***, a small ship.

COBWEB-MORNING. 'A misty morning, *Norfolk.*' *Bailey.* ***Copweb-weather***, misty weather. *Forby.* A.S., atter-***cop***, a spider.

COCK-BRUMBLE. The hawk's-bill bramble, from its curved spines. *Rubus fruticosus, Lin.*

COCKEY. A sewer. The old bricklayers or masoners use the term for a drain. Wel., ***soc***, a sink or drain.

COE. An odd old fellow; Norfolk. *Grose.*

COIT. To toss up the head. Of an affected minx it is said, 'she ***coits*** up her head above her betters.'

Jamieson derives from the Isl., ***kita***, violentu jactare. There is the Wel. ***coeth***, to talk pertly. O. Fr., ***cuider***, to conceit, guess, presume; ***coint***, spruce, fine, tricked up.

COLD-CHILL. An ague fit.

COLDER. Broken ears of corn mixed with short fragments of straw beaten off by the flail. Bret., ***kolo***, straw, the stalk and ear of various grains. See the Lat., collido. See ***Cavings*** and ***cosh***.

COLLAR, COLLOW. I. To sully with soot or coal dust. Chesh., ***colly***. II. Black smut from the chimney bars. A.S., ***col.***, coal; Isl., ***kala***, to smut. ***Colley***, a blackbird. Somerset.

COLLOW. 'Too foulmouthed I am to ***becollow*** or becollier him with such chimney sweeping attributes of smoaking and parching.' *Nashe's Lenten Stuff.*

COLLOGUE. To confer together for mischievous purposes. 'Kinda!' cries out a farmer at a flock of rooks, which he apprehends have a bad design on his corn fields, 'see them there toads ***collogueing*** together.' *Moor.* Cor. of Lat. ***colloquer.*** Yorksh., ***colloge.***

'Unconscionable miscreants care not how they ***collogue***, whom they slander for a private advantage.' *Bp. Hall's Contemplations.*

'If you are Religious, and frequent the church and the sacraments, you're an Hypocrite; and without this, you're an Atheist, or an Heretick. If you are Gay, and pleasant, you pass pleasantly for a Buffoon; and if Pensive and reserv'd, you are taken to be soure, and Censorious. Courtesie is called ***colloguing*** and Currying of Favour.' *L'Estrange's Quevedo.*

COLT. Any person in a parochial or public office attending a public meeting for the first time is called a ***colt***, and must be ***shod***, pay a forfeit of liquor. Ex., 'We shall have a good frolic to-day; we have four ***colts*** to ***shoe***.' *Forby.*

COME-BACK. A guinea fowl – a resemblance to its harsh cry.

COMPANY-KEEPER. A lover. Old Fr., ***compagner***, être en commerce, ou en familiarité avec une femme. *Roquef, Gloss.*

COOK-EEL. A sort of cross bun made and eaten in Norfolk during Lent. Dut., ***koekje***, a little cake.

'A New Year's ***cookey*** is a peculiar cake made only in New York, and at the Christmas Holidays. In the olden time, each visitor on New Year's day was expected to take one.' *Bartlett's Americanisms.*

It was a Norfolk custom not many years back for employers to give a breakfast to all in their employ, on Shrove Tuesday; and boys on that morning were wont to sing when going to work.

'On Shrove Tuesday morning, boys, at the first meal,
I hope my master will give me a ***cook-eel***;
And then up to work without any noise,
And at one o'clock a rare thumping ***froise***.'

The ***cook-eel*** or spiced bread (Fr., ***coquille***, a fashion of a hard-crusted loafe, like our Still-yard Bunne. *Cotgr.*) is a remnant of the old Romish Carnival, remarks Mr. Spurdens.

CONEY-LAND. So light and sandy as to be fit for nothing but breeding rabbits. A common jest is that it may be ploughed with two rabbits and a knife. *Forby.*

CONKERS. Snail shells. Lat., ***concha***, a shell.

CONSTOBLE, a great coat. Also called a ***consloper.***

COOMS. High ridges on bad roads between the ruts and horse path. Wel., ***cwm***, a cup shaped depression in the hills, a valley or dale, a hollow, shelter, dingle. A.S., ***combe.***

Elsewhere, Combe implies a valley. The coomb of corn (and formerly of coals in Norfolk) seems to mean a heap. Lat., ***cumulus.*** The ***comb*** of a bird, its crest. *A. Gurney.*

Comb, the balk or narrow slip which is left in velling the land. *Devon. Dial.*
Combe, a little valley opening into a larger one. *Pulman's East Devon. Dial.*
Combe can hardly be strictly implied to denote a valley. Its Celtic deriv. gives its precise meaning – a ***hollow*** or depression in the bosom or sides of the hills. The combes round Bath, as Lyncombe, are placed in ledges below the hill tops, but lying above the vallcys beneath.

Med. Lat., ***comba***, deep valley. It. dial., ***comba***; Sp. Pr., ***comba***, a hollow or dell; from ***concava***. *Diez.*

COPE. I. A large quantity, or great number. Lat., ***copia.*** II. To chop, exchange, chaffer, barter, deal. Used by the coasters of Norfolk and Suffolk. A.S., ***ceapian***; Dut., ***copen***; Isl., ***kampa.***

'Where Fleminges began on me for to cry,
Master, what will you ***copen*** or buy?' *Lydgate.*

COPPER-ROSE. Fr., ***couperosé***; Lat., ***cupri rosa.*** See ***Canker***.

Ray, in his North country words has '***coprose***, called also ***Head-Wark***, the *Papaver rhœas.*' In Scotland, cock-rose is any wild poppy with a red flower.

COPPLE CROWN. A tuft of feathers on the head of a fowl. ***Coppling***, unsteady, in danger of falling or tippling over. Wel., ***cop***, top of anything. Dan., ***kop***, head.

CORNY. I. Abounding in corn. II. Tasting well of malt. III. Tipsy. Goth., ***kaurn***; Isl., ***kiarni***; Dut., ***keerne.***

Ex. II. 'Now I have dronke a draught of ***corny*** ale,
By God I hope I shal you tell a thing
That shal by reson ben at your liking.' *Chaucer.*

Ex. III. 'A common word for a common condition in New England.' *Elwyn.*

CORRUPTED. Ruptured. Suff.

COSH. The husk, or outer bark of corn, particularly wheat. 'White wheat in a red ***cosh***,' is a favourite local variety. *Forby.* Gael., ***cochull,*** husky. Fr., ***cosse.***

COST or **COAST**. Ribs of cooked meat. Ex., 'Do you choose shoulder or ***coast.***' Lat., ***costa,*** a rib; Wel., ***cyost,*** side; Gael., ***slios.***

COSTLY. Costive.

Moor remarks – 'this word we hear from educated and travelled people.'

COTHISH, COTHY. Faint, sickly. Wel., ***coth.***, sick; A.S., ***cothe.***

Applied in Hampshire to rotten sheep. ***Coathe,*** to bane, applied to sheep. Somerset. ***Cooth,*** a cold. Kotched a ***cooth*** i' his limbs. Salop. ***Coathe,*** to swoon. Linc.

'So fel sche with childe, and sche went onknowing hir tyme fro Seynt Petirs onto Lateran. Hir ***cothys*** fel upon hir betwix the Collise and Seynt Clement Cherch.' *Capgrave's Chronicle – Story of Pope Joan.*

'And this was kept ful grete councelle fro the emperoure, seying that he deyed in a ***cothe.***' *Capgrave.*

COT. I. A covering for a cut thumb or finger. II. A shovel handle.

Dut., ***kot,*** 'widely used,' says Wedgewood, 'in that language, in the sense of hollow receptacle, cavum, loculamentum.' Gael., ***cos,*** handle, haft.

COUCH-HANDED. Left handed. Fr., ***gauche.*** Devon, ***couchy-h.***

COUSIN. Nephew or niece. 'Pandarus calls Cressida his cousin, who was, however, his niece.' *Forby.* See ***kinsman.***

COUSIN BETTY, COUSIN TOM. A bedlamite or rather an impudent vagrant pretending to be such.

Forby says, 'they were wont to enter the sitting-room of a family, having first ascertained that there was nobody in it but women and children, with whom they claimed kindred.'

COWL. A tub, Essex. *Ray.* Dan., ***köle,*** to cool.

Or the root may exist in the Romance dialects, Lat., ***colligere***; O. Fr., ***ceuiller,*** to collect; Pg., ***colher***; Sp., ***colodra,*** a milk pail.

COW MUMBLE. The cow parsnip. *Heracleum sphondyleum, Lin.*

COW-TONGUED. Having a tongue smooth one way, and rough the other, as purpose serves.

COXY ROXY. Merry and fantastically tipsy.

COY. A coop for lobsters. Suff. Dut., ***kouw,*** a cage.

COZEY. Snug, comfortable, warm. Gael., ***coiseag,*** a small nook or corner. ***Coiseagach,*** snug; Isl., ***kios,*** a small place well fenced. Common in Scotland.

CRAB-LANTHORN. A pasty of the apple-jack species, which see.

CRACK. Something to boast of. Ex., 'She is the ***crack*** of the village.' II. A very short time. 'It was done in a crack.'

CRAKE, CRACK. To brag, boast. Dut., ***kraaken.***

'Two good haymakers, worth twenty ***crakers.***' *Tusser.*

'He says we are but ***crakers***,
He calleth vs England men strong harted lyke an hen.' *Skelton.*

CRAMATTING. The process of protecting the surface of newly formed embankments, by layers of straw pegged into the soil and stitched down by an iron chisel. Dut. and Fries., ***kram***, a staple; ***krammen***, to fasten with wire.

CRAMPLED. Affected by cramps. Isl., ***kreppa***, to contract; Ger., ***krumpen;*** Sw., ***krympa***. In Suff., creepled is compressed, squeezed. A stack ***creeples*** when it falls away from irregular pressure.

CRANE-GUTTED. Very thin, herring gutted.

CRATCH. An old Suffolk word for manger. Old Fr., ***créche.***

'And in that infancie of that Church having found it (though as the wise men Christ in the cratch) why did they so adore it?' *Rogers' Lost Groat.*

CRAWLY MAWLY. In a weakly, ailing state. Indifferently well.

Conveys the idea of being able only to crawl on hands and knees.

CREEK. A servant, Suff. It., ***creato***, a servant, from ***crier***, to rear.

CREEPERS. I. Low pattens on iron stumps. II. Grapnel hooks.

I. A.S., ***creopan***; Du., ***krupien.*** II. Gael., ***crub***, a claw, fang.

CREEPLE. A cripple. ***Creeples***, nervous fidgets, uneasy twinges.

'The place must be frequented whence these waters flow, there must be a comming, and (with those ***creeples***) a waiting about the Poole, if we would have comfort.' *Rogers' Lost Sheep.*

CRIBLE. A finer sort of bran, a second sifting. Wel., ***crib,*** to comb, rake; Gael., ***criathair***, to sift. O. Fr., ***crible***.

CRICKLE, CRUCKLE. To bend under a weight, to sink through pain or weakness. Ger., ***kriechen***, to creep, crawl. Lanc., ***cruttle.***

CRIMBLE. To creep about privily, to sneak, wind about unperceived. To ***crimble-i'-the-poke,*** to fly from an agreement, act shabbily. A.S., ***crymbig***, crooked; Wel., ***crwm***.

CRIMP. A dealer in coals, Norf.

CRINKLE, CRUNKLE. To wrinkle, twist, plait or rumple. Frisic and Dut., ***kronkelen***; Dan., ***kringel***. Also to shrink.

Holloway gives crinkle, crunkle, to ***wrinkle, cringle, crumple,*** zigzag, as Norfolk, Suffolk and Hampshire words.

CRISH, CRUSH. Soft bones or cartilage yielding easily to the teeth.

CROAT. A bottle, Suff. Isl., ***krus***; Dut., ***kroes***, a drinking vessel.

CROCK. In Suffolk, the plate or bricks of a fireplace, 'as black as the ***crock***.' To ***crock***, Essex, to black one with soot. ***Crocks***, sooty flakes falling from chimney tops. Dut., ***roet***, soot; ***rook***, smoke. Isl., ***rok***; Sw., ***rok***, smoke. An Americanism.

CROME. A crook, a staff with hooked end for drawing weeds out of ditches, &c. Dung-cromes, turnip cromes, &c. Dut. and Fl. ***krom***; Gael., ***crom***.

CRONE. An old ewe that has lost its teeth. Dut., ***kronie***. Craven, ***crock.***

'In travelling homeward, buy forty good ***crones***,
And fat up the bodies of those seely old bones.' *Tusser.*

CROODLE. To lie close and snug, as pigs or puppies in their straw.

Dimin. of ***crowd,*** to press. ***Croodle***, to crouch like frightened chickens at sight of a bird of prey. *Wilb.* Chesh. Hartshorne in his *Salopia Antiqua*, has 'to bend over the fire in cold weather, to herd together like fowls in the wet.'

CROONCH. To encroach.

CROP-SHIN. A headless herring; a refuse, broken one. Dan. and Sw., ***krop***, the body; Dut., ***krop***, stomach; ***sich kropfen***, to grow amiss.

'There was a herring, or there was not, for it was but a ***cropshin***, one of the refuse sort of herrings.' *Nashe's Lenten Stuff.*

CROTCH. Forked, the meeting of two arms of a tree; the junction of the thighs. Fr., ***croc***, a hook; Dut., ***krook***.

'A lesson good, save ***crotches*** of wood.'
'However ye scotch, save pole and ***crotch***.' *Tusser.*

Of a long-legg'd person it is said he has plenty of ***crotch-room.***

CROTCHED. Cross, peevish, perverse. ***Crotch-boots***, water-boots; ***crotch-bound***, lazy; ***crotch-tail***, a kite; ***crotchety***, U.S. ***crotchical***.

CROTCH-TROLLING for pike, practised by poachers in the Broads and Norfolk rivers. No rod is used, but a reel; and with the help of a ***crotch***-stick the bait is thrown some distance in the water, and drawn gently home.

CROUCE. To catterwaul, to provoke. Fr., ***courroucer***.

CROWD-BARROW, CRUDDEN-BARROW. A wheel-barrow, crowded or shoved along. A.S., ***cread***; Dut., ***kruyden***, to thrust. ***Crudded*** milk, curdled.

'She sent my mother word by Kate, that she should come hither when God sent time, though she should be ***crod*** in a ***barrow***.' *Letter of Margery Paston*, A.D. 1477.

'Which it does, not by shoving or driving it forwards, as a slouch does a ***crowd-barrow***.' *Fairfax.*

CROW-KEEPER. A boy employed to scare crows from new sown land.

'Then stir about, Nicol, with arrow and bow,
Take penny for killing of every crow.' *Tusser.*

Lear exclaims, 'that fellow handles his bow like a ***crow-keeper***!' a passage which wonderfully obfuscated the early commentators.

Crow-time, evening; when rooks fly homeward.

CRUMP, CRUMPY. Brittle, dry-baked; easily cracking; surly. Gael., ***crup.***

Also N. Ang. and Sc. Ger., ***schrumpfen*** and ***krumpen***. In its sense of surly it corresponds to ***grumpy***; A.S., ***grom***; Dan., ***grum***; Wel., ***grwm***; Dut., ***grommen***. A.S., ***crympig***; Ger., ***krumm***; Wel., ***crymn***, to bend, crook.

'When the workman took measure of him he was ***crump***-shoulder'd, and the right side higher than the left.' *L'Estrange's Æsop.*

'He with the Flat Nose is Socrates; the little ***crump*** shoulder'd Wretch was the Famous Aristotle; and T'other there the Divine Plato.' *L'Estrange's Quevedo.*

CRUMPLEN. I. A diminutive mis-shapen apple. II. A little deformed person. Dimin. of A.S., ***crump***, crooked. Wel., ***crwm.***

CUDDLE. To fondle, embrace, press to the bosom.

Mr. Wedgewood derives from ***cruddle***. The Rev. J. Davies, in his admirable paper on the Dialect of Lanc., *Phil. Sy. Trans.*, 1855, p. 230, from Wel., ***cuddio,*** to hide, cover. Still nearer seems the Wel. ***cudawl***, hovering about; ***cudeb***, fondness, affection.

CULCH. Norf. and Essex. In Suff. ***gulsh***, thick dregs or sediment.

At Colchester, the word is thought to have been derived from the oyster trade, in which it is applied to the refuse. In the Devon dialect, ***cauch*** is a disgusting mixture or mess. Gael., ***sailch***, filth, impure dregs or sediment.

Culch, skultch, rubbish composed of broken tiles, pots, and pans, shards of all kinds, laid down in the oyster beds for the oyster spat or spawn to attach itself to. See ante ***culch*** and ***gulsh***.

Corn., ***cauch***, a nasty mixture, filth; O. It., ***gualercio***, dirty, nasty.

CULP. A hard and heavy blow. Ger., ***kolbe***, a club, mace; Dan., ***kolb***, butt-end; ***culpy***, thick set, short.

CULPIT. A large lump of anything. Qy. a cor. of ***collop.***

Wedgewood says, 'collop from ***clop*** or ***colp***, the sound of a lump of something soft thrown on a flat surface.' '***Coup***, a blow, a bit of anything.' *Bailey*. In like manner we have ***dab***, a blow, and a lump of something soft, a ***pat*** with the hand, and a ***pat*** of butter, &c.

CULVER. To beat and throb in the flesh. As a sore advances to suppuration it bulks and ***culvers***. In Suff., ***galver***; Dan. ***skiœlve***, to tremble, shiver; Swed., ***skiülfva***, to palpitate; A.S., ***scylfan***, to waver.

CULVER-HEADED. A stack thatched with straw is said to be culver-headed. C. Bret., ***kôlô***, straw; ***kôlôa***, to cover with straw; ***kôloên-vara***, a thatched summit. Stupid.

CULVER-HOUSE. A pigeon house. A.S., ***culfre***, a dove.

'Or as the ***culver***, that of the eagle is smitten.' *Chaucer*.

CUMBLED. Cramped, stiffened with cold. '***Cumbly-cold***, stiff with cold.' An Old Eng. form of ***clumsy.*** Scot., ***cumbered***, benumbed.

Pl. Dut., ***Klamen, Klomen***, to be stiffened with cold. Isl., ***Klumsa***, suffering from cramp. 'Havi de froide, stiffe, ***clumpse***, benummed.' *Cotgr. Fr. D.*, 1632. '***Aclumsid***, benumbed with cold. Frisic, ***beklomd***; Dut., ***verklemmd. Comelyd,*** for colde.' *Pr. Pv.*, 1440. In Mr. Way's note on the word, occur the following illustrations:—'Our hondes ben ***a-clumsid***.' *Wickliffe's New Test.* 'Thou ***clomsest*** for cold.' *Piers Ploughman*. An old M.S. Eng./Lat. Lexicon dated 1483, the *Cath. Ang.* written apparently in the N.E. of Eng. has '***clumsyd,*** eviratus (cold)' and later on '***cumbryd*** ubi (see) ***clumsyd***'. Earlier, the Pr. Pv. has '***a-comelyd*** for coulde, or ***a-clommyde*** (acomyrd, P. ***a-combred.***)

CURREL. A rill or drain. Dimin. of ***current.*** Lat., ***currere***.

If from the sound, the Gael. ***corrghuil,*** murmuring.

CUSHION-MAN. A chairman.

CUSTARD. The pat on the hand inflicted by a schoolmaster's ferula or patter. The Sc. ***palmie***.

CUTE. Shrewd, sharp, quick in apprehension. Ex., ' 'A's a ***cute*** chap.' A very common Americanism, of East Anglian origin.

In opposition to Mr. Forby, we incline to the Lat. der. of ***acutus***, rather than the A.S. ***cuth.***

CUYP. To stick up. Dut., ***kuipen.***

D

DABBY. Moist and adhesive, like wet linen. ***Dab***, a blow. Dut., ***dabbelen***, to splash. Also to bob up and down.

Dut., ***Dobber***, a fishing float, whence ***dobberen***, to rise and fall with the wave. Hence is derived the name of the waterfowl, the ***dab-chick***. A dab hand, a dabster, quick, doing things at a stroke. ***Dab***, in its sense of to peck or pierce is applied to ***dibbling*** holes in furrows for seed, and dibbling implements were originally called ***dabs***. Fl., ***dabben***.

DAD, DADDY. Father; a word ignored by the march of refinement. Wel., ***tad***; Lapl., ***dadda***.

'Dad, mam, and porridge; Father, mother and broth; Pa, ma, and soup.'

DAFTER, DARTER, and **DOWTER**. A daughter. ***Darter*** is Essex, and has migrated to New England.

DAG. Dew, to bedew. ***Dag of rain***, a slight misty shower. ***Daggy***, dewy. In Norfolk, a shower of rain is called 'a ***dag*** for the turnips;' water ***dogs*** are light watery clouds; the 'sun ***dog***,' a light spot near the sun indicating rain. Sw., ***dag***, dew; Dan., ***dugge***; Old Norse, ***dögg, deigr*** rain; Lanc., ***doage***, wet, damp. 'Meety, ***daggly*** weather like.' Shropsh.

The word which a Lancashire man employs for sprinkling with water is 'to ***deg***,' and when he ***degs*** his garden he uses 'a ***deggin-can***.' *Gaskell.*

DAGGLED, DAGGED. Slashed, torn, ragged. Bret., ***dag***, to stab; Fr., ***dague***; It., ***daga***, whence dagger. ***Dag-prick***, a triangular spade.

'***Dagge*** of cloth, fractillus.' *Pr. Pv.* Chaucer satirizes in his Parson's Tale, 'pounsed and ***dagged*** (slashed) clothing.' His begging Friar, in the Sompnoure's Tale, craves 'a ***dagon*** of your blanket, leve dame.' A.S., ***daag***, anything loose, dangling. A bed covering was termed a ***dagswayne*** – 'some have longe thrumys and jagges on both sides, some but on one.' Harrison writing in Essex, in the days of Elizabeth, relates the old men of his village used to say, 'our fathers have lien full oft vpon straw palletts, on rough mats covered onelie with a sheet under coverlets of ***dagswain*** or hop harlots, and a good round log vnder their heads insteed of a bolster.'

'Never sorry lass so pitifully aweary of her ragged petticoat and ***daggled tail***.' *Gabriel Harvey's Pierce's Supererogation,* 1593.

'Raggid and ***daggid*** and cunningly cut.' *Skelton.*

DAG-LOCKS. Clotted locks hanging in dags or jags at a sheep's tail. Called, also, ***Taglocks*** and ***Claglocks***.

> 'Would it not vex thee, where thy sires did keep,
> To see the dunged folds of ***dag tayl'd*** sheep.' *Bp Hall's Satires.*

Daglets, icicles, from their pointed appearance. *Halliwell.* Called in Northamptonshire, ***daggers***. *Baker.* In later years the original sense of ***daggle*** was merged and obscured in that of ***draggling*** (A.S., ***drag***-an. Sw., ***draga***; Dut., ***trecken***,) a trailing of the clothes in wet grass or mire. The original term, although its derivation is forgotten, exists still in most of our provincial dialects. A ***draggled-tailed trollop*** is a comprehensive epithet for the wearer of skirts and petticoats tattered and torn, splashed and dirty. In Dorset dial. ***Dag*** is a small projecting stump. ***Chill-dag***, a chilblain.

DAGSWAIN. 'In faythe, and he may dreme on a ***daggeswane*** for ony fether bed.' *Skelton.*

DALLOP. I. A patch of ground among growing corn where the plough has missed. II. Rank tufts of corn on the old sites of manure heaps. III. A parcel of smuggled tea. IV. A slattern, var. of ***trollop***. V. A clumsy lump of aught tossed about. VI. To paw, toss and tumble about.

Wel., ***talp***, a lump, protuberance. Isl., ***dalpa***, to give one light blows. ***Dolpr***, a lump, 'and sometimes used as dumpy and thick, said in daily speech of a bouncing new born child.' *Jonsson's Oldnordisk Ordbog.*

'Let ***dallops*** about, be mown and had out.' *Tusser.*

DAM. A marsh, called also drowned-land. Suff. Will derive from its embanking. Su.-Goth. and Ger., ***dam***. In like sense ***dam*** is used, Su.-Goth., for a fish-pond dug out and gained from the land.

DAME. Once applied to ladies of high rank. Now, says Forby, only to the lowest. It would be very offensive used to a farmer's wife.

DAMNIFIED. Indemnified. Ex., ' 'Teent nawn to him – he's ***damnified***.'

DANGEROUS. Endangered. Ex., 'He's sadly-badly; quite ***dangerous***.'

DANK. Moist, damp, as regards weather, the grass, &c. 'A ***dank*** rafty morning.' Ger., ***tunken***, to steep; Dut., ***donker***, dark.

'***Dank*** ling forgot, will quickly rot.' *Tusser.*

A synonym of damp. In Yorkshire, when wool is damp and fusty, it is called ***donky*** or ***thonky***. 'A worthy clothier went to London to buy wool. Having visited a large establishment, he pronounced the fleeces to be ***donky***. "Donkey!" cried the indignant merchant. "***Donky***," replicated the purchaser, while he still smelt at and pulled into pieces the wool.' *Rev. R. Winter Hamilton's Dialect of Yorkshire.*

DANS. Yearling lambs. When cut, they become ***wedders***. In their second year, ***hogs*** and ***hoggets***. Onc, two or three ***shear*** sheep denotes respective ages. ***Shearlings***, the period between the first and second shear. ***Crones***, are old ewes which have lambed and lost their teeth. *Moor.*

Gael., ***uan***; Bret., ***oan***, a lamb. In Vannes, ***duemm***, a kid.

DARE. To pain, afflict. Essex. *Ray.* A.S., ***daru***, hurt.

DARK-HOUR. The evening twilight. The gloaming.

DARNOCKS, DANNOCKS. Hedger's gloves of thick leather.

Gael., ***dornag***, a gauntlet, glove, from ***dorn***, fist. Manx, ***dornaig***, a covering to guard the hand against thorns. *Cregeen.* A convenience we should little expect to have been adopted by a people in the condition of the Celts. *Wedgewood.* Isl., ***dornikur***, stiff boots for wading in water.

DARNED. I'll be. An Essex oath, of wide currency in America.

DASH. To abash. Pl. Dut., ***dwas;*** A.S., ***dwæs***, stupid from fright.

DAUBER. In the large barns and farm buildings of East Anglia, artificers in ***wattle and daub*** – a mixture of clay or mud with stubble or short straw, well beaten and incorporated, sometimes strengthened with laths and hazels, – were formerly in great request. ***Daubing*** was very durable, lasting forty or fifty years. In Suffolk it was employed also for fences. O. Fris., ***dauber,*** to beat.

Tusser calls the process ***Tampring***. The Bible speaks of '***daubing*** with ***untempered*** mortar.' ***Dawber*** or deymann. *Pr. Pv.*

Tapia, Sp., a mud wall; Lomb., ***tabia***, a poor hut; prob. of Eastern origin. Turk. Ar., ***tabiah***, rampart, bastion. *Diez.*

DAUNT. To stun, knock down. Fr., ***dompter,*** to subdue.

DAWL. A cat, to coax it. Dut. ***dauwelen***, to play with, fondle.

DAZE, DAZLE, DAURE. To dazzle, to stun. A.S., ***dagan,*** to brighten, dazzle; Dut., ***daesen***, to be stupified; Pl. Dut., ***dösig,*** dizzy.

> 'Whereby I learne that grieuous is the game
> Which follows fansie ***dazled*** by desire.' *Gascoigne's Flowers.*

Dawzey is a Suffolcism. Ex., 'A ***dauzey*** hiddid fellah.' ***Dozzled*** is another variation; which see. **DAUSEY-HEADED.** Giddy and thoughtless. *Grose.* Var. of ***daze***, applied in U.S. to old people whose faculties are failing.

Dased has also the North Ang. sense of stupified from cold or exhaustion. Isl., ***dasdr***, faint, tired.

DEAL-TREE. Fir tree. ***Deal apples***, fir cones.

DEKE, DIKE, DELP. A ditch, or drain. A.S., ***dic***, a ditch; ***delfan***, to dig; ***deke-holl***, a hollow or dry ditch; A.S., ***holian***, to excavate.

DELK, DALK. A dimple. A cavity or dent in the soil, the flesh, or any surface which should be smooth. Isl., ***dala***, a dint. *Pr. Pv.* ***dalke***, vallis.

DELPH. A catch-water drain in the fens. Fries., ***delven***, to dig; A.S., ***delfan***.

DENES or **DUNES.** The sandy tracts on the East Anglian coast.

Old Fr. ***dunes***; Dut., ***duynes***, sand-hills by the seaside; Gael., ***duin***, to shut in, surround; ***dún***, a heap; Fris., ***döhne***, a sand hillock.

DENT. The worst of anything – the pinch. After a loud clap of thunder, a woman says, ' 'Tis all over. I knew that was the ***dent*** of it.' *Moor.* A.S., ***dynan***, to make a noise.

DERE. Dire, sad. ***Derely***, direly. A.S., ***der-ian***, to hurt.

DEUSAN. A hard keeping apple, which shrivels and turns pale. Hence the simile, 'pale as a ***deusan***.'

Any hard fruit, according to Minshew. Gael., ***deuchainn***, hard.

DEVILTRY. Aught unlucky, offensive, hurtful, or hateful.

DEVING-POND. One whence water is drawn for domestic use, by dipping a pail. ***Deve***, to dive, dip; A.S., ***dufian***.

DEVLIN. The species of swallow, called the swift. *Hirundo apus, Lin.* Also a fretful, troublesome woman.

DEW-BEATERS. Coarse and thick shoes to keep out wet.

DEW-DRINK. The first beer given to harvesters before they commence.

DIBLES, DIABLES. Difficulties, embarrassments. N. Fr., ***dibìllè***, disabled.

DICKY, DICK-UP. An ass. ***Dickey ass***, a male ass; the female a Jenny or a Betty ass. ***Dik-kop***, Flem., is thick-scull.

DICKY-BAHD. The general term for any small bird in East Anglia.

'All little birds are by children called Dicky-birds. We have Jack Snipe, Jack Daw, Tom Tit, Robin Redbreast, Poll Parrot, a Gill-Hooter; a Magpie is always called Madge; a Starling, Jacob; a Sparrow, Phillip; a Gold Finch, Jack Nicker; and a

Raven, Ralph.' *Wilbraham's Cheshire Glossary.*
Moor adds, we have also Jack Curlew, Jenny Wren, Betty Tit, and King Harry, the Goldfinch.

DICK-A-DILVER. The herb periwinkle. Lat., ***per vincà***, ***per***, about, and ***vincere*** to bind, having formerly been used for chaplets.
Forby derives from the O.E., ***delving***, A.S., ***delfan***, 'from its rooting at every joint and spreading.'. More probably from its abounding in East Anglia in the delves or ditches. '***Delph*** and ***delf,***' common terms in the Fens-lands.

DIDAPPER. The little grebe, also known as the ***dab-chick***, the ***dive-an-dop***, ***divy-duck***, &c. Sw., ***doppa***, to dip.
'Such ***dydoppers*** must be taken vp, els theile not stick to check the King.' *Pap with a Hatchet*, 1589. 'The ***diveandop***, to slepe.' *Skelton.*

DIDALL. A spade used for ditching, &c. in the marshes.
'A sickle to cut with, a ***diddall*** and crome
For draining of ditches that noyes thee at home.' *Tusser.*
Mavor, in his *Notes to Tusser*, ed. of 1812, describes a ***diddall*** as a triangular spade for cutting and banking up ditches where the soil is loose. The ***crome*** (see **CROME**) resembles a dung rake, and is used for drawing out the weeds, flags, &c. cut from the bottom of the ditch. At the back of Yarmouth the ***dydle*** is in use and well known. '***Dydleing*** mash ditches,' cleaning or faying them. A dydleing machine was used for cleaning rivers. Grose has '***Didal,*** a triangular spade as sharp as a knife.' Called also a ***dag-prick*** (see DAG) in Norfolk and Essex. Sw. ***dy***, mud, ***dallra***, to shake, ***dela*** to deal out. The Bret. has ***didala***, to remove the bottom of aught.

DIDDER. To quiver with the chin through cold. Dut., ***sidderen***, to shiver; Wel., ***sigaw,*** to shake; Isl., ***titra***.
'***Dyderyn*** for colde.' *Pr. Pv.* ***Didder*** for cold, to say an ape's Paternoster. *Cotgr.* ***Didder*** to ding or dunt (blunt) with cold. Dorset. ***Dother*** and ***dither***, to tremble. North Ang., Heref. and Northampt. ***Dodder***, *Whitby.*

DIDDLE. Dimin. of dawdle.

DIDDLES, DIDDLINGS. Young ducklings or sucking pigs.

DIDDY. The female breast of milk, the ***titty***. Wel., ***didi,*** a nipple, teat, or paps. Ir., ***did***.

DILLS. The paps of a sow. 'More pigs than ***dills***,' a Suffolcism. Dan., ***di***; Norse, ***dili***, to suckle.

DILVER. To weary with labour or exercise. *Forby.* Dilvered, confused, heavy, unwell, out of sorts. *Moor.* Worn out with watching. *Grose.*
Possibly from A.S., ***thyldian***, to endure, suffer. Ger., ***dulden***; Fris., ***dylde***.

DINDEL. Sow-thistle, probably cor. of ***dandelion***. ***Dyndelyn***. *Pr. Pv.*

DING. I. To throw, hurl. Ex., 'I ***dung*** it at him.' In Essex, sling.
Is., ***dengia***, to hammer. A.S., ***dencgan***, to strike; Dan., ***dænge***; Sw., ***dänga.***
'The ***ding-thrift*** heir, his shift-got sum mispent.' *Hall's Satires, B. IV.*
'We, in this age, count him a heathen divine, that allegeth any illustration out of human authors, and makes not all his sermons concloutments of Scripture. Scripture we hotch-potch together, and do not place, like pearl and gold lace on a garment, here and there to adorn, but pile it, and ***dung*** it up on heaps, without use or edification.' *Nash's Christ's Tears.*

'Her alabaster walls were all furred, and some painted, with the bespraying of men's brains ***dung*** out against them.' *Nash's Christ's Tears.*

II. A blow, to beat, violent movement. Ex., 'I could not ***ding*** it into him.' 'A clapp't spurs to 'a's hoss, and awah 'a went full ***ding***.' ***Ding-doulers***, finery in dress. Suff.

DINGE. To rain mistily, to drizzle. Used in the sense of ***dingy*** weather. Isl., ***dyngja***, to rain in torrents; Dan., ***dynd***; Fris., ***duge***; mire, slosh; Wel., ***dihinez***, showery.

Dingin, showery. 'Weather unfit to hoe wheat in, as the weeds do not die.'

DINGLE, to drizzle. 'Dew it rain?' 'No ta ded ***dingle*** just now.'

DIP. A sauce of melted butter, vinegar and sugar for the famous Norfolk dumplings.

DISCOMFRONTLE. To discomfit in an affronting manner. *Forby.*

Dyscowmfortyn. *Pr. Pv.*

DISOBLIGE. To stain or sully. A romp ***disobliges*** a young lady's white frock.

DITHES. Dung of oxen and sheep dried and cut in slabs for fuel. Wel., ***gleiad***, dried cowdung.

DO, DON'T. Used in Norfolk in a remarkably elliptical sense. Ex., 'Has the postman called? I ***don't*** know; du there's no letters for you.' 'Shet yin gate, Jim bor, ***don't*** them pigs'll get out.' *Gillett.*

DOATED. Decayed, rotten, applied to timber. Common also in the U.S. Ger., ***dotteren,*** to totter. Apparently var. of ***dodder'd***; shattered. See ***didder***. ***Dotterill,*** an old doating fellow. *Craven.*

'So it fareth with the same tree in its decay; for it becomes sapless and ***doddered***, one knoweth not well wherefore.' *Stanihurst.*

Isl., ***dotta***, to nod with drowsiness; Dut., ***dödderig***, drowsy, nodding; Ger., ***dotteren***, to totter – roots of our Eng. ***doating***. ***Doated*** timber has its root probably in the Ger. ***todt***, death; ***todten***, the dead; Dan., ***Dödhed,*** deadness.

In Northampts. ***dodderels*** are pollards. ***Dodded***, lopped, occurs in Bailey. ***Doddyd***, without horns. *Pr. Pv.* To ***dodd*** sheep, to cut the wool away about the tail, Teesdale. ***Dodded*** sheep, short-horned,. Whitby. ***Dod***, a round-topped fell, and ***doddy***, a cow without horns, Cumb. ***Doe-headed***, says Carr. *Craven Gloss.* Fris., ***dodd***, a lump, clump. Fr., ***dodu***, round, plump. A ***bog***. – Northampt., from ***dodder***, to shake.

DOBBLE. A local variation of daub.

DOCKEY. A ten o'clock morning meal taken by labourers.

It., ***tocco***, a morsel; vulg. ***tocco di pane***, a bit of bread; Wel., ***toci,*** an allowance, what is cut off; Fris., ***dók***; Bremen, ***dokke***, a little cut shive.

DODDY. Low in stature, small, 'a ***doddy*** bit.' ***Doddy-***mite. Hoddy-***doddy, dodkin, totty***. Dan., ***tot,*** a bunch; Fris, ***dodd***, a lump, clump; Fr., ***dodu***, round, plump.

DODDY-PATE, DODDIPOLE. A blockhead, dunce. Fris., ***doddje,*** a silly-stupid, a blockhead.

'He rayles and he ratis – He calleth them ***doddy-patis***.' *Skelton.*

'Ye hoddy-peakes, ye ***doddy-poules***.' *Latimer.*

'Our curate is an asse-head, a ***dodipoll***, a lack-latine.' *Id.*

'You that purpose with great sums of study and candles to purchase the worshipful names of dunces and ***dodipoles***, may closely sit, or soakingly lie at your books.' *Gab. Harvey's Supererogation*, 1593.

DODGE. A small lump of something moist and thick, as of mortar, clay, &c. Var. of ***dod***.

DODMAN. A snail. See HODMADOD.

'Yt is as great pyte to see a woman wepe as yt is to se a sely ***dodman*** crepe.' *Bale's Kynge Johan*, 1538.

'In that a Snayl or ***Dodman***, which is not only not warm, but to our feeling very cold, is fain to brood its as cold sweaty eggs, nested upon a cold wet earth, bespewing them about with the fuzze of a cold clammy froth, in coldish raughty weather, and all making way to a kind and timely hatching.' *Fairfax*.

'I'm a reg'lar ***dodman***, I am, said Mr. Peggotty.' *David Copperfield*.

Bacon enumerates ***hodmadod*** or ***dodman***, among fish that cast their shells.

DOGGEDLY. Shamefully done. A dogged way, a distance.

DOLE, DOOL. Deal, division or share of anything, as gains, joint property; a distribution, as of alms, food, fuel, or clothing; also a boundary or landmark. A.S., ***dœlan***; Plat. Dut., ***deelen***, to separate, distribute, &c.

Pl. Dut., ***dole***, a ditch, with the sod turned up as landmark.

Dole or ***several*** is a term commonly applied in East Anglia to the divisions of parochial lands or charities, or of common right of pasturage, fuel, &c. ***Dool*** posts were low boundary marks. Also to the half-and-half (in Cornwall, 'one and all') or share principle which prevails in the coast fisheries. In Cumb., ***dote***. Applied on the Yorks. coast to the alms of money or food given at funerals.

'Accursed be he who removeth his neighbour's ***doles*** or markes.' *Homilies*.

DOLK, DOKE. A deeper indentation than ***delk***, a cavity between two swellings. The pit or hollow of the stomach. Fris., ***dolg***, a wound; Gael., ***dochainn,*** hurt, injury; Eng., Gypsy, ***dooka***.

'He hugged her only with his two forefeet, which he had thrust so into the oft of her sides, as to make two deep ***doaks*** there.' *Fairfax*.

DOLLOPT. Badly or over-nursed. Var. of ***dallop***.

DOLVER. Reclaimed Fen ground. A.S., ***dulfon***, dug out.

DOME, DOOM, DUM. Down, as a rabbit's. Dan., ***dunn***. Isl., ***dùn***.

A goose or duck, when beginning to sit, plucks off her plumage to line the nest. This is called ***dumming*** it.

DONE-GROWING. Stunted in growth.

DOOR STALL. A door post. The A.S., ***durusted***.

DOP. A short, quick curtsey. A.S., ***dopettan***, to sink.

DOP-A-LOW. Very short in stature, applied to females.

DOR. The cock-chafer. A.S., ***dora***, a drone.

DORBELLISH. Very clumsy. Gael., ***doirbh***, perverse, untoward.

'Anything that has an unseemly appearance, Ayrsh.' *Jamieson*.

'Will you then hope to beat them down with fusty brown bread ***dorbellish?***' *Nash*.

DORE-APPLE. A firm winter apple of a bright yellow colour; cor. of *pomme d'or*.

DORMER. A large beam.

Halliwell has ***dormant***, the large beam lying across a room, a joist. Also called

dormant-tree, dormond and ***dormer***. Anything fixed was said to be ***dormant***. Fr., ***dormant***, sleeping, lying still.

DOSS. I. To butt with the horns, as a bull, a ram, or he goat. Scot., ***dush***, to push as a ram, ox, &c. Dan., ***dyst***, shock, brunt.

'Potter, the translator of the three Greek Tragic Poets, was nonplussed on first coming into Norfolk as a curate, by the farmer with whom he lodged telling him whilst pointing out to his notice a fine bull, that he must soon make away with him, as he had already '***dossed*** three ***mauthers***.' *Forby.*

II. A hassock, in Chesh., a boss or pess. III. The tussochs or knots of sour rushy grass in marsh land. Gael., ***dos***, and ***dosach***, a bush, tuft, cluster; Manx, ***dossagh***, clustery.

Dossers or ***Dorsers,*** wicker baskets or panniers. Old Fr., ***dorsiers.*** Fr., ***dos***, back.

DOSSERS. A motion of the head in children, caused by affections of the brain. Fris., ***dösig***, giddy.

DOTTED. Giddy, said of sheep that have ***hydatids*** on the brain.

One of the E.A. words imported into Gower, Pembroke.

DOW. A dove. ***Duffy-dows***, their unfledged young. ***Dow House, duffus***, a dove cot. '***Dwfowus***, ***dufhows***, columbaria.' *Pr. Pv.* Isl., ***dufa,*** a dove; A.S., ***duna***; Scot. ***dow, dow-fulter***, a field fare. Sw., ***duf-hus***, a dove-cot.

'With the gardynes berne and ***duffous*** that I purchased therto.' *Bury Wills* (John Barets 1463) *Camden Sy.*

'The fauconer came runnyng with a ***dow***, and cryed, stow, stow, stow!' *Skelton.*

DOW. To mend in health. Of a sick man lying in the same state it is said that he 'neither dies nor ***dows.***'

A.S., ***dugan***, to be well; Fris., ***dodge***, Lanc., ***doesome, dowin***, healthy, prosperous. 'Nayder dee nor dowe,' in a doubtful way. Cumb.

DOWLER. A sort of coarse dumpling.

DOWN-BOUT. A hard set-to; a tough battle. ***Downfall***, rain, hail, or snow; ***down-lying***, lying-in; ***down-pins***, dead drunk.

DOWNY, DOWN I'TH MOUTH. Low-spirited; dull; Dorset, ***dungy***; Cumb., ***dowy***; Teesdale, ***dowly***, the latter from Wel., ***dulyn***.

DOZZLED. Stupid, heavy. Cumb., ***dozent***; O. Fris., ***dösig***, dizzy.

'In such a perplexity every man asks his fellow, "What's best to be done?" and being ***dozzled*** with fear, thinks every man wiser than himself.' *Hacket's Life of Archbp. Williams.*

DRABBLE. To trail or trapes in the dirt, as a ***drabble***-tailed wench. The original word, now obscured by ***draggle***, dim. of drag.

Gael., ***drabh***, refuse, dirt; ***drabag*** a slut; ***drab***, a stain. A.S., ***drabbe***, dregs. Dan., ***draabe***; Du., ***drabbe***, to cover with filth. Plat. Dut., ***drabbeln***, to slobber. '***Drabbelyn***, mud.' *Pr. Pv.*

DRAGGING-TIME. Fair day evenings, when the young fellows towzc the wenches about.

DRAINS. Grains from the mash tub, after the wort has been drained off.

'An oestridge feeding almost upon anything, ours refused nothing but the

draines from the brew-house.' *Sir T. Browne,* v. I. 459.

DRANT, DRAUNT. To drone or drawl in speaking. The Norfolk characteristic, as distinguished from the Suffolk whine. A.S., ***drean***.

'Than, be ydilnesse, began mech debate in the cite, evil ***drantes*** in the puple.' *Capgrave's Chronicle.*

'I long since found by experience, how ***Dranting*** of verses, and Euphuing of sentences did edify.' *Gab. Harvey's Pierce's Supererogation,* 1593.

DRAPS. Fallen fruit picked up in orchards and gardens.

DRAWK. The common darnel-grass. *Lolium perenne, Lin.*

DRAW-LATCH. A dawdling loiterer. Isl., ***latr***; Dan., ***lad,*** slow.

Drawlatchet, walking lazily. ***Latchet*** means to saunter. *Barnes' Dorset Dial.*

DREDGE. A mixture of oats and barley, now rarely sown; '***dragge***, menglyd corne; (***drage,*** or mestlyon).' *Pr. Pv.*

In the 13th cent., the grain crops chiefly cultivated in England were wheat, 'berecorn, ***dragg***,' or a mixture of vetches and oats, beans and pease. The regulations, for the brewers of Paris in 1254, prescribe that they shall brew only '*de grains, c'est a savoir d'orge, de mestuel, et de* ***dragèe***.' Tusser speaks of ***dredge*** as commonly grown in the Eastern Counties –

'Sow barley and ***dredge*** with a plentiful hand.
Thy ***dredge*** and thy barley so thresh out to malt.'

'***Dredge*** mault, malt made of oats mixed with barley malt, of which they make an excellent quick sort of drink, used in Staffordshire.' *Bp. Kennett's Gloss. Coll.* '***Dragée*** *aux chevaux*, provender of divers sorts of pulse mixed together.' *Cotgr. From Way's Notes to Pr. Pv.*

DREPE. To drip or dribble. A.S., ***driopan***; ***dreeping wet***, dripping wet; a ***dreep***, a fall of water; ex., 'three inches in a foot is sufficient ***dreep*** for pantiles.' Isl., ***driupa***; Fris., ***drepe***.

DRINDLE. I. A small slow channel to carry off water. A drill or small furrow for receiving seed. ***Drindly, dringly***, slow; ex., 'He's the ***drindlest*** man I ever did business with.' Gael., ***drill,*** a drop; Manx, ***drigey***, falling in drops. A.S., ***trindelyd***, made rounded. Su.-Goth., ***trind***. II. Slow. Wel., ***trymly***, sluggish, flagging.

DRIVING. To go fishing, used in the herring fishery. A.S, ***drifan***.

DROLL, pron. like doll, to put off, amuse with excuses. Gael., ***dàil,*** procrastination.

DROP-GALLOWS, a foul-mouth'd person.

DROPE. To perspire, to drip as tallow. Preterite of ***drepe***, which see.

DROPPERS. Women and children employed to drop seed and grain into the holes made by the ***dabs*** or ***dibblers***. The portions of work allotted to each are called ***rockets***. *Moor.*

DROUCHED. Drenched with rain, drowned. Scot., ***droukit***; Isl., ***dreckia***, to plunge in water. 'Fr., ***druger***, said of a sound shower, that wets thoroughly.'*Cotgr.* Sw. ***dränka***, to drown.

In *Robert of Brunne's Chronicle*, ***drenkled, dronkeld***, and ***dronkled***, are used indifferently.

'This man was wikked in all manere thing; therefore he was ***dronchin*** in a small water.' *Capgrave's Chronicle.*

'And took of hem to hundred and XXVIII. schippis. Thei bored and ***drenched*** hem.' *Capgrave.*

'There came up eleven hundred Flemings at Waxham, thereof were taken and killed and ***drowchyn*** eight hundred.'*Paston Letters*, A.D. 1440.

DROVE, DRIFT. An unenclosed road in the fen districts. Fris., ***droven***; Walloon, ***drovi***, to open, ***drovi n'voie***, a road, path.

DROVY, DROSY. Itchy, scabby, lousy, or even all three. A.S., ***drof***, dreggy, dirty; Dan., ***drav***; Manx, ***drouse***.

'Thus much I can say of my selfe, that these drunken ***drosie*** sonns go a tooting abroad as they themselves tearm it.' *Green's Quip for an Upstart Courtier.*

DROY, a scullion, a drudge-of-all-work; Dan., ***dröi***, heavy, stout.

DROZE. To beat very severely; ***drozings***, a sound drubbing.

North. Ang. ***drove***, to afflict trouble; Dut., ***droeven***, to afflict; ***droes***, the devil; Ger., ***drohen***, to menace; A.S., ***drefan***; Isl., ***dreyssa***, to act haughtily.

DRUG. A strong carriage with four wheels, for conveying heavy timber. Gael., ***dragh***, and ***tarruing***, to drag; Manx, ***drug***, a dray.

A ***jim***, for the same purpose has one pair only of wheels. Timber is laid upon the ***drag***, but under the axle of the ***jim***.

DRUMBLES. 'He dreams ***drumbles***.' He is half asleep. Dan., ***dulme***, to doze; Sw., ***drumla***, to be drowsy; Manx, ***dromm***.

DRY-FATS. Large wooden vessels. A.S. and Fris., ***fat***, a vat.

DUDDLE-UP. To snuggle up closely and snugly. Ex., 'How he do ***duddle*** his self up.' ***Duddle*** may be a dimin. from the Su.-Goth., ***tudda***, conglomerare, convolvere. Sax., ***tüdern***.

Moor gives an illustration overheard at a pigsty, where an old sow, who had been stingy to her clamorous litter was defended by a byestander. 'Aa, she fare ta stunt em neeyeow – but she'll lah down an ***duddle*** em present.' Derived probably as a dimin. from Dan., ***dægge***, to suckle, fondle; Sw., ***dæggja***.

Duddles, little dumps; ***thick-duddle***, flour and water. *Barnes' Dorset Dial.*

DUGGLE. A variation of the above.

DUDDER. To shiver. See ***didder.***

DUFFIN, DUTFIN. A cart-horse bridle.

Etymology obscure. It may be from the Old Fr., ***duire***, to lead, guide; and ***frein***, bridle, rein.

DULLER. To sorrow with pain; ***dollour***, a fretting plaint. Lat., ***dolor***, Wel., ***dulyn***; melancholy.

DULLOR. Loud speech. An old woman rather deaf would go to hear Parson H., for she could understand him, he made 'sich a ***dullor***.' Wel., ***dolur***; Fr., ***dolour***.

DUMBLE. To muffle or wrap up. From Su.-Goth., ***tumla***, to roll round and round. Is., ***tumba***, dark colour.

DUNDUCKYTIMUR. A dull, indescribable colour.

DUNDY. Of a dull colour, as ***dundy grey***. A.S., ***dun***; Isl., ***dumba***.

DUNK-HORN. The short blunt horn of a beast. ***Dunk-horned***, pitiful, sneaking, applied to cuckolds.

DUNSH. A shove, push. Scot., to jog with the elbow. ***'Dunche.'*** *Pr. Pv.* Gael., ***tuinnch***, tossed or dashed as it were by the waves. Dan., ***dundse***, to thump; Sw., ***dunka***, to fall clumsily.

DUNT. Stupid or dizzy as from a blow. Isl., ***dyntr***, shaking up and down; Sw., ***dunka***, to beat heavily.

A dull boy is said to be 'kiender ***dunt*** hidded.' A ***dunt*** sheep, one that mopes about from a disorder in the head. 'Words are but wind, but ***Dunts*** are the devil.' *Ray's Proverbs.* ***Dunt,*** a common abrupt pronunciation of done it. ***Dunch***, Dorset, Sus. is deaf, dull; ***Dunny***, hard of hearing. Heref. and Shrops.

DWAIN, DWAINY. Faint, sickly. A.S., ***dwinan***, to pine, waste away; Wel., ***gwan***, weak, feeble; Gael., ***fann***.

DWILE. A refuse lock of wool, a mop, any coarse rag. '***Dweyl***, a clout to wash the floor'; ***dweylen***, to mop. *Sewel's Dut. Dicty.*

According to Forby, an awkward rustic perversion of ***doiley***, which it clearly is not. The use of ***doileys*** as a small napkin at dessert is thought to have been imported with the name from Holland, or derived from the name of the dealer by whom they were introduced.

DWINGE, DWINGLE. To shrivel, dwindle, shrink. Isl., ***dvina***; Ang. and Fris., ***dwine***; A.S., ***dwinan; dwined***, vanished away, *Verstegan.*

Dwain, faint, sickly, a swoon. Suffolk. Craven, a ***dwine***. Whitby coast, a ***dwain***; ***dwiney***, puny; ***dwined***, shrivelled.

'And it is possible some may be sent thither by no default of their own, or visible cause from others; but merely from Divine Justice, insensibly ***dwingling*** their estates, chiefly for trial of their patience.' *Fuller's Worthies – on the Suffolk Proverb, 'You are in the Highway to Needham."*

DYMOX. A sturdy combatant. From ***Dymoke***, the name of the hereditary champion of the sovereign. ***Dummuck***, a blow.

E

EA. Water. A.S., ***ea***. Still retained in the proper names of many places in the fens. ***Ea*** brink; Pophams ***ea***, and other water courses cut in the Bedford Level drainage.

Eay, a pond or pool, drain or watercourse. Northampts.

EAGER, HIGRE. The swell and inundation caused by a peculiar tidal action in some rivers, as the Severn.

Forby states its occurrence in the Ouse, near Downham-bridge; and in the Nene between Wisbeach and Peterborough. '***Akyr*** of the see flowyng, *impetus maris*,' *Pr. Pv.* North Fris., ***hieen***, to rise or swell as water; or it may be A.S., ***ea***, water, and ***cer***, a turn. At Howden, Yorks., a sudden inundation of the Humber is called an ***egor***. In Craven dial. ***acker*** is a ripple.

EAR. The kidney, or adjacent fat, applied to veal. Also called ***near***, or ***neah***, ***aiyah***, and ***niyah***.

Gael., ***àra***, plur. ***àirnean***, the kidney, fat of the kidneys. Wel., ***aren***; Ger., ***mere***.

EARTH. One plowing. A.S., ***earian***, to ear or plough. Wel., ***aru***. Dut., ***eren***.

'***Eryyn londe*** (Lat.) ***aro***' *Pr. Pv.*

Goth., ***arian***, the earliest labour having been the tillage of the field.

'At the very point where man parts company with the brute world, at the first flash of reason as the manifestation of the light within us, there we see the true genesis of language. Analyse any word you like, and you will find that it expresses a general idea peculiar to the individual to which the name belongs. What is the meaning of moon? – the measurer. What is the meaning of sun? – the begetter. What is the meaning of earth? – the ploughed. The old name given to animals, such as cows and sheep, was ***pásu***, the Lat. ***pecus***, which means feeders.' *Max Muller on Language.*

EASLES. Hot embers. Essex, ***esse***. Cumb., ***ess.*** Salop, – Isl., ***eysa***.

EBBLE. The aspen tree. O.E., ***abele***; Dut., ***abeel***; the white poplar; Lat., ***albus***, white.

EDDISH. Aftermath, the ***eatage*** on land after a hay or grain crop. Fris., ***etten***, pasture; A.S., ***edisc,*** aftermath.

In *Ray's East Ang. words*, ***ersh*** is given, 'the same that ***Edish***, the stubble after the corn is cut.'

'When wheat upon ***edish*** ye mean to bestow,
Let that be the first of the wheat ye do sow.' *Tusser.*

EECHANNONNUM. Each one of them.

EERIE. Grand and causing fear. Common to Norfolk and Scotland. Dut., ***eeren***, to reverence.

ELVISH. Peevish, tricksy. Applied also to bees, as 'the bees are very ***elvish*** to-day.' A.S., ***ælf***; Isl., ***alfr***, an elf or fay.

'The mere spirit that is in you lusts to envy, inclines to crossness, ***elvishness*** and self-willedness of spirit.' *Rogers Matrimonial Honour.*

ERRIWIGGLE. An earwig. '***Erwygle.***' *Pr. Parv.*

A.S., ***ear-wigga***, or worm. O.E., ***yer-wigge***, Leic., ***wiggen-ear***; West Somerset, ***yerriwig***; ***earwicke***; East Anglia, ***erri-wiggle, err-igle, ear-wrike, narrow-wriggle;*** Northamph., ***arra-wig***; South, ***pincher-wig***; North, ***forkin robin, twinye*** and ***cat with two tails***. Lowl. Scotch, ***Gelloch*** and ***gavelock***. *Adams. Phil. Trans.*, 1858.

A.S., ***wickga***, a worm, beetle. See ***polwiggle***.

It is curious that in most European languages a name is given to this insect implying the habit of entering the human ear, – a popular error in entomology.

'ESSEX MILES, Suffolk Stiles, Norfolk Wiles,
Many Men beguiles.' *Old East Anglian Saw.*

Essex Miles. 'These are cryed up for very long, understand it ***comparatively*** to those in the neighbouring county of Middlesex. The truth is this, *good way* and a *good horse* shorten miles, and the want of either (but both especially) prolong them in any county whatsoever.' *Fuller's Worthies.*

Fuller might have added that no miles are so long to the pedestrian as those which traverse flat and uninteresting scenery like that of Essex.

ESSEX CALVES. As valiant as an Essex Lion, i.e. calf. *Local Saw.*

'Essex producing calves of the fattest, fairest and finest flesh in England (and consequently in all Europe). Sure it is a Cumberland cow may be bought for the price of an Essex calfe in the beginning of the year. Let me adde that it argueth the goodnesse of Flesh in the county, and that great gain was got formerly by the sale thereof, because that so many stately monuments were erected antiently therein for Butchers (inscribed *Carnifices* in their Epitaphs), in Cogshall, Chelmsford Church, and elsewhere, made of Marble, inlaid with Brass, whereby it appears that these of that trade have in this county been richer (or at least prouder) than in other places.' *Fuller's Worthies.*

ESSEX STILES.

'For stiles Essex may well vie with any county of England, it being wholly divided into small closes, and not one common field that I know of in the whole county.' *Ray's Proverbs.*

ESH. The ash tree. A.S., ***esc***. *Pr. Pv.*, ***esche***; Isl., ***eski***.

ETHER. To wattle or intertwine, in making a staked hedge; 'to bond a hedge,' finishing its upper part with stouter materials to bind firmer the lower. A.S., ***ether*** and ***edor***, a hedge. Also called ***edder***. ***Etherings***, pliant, hazel wands, Northampts.

'Save ***edder*** and stake – strong hedge to make.' *Tusser.*

EVERY-FUTNON. Every now and then. ***Every-each***, every other.

EVEN-FLAVOURED. Unmixed, unvaried. Current, says *Forby*, in North Suffolk, in phrases like the following 'An ***even-flavoured*** day of rain;' i.e. incessant.

EWE. Preterite of owe. 'He ***ewe*** me five pound.'

EYND, or water-smoke, as it is called in Norfolk. A remarkable phenomenon, occurring mostly between spring and autumn, and with peculiar suddenness. All at once a damp cold mist sets in from the sea, and spreads at times many miles inland, refreshing the vegetation, but imparting a dreary aspect to the landscape. Sometimes it remains the whole day, at others not more than an hour or two, then gradually vanishes. It has a faint smoky appearance, as if entirely distinct from ordinary fog.

'I have made many enquiries concerning this curious word, ***eynd***, among dwellers in Norfolk, and philologers, in the hope of learning at least how to spell it, but in vain.' *Walter White's Eastern England.*

Isl., ***oend***; Su.-Goth., ***ande***; Dan., ***aande***; A.S., ***ond***, vapor, breathing; Sc., ***aynd***.

EXE. An axe. A.S., ***ex***.

F

FADGE. To suit or fit – to answer expectation. A.S., ***gefegan***.

'The single shove or heave of the spring, which if the pieces of the watch were unhing'd and born upon by it, would only be pusht forwards or by-wards puts the Watch thus ***fadg'd*** together and in tilter into motions round, right, or level, swingling, forwards, backwards, upwards, downwards, and other wayes, all because 'tis a knack or engine.' *Fairfax.*

A bundle, Lanc. A bundle as of sticks; North Ang. ***Fadge-te-fadge***, a slow trot. Cumb. ***Fay,*** to ***fadge***, Dorset, used in our dock-yards. Applied to a child walking – Teesdale. To walk as if tired – Westmoreland. A half-filled sack; to suit, agree –

Northampts. A short, fat, ***fudgy*** individual; to straddle along like a fat man – Whitby.

FAGOT. A contemptuous appellation of a woman. 'A lazy fagot.'

'Qu'il y a bien de difference entre une femme et un ***fagot***,
Qu'une femme parle toujours, et qu'un ***fagot*** ne dit mot.'

French Proverb.

'In Glouc., to call a woman an old ***fagot*** is almost the greatest insult that can be offered to her.' *Sir G. C. Lewis.*

FAIRY BUTTER. A species of tremella of yellowish colour and gelatinous substance found on furze and broom, and the roots of old trees, and after heavy rains and putrefaction reduced to a colour and consistency not unlike butter.

FALL-LALS. Flaunting and flaring ornaments.

FALLS. The cliff sides. Elsewhere ***fells***.

FAMBLE-CROP. The first stomach in ruminating animals.

Synonymous with ***fumble***, signifying imperfect action. Dan., ***famle***, to fumble, handle; Sw., ***famla***, to feel for; Pl. D., ***fummelen***. In Cumberland, a ***fummelen feast*** is held, when a new married couple are dilatory in producing issue, the neighbouring wives assembling unbidden at the house, invite themselves to tea, and make merry, wishing better success to follow.

FAN. To urge along. '***Fan*** um along,' said of a horse urged on by the whip. Gael., ***fannan***, a gentle gale.

FANG. A fin. North Ang., a paw or claw.

FANGAST. Ripe for wedlock, a marriageable maid. *Sir Thomas Browne.*

An old Norfolk word, long obsolete. The derivation is obscure. Ray's is by no means satisfactory: ***fangan***, to take, ***gast,*** amor! the latter a forced interpretation, but adopted by *Forby*. It may be the Gael ***fann***, to languish, weary for; ***fann***, *adj.*, apt, prone; ***fanntais***, languishing; ***gaol,*** love; ***gasda***, a beautiful or blooming maid.

The A.S. has ***fœmne***, a maiden; ***fœmne-had***, woman-hood; ***gehœman***, to cohabit; also ***hægsteald***; Pl. Dut. ***hagestolt***, a virgin. ***Fangast***, is probably a compound of ***fæmne***, and ***ghast***, an old word of wide spread and import. See the latter under ***gosgood***.

FAPES, THAPES, or **THEBES**. Gooseberries or feaberries. The names are applied in the unripe state only.

At Norwich *Forby* remarks that ***fape-tarts*** are indispensable on every table on the Guild-day, the Thursday before June 22. Wel., ***ffebris***, berries. *Roderick's Eng.-Wel. Dicty*, 1737. Used in the mining district when colliers talk of a ***faeberry*** pie; Dan., ***rips***. In *Gerarde's Herbal*, 1636, ***faeberry*** is given as synonymous with gooseberry; Lanc., ***fayberry***. ***Febe*** seems applied to berries in general, as whinberries. Ger., ***Pfebe,*** a melon.

FARE. To be, feel, seem to do. A.S., ***faran***, still in constant use in East Anglia, and with an infinite variety of meanings. Ex., 'She ***fared*** sick'; 'they ***fare*** to be angry'; 'how do you ***fare*** to feel.' A venture or enterprise is called a faring; as the herring and mackarel farings.

FARE. A litter or farrow of pigs. A.S., ***fearh***; Dan., ***fare***, a litter; Old Norse,

fara, to procreate. ***Ferry*** and ***fezzle***, other dial.

FAREING. Seeming, feeling. ' "I've had sich ***fareings*** myself," said by an experienced dame of the indescribable ailments of a lovesick damsel.' *Moor.* The immediate der. of this is obviously the Dut. and Fl., ***vaaren***, to put into a fear or melancholy.

FARMER. A term of distinction, says *Forby*, commonly applied in Suffolk to the eldest son of the occupier of a farm. He is addressed by the labourers as 'the farmer,' whilst the occupier himself is called master.

FARRISEE. A fairy. A ***fairidge***, says Moor, in Norfolk. The green circlets in pastures were called ***farrisee-rings***. ***Ferrier***, a fairy – Suff. ***Fairishes***, North and Mid. Ang.; Manx, ***ferish***.

FARROW. Barren, applied to cows. Frisic, ***vare kou***.

FARTHING-BOUND. Costive.

FASGUNTIDE. Shrove-tide, fasting time.

Given by Blount in his *Dictionary of Hard Words*, 1680, as a Norfolk word. Now obsolete. A corruption of Dan., ***fasten-tiden***, Lent; Dut., ***Vasten-tyd***.

FAT-HEN. Muck weed or goosefoot. *Chenapodium album*, *Lin.*

Ger., ***Fette Henne***. Also called *Good Henry*, which a correspondent of *Seeman's Journal*, vol. 1, p. 151, asserts to have been used formerly for fattening poultry, a statement requiring confirmation. *Dr. R. C. A. Prior.*

FATHOM. To spread or fill out. 'The wheat ***fathoms*** well.'

FAUTOUR. A supporter, believer in, protector. **FAUT.** To find out, discover. Fr., '***fauteur***, a favourer, furtherer.' *Cotgr.*

'He had consenting onto him a grete ***fautoure,*** to his erroure, on Anastase, fals Patriark of Constantinople.' *Capgrave.*

'I confess his memory has suffered much in many men's judgments, for being so great a ***Fauter*** of the fancifull opinion of the Millenaries.' *Fuller's Worthies, on Mede.*

Skelton has flaytering ***faytors,*** i.e. deceivers. '***Fawtour***, or meyntynore,' (liar). *Pr. Pv.*

FAY, FEY, FIE. To clean out the inside of a decayed tree or ditch.

In Chesh. to ***fay*** is to remove the soil to get at the marl; ***fey***, loose earth, Craven; ***feigh***, stone, soil, &c. carted away as useless. – Derbysh.; ***faigh***, soil superincumbent on coal, marl, stone, &c. – Salop. Ray says 'to ***fey*** or ***feigh*** it,' to do anything notably. 'Mind an' ha' t' house ***fey'd*** up ageain I come back.' *Yorks. Dial.* To ***fey*** meadows, to cleanse them; to ***fey*** a pond, to empty it. East Anglia. Dan., ***feie,*** to sweep out; Isl., ***fægja***, to rinse, purify. There is also the A.S., ***feoran***, to remove; ***feormian***, to cleanse, purge, corrupted in the West Country and Northampts. dialects to ***farm***.

> 'Such muddy deep ditches and pits in the field,
> That all a dry summer no water will yield,
> By ***fieing*** and casting that mud upon heaps,
> Commodities many the husbandman reaps.' *Tusser.*

FEAGUE. To be perplexed. ***Feaks***, a lover's anxious flutterings. Dan. and Ger., ***feig***, faint-hearted.

FEATHER-PIE. A hole in the ground, filled with feathers fixed on strings, and kept in motion by the wind. Used to scare birds.

FEFT. To persuade. One of Sir T. Browne's obsolete words.

In his own county, Essex, *Ray* says 'to put off wares.' Possibly from Wel. ***fest***, adroitness. A.S., ***fus***, prompt, ready; Dan., ***fif***, contrivance, finesse.

FEGARY. Cor. of vagary.

FEISTY. Fusty. Fr., ***fusté***, smelling of the cask.

FELL. Fill. Also a ***fall*** or drop of lambs.

FELL. To call round periodically. Essex. A.S., ***fela***; Ger., ***viel***, many times. Dut., ***veil***, to set out to sale.

FELON. A sore, a whitlow. Gael., ***feolan***, proud flesh, an excoriation; ***fealb***, a lump in the flesh, carbuncle; from root, ***feoil***, flesh.

'This is the camell which suffers not the soule to goe through the needle's eye. Somewhat is the cause why the ***felon*** upon the hand swells, it is an humour which is not yet let out; if that were out, the ***felnesse*** would cease.' *D. Rogers' Naaman.*

FELT. A bank or field foul from spear grass is said to be all of a ***felt***, matted. Low Sc., ***felt***, creeping wheat grass.

Gael., ***falt***, hair; ***faltan***, tough mountain bulrush. Wel., ***fyll***, overgrown, shaggy, full of brakes; ***gwallt***, hairy, also faulty, neglected.

Feltered, entangled, Yorks.; felt-haired, matted, Craven.

FESS. To force or obtrude aught. Ger., ***feste***, firm, fixed. Fr., ***fiché***, resolute on; Sw., ***foss***, forward, impudent; ***Fest***, to make a fuss, is used by Robert de Brunne.

Fess, fussy, meddling, eager in what is going on. *Dorset dial.* Su.-Goth., ***foss***, forward, vehement, trampling over, bursting headlong forth; from the Old Goth., ***fus***.

FIFERS. Fibres, roots or shoots of trees, weeds, grain.

Wel., ***tyviad***, shooting, vegetating; Gael., ***fiar***, twisting, wreathing, ***fiuran***, sapling, branch, shoot. Or it is probably a cor. of fibre.

FILE. To defile. The Old Eng. form. A.S., ***fylan***; Dut., ***vuylen***, to pollute. It occurs also in *R. de Brunne's Chronicle.*

FILLA or **FELLER**. The shaft horse of a cart or tumbrel, the ***filler***. Also ***thiller*** and ***thill-horse***. West country, ***viller;*** A.S., ***thille***.

Fill-bells, the chain tugs to the collar of a cart-horse, by which he draws.

'***Thiller***, the horse near the ***thills***, or forepart of the cart.' *Cocker.*

'Thou hast more hair on thy chin, than Dobbin, my ***thill*** horse has on his tail.' *M. of Venice,* ii., 1.'

'With collars and harness for ***thiller*** and all.' *Tusser.*

FILLER. To go behind. To draw back. Apparently a cognate of the above. A.S., ***filian***, to follow.

FIMBLE. I. To touch lightly with the ends of the fingers. II. To pass through without cutting. Ex., 'my scythe ***fimble*** the grass.' The thistle or female hemp. Essex.

The ***fimble*** to spin, and the carle for his seed. *Tusser.*

Not a ***dimin.*** of fumble as Forby asserts, but of the Frisic ***fample***, to clutch with the fingers. Sw., ***famla***, to feel for; Dan., ***fiple***, to handle; ***fip***, tip, ***famle***, to fumble; Dut., ***fimelen***, light action of the fingers. ***Fimble***, a wattled chimney.

Heref.

FINGERS. Mr. Halliwell gives from a MS. of the XV. century, the following rhyming list of popular names of the fingers in Norfolk, 'Tom-thumbkin, Will-wilkin, Long-gracious, Betty-bodkin, Little-tit.'

FISHERATE. To provide for. 'I een't able to fisherate for 'em all.'

A Suffolcism. Moor says very common. Forby has not got it. See ***Beein***.

'But ***fischereres*** fond the body, and brout it to St. Petir Cherch.' *Capgrave.*

FISSLE. A thistle.

FITTER. To shift from one foot to the other. Dan., ***flytte***, to transfer.

FIVE-FINGERS. A star fish. A disease in turnips, also called ***Hanbury***. In Norfolk, oxlips, *Primula elatior.*

'A fish like a spar-rowel, destructive to oysters, destroyable by admiralty law.' *Cocker.*

FIZMER, FIZZLE. To fidget unquietly.

Fizzling, fidgeting – Whitby dial.; nestling, – Cumb.; rustling, – Teesdale; Ger., ***fusseln,*** to play with the feet; ***fiz-gig***, a flirting wench, – Craven. Wel., ***fysg***, of quick motion.

FLACK. To hang loose. A blow with something loose and pliant. Also ***flick***; Ger., ***flackern***, to flare, flutter. Su. Goth., ***fleckra.***

FLACKER, to flutter – Leeds. To flutter as a bird – Whitby. To quiver, shiver – Cumb. To palpitate – Craven. ***Flack,*** a blow with aught pliant – Northampt.

FLACKET. A tall flaunting wench, whose clothes hang loose or flop about her. Also women's ribbons and such loose gear. Used also as a verb. Ex., 'She go ***flacketten*** about.' ***Flacky***, hanging loose. The Dan. has ***flagren***, dishevelled, ***flakke***, to rove about. Isl., ***flaka***, to hang loose down behind.

FLAG. Turf, sod. Also heathy land turned up by the spade and heaped to dry for fuel. The surface of a clover ley of the second year turned up by the plough; the portions turned at once by the plough being called ***flags***. 'One hole on a flag' is one row of holes dabbled or dibbled on each of such portions for dropping the seed wheat into. *Moor.*

Cocker has '***flags*** – a Norfolk word – turf pared off to burn.' Ray – '***flags***, the surface of the earth which they pare off to burn, the upper turf, Norfolk.' – *E. W. Jamieson's Scot. Dict* – '***flag***, a piece of green sward cut with a spade.' Isl., ***flaga***, to cut turf; ***flag***, a patch of ground. Prov. Dan., ***flag, flad***, a sod. Fris., ***flaggen***, thin sods. Sw., ***flaga***, to scale off; ***flake***, the primary sense of the word in various dialects. A.S., ***fle-an***; Dut., ***vlaegh-en***; Wel., ***flag. Flaks***, turfs – Cumb.

FLAGELUTT. A small rent or hole in a garment. Dimin. of Isl., ***flaga***, a splinter, rent.

FLAITE. To affright or scare. Used in conjunction with ***gaster***, an Essex word, with the same meaning. *Ray*. Hence has arisen ***flatter, flapper, flamber***, and ***flabbergaster.***

'Desire to God to ***flayte*** and ***gaster*** thee out of that lap and bosom, and Samson out of Delilah's.' *Rogers' Naaman the Syrian.*

Flay, to fright; ***flowtered***, affrighted, a ***flowter***, a fright, North Ang. – *Ray*. ***Flain,***

frightened; ***flaay***-crow, a scare-crow – Leeds. 'They ***flaid*** her intiv a fit'; ***flay***-boggle and ***flair***-cruke, a scare-crow; ***flaysome***, fearful – Whitby. ***Flaytly***, timidly,– Cumb; ***flayed*** – Teesdale; ***flowtered*** – Northumb.; ***flaide***, afraid; ***flay***-somer, more frightful – Craven.

Flay, to terrify, Old North Ang. Dial., is from Isl. ***flœja***, to terrify, says Mr. Morriss – *Gloss. to Pricke of Conscience.* The latter would seem rather to imply to abandon, desert, shun. The Gael. has ***fuadaich***, to put to flight; the Dut., ***flaauwte***, a swoon, fainting fit; A.S., ***flitan***, to chide.

'To behold the sad and dead point which many of us doe and long have stood at, would ***flait*** any honest heart to think of.' *D. Rogers' Naaaman.*

> 'Then Phœbus gathered up his steeds, that yet for fear did run
> Like ***flaighted*** fiends.' *Golding's Ovid's Metam, b. 2.*

FLANG. To slam a door; Sw., ***flänga,*** to bang, move violently.

FLAP. A slight stroke or touch. Ex., 'I have got a ***flap*** of cold.'

FLAP-JACK. A flat thin joint of meat, as the breast of a lean sheep or calf. See also ***Apple-Jack***. In New England, ***flap-jacks*** are pancakes, not apple puffs.

FLAPPERS. Young wild ducks or rooks just able to fly. 'Full flappers,' very near flying. 'Ar yar rooks fliers?' 'No; but th'ar full ***flappers***.' Dut., ***flabberers,*** to flutter, ***flabbe***, a slap.

FLAPS. Large broad mushrooms.

FLARNECKING. An ostentatious flaunting. Dan., ***flane,*** giddy girl, coquet.

Alongside of the numerous onomatopœas in our language, those words produced by direct imitation of the sound given out by a variety of animate objects (as *cuckoo*) and by collision, resonance and percussion (as *thud*), are a number appealing to man's other senses. Among these latter occurs a large class called into existence by the action of the elements upon our vision. The movement rapid, irregular or continous of air, fire and water acting upon the retina and nerve of the eye has led to the coinage of many words both in the Teutonic and Romance languages, with the prefixes respectively of *fl, gl, sl,* which give expression to a multitude of its sensations, striving more or less felicitously to define their most subtle gradations of intensity.

In some words as the *flapping* action of a sail or the *splashing* of water the sensations produced both upon sight and sound seem equally interpreted. Fertile in suggestion and tempting as is the theme, space precludes our dwelling on it. The words falling under *gl* which pertain to the action of light and *sl* to that of water, are noticed under those letters.

Under *fl*, the most prolific derivation, a classification representing each element might be made, ranged under the heads of *flying, flaming*, and *flowing*, the first by far the most copious in its vocabulary. There are many words conveying the joint impressions of the eye and ear, as *flap, flicker, flutter, flop*, &c. There are those borrowed from the visible phenomena of common objects in which are also expressed, wavering, unstable, insolid action or condition of mind and body, *flashy, fluent, flighty, flippant, flatulent, flabby*, &c. The class, however, which comes most legitimately within the scope of this glossary, is that in which the sense of female untidiness is conveyed, arising from the fluttering of garments, loosely hanging round the limbs; or of dishevelled hair, left for the winds of heaven to visit freely. It is in the invention of *flouting* words of this class that village wit finds its amplest scope, and in this domain of language are forged those missiles of clumsy sarcasm, those flint implements of satire over which the rude ingenuity of rustic life, toils, and boggles, as it strives with a slow elaboration to give them edge and sharpness.

We append a list gathered from our dialectic glossaries of epithets, used mainly in disparagement of *flaunting,* the characteristic failing in rural finery, and with which a sense of untidiness seems instinctively associated. Almost all occur in our Anglian dialects, North, Midland, and Eastern.

Flawps, an awkward slovenly female; ***flee-be-sky***, one who dresses ridiculously, a ***flipperty-flop***; ***floaping***, said of a girl with flying bonnet ribbons, flossy-dolly, a giddy, impudent female – Leeds. ***Flappery***, minor equipments; of dress; ***flaumy*** or ***flaupish***, vulgarly fine. All wind and ***flaup***; a ***flaupy*** body, fawning and canting; a ***floutersome flee-be-skie***, a flighty, sky-high body, a gaudy female; a ***flirtigigs***; ***flobb'd up***, inflated; ***flumpy***, squat – Whitby. ***Fallops***, untidy ragged clothes; ***flakker*** and ***fliar***, to laugh heartily like a child – Cumb. ***Flig-me-gairy***, a gaudy, untidy girl, said also of useless fripperies – Westmoreland. ***Fal-lals***, foolish ornaments; ***flisk***, to skip or bounce, 'a ***flisky*** jade' – *Brockett's North Country Words.* ***Flaff*** to fan, a fop; ***flaffer***, to flutter; ***flam-foo***, any gay trapping, flaunty, capricious; ***fleegeries***, gewgaws; ***fliskmahaigo***, giddy – *Jamieson's Scot. Dial.* ***Flarin***, shewy; ***flowsy***, a slattern – Craven. ***Flop***, quickly, smartly – Salop. ***Flarnecking***, giggling, flaring; ***flobbering***, hanging loose; ***flommac***, a slattern; ***flurrigigs***, finery – Northampts. ***Flammakin***, a blowsy slattern; ***floistering***, skittish, hoydenish – Devon. A ***flantum-flatherum*** piebald dill, a woman fantastically dressed – *Grose.* ***Flapse***, an impudent trollop – Beds. ***Flippety-flop,*** draggle-tailed, awkward in fine clothes – Warwicksh. ***Flummuck***, a sloven – Heref. ***Fly-a-boster***, outrageously shewy – Somerset.

FLASH. A hedge, to clip off the lower parts of the bushes which overhang the bank or ditch; cutting it flat or flush. Dan., ***fleske***, to cut, slash.

FLATS. Flat marshy sites. Also the oozey levels left by high tides on the flat East Anglian shores. O.E. ***flat***, to dash down water; Dut., ***plat, vlak***.

FLATS. A general term for small fresh-water fish.

'Item in ***Flathe*** and Thornbacke, xijd.' *L'Estrange Household Accounts.*

FLAZZARD. A stout broad faced woman loosely, flaringly dressed.

FLEACHES. The slices into which timber is cut by the saw. Var. of ***flitch*** and ***flake***. Dan., ***flœkke,*** to split; Isl., ***fleki***, timber slices.

'Martin, this is my last straine for this ***fleech*** of mirth.' *Pap with a Hatchet.*

Fleak, a gate set in a gap, or a hurdle – North Ang. Dut. ***vlaek***. '***Fleyke*** or hyrdylle.' *Pr. Pv.*

'Botes and barges ilkin, with ***flekes*** make them tight.' *R. de Brunne.*

FLECK. The down of hares or rabbits torn off by the dogs. A.S., ***flix***, down, soft hair. Also to deprive. Ex., 'I ***fleckt*** him of all his marbles.' Fr., ***flic***, a jerk.

FLECKED, FLECKERED. Dappled, speckled. Ger., ***fleck***; Isl., ***flekka***, to spot, stain, speckle.

'As well appeared by his ***flecked*** cheekes,
Now cherrye redde, now pale and greene as leekes.' *Gascoigne.*

'The janglynge jay, to rayle; the ***fleckyd*** pye, to chatter.' *Skelton.*

FLEET. To skim the cream from the milk. A.S. and Fris., ***flete***, cream; Isl., ***flot***, what floats on the surface; Pl. Dut., ***flot.***, cream.

In Lanc. ***fleetins*** are curds of milk. ***Fleet-time***, day break, from the clearing off of vapours. In Suffolk, ***flet*** cheese is the cheese made of skimmed milk, which enjoys such ill repute for its flinty properties. In Chesh., ***fleetings*** or ***flittings*** are the refuse milk in cheese-making.

FLEET. A shallow piece of standing water, when very shallow a ***plash***, when deep a ***meer. Fleet***, shallow. Sussex, ***flit.***

Fris., ***flaak***, shallow; Sw., ***flata***; Dut., ***vlacke***.

At Lynn, and on some parts of the Suffolk coast, a ***fleet*** is a channel left shallow at low water by the tide, a creek.

'My various ***fleets*** for fowl, O who is he can tell.' *Drayton.*

'Its fur from being ***fleet*** water in his mind, where them thowts lays. It's deep, Sir, and I can't see down.' *David Copperfield.*

FLEET. Of nets. The train of drift nets paid out by a herring or mackarel boat. A.S., ***fleotan***; Dut., ***vlieten***, to float; or it may be from the Dan., ***flette***, to plait, braid.

Is it not a ***float*** of nets? A.S., ***fleotan***, Ger., ***fluten***, Sw., ***flyta***.

'The fishes ***flete*** with new repaired scale.' *Surrey.*

FLETCHES. Green pods of pease. Also ***fletshards*** or ***fletshads***. Of the same derivation apparently as ***fleaches***, as is also

FLICK. I. A smart stinging slap. II. The flake or flank of a hog cured in a 'powdering tub.' Ex., 'Dew ye powder all yar ***flick*** ta year.' A ***flitch*** of bacon. Fr., ***flique de lard***; Isl., ***flicki***; A.S., ***flicce***.

'Another brought a spycke – of a bacon ***flicke***.' *Skelton.*

FLIGGER, FRICKER. A fluttering movement. A.S., ***fliccerian***.

'And now he and all his old fellowship put out their fins, and are right ***flygge*** and merry, hoping all thing is and shall be as they will have it.' *Paston Letter,* A.D. 1460.

'Fain would she seem all ***frize*** and frolic still.' *Hall's Satires, p., VI.*

FLIGGERS. The common flag. *Iris pseudacorus, Lin.*

FLITCH, FLIT. To move from place to place. To remove from one house or farm, to another.

Common to other dialects, as the Lanc. Old Norse, ***flytia***; Dan., ***flytteri***, bustle or trouble of moving.

FLITTER-MOUSE. The bat, from its fluttering wavering movements. Ger., ***fledermaus***. In Wessex, the ***rere-mouse***. A.S., ***hreran***, to flutter.

FLIZZOMS. Flying particles, or small flakes in bottle liquors, their ***beeswing***.

'Flizz, to fly off.' *Bailey.* Isl., ***flus***; Sw., ***flisig***, scaly; Dan., ***flise***, to splinter.

FLOCKY. Over ripe, or badly ripened, tasting woolly, dry, or stringy. ***Flocks,*** sediment. Lat., ***floccus***.

'Not to leave anie ***flockes*** in the bottom of the cup.' *Nash's Pierce Penilesse.*

FLOP. Souse, plump, flat. Ex., 'A fell full ***flop***.' 'I'll gi yeow a ***flop***.' 'A ***floppt*** his affections on that flacketty wench.' 'She ***floppt*** down into ar seat.' Also

flump. An awkward person ***flumps*** into a chair. Var. of ***flap***.

Flop, a mass of thin mud. Dorset.

FLUE. I. Shallow. II. The coping of a gable end, an end wall.

I. '***Flew*** or scholde, as vessell or other lyke.' *Pr. Pv.* Ger., ***flau***, shallow; Fris., ***flüe***; Isl., ***flaa***, a marsh. II. Wel., ***flu***, a prow, a projecting out; Fris., ***fleuer***, a vane, summit of a roof. Ger., ***flügel,*** a wing or aisle.

Flowe, a large peat bog, as Solway ***Flowe***. – Cumb. dial.

FLUSH. The stream from a mill head. Scot., ***flusch***, a run of water. Isl., ***flust***, abundance. Dut., ***fluysen***, to flow violently.

FLY-TIME. The season in which flies are troublesome.

Amongst the most popular of American similes is – 'Threshing round like a short-tailed bull in ***fly-time***.'

FODDER. Yarmouth dialect. A very small trader, an intermediate collector of eggs, poultry, etc., between the producer and retailer.

Of difficult etymology, from its multiplicity of meanings in various languages. ***Fodder*** has I. a primary sense of to forrage, collect and distribute food. A.S., ***foder***; Dut., ***voeder***; Su.-Goth., ***foder***; Fr., ***fourrer***. II. Su.-Goth., ***fodra***, to solicit, dun, seek, importune, sell; Ger., ***fordern***, to call for; Su.-Goth., ***foga***, to adapt, fit one's self to, fudge; '***fog***, proprie, quod sese alteri adaptat, commissura.' *Ihre*. III. ***Foder***, in the Norse and Teut., dial., has the senses of a skin, fur, covering, sheath, case, Ger., ***futter***, a case, fur, fodder, forage, ***futterer***, a huckster. IV. L. Ger. and Fl., ***voeder***, a carrying thing, a cart, wain, etc., hence to convey, lead, carry. V. Su.-Goth., ***föga***, petty, small. Many other meanings occur, as Fl., and Dut., ***vod***, a rag, ***voddery***, trifles, ***vodderaaper***, a rag-gatherer, Dan., ***vod***, a fishing net, etc. Lastly, the untenable Gael. der., ***foghar***, a vagabond, robber, thief, and the Ir. ***fogarach***, noisy, clamorous, proclaiming aloud.

FOG. Long grass, growing in pastures in late summer or autumn; not fed down but allowed to stand through the winter, and yielding early spring feed. By its length and thickness the outer part forms a cover or thatch for the lower; which is kept fresh and juicy, at least through a mild winter. *Forby.*

Fog occurs in almost every Eng. dialect, with varying meanings. *Ray* has '***fog***, coarse sour grass that cattle will not eat, till it be frost-nipt – or little else be left on the pasture.' *North Country Words*. In his *East Words* he gives '***fogge***, long grass remaining in pastures till winter.' *Nares* has '***fog***, rank, strong grass.' ***Fog cheeses*** in Yorksh. are such as are made from this latter grass, as ***eddish*** cheeses in some other counties. The *Yorks. Dialogue*, 1697, has ***fog***, fresh grass that comes after mowing.' *Blount's Glossographia*, 1656, has '***fogage, fog*** or ***feg***, rank grass not eaten in summer.' *Baily's Dicty.*, 1730, has '***fog***, corn which grows after autumn and remains in pasture till winter.' *Jamieson's Sc. Dict.*, '***fog***, to be covered with moss, to eat heartily; ***foggage***, rank grass which has not been eaten in summer, or which grows among grain, and is fed on by horses or cattle, after the crop is removed.' *Ducange* has ***fogagium***, winter fodder. Carr, in his *Craven Dialect*, writes '***fog***, after-grass, after math, not winter eatage in the sense of Ducange;' but immediately after contradicts his explanation by his illustration, 'when farmers take the cattle out of the pastures in the autumn, they say 'they are bound to ***fog*** them,' that is, feed them on dry food. *Baker's Gloss. of Northampt.* renders '***fog***, coarse grass which cattle will not eat.' Hartshorne in *Salopia Antiqua*, gives '***foggy***, a horse is said to be so, when for a time having been fed upon grass, he has grown dull and stupid.' *Palsgrave's Dicty.,* 1530, has '***foggy***, too full of waste flesshe.' Brockett's *North County Words* renders ***fog***, grain grown in autumn after the hay is mown. ***Fog***, long coarse grass, – Northampts. ***Pheg***, – Salop. ***Feg***, grass withered on the ground, without being severed from its root – *Sir G. C. Lewis, Heref. dial.* The Rev. J. Davies, in his paper on the *Dialect of Lancashire, Phil. Sy. Trans.*, 1855, seeks to affix to ***fog*** the meaning of dry food, as hay, in opposition to the fresh grass, basing it on the Wel., ***fwg***, long dry grass, but this seems to imply ***standing*** grass, ***gwair***, applying to hay on every description of land, ***gwair rhos***, meadow hay, ***gwair hallt***, marshland hay, &c. The Gael. has ***fog-har***, under crop, harvest, also ***foghnan***, thistle. Sw., ***föga,*** herbage.

From this conflict of authorities, two distinct interpretations of ***fog*** are extractable – an aftermath, ranker grass than the first crop, a meaning attached to it in the North; – and a winter pasturage of coarse tufty grasses, disdained in the summer by the cattle but relishable with its young shoots in the scantier herbage of winter.

'Her face glystrying like glass; all ***foggy*** fat she was.' *Skelton.*

'Then green and void of strength and dark and ***foggy*** is the blade.' *Golding's Ovid,* 1587.

'Those who on a sudden grow rather ***foggy*** than fat by feeding on sacriligious morsels, do pine away by degrees and die at last of incurable consumptions.' *Fuller's Pisgah Sight.*

FOGGER. A huckster, petty chapman, small dealer in fish, poultry, game, and vegetables. Whence ***pettifogger***.

In Gael., ***foghar*** is a robber, and huckster is synonymous with cheat.

In the old Yarmouth assembly books, the term fish ***fogger*** occurs, applied to the small dealers.

FOISON. Succulency; the juicy properties in herbage. Ex., 'There is no ***foison*** in this hay.'

'I will gyvi kynge Johan thys poyson
So matynge hym sure that he shall never have ***foyson***.' *Bp. Bale.*

Sc. ***foison, fusioun***, pith, essence or spirit of a thing. Ex., 'What are ye glouran at me for, whan I'm at my meat? Ye'll tak a' the ***fizzen*** out o't.' *Roxb.* 'He has nae ***foison*** in him,' no energy. *Jam.* ***Foisonless***, sapless, dried, withered. Fr., ***foison,*** abundance, from Lat. ***fusio***, effusion.

'Beware of it then, the sin it selfe is sad; but that it should be the canker that should eate out the ***foyson*** of grace, and destroy all my hearings, and make my devotions as odious as the cutting off a dogge's neck.' *D. Rogers' Naaman.*

FOKY. Bloated, unsound, soft and woolly. Ex., 'a ***foky*** turnip.' Wheat is said to be ***foky*** when the grain is inadequate in quality to the promise of the ***boke*** or bulk. Boggy land is ***foky***.

Sc., ***fozy***, spongy, porous; ***foziness***, duffiness, obtuseness, '***fozy*** Tam.' Cumb. dial. ***fozzy***, soft as a frosted turnip. *Brockett's N.C. Words*, ***foxy, fuzzy***, light and spungy. Fris., ***fozy***; Dut., ***voos, vooze raapen***, spongy turnips.

Brockett and others derive from A.S., ***wosig***, juicy, moist, succulent, which seems rather a der. of ***foison.***

FOLD-PRITCH. A heavy pointed iron to make the holes to receive the toes of hurdles. A.S., ***pricca***; Isl., ***prik***, a point.

FOLLOW, to. Applied to the pursuit of trades and callings.

FOLLOWING-TIME. A wet showery season. Also ***falling-time***. Common now in the U.S.

FOND. Luscious, fulsome, disagreeably sweet to taste or smell.

FOOL. A pet. Cumb., a ***fout***.

FOOTING-TIME. The time of recovery from a lying-in or foot-falling.

FORCE. Used in a neutro-passive sense. Ex., 'I ***forced*** to go.' I was obliged, I could not help.

FOREIGNER. Applied disparagingly to those not born in East Anglia.

Applied in U.S. to persons not born in America. In the Southern States to those born in another State.

FORE-SUMMERS. The fore part of a cart, formerly much used in Norfolk. A sort of platform projecting over the shafts, was called the ***fore-summers***.

Wel., ***swmer*** (Wel. ***w*** like Eng. oo), that supports or keeps together, a beam; ***swmer càr***, the hind part of a drag or dray, which holds up the load. In the Gaelic, ***sumhlas*** is a packing close together.

FORGIVE. To begin to thaw.

FORHINDER. To prevent.

FORLORN. Worthless, reprobate, abandoned. 'A ***forlorn tyke***,' a sad dog. A.S., ***forloren***, lost; Sw., ***fær-lora***.

'*Goed verloren, niet verloren; moed verloren, veel verloren; eer verloren, meer verloren; ziel verloren, al verloren.* Fortune lost, nothing lost; courage lost, much lost; honour lost, more lost; soul lost, all lost.' *Dutch Proverb.*

> 'Of heav'n and earth, and God and men ***forlore***,
> Thrice begging help of those whose sins he bore.'
>
> *Giles Fletcher. Christ's Triumph over Death.*

'I'm a lone ***lorn*** creetur' myself, and everything that reminds me of creeturs that ain't lone and lorn, goes contrairy with me.' *David Copperfield.*

'Thou hadst not spent thy travail thus, nor all thy pain ***forlore***.' *Surrey.*

FORTH-ON. A general idiom for an indefinite period. Ex., 'Come a month on liking, and if we agree you may stay ***forth on***.'

FOSTAL. A paddock near a farmhouse, or a private way leading thereto. Also a farmyard; in former days in front of the house; A.S., ***forestal,*** a stoppage of the way; Ger., ***forststallung***, an enclosure in a wood.

FOUR-EYED. Applied to dogs which have a distinct mark over each eye, of a different colour, as tan upon black; common to terriers, spaniels, &c. One wearing spectacles is said to be ***four-eyed***.

FOUREY-LEET. Four cross-ways. In the North, four lane ends. Ger., ***leiten***, to lead, conduct to.

FOURSES. The four o'clock snack of labourers in harvest.

FOUTRY. Paltry, trumpery, despicable.

'A ***foutra*** for thine office,' exclaims Pistol to Justice Shallow. Explanation of the term seems to be shirked by the commentators. Nares also overlooks it. Forby inclines to its being one of the Spanish colloquialisms current in England in

Shakespeare's time. *Cotgrave's Fr. Dict.*, 1632, has ***fouter***, a scoundrel, *Jamieson's Sc. Dict.*; ***fouty***, ***futie***, mean, base, obscene, Lanarksh.; ***foutilie***, Clydesdale; ***fouttour, foutre***, a term expressive of the greatest contempt, *Lyndsay*. The Gaelic has ***fotrus,*** orts, offal; ***fotus***, refuse, corruption. ***Fouter***, a despicable low fellow; ***fouty***, base, mean, North Ang. ***Footy***, little, insignificant – Dorset. ***Fouty***, said of a dress misfitting or sticking out, unseemly – Whitby; mean, paltry – Northampts.; silly, foolish – South Coast dialects; a scurvy fellow – Somerset.

FOWL. A term applied to all large birds. A.S., ***fug-el***.

Also North Ang. 'We saw all maks o' feather ***fewl***.' – Whitby Dial.

FOY. A supper formerly given by owners of fishing vessels at Yarmouth, to the crew at the beginning of the season, otherwise called a ***bending-foy***.

Forby says it must be from the Fr., ***foi***. If so, it could here be only used in the sense of a contract. *Bailey's Dicty.*, 1735, has '***foy*** (***foy***, Belg. ***voye***, Fr. a way) a treat given to their friends by those who are going a journey.' This would be given as a ***fare-well***. *Jamieson's Sc. Dict.* has '***Foy***. I. An entertainment given to one about to leave his residence or go abroad. II. Metaphorical, as equivalent to wishing one a good journey. Belg., ***de fooi geven***. [This in *Sewel's Dut. Dicty.*, 1708, is – ***to give the foy***.] Sw., ***drickaa foi***, a departure supper. The Gael. has ***fleadh***, a ***foy***, feast. – *Highl. Sy. Dict.*

Nares has altogether missed the meaning of the word whilst quoting from *Pepys' Diary* the following::'To Westminster with Capt. Lambert, and there he did at the Dog, give me and some other friends of his, his ***foy***, he being to set sail to-day towards the Streights.'

FOYSTING. Swaggering, intruding upon. Also pocket-picking. ***Foist***, a cut purse, a juggling trick. ***Foist, feist, fizzle***, to break wind in a noiseless manner. Dut., ***veest***; A.S., ***fysan***, to expel.

'All the bravery comes by nipping, ***foysting***, and lifting.' *R. Greene's Theeves falling-out*, 1637.

'Thereupon appeared a little Remnant of a man; a dapper Spaniard, with a kind of a Besome Beard, and a voice not unlike the yapping of a ***foysting*** Cur.' *L'Estrange's Quevedo*.

FOZY. See ***Foky***.

FRACK. To abound, swarm. Ex., 'the church was ***fracking*** full.' 'My apple-trees are as full as they can ***frack***.'

Dut., ***vracht***, a load; Isl., ***frek-r***; Su. G., ***fraeck***.

FRAIL. I. To fret or wear out cloth. Fr., ***frayer***. II. A flat rush or mat basket, in which fruit and fish were formerly packed. O. Fr., ***frayel***, a mat basket; It., ***fragli***, an interweaving of boughs.

'Two hundred ***frailes*** of figs and raisons fine.' *Mirrour for Magistrates*, 1587.

'Three ***frails*** of sprats carried from mart to mart.' *Beaumont and Fletcher*.

FRAME. Affected demeanour or speech. In Low Scotch 'framed manners,' ***frame-person***, a visitor to be received ceremoniously.

Isl., ***fram***; Dan., ***fremmed***; Swed., ***främmande***; A.S., ***fremed***, strange, from afar, a guest. In Chesh., ***frem'd*** and ***frim***. In the North, ***frem'd***; foreign. Also used in the sense of uncommon. Ex., 'It's rather ***frem'd*** to be ploughing with snow on the ground.' *Brockett*. ***Frem-sted***, deserted, abandoned, Low. Scotch.

FRAMPLED. Cross, ill-humoured, peevish. See ***Frump.***

Apparently synon. with rumpled, crumpled, ruffled. ***Plionner***, to ***frumple***. *Cotgr.* Ger., ***krumpen***; A.S., ***hrympelle***; Scot., ***frample***.

'I wiss ye dele uncurtesly;
What wold ye ***frompill*** me? now fy!' *Skelton.*

'He has good have took Meat, Drink and Leisure, for the churlish ***frampled*** waves gave him his Belly-full of Fish-Broth, before out of their Laundry or Wash-House they would grant him his Coquet or Transire.' *Nashe's Lenten Stuff.*

'And I do think myself so much the more bound to take heed how I handle the Good name of others, by how much the more I see, how an ill-willed and ***frampled*** waspishness has broken forth, to the royling and firing of the age wherein we live.' *Fairfax.*

'It doth not use to be so forward; meere necessity must drive her to say, tis ***frampole***.' *Rogers' Lost Sheep.*

FRANK. The large, slow-flying, fish-eating heron, the name derived, conjectures Moor, from its monotone note, called also a ***hahnsey***.

FRAWL, FRAZLE. To unravel awkwardly, as skeins of thread, &c. ***fraizlins***, threads of cloth. ***Fraisler***, to break into many small pieces. *Cotgr. Fr. Dict.*, 1632.

Fraise. To break. '***Frees***, freyl or brokulle.' *Pr. Pv.* Lat., ***frangere***.

In the North, a ***fraze*** is an eighth of a sheet of paper, called in East Anglia a vessel. *Pegge's Suppt. to Grose.*

FRAWN. Frozen. 'I'm ***frawn*** to dead almost.' Dut., ***vervroren***, frozen; Ger., ***friéren***; 'Ta ***frize***,' it freezes; A.S., ***frysan***; Sw., ***frysa***; Dan., ***fryse. Frore*** is also used for frozen.

'A ***fresy*** thowe, a melting ***fryse***.' *Lydgate.*

FRAWSY. Frisky, pettish; Gael., ***fraigeasach***, smart, lively.

FRAZY. Grasping, voracious; Ger., ***frassig***, greedy; Dan., ***frasnige***, to trick out of.

FRECKENS. Freckles. Gael., ***breac***.; Wel., ***brycan***.

Chaucer has ***fraknes***. ***Frekens,*** says Tyrwhitt is Sax. for spots. Dan., ***fregnet***; Isl., ***frekna***. The A.S., ***fretan***, is to gnaw, devour; ***fretnes***, a devouring. In Suffolk and in the North, ***fretten*** is pockmarked; ***pock fretten***, eaten by small pocks. Lat., ***fricare***, to rub; It., ***fregare***; North Ang., ***farntickle***.

'Were not wormys ordeyned theyr flesh to ***frete***.' *Skelton.*

FREE-MARTIN. Twins of different sexes, or rather the female calf of a twin, of which the other is a bull.

'When twin calves are born, they may be both perfect bull or perfect cow calves. When one is a bull calf and the other a cow-calf, the latter, in general, will not breed, from malformation of the genital organs.' *Mayo's Philosophy.*

FREELI-FRALIES. 'Light, unsubstantial delicacies, frothy compliments, frippery ornaments, trumpery finery, corresponding somewhat to the O. Fr. ***fan freluches***, fopperies, fooleries, loose threds, shreds and rags.' *Cotgr.* See ***frawl***.

FRENCH. Very bad, in great trouble. *Halliwell.* Dut. and Ger., ***krank.***

FRESH. Handsome, blooming, beautiful. '***Fresche***, ioly and galaunt.' *Pr. Pv.*

See *frycke*.

'The ***freshe*** beautee sleth me sodenly.' *Chaucer's Knight's Tale.* '***Fresshe***, gorgyouse, gay, or well besene.' *Palsgrave.* Sw., ***frysk***, sound, healthy, fresh; Ger., ***frisch***.

FRESHER. A young frog. In *Pr. Pv.*, ***froske***, ***frosche***, a frog. Ger., ***frosch***; Dan., ***frosk,*** a frog. Craven and N. Ang., ***frosk***.

FRESHES. The overflow of water in rivers, after heavy rains.

In America, ***freshets***, used in the North and East States. Bartlett, *Dict. of Americanisms,* remarks 'that it is an old English word is evinced by the following extract from the description of New England, written and published in England, in 1658. "Between Salem and Charlestown is situated the town of Lynn, near to a river whose strong ***freshets***, at the end of the winter filleth all her banks, and with a violent torrent vents itself into the sea." '

Fresh. A flood or overflow of a river. N. Ang.

FRIAR'S LOAVES. Fossil echini.

FRICKE, FRYCKE. Fresh, active, lusty. '***Fryke***, or craske or yn grete helthe.' *Pr. Pv.* See ***fligger*** and ***fresh.***

'When thou art ***fryke*** and in thy floures.' *Lydgate.*

O. Fr., ***frique***; Goth., ***friks***, brisk, lively; Fris., ***freck***. Su.-Goth., '***fræck***, alacer, strenuus, tumidus, insolens.' *Ihre.* Dan., ***fræk***; Eng., ***freakish***.

FRIGHTFUL. Fearful, timorous. Ex., 'Lawk! Miss, how ***frightful*** you are! says an homely wench, when Miss screams at the sight of a toad or spider.' *Forby.*

FRIMICATE. To play the fribble, to affect delicacy.

In Lanc. ***frum*** is tender, delicate, easily broken. In Chesh. ***frim*** is applied almost solely to young tender grass. Bailey has '***frim folk,***' outlandish men, Linc. ***Frem***, handsome, new – Northampts. Fresh, plump – Glou. ***Frum***, forward – Salop. Dan. ***frönnet***, brittle.

Under this are given: I. ***Frim***, tender; the Isl., ***frum***, first growth. II. ***Frim folk***, outlandish; the Teut. and Norse, ***fremd***, from afar. III. ***Frum***; Su.-Goth., ***from, frami***, bold; Dan., ***frem***, forward.

FRINGEL. The limb of the flail which strikes the corn. The other is the head-staff. See ***Swingel.***

FRIZZLE. Used in the sense of a rumpus; a difficulty. ***Friser***, to ruffle. *Cotgr. Fr. Dict.,* 1632. Sw., ***frisera***, to frizzle.

'A precious nip and ***frizzle*** of a fix' is a popular Americanism. A few years ago, when visiting an East Anglian church, we expressed to the clerk who acted as cicerone, our admiration of the elaborate character of its restoration, we elicited the dry rejoinder, – 'Ay, an' a pretty ***frizzle*** there wur when the bill cum' in.'

FROISE. A large thick pancake the size of the pan, sometimes containing small pieces of bacon mixed in the batter. To spread thin – Suff. '***Froyse*** of egges.' *Palsgrave's Fr. Eng. Dict.,* 1530. Wel., ***froes***, an omelet.

Froisser, to knock or clatter together. *Cotgr. Fr. Dicty.*, 1632. An old Norfolk proverb is, 'If it wont pudding, it will ***froize***;' if it won't do for one purpose, it will do for another. Bailey has '***froyse,*** a pancake with bacon.' With apples intermixt they are called ***fritters***.' Linc., ***frits***.

FROLIC. Pron. ***frolluck***. A common East Anglian term for a merry-making, specially applied to aquatic gatherings on the inland broads. Ger., ***froli***, rejoiced, happy, ***fröhlich***, gladsome, jovial.

FROSLING. Anything as plant or animal, nipped or injured by frost.

'Another brought two goslynges, That were noughty ***froslynges***.' *Skelton.*

FROUZY. Blouzy, with disordered and uncombed hair.

Not applied in East Anglia to what is offensive to the nose as well as eye, the sense attached to it in the Salop, Northampts and other dialects; but what offends the eyes. In Craven, Leeds, and the North, ***frow, frowdie***, is a dirty woman. Ger., ***fraw***, Dut., ***vrowe***. ***Frowzy***, sour, countenanced, forbidding, a fustilugs – Whitby; ***frowé,*** a fat and morose woman – Cumb.; a slattern, a lusty female – Northumb.; ill-looking and dirty – Salop; red in the face from exertion and heat – Sussex. ***Frowchy,*** (Dut., ***vrowtjie***.) a furbelowed old woman – New Yorkism. ***Frounty***. Very passionate – Linc.

FROWNCED. Frowning, wrinkled. See ***Frampold*** and ***Frump***.

'Caron with his beerd hore,
That roweth with a rude ore,
And with his ***frownsid*** foretop,
Gydeth his bote with a prop.' *Skelton.*

FROWY. Stale, musty, fusty; ***frousty***; meanings attached to ***frowzy*** in other dialects. Applied also to cattle feed.

FRUGAL. The reverse to costly, which see. Ex., 'Good woman,' quoth the village doctress, 'is your child costive?' '*Costly!* ma'am, no, quite the contrary, sadly ***frugal*** indeed.' *Forby.*

Mistress Page, on receiving Falstaff's love-letter, soliloquises – 'What an unweighed behaviour hath this Flemish drunkard picked (with the devil's name) out of my conversation, that he dares in this manner assay me? Why he has not been thrice in my company! What should I say to him? I was then ***frugal*** of my mirth – heaven forgive me!' The word has been a puzzle to the commentators, free, rather than sparing, appearing the sense implied. Johnson says he once thought 'not' should be prefixed.

An O.E. form derived from A.S. ***frig***, free. ***Frugal***, frank, kind, affable, Aberdeen. *Jamieson.* Gael., ***frogan***, lively, cheerful.

FRUMMETY. Wheat boiled in milk, with cinnamon and sugar, an excellent thing. 'When ta rain ***frummety,*** mind ye heent a dish to seek.' Lat., ***frumentum***, wheat; common to other dialects.

'Remember thou therefore, though I do it not
The seed cakes, the pasties, and ***furmenty*** pot.' *Tusser.*

FRUMP. A sour, ill-humoured person or look. Said more particularly of old women. Synon. of ***frampold***.

In Lanc. to sulk, to take offence. Also a taunt, 'and vex'd with jeers and ***frumps***. *Tim Bobbin.* Wel., ***from***, to chafe, fume. Dut., ***frump***, an unseemly fold, from the puckering of the features under the workings of ill-temper. Bailey has ***frump*** (***frumpeten***, Teut., to frizzle up the nose, as in derision) to flout, taunt, snub. Craven dial., to treat rudely. Leeds, cross-grained, to rebuke angrily. Sussex, one with badly-made clothes ill put on.

Frump, a fidgetty woman – Bristol; cross, ill-tempered, an old ***frump*** – Americanism.

'I gave him slender thankes, but with such a ***frumpe*** that he perceived how light I made of his counsell.' *Greene's Theeves falling out*, 1637.

'How scornefully doth she reject the water hee offers her? How doth she scoffe and ***frumpe***, and breake jests upon him.' *Roger's Lost Sonne.*

FRUSH. To bruise, rub, or scrub. 'To ***frush*** a chicken,' to carve it. Fr., ***froisser***.

'And with his berde he ***frushed*** hir mouthe un-mete.' *Lydgate.*

FULLA. Fellow. Moor thus illustrates: 'The day on which I write this, the following conversation passed between me and an honest neighbour, a labourer: "Why that there daater 'a yars grow a fine swacken gal?" "Ah! she dew, she'll be a wappa if she git on thussens." "Wha's she the pitman, eh?" "Is – no – why I don't fare ta know – she's a twin – I've got the ***fulla*** tew ar a toom.'

FULL-DUE. A final settlement and acquittance.

FULL-FLOPPER. A young bird fledged enough to quit the nest.

FULL-FROTH. Said of a cow in full milk.

FUMBLE-FISTED. Awkward in handling.

FUNK. Touch-wood, in other dialects, ***spunk***. '***Funke***, or lytylle fyyr.' *Pr. Pv.*

Dut., ***voncke***; Ger., ***funke***; Dan., ***funke***, a spark, tinder, touchwood.

FURTHER. Pronounced ***fuddah***, used in negative senses. Ex., 'If I dew, I'll be ***fuddah***,' i.e. I'll never do it.' 'I wish that fellow ***further***.' 'I'll see you ***fuddah*** fust.'

FUSSLE. ***Fussment***, a slight confusion, bustle, Suff.

FUSSOCK. ***Fissock***, a large coarse woman. N. & E. Ang. dialects.

FUTNON, FRUTINON. Now and then.

G

GAG. To nauseate, to reject with loathing. To make an unsuccessful effort to vomit. '***Gaggyn***, or streyne be the throte – suffoco.' *Pr. Pv.*

Gael., ***gagach***, to stammer; Wel., ***gogen***, to yawn; ***gwagau***, to empty or void; Breton, ***gag***, to sputter; A.S., ***geagl***, the jaw.

'The heron so gaunce, And the cormoraunce,
With the fesaunte, And the ***gaglynge*** gaunte.' *Skelton.*

'There's such a Singing, Bawling, ***Gaggling***, Leaping, and Thundring up and down that there's no hearing one another.' *L'Estrange's Erasmus' Colloquies.*

GAGE. A bowl to receive the cream as it is skimmed off. ***Gage***, lytyll bolle. *Pr. Pv.*

GAGGER. A Nonconformist. 'An old Puritan' originally, says Forby.

GAHUSEY. A warm worsted short shirt with sleeves; cor. of ***Jersey***. [Guernsey?] The sailor's and fisherman's every day over-garment, a coarsely-knitted blue worsted shirt with or without sleeves; vulg., a ***jersey***. O. Fr. and Romance, ***jaseran***, a coat or shirt of closely woven chain mail. *Cotgr.* A cuirass, says Roquefort, used as far back as the 12th cent. Sp., ***jacerina***; It.,

ghiazzerino. Probably der., says Diez, from Sp., ***jazarino***, Algerian; from Ar. ***al-jazäir***, Algiers. ***Jasque***, Romance dial., a little quilted jacket worn under the cuirass. *Roquefort*. O. Fr., ***jargot***, a coarse garment worn by country people; Languedoc, ***jhergaou***, an overcoat; Dut. and Fl., ***jurk***, a frock drawn over the other clothes. Hence the O. Eng., ***jerkin***.

GAIN. Has in East Anglia beyond its ordinary meaning of handy and dexterous, other significations. Ex., 'I bought this horse very ***gain***,' (cheap). ***Gain***, quiet, pretty quiet. 'The land lies very ***gain*** (near) for me.' ***Geany***, gainful; ***gayn-cope***, to take a short-cut.

In Lanc., ***gainest*** way is the nearest way. Dan., ***giensti***, a short cut; Isl., ***gagn***, against, through; Sw., ***genasti***, nearest. The secondary meaning of ***gain*** as profitable, convenient, handy, in opposition to ***ungainly***, provincial ***on-gain***, is the Isl., ***gegn***, suitable. Scot., ***gane***, fit, useful; Su. Goth., ***gagnelig***.

'Fulle sone the yong kyng with gode man that wer ***gayn***.
Purveid his wendying.' *Robert de Brunne*.

'GAL, for girl,' writes Elwyn, 'that every New Englandman has heard so often, is from Essex.'

Whether a cor. of girl, or from the A.S., ***gal***, light, pleasant, merry, wanton, wicked, deponent saith not. It would not be so far-fetch'd as Horne Tooke's deriv. of ***wench***, from ***wine-ian***, to ***wink***, ergo, one to be ***winked*** at. ***Girl*** is the O. Fris., ***görl,*** a young and foolish maiden; Pl. D. ***gör***.

Isl., ***gola***, giddy girl, coquette.

'Sen John's kep comp'ny with that ***gal***,
He's quite transmogrified.' *John Noakes and Mary Styles*.

GAL-BOY. A rough, romping girl, hoyden. Americanism.

GALDER. To prate in a coarse, vulgar, noisy manner. Sc., ***gandy***.

The Gael. ***goileadair***, a boaster, chatterer. Wel., ***gwagher***, vain bravado, are more obvious derivations than Forby's A.S., ***galdor***, an incantation.

GALE. Sweet, or Bog Myrtle. *Myrica Gale, Lin.* '***Gawl,*** wode or fowayle; ***mirtus***,' *Pr. Pv.* Wel., ***ysgewyll,*** osiers, twigs.

Formerly grown very largely for fuel in the East Anglian Fen districts. The *Myrtus Brabanticus, Gaule*, sweet willow, or Dutch myrtle, grows plentifully in the Isle of Ely and thereabouts, writes Gerarde in his Herbal. 'Whereof there is such store in that country that they make fagots of it, and sheaves, which they call ***Gaulesheaves***, to burn and heat their ovens.'

Hence comes probably ***goll-sheaves***, a phrase which appears in Hacket's *Life of Archbp. Williams*; a term which Archbp. Trench observes, one meets in no glossary or Dictionary, and adds, 'I only guess at the meaning of it.' 'All the rest of the articles, (i.e. of accusation,) were ***goll-sheaves***, that went out in a sudden blaze.' *Hacket*, pt. 2, p. 92.

Formerly used in lieu of hops, to give an intoxicating quality and bitter flavour to ale.

GAL-KA-BAW. An old East Anglicism for a girl cow-boy, say its writers. We doubt it. The Dorset dial. Has ***gally-crow***, a scarecrow; ***gally***-bagger, a scare-beggar, from the O.E. ***gale***, to cry, holla; Isl., ***gala***; Dan., ***gale***; or more probably the Wessex ***gally***, to terrify; A.S., ***gælan***.

'The Greeks have preserved more perfectly than the Latins the Gaelic pron. of the word for cowherd, which is bochoill; bubulcus, Lat.; boukolos, Gr. The word signifies literally, cowherd, being a compound of ***giull, cow***, and ***bo***, boy or young man.' *Grant on the Origin of the Gael.*, 1814

GALL. A vein of sand in a stiff soil, through which water oozes to the surface at soft places – called ***sand-galls***. ***Galty***, boggy, clayey.

Several derivations are open. I. Ger., ***quellen***, to gush, well up, soak. II. Gael., ***gail***, water-bubble. Wel., ***gwall***, faulty, defective; Sw., ***gall***, sterile; Dan., ***gal***, wrong, provincially sore. Isl., ***gall***, a blister. The latter corresponds with our dialectic English sense of ***gall***, a sore or bare place in a crop, from wet or liability to scorch. Dorset, ***gawly***. Heref and Shropsh., ***gally***, spungy and wet, said of sand; ***galls***-springs, Craven. Sir G. C. Lewis adopted the first cited deriv. in his *Heref. Gloss.*

'Bare plots full of ***galls*** if ye plow over thwart,
And compas (? compost) it then is a husbandly part.' *Tusser.*

'I see in some meddows ***gaully*** places, where little or no grasse at all groweth, by reason (as I take it) of the too long standing of the water.' *Norden's Surveyor's Dialogues*, 1610.

'In the Southern States, as in Florida, ***gall*** is low spongy land, treacherous to the foot, unpleasant to cross.' *Vignoles' Florida.*

Gall-apples, oak-apples, excrescences produced by insect deposit, used for ink. Lat., ***galla***; Wel., ***ysglin***, to form a knot; ***ysgwl***, a scab.

GALLOPPED-BEER. Small beer for immediate use, made by boiling small quantities of malt and hops together in a kettle.

GALLOW-BALK. The iron bar to which pothooks or hakes are appended in the open kitchen chimney. North Ang., ***galley-bauk***.

Isl., ***galge,*** gallows, from ***gagl***, says Ihre, the branch of a tree, its earliest substitute. ***Gallowses***. N. Ang., dialect, braces, or suspenders.

GALVER or **GALVA**. To throb. An inflammation or push is said to ***galva*** or ***galver,*** or ***boolk***, bullock. For deriv., see ***Culver***.

GAMBREL or **BUCKER**. The crooked piece of wood on which the carcases of slaughtered beasts, hogs and sheep are expanded and suspended. ***Cammerell***, N. Ang. dial.

'Soon crooks the tree that good ***gambrel*** would be.' *Ray's Proverbs.*

From ignoring the Celtic roots of our language, Forby and Moor overlooked the true derivation of this as of so many other East Anglian words. Forby derives from Ital., ***gamba,*** leg. It comes from the Wel., and Gael., ***cam***, crooked, bent awry; ***cambrel, cambren***, a crooked stick with notches in it on which butchers hang their meat. In Northampt. and Lanc., ***gambrel***. In the latter, wearing shoe heels on one side is called ***camming***; a fit of ill-temper, a ***camm'd*** humour. In ship-building an arched deck is ***cambered***. Fr., ***cambrer;*** Sp., ***gambote***. Sc., ***cameral***, a large, ill-shaped person; ***cammel***, crooked wood, used as a hook for hanging anything on. Fr. ***jambe***, a leg. ***Gambrel,*** a cart with rails or thripples. Heref. Manx, ***gammag***, a crutch, awry.

In his assault on Wolsey the East Anglian satirist declares

'All that he doth is ryght, as ryght as a ***cammoc*** croked.'

Of the Trumpington Miller in Chaucer's Reeve's Tale, it is said,

'Round was his face, and ***camois*** was his nose.'

Camois his editors read flat. It should be crooked or hook-nosed.

Bucker, used in East Anglia in a sense similar to that of Gambrel is from Ger., ***bucken***, to bend; ***buckelig***, hunch-backed; ***buckling***, a bow, a red-herring, bloater; Dan., ***buk***, to bow; Isl., ***bukkr***, to bow.

'As straight as a maypole, as little as a pin,
As bent as a ***bucker***, and as round as a ring.' *Old Suffolk Riddle.*

GAME-LEG. A bent leg, a sore or wounded one. Wel., ***cam***, crooked.

In Lanc. and Yorks. ***gam***-legg'd is crooked; ***gammerel***, hocks or lower hams of an animal – Devon.

'A hipped roof to a house is called a ***gambrel***, from its resemblance to the hind leg of a horse, which farriers call a ***gambrel***.' *Bartlett's Americanisms.*

GAMMICKING. Gossiping, idle. Essex. A.S., ***gamenlice***, sportive.

GANDER. To gad, to ramble. A.S., ***gan***; Low Sc., ***dander***, saunter.

GANG. To go or come, as in Scot. Used also as a sub. 'A ***gang*** of harrows'; 'a ***gang*** of feet for making jelly.' A gang is a row or set of teeth, or the like. *Ray.* Dut., ***gang***, a pace; A.S., ***gan***; Isl., ***ganga***, to walk.

GANT. I. A village fair or wake. Not common, says Forby, but occurs in noted instances like Mattishall Gant. II. A gannet.

From A.S., ***gan***, he adds in the sense of a gathering, assemblage. The Dan. has ***ganteri***, foolery, banter, horse play, ***Ganse*** or ***Gants***, merriment, hilarity. – Sussex, ***galliganting***, or gallivanting, wandering about in gaiety – applied to associations of the sexes. *Jenning's Somerset Dial.* ***Galligant***, to play the hoyden, to flirt – Devon. ***Ysgont***, to whisk about, Wel.

GANT, scanty, cor. of gaunt. Used in the epithet ***ganty***-gutted. A.S. ***gewant***, dwindled. '***Gawnt***, ***gawnte***, or swonge or lene (or slendyr).' *Pr. Pv.*

GAPE-STICK. A large wooden spoon, a clown. A.S., ***geapan***, to gape. Isl., ***glapa***.

GARLE. To mar butter in making, by handling in summer with hot hands, turning it to a curd-like substance, with spots and streaks of paler colour.

Garled is streaky, spotted, applied to the colour of animals. Dismissing Forby's conjecture of a derivation of ***garle*** from A.S., ***geara***, prepared, a clue to its origin is gained from the senses last quoted. Dut., ***kakelbout***, speckled, streaked, spotted. Dan., ***kal***, veins in a tree round the pith. The Wel. has ***calen***, a lump of butter, ***caleard***, enamelled, streaked. Fr., ***biggarré***, motley, pied.

GARTLE-HEAD. A thoughtless person, gartless.

GARTLESS. Heedless, thoughtless; cor. of regardless.

Su.-Goth., ***garfwa***; A.S., ***gearwian***; Isl., ***giorwer***, prepared, ready.

GAST or **GHAST COW**. A barren cow, called also a ***farrow-cow***. Dut., ***guste koe***; A.S., ***gasen***, barren, wanting, deficient.

Among the items of stock at Hengrave Hall, in 1607, under great cattle, were, '***gastware***, of the last remaynti ij.' Among the customs at Campsey Ash, Suffolk, in 1662, were, 'for every ***gast***-beast, and heifer, ***gast***-ware, and bud, 1½d., each.'

GAST BIRD. A single partridge in the shooting season. Suff.

a. Su.-Goth., ***gast***, strange, foreign.

GASTER. To startle, scare or affright – Essex. ***Gashful***, frightful; A.S., ***gæston***, afflicted; ***gast,*** a ghost.

'Whose ***gashful*** halls do seem to pelt the skies.' *Quarles' Jonah.*

'Since thou must goe to surge in the ***gastfull*** seas, with a sorrowfull kisse, I bid thee farewell, and I pray the gods thou maist fare well.' *Greene's Pandosto.*

'If they run at him with a spit red hote, they ***gaster*** him so sore that his dame shall go her selfe if she will; he will come no more there.' *Gifford's Dialogue on Witches. – Essex,* 1603.

'The word seems to have done working upon the consciences of the most, few are ***gastred*** by the terrors thereof.' *D. Rogers' Naaman.*

GATS. Openings like those in the sand-banks of the Yarmouth Roads. Isl., ***gat***, a gap, aperture, opening; ***gata***, footpaths, narrow ways; ***gatt,*** a door-opening. In Dan., ***gat***, a narrow inlet. Also Dut., a channel, harbour, ***gaten***, holes, straits; Sw., ***gata***, street, lane, common pavement; A.S., ***gat***, a gate; ***geat***, a gap, opening, door; ***geath***, a street.

The Rev. I. Taylor finds the root in the A.S., ***geat***, gate; Dan., ***gata***, a street or road, respectively passages *along* or *through.* Sanskrit, ***gati***; Zend., ***gâta***, a road. From the same root come ***gut***, and the nautical ***gat***, a passage through a narrow channel, as the Catte***gat***. Other***gates***, Sussex provinc. for otherways. The ***ghats***, or ***ghauts***, of India, are the passages to the river side, and the passes through the western line of hills.

Gat, says *Bartlett, Dict. of Americanisms*, 'is applied to several straits in the vicinity of New York,' named by the Dutch settlers.

Gates, on the Kentish coast, are waggon tracks, cut on a slope through the face of the cliff down to the beach below, and used for drawing up sea-weed on to crops for manure. *Wright's Provinc. Dict.*

'***Gate, gyet***, a way, path or street. In many North Country towns the names of streets which end with ***gate,*** as Narrow-gate, &c., have no allusion to gates having ever been there.' *Brockett's Gloss. North County Words.* ***Gate,*** way, path – Teesdale. 'Let him e'en gaing his ain ***gate***,' Sc. Saying. 'Town-***gate***,' the street – Craven. ***Gaut*** or ***gote***, a narrow opening or slip from a street to the shore – Whitby. ***Gate***, a road, a fence, a bar that opens – Lanc. A farmyard – Sussex. A road – Chesh. ***Glat***, a gap in a hedge – Heref. and Salop. ***Gatless***, heedless, careless – East Ang.

Chaucer's line, '***gat toothed***, I was, and that became me well,' – Wife of Bath, – has perplexed his editors. It is generally regarded, remarks Archbishop Trench, in his *Deficiencies in our English Dictionaries*, as a solitary appearance of the word in print. He finds, however, two centuries later, two instances of gap-toothed, in one of which, the word is exchanged for 'tut-mouthed,' projection of the lower jaw. [The derivation of ***gap***, is distinct from that of gat. A.S., ***geapan***; Sw., ***gapa***.]

'Thy mone pynnes bene lyche old yvory,
Here are stumps feble, and her are none,
Holes and ***gappes*** ther are, I nowe for why.'

Lydgate's Advice to an old Gentleman who wished for a young wife.

'She was ill-shaped and ugly, had six fingers, a ***gag-tooth***, and a tumour under her chin.' *Saunders' Account of Anne Boleyn.*

Wedgewood derives from Norse ***glestent***, having teeth apart; ***glisa***, to shine through; ***glett***, an opening in the clouds; ***gletta***, a peep; ***glott***, an opening, hole, the l being dropt. ***Glestand,*** Sw., is ***gap***-toothed.

The music of 'sweet satyric Nash,' was characterised by one of his contemporaries, as 'armed with a ***gag***-tooth,' a tusk, says Disraeli. His bitter foe Gabriel Harvey pounced upon the simile, and in the prologue to his lengthy tirade against Nash, the *Pierce's Supererogation*, 1593, exclaims, 'I'll lead the ***gag***-toothed fop a new-found dance.' ***Gag***-teeth, said of prominent ones, occurs in var. Eng. dialects; ***gag***, Gael., is fissured, cleft, gaping; Isl., ***gagr***, oblique, awry. 'The poets were ill-advised, that fained him to be a leane ***gag-toothed*** beldame, with hollow eyes, pale cheeks, and snakie haire.' *Nash's Pierce Penilesse,* 1592.

GATTER-BUSH, GATTRIDGE, GADRISE. The wild Guelder-rose, *Viburnum opulus*; the wild dog-wood, *Cornus sanguinea*; the spindle, *Euonymus Europæus, Lin.* ***Gatteram,*** a green lane, Linc.

A.S., ***gad***, a goad; ***treow***, tree. Also ***gad***, and ***loris***, a rod; Dan. and Dut., ***rüs***, so called, says *Turner's Herbal*, 1551, 'because butchers make prickes of it.' Dorset, ***gad,*** a hedge stake. ***Gad***-fly, a goad fly. ***Gutteridge; gaitre, rouge***; Fr., ***verge sanguine***; from the red colour of the twigs and autumn foliage of the spindle and carnel trees.

'Doubtless the gad to which these names refer, is the A.S., ***gad*** a point; Sw., ***gadd***, a sting; Isl., ***gaddr***, a pin; and the shrubs so named, from rods cut from them, being armed with such points, and used for driving oxen, and thence explained in the *Pr. Pv.* as a "ghyp, or whyppe."' *Dr. R. C. Prior's Pop. Names Brit. Plants,* 1863. Wel., ***ysgwd***, to push, thrust.

GATTIKIN. Clumsy. 'A great ***gattikin*** mawther.' Dimin. of ***gawky***. Isl., ***gaurr***, a tall, clumsy person. Dut., ***gek***; Ger., ***gauch***, a fool. ***Gauk***-handed, left-handed; Fr., ***gauche***.

GAVEL, GAVIN. A sheaf of corn before it is tied up. ***Gavellers*** gather mown barley or oats or hay with hand rakes into rows and loose cocks ready to pitch on to the waggon. The corn in such rows is said to be in ***gavels***. See ***Gofe***.

Gawler, to swathe or ***gavell*** corne; to make it into sheaves or gavells. *Cotgr. Fr., Dict.*, 1632. Dut., ***geveld***, cut down; Sw., ***kärfve***, little sheaf; Wel., ***gavyr***, to tie in little whisps, to rear up corn in little whisps; ***ysgavyn***, to stack corn; ***ysgubell***, a sheaf; ***gavyl***, a pitch fork; Gael., ***gob-hal***, a fork. Dan. and Ger., ***gaffel***.

GAVEL, a tribute, impost; A.S., ***gafel***, from ***gaf***, gave; Fr., ***gabelle; gavel***-bread, a corn rent; ***gavel***-erth, a tenant's duty of ploughing so much land for his lord, as was also ***gavel***-med, of mowing, and ***gavel***-rep, of reaping.

GAVEL, a gable; from the Dan., ***gavl***; Fris., ***gavel***; ***G'yavel***-end, N. Ang.

GAVEL-KIND, the custom in Kent, by which all sons of a family shared the property equally; Gael, ***gabhail***, division of land by lot among the members of a family or tribe, as practised by the ancient Gaels; Irish and Welsh, ***cîne***, kin; Wel., ***gavael***, the family tenure, tenacious; ***cenedyl,*** family, clan; ***cen***, in possession of.

GAWMLESS. Silly, heedless. ***Gawm***, to give heed to, to consider. Isl., ***gaumr,*** attentive, heedful. A.S., ***gymeleas***, careless, negligent. Mæs. Goth, ***gaum-jam***, to apprehend.

The roots apparently of ***gumption***. A Lanc. man says, 'I conno ***gaum*** what tha means.' In the Ulphilas Gospels, Mark XVI. 4. ***gaum***, appears for perceived. ***Gawmin***, foolish, ignorant, Cumb. Persons dead drunk are always spoken of as ***gaumless***, Leeds; ***gaumish***, cute, knowing, Whitby; ***gawmble*** to try to comprehend, Lanc. To ***gaum***, implies to discern, perceive, rather than amount of knowledge, in the Yorks. dial.

GAWP. To gape very wide. Intens. of ***gape***. Dut., ***gaapen***; Isl., ***gapi***; A.S., ***geapan***.

GAYS, GAHS. Pictures, prints in a book. Seemingly used in the senses of a ***gawd***, a gew-gaw. ***Gay-cards***, the picture cards in a pack. ***Gay***, gawdy, said of speckled cattle.

'Item to Kateryne Druy my best ***gay*** cuppe of erthe kevvryd, or ellys oon of the frerys to chese of bothe.' *Bury Wells (John Barets)*, 1463.

'Like children, they take more delight in the gilded out-side of a book, and to look upon the ***gayes***, and pictures that are therein.' *Rogers' Rich Fool.*

'There are it is true, a certain set of morose and untractable spirits that look * * * as upon ***gays*** and pictures, that are only fit for women and children.' *L'Estrange's Æsop's Fables.*

GEAR. Stuff, tackle. Doctor's ***gear***, household ***gear***. A man exerting himself, is '***going gears***.' A.S., ***geara***.

GEASON. Rare, wonderful, scarce. Used by Bp. Hall. Old Norse, ***gisiun***; A.S., ***gæsen***, rare.

'Graffes of such a stocke are very ***geason*** in those days.' *Gascoigne.*

'Trusting to treason, And not to reason,
Which at that season, To him was ***geson***.' *Skeltonical Rhymes*, 1589.

'Hard to attain, once gotten, not ***geason***.' *Surrey.*

GE, GEE, or **JEE.** Fit, suiting. Used negatively. Ex., 'Ta dont fare to ***jee***.' 'This does not ***ge*** well with that.' 'He and she will never ***gee*** together.' ***Geed***, went, – '***getting*** away for,' near, approaching to. A.S., ***gegan***, to go.

GENERALS. The Archdeacon's Visitation or General Courts. A Norfolk phrase.

GET. To get ***shut*** of, to get quit of. 'To ***get*** over the left shoulder,' to be a loser.

GIBBET. A violent fall. In Norfolk, a swattock.

Sw., ***gippa***, to whip up into the air, ***guppa upp***, to tilt up. *Wedgewood.*

GIBE. I. To fit, agree, suit. Dan., ***gide***. II. A harvest fork. The root may be the Wel., ***ci*** (ch), a catcher, holdfast; ***cib***, (chib) what turns round with a tendency to grapple or hold.

GIB-FORK, a two-pronged harvest fork. Gael., a ***gobhal***; Ger., ***gabel***; Dan., ***greb***; Fris., ***greepe.***

GIFFLE, JIFFLY. To be restless, unquiet, fidgetty. A ***jiffy***, an instant, in the twinkling of an eye. A.S., ***geflea,*** trifles.

Wedgewood derives from Wel., ***cipio, ysgipio***, to snatch. This seems too remote. A nearer is ***ysglyvu***, to snatch, ***scuffle; gwyllt*** and ***ysgavn***, full of starts and turns, skittish. Forby ders. from ***gliff,*** a glimpse, Sc.

Gifeling, idle, flighty, applied to young girls. *Baker's Northampts. Gloss.*

'Bodies so stirr'd do not gain for every minute of time a point of room, but jugging on in a ***giffling*** way, they lay behind at every bearing, as they come up more or less at every jetting.' *Fairfax.*

GIFTS. The white spots under finger or thumb nails.

GIG. A trifling silly fellow. **GIGLET.** A flighty girl.

Imitative of flighty movement, O.E., ***gig***, a top; Swiss, ***gagli***, a girl that cannot sit still; ***giggling, giggish***, have similar meanings; Dut., ***gichgelen***, to laugh, sniggle; Swiss, ***gigelen***. *Wedgewood.* The A.S. has ***gagol, gægl,*** wanton. The Somerset ***gigletin***, is trifling, wanton, said of the female sex; Devon, ***gigglet***, a laughing romp, a tom-boy, whence says Miss Palmer, wakes and fairs are sometimes called ***gigglet-fairs***.

'A wanton ***giglot***, maye cal me to sorrowful repentance, whilst she is yat in her gawdes.' *Bale's Apology.* 'Ye fayrare woman ye more ***gyglott***.' *Sloane M.S.*

'B. And how went matters in your Chambers? G. Why, there we had the girls about us again, ***gigling*** and toying with a thousand Ape's tricks; and their main business was to know what Linnen we had to wash.' *L'Estrange's Erasmus' Colloquies – The French Inn.*

GILVER. To ache, throb, same as **CULVER**, which see.

GIM, GIMMY. Spruce, neat, smart. Wel., ***gwym***, sleek, glossy; Gael., ***grinn***, neat, elegant; A.S., ***gym-en***, heed, solicitude.

GIMBER. To gad about. Is most probably the Su.-Goth., ***gina***, to run and get together. Gael., ***sgilmeil***, given to prating; ***sgeilm***, garrulous idle talk. Or it may be the O. Fr., ***gimbreter***, to play the wanton.

GIMBLE. To grin or smile. It., ***ghigmare***; Fr., ***guigmer***, to wink, leer; from A.S., ***ginian***, to gape, says Diez. O.H.G., ***ginen***, or from O.H.G., ***kinan***, to laugh. The A.S. has ***gamenian***, to joke, be merry; ***gamnigende***, jesting.

GIMMERS. Small hinges. Dorset, ***gimmy***; O.E., ***gimmal***; Somerset, ***gimmace***. *Sherwood's Eng. Dict.*, 1632, has ***giminewes***, joints of a spur. Fr., ***geminé***, twin, two-fold. See long note, *Pr. Pv. Way's Ed.*

'The dry rusty creeking of whose hookes and ***gymmes*** might be heard a mile off.' *Nash's Christ's Tears.*

GIMSON. A gim-crack. ***Gimsoner***, an expert in making them.

GINNICK. Neat, spruce, figg'd up. Essex and Suff. Var. of ***gim***, or the Ger. ***genau***, fitting close, exactly. Or a contraction of the Gaelic, ***gilmeanach***, dainty, foppish; ***sgeinheach***, handsome, elegant, adorned, well-dressed.

GINPIE. Made of a calf's entrails, dressed with lemon, currants, &c.

GIP, GIB. To cheat, swindle; A.S., ***gæp***, shrewd. Wel., ***ysgip***, snatching, rapacious.

'She is a tonnish ***gyb***, The devil and she be syb.' *Skelton's Elinour Rammynge.*

GIRTY-MILK. Porridge of oatmeal or grits. A.S., ***grœtta***, groats.

GIVE. To give one it; to rate soundly – 'give one his own,' – to tell him plain unwelcome truths, to give him it like a Dutch uncle, – to pay one in his own coin – 'to give one the bag,' to dismiss – 'to give one white-foot,' to coax him – to give one the seal of the day, to greet suitably to the hour of meeting. A.S., ***sæl***. To give grant, to allow authoritatively.

GLENT. A glance, start, glimpse, gliding aside, slip; also intens. of ***gleaned***; Wel., ***ysglentiaw***, to slide.

'Fro Cawod scho ***glent***, to Donnefermelyn to fare.' *R. de Brunne.*

'In at a gape as he ***glent***. By the medylle he was hent.' *Lydgate.*

'But for all that he is lykely to have a ***glent*** (fall).' *Skelton.*

'Go softly, she sayd, the stones be full ***glent*** (slippery).' *Skelton.*

GLICK. A jest, joke, repartee, retort. Isl., ***leikari***, a juggler.

'A ***glicking pro***, and a frumping ***contra***, shall have much ado to shake hands in the ***ergo***.' *Gab. Harveys' Pierce's Supererogation*, 1593.

GLIES. Blinkers. Isl., ***glja***, a glance. Leeds dial., ***glee,*** to squint; Lanc., ***gley***. '***Glyare, gloyere***, or ***gogyl*** eye.' *Pr. Pv.*

GLIMSE. To shine, gleam, glimmer. Dan. ***glindse***; Isl., ***glys***.

'The christal glass, which ***glimseth*** braue and bright.' *Gascoigne.*

GLISTER. To sparkle, glisten. Sw., ***glistra***; Dut., ***glinsteren***.

> 'She dranke so of the dregges, The dropsy was in her legges,
> Her face ***glystring*** like glas, All foggy fat she was.' *Skelton.*
> 'As a glede glowynge, your ien ***glister*** as glasse.' *Id.*

'The ***glistering*** glosse of bewties blaze, than reason should it deme.' *Gascoigne.*

'And with that word his ***glistering*** sword unsheathes.' *Surrey's Æneid.*

GLOTTEN. To be scared, perplexed, affrighted. N. Ang., ***gloppen***; Isl., ***glapa***, to gape; ***glappi,*** a dolt.

'Come hither, Sirrah,' cries Lucifer; 'and so the poor cur went wriggling and ***glotting*** up toward his Prince.' *L'Estrange's Quevedo.*

GLOUSE. A strong gleam of heat from sun or fire. Isl., ***glæsa***, to sparkle; Gael., ***loisg***, to burn, blaze.

GLOUT. To look sulky, angry. Isl., ***gletta***; Sw., ***glutta***, to look out of the corner of the eye; ***glott***, a bitter smile. Teut., ***gluyeren***, to look asquint. Fris., ***gloare***.

GLUSKY. Sulky in aspect, looking awry. The *Pr. Pv.* has ***gluscare*** and ***gluskynge***, squinting.

Under ***gl*** an extensive group of English words, both written and colloquial, is noticeable, embodying the varied impressions which light conveys through the vision to the brain. They are specially noteworthy as not deriving from Greek or Latin sources, but from the Scandinavian and Teutonic.

The Greek and Latin have a few words from the roots of ***gl***aukos, ***gl***eukos, and ***gl***oios, describing respectively the qualities of I. Bright, ***gl***eaming; also light blue or grey, tints most nearly expressing the colour idea of atmosphere, sun-illumined. II. and III. Sweet and sticky properties of wine, must, gum, glue. There are also a few words in these languages from the root ***glu***; Sanscrit, ***gri***, on the tongue and throat; Gr., ***gl***otta, tongue; Lat., ***gula***, throat, whence ***gulp,***

glutton, glotting, glosing, &c.

The root of the words loosely strung together in the passage beneath seems to lie in the Isl., ***gulr,*** yellow, the colour of ***gold***. They all reflect in their degree the ***gl***addening (Isl., ***gladr***, bright) action of the light of the sun direct, borrowed, or refracted, upon the unsophisticated mind of the Northmen, the root appearing ever as a prefix, – whether the dewdrops ***gl***isten in the sun's morning rays, or its beams ***gl***ance downward in the full ***gl***are of noontide heat – now veiling their brightness by momentary ***gl***eams through the clouds – now ***gl***oomed over with gathering storms – now ***gl***owing in a sky of unsullied blue – now dappling the woodland ***gl***ades with chequered light and shade. Anon it sinks beneath the eastern heaven in a dying blaze of glory. The ***gl***oaming gathers o'er the landscape, – darkness deepens, – afar, in cottage homes, we mark the taper's glimmering ray, or the flickering shadows cast from the hearth by the fitful flashes of the expiring ***gl***ead. Soon the moon takes up 'the wondrous tale' – its pale beams ***gl***iding across the ***gl***assy lake or flinging fitful ***gl***impses athwart the driving rack. Now turn we to the ball-room's borrowed light, where midnight strives to mimic day. Myriads of lustres ***gl***inting from prismatic mirrors dazzle the eye. In the hair of beauty diamonds sparkle with a ***gl***itter outvieing the modest taper of the ***gl***ow-worm. The ***gl***ances of her bright eyes fill the soul with a strange ***gl***amour. Wrapt in the sheen of ***gl***ossy silks, she moves proudly along amid the ***gl***oating gaze of admirers, the ***gl***ouring looks of envious rivals.

We have quoted here words only of common significance – the student of our provincial glossaries will find they have furnished to the popular imagination themes for infinite variations and embroideries, and the glossaries of the Northern languages are equally prolific.

GLY-HALTER. A halter or bridle with winkers. Wel., ***llwg***, eyesight. '***Gly,*** to look asquint.' *Ray's N.C. Words.* From the Isl. and Su.-Goth., ***glia***, to shine, ***glo***, to see with the eyes.

GNATTLING. Idle talk, busy about nothing.

GOB. I. The mouth. II. A greasy, mouth filling morsel.

'What great ***gobs*** of mutton, and pieces of fat,
My mother gave me, when I was a brat.' *Old Suffolk Song.*

Gael, ***gob***, bill or beak of a bird; Isl., and Dan., ***gab***, the mouth; Polish, ***geba***, the mouth; Russ., ***gaba***, the lips; It., ***gobbio***, a goitre; Fr., ***gober***, to gulp down; ***gobe-mouche***, a gape-mouth, fly-catcher. In Suffolk, ***gobben***, is to chatter, idle; 'yeow tew e'ent a dewin a nawn – you only go ***gobben***, about all day.' ***Gobble*** cock, a turkey cock; in the U.S., a ***gobbler***; in Sc., a Bubbly-Jock. ***Gob-locks***, large mouthfuls, Yorks.

GO-BY-THE-GROUND. A person of small stature.

GOFE, GOAF. A corn rick in the straw, laid up in a barn.

Goaf-flap, a wooden beater to knock the ends of the sheaves, and flatten the goaf; ***goaf-sted***, every division of a barn in which a ***goaf*** is placed, a large barn has four or more. The threshing-floor is the middle-sted; A.S., ***stede,*** a place; ***Goave***, to stow or stack corn in a barn; ***goffe***, a mow, Essex.

Palsgrave's Fr. Eng. Dict., 1530, has ***goulfe***, of corne, so moche as may lye bytwene two postes, otherwise a baye; Dan., ***gulv,*** a floor; ***gulve***, to lay corn sheaves on the barn floor; Isl., ***golf***, a floor, partitioned room.

'In ***goving*** at harvest, learn skilfully how,
Each grain for to lay by itself on a mow;
Seed barley, the purest, ***gove*** out of the way,
All other nigh hand ***gove*** as just as ye may.' *Tusser.*

The Sw., has ***Kärfve***, little sheaf; Gael, ***sgiobal***, a barn, granary; ***sguab***, a sheaf; Wel., ***ysgwbawra***, a barn; Heb., ***schibal***, an ear of grain.

GOFERS. Tea-cakes of flour, milk, eggs, and currants, baked on a ***gofering*** iron, divided into compartments which crimp the cake. ***Gofering***, applied to the crimping of shirt frills, caps, &c.

We have occasionally witnessed a brisk demand for ***goffre*** cakes from itinerant vendors on the Boulevards of Paris. They are there a very light species of pickelet or pancake, served hot, and ***goffred*** the moment before handing to the purchaser in a small machine, from which the cake emerges wafer-thin, and stamped in a number of small squares puffed out. Cotgr. Fr. Dict., 1632, has ***goffre***, a wafer, a honey-comb; modern Fr., ***gauffre***; Eng., ***wafer***; Low. Lat., ***gafrum***; Gael., ***gearr***, a wafer. The primary root seems to lie in the act of dividing, incising with a stamp or impress, the Gael, ***gearr***, the act of cutting; Wel., ***cyfran***, to divide. ***Gaufers***, tea-cakes of the muffin sort, square, made of pancake batter, – Whitby dial.

'In the valleys of the Mississippi and Missouri immense tracts are covered with hillocks of earth, burrowed by a species of mole twice the size of the common field mole, called ***Gophers***.' *Flint's Geogr. Miss. Val.*

GOFFLE. To eat fast and greedily, Essex. Var. of gobble, so the Ger. has ***gähnen*** and ***gaffen***, to gape; Ger., Sw. and Dan., ***gaffel***, a fork.

When vainly trying to make a dolt understand aught, an irate German will exclaim – 'I will pitchfork (***gaffel***) it into you.

GOING. A right of pasturage on a common.

GOINGS-ON. 'Pretty ***goings-on***,' fine doings.

From Essex, says Elwyn in his Americanisms, and adds 'How often has every mischievous boy heard this!'

GOLDEN-DROP. The plum, ***drop d'or***.

GOLDEN-KNOP, the lady-fly or golden-bug. In Dorset, 'God Almighty's Cow.'

GOLE. Full, florid, rank, as grass, &c. Ger., ***geil***, rank, fat, rich, well-manured.

GOLES, GOSH, GOMS. Foolish evasions of profane oaths. Mr. Peggotty's '***gormed***' may have been a var. of the last.

GOLLS. I. Fat chops; ridges of fat on the fleshy parts of a corpulent person. Gael., ***giall***, jaw; A.S., ***geahlas***; O. Fr. ***golle; jol***, *Pr. Pv.* II. Also hands or fists. (Northumb., ***glams***, hands.) 'By ***goles*** or ***golls***, an ancient oath. ***Goll***, Suff., a clumsy fist. Isl., ***kolla***, a handgripe; ***kollr***, applied to chilled, swollen hands. III. Mucus hanging from the noses of dirty children or ***grubs***. Gael., ***sglon***.

GOMMACKS. Tricks, mischief, foolery. ***Gomeril***, a fool.

Prov. Gael., ***gomag***, a nip, pinch; Gael., ***guaineach***, giddy, sportive, frolicking; ***goimheil***, causing annoyance, hurt, vexation. From this root ***gomeril***, a fool, seems to derive, as ***haveril***, also Sc., from ***aifir***.

GON. Gave, given. **GINT,** gave it. 'I ***gint*** em properly.'

GONG. One half the stitches which form the aperture or mesh of a net. '***Goonge***, hole.' *Pr. Pv.* The A.S. has ***gong***, a step, ***gongel-wœfre***, a spider; Dan., ***gænge***, a thread, groove. Isl., ***göng***, a small step.

In the Sicilian dialect, ***gangama*** is a fisher's net. Gr., ***gaggamon***, a small round net.

GONG. A jakes. '***Goonge***, preuy.' *Pr. Pv.* A.S., ***gang***; Wel., ***ysgoth***.

'And al this persecucion was for on Arrian, which deyed at Constantinople ful schamefully. For as he went to church with his clientes and mech pride, there fell upon him a appetite for to go to a sege; and with his issew went alle the guttes out of his wombe down in to the ***gong***.' *Capgrave's Chron.*

GORE. Mire. 'Slush and gore' go together, the former expressing the thin, the latter the thick part of the mire. '***Gore*** or slory.' *Pr. Pv.* A.S., ***gor***, dirt, mud; Fris. and Dut., ***goor***; Sw., ***gorr***; Gael., ***gaorr. Gor***, rotten, decayed; ***gorry***, nauseously fat – Craven.

GOOD-DOING. Charitable. **GOOD-MIND, GOOD-SKIN,** in a good humour. ***Good'n, goody***, contractions of goodman and good-wife. ***Good-tidy***, reasonably, not amiss; ***good-outs***, doing well; ***no-outs***, the reverse. In Linc., ***good***-woolled, a fine fellow, a good sort.

GOOSE-HOUSE. A parish cage or lock-up. Suff.

GORMED. A word which appears in no East Anglian vocabulary.

'He struck the table a heavy blow with his right hand, (had split it on one such occasion,) and swore a dreadful oath, that he would be "***Gormed***," if he didn't cut and run for good, if it was ever mentioned again. It appeared, in answer to my inquiries, that nobody had the least idea of the etymology of this terrible verb passive, to be ***gormed***; but that they all regarded it as constituting a most solemn imprecation.' ***David Copperfield***.

Assuming that Mr. Dickens picked up the word from the beachmen of Yarmouth, the task of hunting down its probable derivation is worth an effort. The old Norse has **gormr**, mud, mire, filth from butchers' shops, intestines, entrails; hence the North Country, ***gorm***, to smear, daub; and a Staff. dialectic word I have never seen in print, the ***gormaruttles,*** pain in the bowels, diarrhœa. The Gael. has ***goinih***, hurt, damage, anguish; ***gorm***, to become blue; Wel., ***gorne; gor***, Fris., Dut., and our North Country, is rotten, dirty; lastly also, and most probable, the true der. is Sw., ***gorma***, to insult, abuse.

GOSGOOD. Yeast, a word of Sir T. Browne's collection. Extinct, says Forby. Ray derives from ***God's-good***; Forby, from A.S., ***gos***, goose; a bird fondly associated in the Norfolk mind with yeast dumplings; ergo, good with goose, ***goose-good***.

The Sw., ***gasa***, to ferment; ***gas-ning***, yeast; ***gas-deg***, leaven; ***god***, good. Gael., ***dèasgann,*** yeast; Wel., ***ysg***, froth, foam, are more likely.

Isl., ***gusa***, to spurt out; ***gjosa***, to hurl up with whizzing force.

'Even in the other great class of languages – the Indo-Germanic – the same figure appears, and may fairly be taken to illustrate the Eastern metaphor. ***Ghost, Geist***, the moving inspiring spirit, is the same as the heaving, fermenting ***yeast***, the boiling, steaming ***geyser***.' *Stanley's Lectures on the Jewish Church.*

'***Ghost***, the German ***geist***, is connected with ***gust***, with ***yeast***, with ***gas***, and even with the hissing, bubbling ***Geysers***.' *Max Müller.*

Giest, the inspiring working spirit of things animate and inanimate, as of love, impulse, affection, is from the O. Ger., ***gäsht, gisten***, fermentation, leaven. *Heyse.* Carried south to Italy it appears in ***gasto***, a lover; Lake of Como., ***gast***, the beloved one. *Diez.* See ***Fangast***.

GOSLINS. The beautiful early blossoms of the willow, *Salix, Lin.* A.S., ***wilig***.

So called from the resemblance of the soft down and yellow colour of the antheræ of the catkins, to young geese.

GOTCH. A large pitcher, a big-bellied jug. Also Flemish. It., ***gotto,*** a pot. ***Gotch-gutted***, pod-bellied.

GO-TO. Of a knife, it 'Don't go to open' is not made to open – 'don't go to come out' – 'Ta don't go ta come off, dew it?' – 'Is, ta dew.'

GO-TO-BED-AT-NOON. The common goat's-beard. *Tragopogon pratense, Lin.*

GOUNDY. Said of eyes running from secretions. A.S., ***gund***, matter, pus; Yorks., ***gunny***; Westm., ***gunded***. '***Gownde*** of the eye, ridda.' *Pr. Pv.*

'A ***goundy*** eye is deceyved soone.' *Lydgate's Warres of Troy.*

'Her even ***goundy***, Are full unsoundy.' *Skelton.*

GOW. Let us go; abbr. of go we. A Suffolk farmer, speaking of the difference between the old and modern farmers' wives, observed, 'that when his mother called the maids at milking-time she never said go, but ***gow***.' *Forby.*

Ray has a proverb.– 'Do not say go, but ***gaw***, i.e. go thyself along.'

GOWT. A drain, sluice; pron. ***gote***. O. Fr., ***goutliere***, a gutter, ***égout***, a drain.

GRAIN. To gripe the throat, to strangle. In Suff., ***green***. Not A.S., ***gryne***, laqueus, *Forby*; but the Gael., ***greimich***, to grasp, gripe. ***Grained***-fork, a pronged fork. Sc., ***grain***; Sw., ***gren***, a branch, a prong, fork.

GRASS-WIDOW. In Suffolk, ***Grace-widow***: a betrayed and deserted fair one.

GREASE. A faint suffusion over the sky, supposed to portend rain. Ex., 'the sky begins to ***grease*** up.' ***Greasy***, foul, grassy, said of fallows. Also slimy, as of roads, after rain.

The ground is said to be ***greasy***, in a thaw, after slight frost. *Baker's Northampt. Gloss.* Gael., ***cries***; Lat. ***crassus***; Fr., ***gras***, fat.

GREEN-OLF. The green-finch, or green grosbeak. *Parus viridus.*

GREFT, GRIFT. To graft, to dig. ***Grift,*** in Suffolk, slate pencil.

A.S., ***græft***, carved, cut; Fr., ***greffe***, a shoot for grafting; Dut., ***greffie***, a cutting, also 'a slate-pen,' from ***graphium***, a stylus, Gr., and Lat. ***Graft,*** a ditch, Frisic; ***griffel***, slate pencil, Sw.

Graft, Craven and N. Ang. is the depth of a spade's bit in digging, from A.S., ***grafan***, to dig, to carve; Isl., ***grafa***, hence grave. Dan., ***gröfte***, to ditch, trench.

Cumb., ***greaav***, to cut peat, dig; Whitby, ***turf-greaving-time***, – autumn, when farmers near the moors ***greave*** or slice the turves off the surface with a spade, and stack to dry for winter fuel. ***Graff***, to dig with a spade, Heref. Sir G. Lewis remarks, 'ground can be ***graffed*** when soft enough not to require a mattock.' In Yorks. (says Grose in *Dig.*) they distinguish between digging and graving; to dig is with a mattock, to grave with a spade. In Gloucest. a 'grafting tool' is the strong spade in shape of a segment of a circle, used in digging canals and other very heavy work; in Northampts. a long tapering spade. ***Gruff***, Somerset, is a mine; ***gruffiers***, miners; Sw., ***gruffva***, a mine; E. Ang., ***grufted***, dirtied begrimed.

GRETT. A snare for hares. Also called ***grynes, grynnies***. A.S., ***gryn***, a snare; ***grytte***, a spider's web.

'He spared nother hylle nor holte, busche, ***gryne*** nor ***grett***.
Lord! he was fowle scrapyd!' *Lydgate's Prioress and her Lovers.*

GREWIN. A greyhound. In Scot., ***gru*** and ***grew***. N. Ang., ***grewnd***. The Isl. has ***grey***, a hound; the A.S., ***grig-hand***.

GREY-COAT PARSON. A lay impropriator of tithes.

GRILL OR GRIZZLE. To snarl or snap. 'How them there tew warment dew grill and grizzle at one another.' *Moor.*

In Devon, to laugh or grin. *Miss Palmer.*

Both convey the same idea. Dut., ***grillen***, to shiver; Ger., ***grinsen***, to snarl; ***griseln***, to grin, simper, show one's teeth; Sw., ***gräl***, a quarrel. Wel., ***grillian***, to gnash; ***grunsgul***, to grin, snarl; Manx, ***gyrn***.

'Tell you I chyll, If that ye wyll,
A whyle be styll, Of a comely gyll,
That dwelt on a hyll, But she is not ***gryll***.'
Skelton's Elinour Rummynge.

GRIMBLE. To begrime. A diminutive. Isl., ***grima***.

GRIMMER. A pond or mere with weed covered surface. A.S., ***gren***, green; ***mere***, pool.

'An old woman said "the ground was so wet, I stuck all in the ***grammer***." I find no authority for the word, it is very local, but in some parts of the county well known. *Miss Baker's Northampt. Gloss.*

GRINDLE, *grindlet, grip, grup, gripple* or ***groop***. A little ditch or trench. A.S., ***grœp***; Dut., ***greppel***; Fris., ***groppe***, a trench, furrow, drain; Gael., ***grinneal***, deep, gulphy.

Grip, groop, N. Ang. and Lanc., is the hollow running between a double row of cow-stalls in which the dung falls. – '***Growpe***, where beestys, as nete standyn.' *Pr. Pv.* A.S., ***grœp***, latrina, says Skinner. '***Grype*** or a ***gryppel***, where watur rennythe a-way in a londe, or watur-forowe.' *Pr. Pv.* ***Grip***, to make an open ditch, Heref; the hollows between furrows, Whitby.

'Item there is vij acres lond lying by the high weye toward the ***grendyll***, not ferre from Herdwyk.' *Bury Wills (John Baret's*, 1463) *Camden Sy.*

GRINT. *Grit.* A participle of ***grind.***

GRISSENS. Stairs. Craven, ***grees*** and ***grice***. '***Grece***, or tredyl, or steyre.' *Pr. Pv.* Fr. ***degré***, a staire, step, ***greese***. *Cotgr.* Hence comes the der. of the ***Grecian Stairs*** at Lincoln. From the Wel., ***gris***, a step; ***grisiaw***, a staircase.

Greece, a little brow, stairs, an ascent, Lanc. Manx, ***greeish***.

'This Pope went down into the erde a hundred ***grecis*** and fifty, and bond a dragon.' *Capgrave's Chron.*

'To parte the litil botrie vnder the ***gresys***.' *Bury Wills (John Baret*, A.D. 1463) *Camden Sy.*

GROANING. A lying-in. ***Groaning-cake*** is made on such occasions.

Not to be confounded with the Manx ***groonoays***, biestings or new curd of the milk of a cow, newly calved.

GROPE. 'Teach your grandame to ***grope*** her ducks.' *Ray's Proverbs.* Now-a-days the good old lady is taught 'to suck eggs.' 'Gropyn or felyn wythe hande.' *Pr. Pv.* A.S., ***gropian***.

'Sum medelynge spyes, by craft to ***grope*** thy mynde.' *Skelton.*

'In remote country villages was (in my early days) an old woman exclusively possessing the secret of ascertaining whether or not a goose was duly impregnated, by ***gropeing*** in a peculiar manner with her finger. I recollected few things that I ever enjoyed more than palming a gander on a sapient beldam of this description, witnessing her sage researches, and listening with my wicked compeers to her remarks.' *Major Moor.*

'It is not the Primitive Church shall beare out the Vicar of Little Down, in Norfolk, in ***groaping*** his own hennes, like a Cotqueane.' *Nashe's Almond for a Parrot,* 1589.

'Let him alone, and if he doe not know by a cowes water how many pintes of milke she will give in a year, then wyll he neuer help his wife to make cheese again whiles he liues; and without offence to his Pastorshippe bee it spoken, hee will saie pretyly well to a henne, if she bee not too olde, always prouided shee haue a neaste of cleane strawe in his studie and hee ***groape*** her with his own hands evening and morning. Then see if he do not make three pounds a yeere of her over and above all costes and charges.' *Ibid.*

GROUND-SWEAT. A person buried some time is said to have taken a ***ground-sweat***.

GROUT. The thin fluid mortar used in building with flints.

Dut., ***gruisje***, morsels of stone; Isl., ***grut***, dregs; ***gruten***, muddy; '***grute***, fylthe;' *Pr. Pv.* A.S., ***greot***, sand, dust.

Grouty, muddy, lees, dregs, in var. dial. ***grout***, wort of the last running; N. Ang., from O. Fr., ***gru***, malt; ***grout***, implying ground malt; '***growte*** for ale, granomellum.' *Pr. Pv.* In Med. Lat., ***grutum***. In Leices. says Bp. Kennett, malt infused for ale before it is fully boiled is called ***grout***, and before it is turned, wort. In the West a thick ale, called ***grout-ale*** is drank. *Way's Notes to Pr. Pv.* ***Grout***-headed, stupidly noisy, Sussex.

'Whilst I am shuffling and cuttling with these long-coated Turks, would any Antiquary would explicate unto me this Remblere or Quidity? – Whether these Turbanto ***Grout-heads*** that hang all men by the throats on iron hooks, even as our ***Towers*** hang all their Herrings by the throats on wooden spits, first learned it of our Herring-men, or our Herring-men of them?' *Nashe's Lenten Stuff*, 1599.

GROWER. A cultivator. 'A great ***grower*** of hemp;' 'a ***grower*** of turkies, lambs, &c.'

GRUB. I. Idle, nonsensical talk. II. Constant toil, Essex. I. Ger., ***grublei***, trifles. II. ***Gruben***, to dig.

GRUB. A dirty little animal or child. Wel., ***ysgrubyl***, beast like.

GRUBBLINS. Lying grovelling on the belly. A nurse lays a crying child ***grublins*** on her lap to quiet it. – 'I sah dew yeou lah that there child ***grublins*** – 'tull far the buttah faught.'

L. Sc. ***gruffling***, Isl., ***liggia a grûfu***, to lie face downwards; ***grufla***, to grovel.

GRUFFLE. To make a growling noise in the throat.

L. Sc., ***gruff***, discomposed slumber; Grisons, ***grufflar***, to snore. *Wedgewood.*

GRUMPY. Surly; in Suffolk, snaggy. A.S., ***grum***; Gael., ***gruaim***, fierce; Wel., ***grwm***, a growl.

GRUNNY. A hog's snout. ***Grunnying***, the rootling of a pig's snout.

Isl., ***tryni***; Fr., ***groine***; N. Ang., ***grune***; A.S., ***grunan***, to grunt.

'The ***Gruntyng*** and the ***groynninge*** of the grounyng swine.' *Skelton.*

GRUTCH. To grudge. '***Grotchynge***, ***grutchon, gruchyn***.' *Pr. Pv.* Fr., ***gruger***. *Cotgr.*, 1632.

GUBBINGS. Parings, fragments, fish scraps, &c. See ***Kiplins***.

Gubbins, fish fragments, bait, parings of haberdine, cod-fish, dog-fish, (Gael., ***gobbag***, and ***goibin***, sand-eel) &c. O. Fr., ***gobeau***, a bit, gobbet, or morsel. seems to be the Wel., ***ysgubion***, sweepings.

'All the meat that we eat we catch out of the sea, and if there we miss, well-washed and salted we sneak home to bed supperless; and upon the tail of it he bringeth in a parasite that flowteth and bourdeth them thus: 'Hough you hunger-starved ***gubbins*** or offals of men, how thrive you, how perish you?' *Nashe's Lenten Stuff.*

GUG. Is der. from the O. It., ***guiggia***, a whip or scourge wherewith friars discipline and whip themselves; ***guiggiare***, to scourge with a ***guiggia***. *Florio's Ital. Dict.*

GUGGE. A term which occurs in the Puritan Divinity of Essex.

Hardly the sense of '***gugaw***,' *Pr. Pv.* to pipe, to trifle with disport, the Fr., ***goguer***; or of the Fr., ***guigner***, to wink, blink, aim at with one eye; but rather a vulg. like the Walloon ***geug***, to judge, admonish.

'The Divell and his eldest sonne know well the complexions of carnall people, and when the gospel hath been preached twenty yeare together, yet people will long after the garlick and onions of old religion; and carnall reason, with her taile, sweepes downe a great part of the starres of heaven; we do but ***gugge*** and tire most men with our preaching of self deniall and faith.' *D. Rogers' Naaman.*

'One day this error of thine will ***gugge*** thee to the quicke, and cause thee to cry out.' *D. Rogers' Naaman.*

GULL. To sweep away by force of running water. Ex., 'The bank has been ***gulled*** down by the freshet,'. ***Gull***, a breach made by the force of a torrent. ***Gully-hole***, the mouth of a drain or sewer.

Dut., ***gullen,*** to suck down; Sc., ***guller***, to gargle, guggle, *Jam*; Wel., ***gwyll***, wild, savage, rapid; Sui-Goth, ***goel***, a whirlpool; Lat., ***gula***, a throat, swallow.

'Take heed of filling thine heart and thoughts with earthly things; the cares for earth will eat in so dangerously, and winne upon thee, as the sea tydes ***gull*** down the bankes.' *D. Rogers' Naaman.*

GULLION. Stomach-ache, colic. Essex. O. Ger., ***gölle***, bile. Gael., ***goile***, the stomach; ***caolan***, the intestines; Manx, ***gollane***.

GULP. I. The young of animals in their softest tenderest state; Dut. ***welp***. II. A squabby diminutive person; in the sense of ***collop***, a lump. III. A severe blow or fall; var. of ***culp***.

I. Sui-Goth, ***gul***; A.S., ***geole***, yellow. Applied in Chesh., says Wilbraham, to young unfledged birds, from their yellowish plumage. Heref., ***gull***, a gostling. The deriv. may be from the Wel., ***gwylaw***; Gael., ***gul***, to cry; the Sc. has ***gulpin***, a young child.

Whitby, ***gorps***, a bird just hatch'd. 'As naked as a ***gorpin***.' Teesdale, ***gorbin***; Cumb. ***gorlin***; Sc. ***gorblet***. In the above N. Ang. dial. the derivation seems an intens. of ***gape***. ***Gorby*** being the term for a rustic, with eyes and ears wide agape. Sw., ***grobian***, a clown.

'As that ungentle ***gull***, the cuckoo's bird.' *Henry IV, v. i.*

GULSH. Mud; also ribaldry, silly talk. See ***culch.*** Also plump, souse, applied to a heavy squashy fall, a squelcher. In the latter senses the word is also Mid. Ang. Wel., ***golch***.

GULSKY. Corpulent and gross. In Northampts., ***gulshing***.

Gael., ***sult***, Isl., ***svil***, fat; Dut., ***gulzig***, gluttonous. Nares has ***gulch***, a glutton, Latinized ***ventricosus***; ***gulschy***, gross in the body, Clydesdale; ***gulsoch***, voracious. A ***gulching***, or huge bellie, a bellie as big as a tunne. *Cotgr.*, 1632. ***Golsh***, to gulp down voraciously, Craven and Lanc.; to belch, Leeds; to ***gulk*** or ***gulge***, to gulp greedily, Devon.; ***gocken***, to be ravenous, Linc., ***gulschy***, greedy of drink. Salop.

GUMBLED. When waking, the eyes are said to be ***gumbled*** when not easily opened, but glued or gummed together. N. Ang., ***gowled***; Northampts., ***gubbed*** up.

GUMSHUS or ***Rumgumshus***, quarrelsome. ***Bumshus*** and ***Rumshus***.

Var. of ***grumpy***, which see. Gael, ***gruamach***, morose, surly. To ***take the grumps***, to be ill-tempered; Scot., I am ***gumple-fisted***, sulky, see *Redgauntlet.*

GUNNER. A shooter; ***gunning***, shooting; ***gunning*** boat, a light and narrow one used by the fenmen to pursue wild fowls along the drains and cuts.– East Anglicisms, common in the U.S.

'***Gunnare***, or he that swagythe a gunne.' *Pr. Pv.*

GURN. To grin, as a dog. Old English, says Forby.

The Sc. has ***gurr***, and ***gurl***, to snarl as a dog; Isl., ***kurra***, Gael., ***grunsgul***.

GUSH. A gust of wind. ***Gussock***, a sudden gust.

It ***guscio di vento***; Isl., ***gustr, giostr***, a cold blast. *Wedgewood.* Ger., ***guss***, a gush.

GYLE. Wort. Dut., ***gyl***. **GUILE-FAT**, a wort tub.

It occurs also in the *Gloss. of Brockett, Jamieson and Ray.* '***Gyylde***, or new ale.' *Pr. Pv.* A ***guile*** of beer, a brewing.

GYP, to gut a herring, Sc.

The Scotch process of disembowelling a herring, done with instantaneous rapidity. In this the der. perhaps lies, as the term is neither Norse or Dutch. Sc.,

gype, keen, ardent in any operation; ***gypelie***, nimbly, quickly; Isl., ***gypa***, vorax, says Jamieson. The Sw. has ***gippa*** to whip up. ***Gyp***, Leeds dial., to gasp for breath; a bather pushing another into the water makes him ***gyp***. A fish ***gyps*** when out of the water. Ger., ***giepen***, to gape for breath. ***Klip-fish*** is the term applied to the split and dried cod; the staple of the Norwegian fishery. Sw., ***klippa***, to cut, shear.

Under ***g*** the absence in East Anglia of certain words common to the North Anglian dialects, is noticeable, such as ***gaily, gar, goupen, girt, gloaming, gradely, graith,*** &c.

H

HA'. To have. 'I'll ***ha'*** you bor, I'll ***ha'*** you.'

HACK, HECK, HALF-HACK. A hatch, a door divided across.

Heck, a latch; ***heck-door***, the inner door; ***half-heck***, the half or lower part of the door. *Brockett's North Country Words.* ***Heck-board***, a cart tail board, which lets down, is common to several Eng. dialects. '***Hec, hek***, or ***hetche***, or a dore.' *Pr. Pv.* ***Hack*** or ***heck***, a hay rack. – 'With ***hek*** and mangeoir.'—*Archæol. xvii, 203.* ***Guichet***, a wicket or hatch of a doore. *Cotgr. Fr. Dict.* Dut., ***heek***, a barrier of lath or trellis, a grating, gate. A ***heck-door***, N. Ang., is one partly latticed and partly pannelled.

'Theyre browys all to-broken, such clappys they cach;
Whose jawlawsy malycyous makyth them to lepe the ***hach***.' *Skelton.*

HACK. To stammer, to chop words in pieces. Dut. and Ger., ***hacken***, to chop up; Dan., ***hakke***; Fr., ***hacher***; Bret., ***hakein***; Cumb., ***hakkar***. Applied also to a violent cough.

'A faint, tickling, incessant cough, is its Norfolk meaning; a short, hard, cutting cough in the South. The last is the American application of the terms.' *Elwyn.*

Dorset, ***hacker***, teeth chattering from cold or fright. In the N. Ang., ***hacked*** is applied to chapped hands or feet. In Cumb. ***hag*** is to cut or hack. In Northampts., hay is ***hacked*** or ***hackled***, when after tedding it is put in small rows. ***Hack***, Somerset, the spot where bricks are ranged to dry.

'Thus shall we sort out eternity into as many kinds and lengths, as the Darbyshire huswife does her puddings, when she makes whitings and blackings, and liverings and ***hackings***; and 'tis pitty for fooling sake that we cannot tye a string at the end of all alike.' *Fairfax.*

HACK. A hard-working man – Suff. Also a hedge. Su.-Goth., ***hæck***, an enclosure; A.S., ***haca***, a hedge. Dut., ***heck***.

Hack, a hoe or pick-axe, Dorset and N.A.; Dut., ***hak***, grubbing axe.

HACKLE. I. To shackle. II. Also a fastening applied to cows to prevent their kicking when being milked. Var. of Sc. ***hapschackle***. ***Hackle***, N. Ang., to dress, as flax, to trim up.

HACK-STAMMERING. Stammering and sputtering like a dunce at lessons. Dut., ***hakkelen***, to stutter. Dan., ***hakke***; Cumb., ***hakkar***.

HAFEREN. Unsettled, unsteady. 'A go ***haferen*** about.' Scot., ***haver***, to talk foolishly; ***haverel***, a fool. N. Ang., ***haffle***, to waver, stammer. To '***haffle*** and snaffle,' to stammer and speak through the nose; to hesitate –

Whitby. ***Hifer***, to loiter – U.S. ***Huffle***, to waver – Devon.

Isl., ***gifr-a***, loquitur ***hefer***, garrulous, writes Jamieson. Dut., ***haperen***, to stammer; Sw. ***happla***. The Wel. has ***yuvyd***, foolish; Gael., ***aifir***; Heb., ***epher***, symbolum levitatis.

HAGGY. Applied to the broken surface of the soil, when wet. The same when dried and hardened is termed ***hobbly***.

In the North, a ***hag***, is a boggy quagmire. Ex., a peat-***hag***; Isl., ***hagga***, to shake. On the Yorks. coast a ***hag*** is a mist, cor. of ***haze***. ***Haggy***, applied to coarse uneven ground in Mid Ang. woodland districts. Isl., ***hagi***; Sw., ***hage***.

HAHM or **HAWHM**. Wheat stubble. Applied also to ***risps***, the green straw or runners of potatoes and pease, and the stubble of beans. Fr., ***chaulme***. – *Cotgr.* Dorset, ***hame***.

'Mown ***haulm*** being dry, no longer let lie.' *Tusser.*

It occurs in a similar sense in *Ray's S. & E. Country Words.* A.S., ***healm***, Fris., and Dan., ***halm***; Isl., ***halmr***, stubble.

'The ***haulm*** is the straw of the wheat or the rye,
Which once being reaped, then mow by and by.' *Tusser.*

HAHNET. A hornet. 'Nine ***hahnets*** 'al sting a hoss ta dead,' – Suffolk saying. Ray has ***hornicle***, a Suffolcism for hornets; a term Moor says he never heard.

HAHNSEY. The large heron or hernshaw. Called also from its note, ***frank*** or ***fraank***. Doubtless the original of Shakspeare's—

'I know a hawk from a hand-saw.' *Hamlet II. 2.* That is, a hawk, from the heron it pursues. A cor. of Fr., ***heronceau***, a young heron.

'Item a ***Hernesew*** of Store.' *L'Estrange Household Account*, 1519.

HAIFER. I. To toil. II. Suff., to higgle, from A.S., ***heofian***, to mourn. *Forby.*

I. Isl., ***Haf***, to heave; ***hafandi***, burdensome; ***hafferma***, to load heavily; or the Wel., ***traferth***; Gael., ***saothair***, to toil, labour, trouble; Bret., ***chifa***, inquieter, are more likely der. II. See ***Haferen***.

HAINISH. Unpleasant, Suff. The Gael., ***ainideach***, vexing, galling. A.S., ***hean***, needy, despised. N. Ang. ***hooned***, ill-treated.

Fr., ***honteux***, and ***honni***, to shame, insult; Goth., ***haunjan***; Ger., ***höhnen***, to scoff; O. Sax., ***hönda***, shame; Su.-Goth., ***hän***.

HAKE. A pothook; the dentated iron head of a foot plough. Isl., ***haka;*** Dut., ***hake***, hook; Dan., ***hage***. Bret., ***higen***, a fish-hook.

HAKE. To toil, particularly in walking. Often joined with ***hatter***. 'He has been ***haking*** and ***hattering*** all day long.' Also to loiter.

'At euery ale stake, With welcome ***hake*** and make, (mate)
By the bread that God brake, I am sorry for your sake.' *Skelton.*

Sc. and N. Ang., ***haik***, to saunter; ***haigle***, to walk, much fatigued; Bailey has ***hake***, to gape after, to sneak, loiter; Dut., ***haaken***, to hanker after; ***Hakes***, an idle lounger, Craven; a ***Hallacks***, Leeds. ***Haltering***, the Sc., ***hatter***, to be in a confused but moving state, '***a hatterin***,' Dumfries. See ***hatter***.

Hake, to tire, distress, applied in Cumb. to over-cropped, exhausted land; 'haking about,' prying, Whitby; also to teaze, worry one with askings. ***Hakasing***, tramping about, Linc. Possibly a cor. of ***hawk***.

The Ger. has ***hocker***, a huckster, from ***hocken***, to heap together, to take upon the back. Our ***hawker*** may der. from this or from Isl., ***hauga***, to heap up, or as Wedgewood suggests, Norse, ***hauka***, to cry, shout; Fr., ***hucher***. The Sw. has ***hökare***, chandler; ***hökeri***, haggling.

HALF-HAMMER. The game of hop, step, and jump.

HALF-ROCKED. Oafish, silly. Elsewhere half-baked, half-saved.

HALSE. To hug, embrace, hang on to. A.S., ***hals***, the neck.

Dut., ***halsen***, to embrace. '***Halsynge*** or dallynge, amplexus.' *Pr. Pv.* Isl., ***heilsa***; Dan., ***hilse***, to salute; ***hilsen***, greeting.

Halsethe and kissethe and wol hym not with-seyne. *Lydgate.*

'The ryuers rowth (rough), the waters wan;
She sparyd not to wete her fete;
She wadyd ouer, she found a man,
That ***halsyd*** her hartely and kyst her swete.
Thus after her cold she coughte a hete.' *Skelton.*

HAMBER. A hammer. So also in East Anglia, manner is pronounced mander; banner, bander, &c. Heref., ***homber***.

'The foreseid Jubal proporcioned his musik after the sound of Jubal ***hamberes***.' *Capgrave.*

'Masyd, wytles, smery smyth.
Hampar with your hammer upon thy styth.' *Skelton.*

HAMMER-SPOTS. The dappling of a fine coated horse. Isl., ***hamr***; A.S., ***hama***, skin. 'Hence yellow-***hammer***, ***hammer***-cloth, the skin cloth, usually of bear's skin.' *Miss Gurney.*

Hame, thyn skynne of an eye or other lyke.' *Pr. Pv.*

HAND. To sign. 'They made me ***hand*** a paper.'

HAND. Performance. To make a hand on, to waste, to destroy.

HAND of pork. The shoulder joint, cut without the blade bone.

HAND OVER HEAD. Thoughtlessly extravagant, ***hand***-smooth, worn threadbare, or anything very smooth.

HANDLE, the, of a knife or small tool is called a ***haft***; of a hatchet or axe, ***helve***; of a flail, ***handstaff***; of a spade, ***skuppatt***; muckfork, ***tiller***; rake or long fork, ***stale***; of a pump, ***swake***; long pitch-fork, ***sheath***. A scythe-stick is a ***sneath*** or ***snaithe***. *Raynbird's Agr. of Suffolk.*

Haft. A.S. and Dan., ***hœft***; Sw., ***häfte***; Isl., ***hefti***, a handle. ***Helve***. A.S., ***helf***; Ger., ***helm***. The remainder see under their heads. The nomenclature of our Agricultural Implements is Teutonic and Scandinavian.

HAND-STAFF. The longer limb of the flail, held by the thresher.

HANG. I. A crop of fruit. 'I've a fairish ***hang*** o' nuts ta year.' II. A declivity. Is., ***hanga***.

HANG-SLEEVE. A dangler; an officious but unmeaning suitor.

HANG-SUCH. A worthless fellow. N. Ang., ***hang-gallows***.

HANK. A door or gate fastening. Isl., ***hanki***, a strap or chain; Sw., ***hank***, a tye-band. A chain or hook fastening is a ***hasp***, writes Moor. Ger., ***hespe***; Swed., ***haspe***; A.S., ***hœps***.

HAP. To cover, wrap up. E. and N. Ang., ***happing***, a coverlet; ***Hap-***

harlot, a coarse coverlet. A.S., ***heapian***, to heap together.

The Gael. has ***brat-uallach***, a coverlet, swathing. Bailey has ***happerlet***, a coarse bed covering; ***Harle***, is the stem or straw of flax, separated from the filament. *Jamieson*. '***Lappyn***, or whappyn yn clothys, (happyn to-gedyr) wrap to-geder in clothes, involvo.' *Pr. Pv.* See note *ante*, on ***daggled***, from which ***hop harlots*** seem to have been bed coverings of a coarse material. ***Hop***, in East Anglia, was used in the sense of wrap or ***wlap***, of which Wedgewood conceives it to be a corruption. In the *Paston Letters*, John Paston writes, 'I pray yow ye woll send me hedir ij elne of worsted for dobletts, to ***happe*** me thys colde wynter.' **BIRLET** was an old English form for a coif, hood or knitted cloak, see Bailey. *Cotgr.* 1632, has '***bourlet***, a wreath, or a roule of linnen cloth, or leather; also the hood worn by graduates, lawyers, and citizens at their assemblies.' Possibly ***hap-harlot*** is a cor. of the two words.

Happin, Craven, is a rug or coverlet; also any clothing, thick and warm. ***Happins***, thick woollen bed covers, woven carpet wise, Cumb.; bed clothes, Leeds. ***Hap***-harlot, a coverlet for a servant. *Brockett's N. Ang. Words*. ***Harlot*** was originally not appropriated to a female, nor even to a person of bad character.

'He was a gentel ***harlot*** and a kind,
A better felaw sholde a man not finde.' *Chaucer*.

'Harlot,' remarks Wedgewood, 'simply signified a young man;' Wel., ***herlod***, a youth, stripling; ***herlodes***, a damsel.

HARBER. A cor. of the ***horn beam*** or ***hard beam***.

HARDS. I. Coarse flax, otherwise ***tow-hards***. ***Harden***, strong, coarse, hempen cloth; N. Ang., ***hurdis***, ropes; A.S., ***heordas***, refuse of tow. 'Fr., ***hard***, string, ***harde***, rope.' *Diez.* II. Very hard cinder, the calx of pit coal imperfectly vitrified. Sw., ***härd***, the hearth of a forge.

'No such iron-fisted Cyclops to hew it out of the flint, and run through anything as these frost-bitten, crab-tree-faced lads, spun out of the ***hards*** of the Tow, which are Donsel Herring Lackies, at Yarmouth every fishing..' *Nashe's Lenten Stuff.*

HARNSEY-GUTTED. Lank and lean. See ***Hahnsey***, ante.

HARREN. Made of hair. Dut., ***haren***.

HARRIAGE. Confusion. 'I think I have heard that, in the south part of Suffolk, the phrase "he is gone to Harwich," means he is gone to rack and ruin.' *Forby*.

It may be a local manufacture from the verb ***harry***; A.S., ***hergian***, to plunder, afflict., Isl., ***heria***, to plague; Dan., ***hærje***, to ravage. O. Fr., ***harier***, to vex, trouble. *Cotgr.* 'I'm sadly *harrish'd,'* worn out; harrishing weather, cold and stormy, Craven. ***Harry***, a country man, boor, Craven. ***Hare,*** to make wild, ***harum-scarum***. *Ray's E.A. Words*. A sea-***harr***, a storm, Linc.; A.S., ***hærn***, a wave. A ***Harry-gaud***, a rigsby, a wild girl. *Ray's N. Ang. Words*; a blackguard. *Brockett*.

HARRY-CARRIERS. The Yarmouth Trollies. See ***hurry-carriers***.

HARVEST-BEEF. Any kind of butcher's meat, eaten in harvest.

HARVEST-LORD. The principal reaper who goes first and regulates the movements of the rest. ***Harvest-Lady***, the second reaper in the row. In

Cambridgeshire, the ***harvest queen***. The man who goes for the beer and pours it out is called 'the steward.'

HASE, HASLET. The heart, liver, &c., of a hog, seasoned, wrapped up in the omentum and roasted. Old Fr., ***hastille,*** entrails.

A small pig's fry or roast; Fr., ***haste***, a spit or broach. *Cotgr.* '***Hastlere***, that rostythe mete,' *Pr. Pv.* Lat., ***assator***; Scot., ***fraise***. Dut., ***harst***, a roast.

HASSOCK. I. Coarse grass growing in rank tufts on boggy ground. II. A bass of matted rush. ***Haske***, a fisher's basket.

'These ***hassocks***, in bogs, were formerly taken up with a part of the soil, matted together with roots, shaped, trimmed and dressed, a sufficient part of their shaggy and tufted surface being left to make kneeling much easier than on the pavement of the church, or the bare-boarded floor of a pew. Some remains of them are still to be found in some of our meaner parish churches, particularly in the fens.' *Forby*. Scot., a besom, anything bushy, as a ***hassick of hair***; a large round turf, used as a seat. *Jam.* Sw., ***hwass***, a rush. Sp., ***has***, a bundle of hay or grass.

'Then till the sun, which yet in fishes ***hasks.***
Or wat'ry urn, impounds his fainting head.' *P. Fletcher.*

HASSOCK-HEAD. A shock head, bushy, matted and entangled. Fin., ***hassa***, tangled, shaggy; Sw., ***hässla,*** a bunch of flax.

HASTINGS. An early variety of pea. Suff.

'Some indeed are so base and perverse, that they rather are moved to prich and disdaine by their inferiour's forwardnesse, calling them ***hastings***, soone ripe, soon rotten; ragged colts make the better horses.' *D. Rogers' Naaman.*

HATTER. To harass and exhaust with fatigue. Sc., ***hatter***, to be in a confused moving state, to totter. ***Hottering***, limping lame, Whitby. A.S., ***ateran,*** to fatigue, tire; Isl., ***haltra***, halt, lame. See ***Hake***.

The N. Ang. ***hetter*** (Craven, ***hitter***) has an opposite meaning, that of eager, earnest, keen; Chesh., ***hattle***.

HAUGHTY weather. Windy, blustering.

HAW. The ear of oats. **HAVER**, oats. See **AVEL**.

Craven, ***havver***; Old Fr., ***haveron***, wild oats; Sw., ***hafre***; Dut., ***haver***; Manx, ***heel***, threshed oats.

HAWKEY, HOCKEY, the feast at harvest home. ***Hawkey-load***, the last load crop, formerly led home with rustic pageantry, decorated with flags, streamers and garlands, and attended by masquers and mummers, foremost among whom revelled my Lord and Lady.

In Suffolk, called ***horkey***. 'Now, writes Raynbird, in his Prize Essay on Suffolk Agriculture, the horkey is kept at public houses or cottages instead of at the master's; a sum of money being allowed to each man in place of supper. The same writer quotes from Sharpe's Mag., Vol. II, a lengthy account of the usages attending the East Anglian ***horkey***, its songs, ditties, healths, &c. Bloomfield has a ballad on the Suffolk ***Horkey***, modelled *longo intervallo* on Burns' Halloween.

Intractable to an etymologist, remarks Forby, not unlikely derived from the hallooing which forms so marked a feature of the ***horkey***.

Norse, ***hauka***, to shout. Wel., ***hwa***. Med. Lat., ***huccus***, a cry. Hence ***hawker, huckster***.

HAY. A hedge, specially one of clipt quickset. Old Fr., ***haye***; A.S., ***haga***; Ger., ***hag***. ***Hay-net***, a hedge-net. ***Hay***-jack, the lesser reed-sparrow, or sedge-bird.

A ***hay-net*** is a long low net, 30 or 40 yards long, by one yard high, placed upright by stakes along hedges, or in ***slays*** cut through whim covers, &c., to prevent the transit of rabbits from side to side when hunted by dogs.

'Paid to Stephen Percye for a ***haye***, of l fadom long, *xs.*' *L'Estrange's Household Accounts*, 1519.

HAZE, HAZLE. To dry linen, &c. by hanging it in the fresh air.

Rows of Corn are said to be ***hazed*** when a brisk breeze follows a shower. Land drying after being turned up by the plough is left to ***haze*** before harrowing. ***Hazle***, dim., to grow dry at top. Fr., ***Hasler***, to scorch in the sun. *Cotgr.* Isl., ***hœsa***, to dry in the wind. Dan., ***hœs***, stack, rick. ***Hazle,*** stiff as clay, &c., Essex.

'Thou, who by that happy wind of thine didst ***hazle*** and dry up the forlorn dregs and slime of Noah's deluge.' *Rogers' Naaman, the Syrian.*

HEAD. Face. 'I told him so to his ***head***.'

HEAD-ACHE. The wild field poppy.

HEADS and **HOLLS, HUMPS** and **HOLLS**. Pell-mell and topsy-turvy.

Sw., ***härs och tvärs***; Fr., ***pesle-mesle***, all on a heap. *Cotgr.* Fris., ***hulta de bulter.***

HEADSWOMAN. A mid-wife. N. Ang., ***howdy***.

HEART. The stomach. ***Heart spoon***, the pit of the stomach.

HEAVE. To pour corn from the skuffle before the wind. Isl., ***hefia***. Also to swell out, elevate; go before the wind. See ***hefty***.

'Nor walking in the streets (of Yarmouth) so many weeks together, could I meet with any of these swaggering Captains (Captains that wore a whole ancient in a scarf, which made them go ***heave-shouldered***, it was so boisterous), or huftitufty, youthful, ruffling comrades, wearing every one three yards of feather in his cap for his mistress's favour, such as we stumble on at each second step at Plymouth, Southampton, and Portsmouth.' *Nashe's Lenten Stuff.*

HEAVING and **SHOVING**. Jostling, hustling, lifting and thrusting.

'And here is great ***heaving and shoving*** by my Lord of Suffolk and all his counsel for to espy how this matter came about.' *Paston Letters*, A.D., 1440

HEDGE-ACCENTOR. The hedge sparrow.

HEFTY. Rough. ***Hefty*** weather; a ***hefty*** sea. Dan. and Ger., ***heftig***.

HEIFKER. A heifer, a metathesis. A Runcton will, Norfolk, in 1579, bequeaths certain ***heckfordes*** or ***heckforthes***, heifers.

Hekfere, beeste or styrke. *Pr. Pv.* ***Heckford,*** a young cow. *Palsgr.* A.S., ***heahfore***; Dut., ***hokkeling***.

A 'black hewed ***hecfurth***' occurs in the will of Thomas Hovell, of Burwell, 1540. 'A black stered ***heckforde***' in the will of Rycharde Kanam, Soham, 1579.

HEIGH'N. To heighten. Invariably applied to increase of prices, wages, &c. *Forby*. '***Hawnayn***, or ***heynyn***, heightyn, exalto.' *Pr. Pv.*

'***Heyning money***' was levied on herrings by the Yarmouth Corporation.

'Where by the way in a green meadow, thou espied'st a poor drunken beggar, (his belly being full,) ***heighing***, leaping and dancing.' *Nashe's Christ's Tears.*

HEIR. To inherit. 'His son will ***heir*** his estate.'

HEIT. The cry by which cart horses are turned to the left. ***Ree***, prolonged with a shake, to the right.

The carter smote, and cryde as he were wode,
Heit Scot! ***Heit*** Brok! what, spare ye for the nonce,
'The fend ye fetch,' quoth he, 'body and bones.' *Chaucer's Freer's Tale.*

'Scot and Brock are still Suffolk names for cart-horses.' *Moor.*

Heck, applied to draught horses to come near. ***Gie***, to go to the right. ***Helt***, ***heck***, and ***hauve***, to turn to the left, Craven. In Germany ***hott*** is the driver's cry 'to the right;' ***ho***, to the left.

HELP-UP. To assist or support; Ironical. 'I am finely ***holp***-up.'

'A man is well ***holp up*** that trusts in you.' *Comedy of Errors.*

HEN-POLLER. A poultry loft or roost. Ital., ***pollajio***, a hen-roost.

HEN'S-NOSE-FULL. A very minute quantity.

HERNE. A nook of land projecting into another district, parish or field. A.S., ***hyrne***, a horn, corner; Sw., ***hörn***. 'Halke or ***hyrne***, angulus.' *Pr. Pv.* A.S., ***heal***, an angle.

HERRING.

A.S., ***hæring***; O.H.G., ***harine***; Ger., ***hering***; Dut., ***haering***, also ***nëring***; Ger., ***nährung***, nourishment, food. In Sp., ***arenque***; Wal., ***hëring***. Baltic, ***ströhmling***; when smoked, ***bückling***. ***Konn*** and ***kenge***, Livonia; ***sill***, in Swed., when large; ***ströming***, when small; ***Sild, Quale-Sild***, and ***Graben Sild***, Denmark, large, and when small, ***strömling***; ***Straale-sild*** and ***gaate-sild,*** Norway; ***kapeselikan***, Greenland; ***Beltschutsch***, Kamtschatka. ***Jyder***, dried herring Dan.; ***Sgadan***, herring; Gael. and Wel., also ***penwaig***, Wel.

In England a herring is popularly known as a Yarmouth capon. In Scotland, a Dunbar wether, a cuddy's legs; in the U.S., a Taunton Turkey.

HET. Heated, (Dorset, Suff., and U.S.,) 'Ta ***het*** i' th' goof.' A.S., ***hete***, heat. Also abbr. of have it. 'I oont ***het***.' N. Ang., ***hett.***

HEW. Hooed. A.S., ***hiewe***. Also who. 'Hew ***hew*** them there tahnups.'

The usual Suffolk mode of pronouncings preterites of verbs ending in ***oo*** or ***ow*** is with an acute ***u***; a most striking Suffolk localism remarks Moor. 'He ***mew*** that there stuvva.' ***Ewe***, for owed; ***snew***, for snowed, ***thew***, thawed. The acute ***u*** appears in such words as the following:– fule, guse, lewse, mune, skule, stule, sune, tule, &c.

HEW'D. Held. 'A nivva ***hewd*** up a's hid aater.' Also 'who would', abbreviated.

HEY-HOWING. Thieving of yarn from the master weavers. A.S., ***heueld***, thread; ***helan***, to hide.

HICCUP, SNICKUP. The hiccough or hiccup. Dan., ***hikke***.

HICK. To hop or spring. Wel., ***dyclam***, a leap; A.S., ***hicgan***, to struggle.

HICKLE. To make shift with indifferent quarters; to double up, as two beds in a room; to gather in a little heap.

To hickle one's self into lodgings, – or a pig into a sty already sufficiently occupied. Wel., ***dycluz***, hemmed in; A.S., ***hicgan***, to wriggle.

HIGGLE. Apart from its sense of chaffering and bargaining, has in East

Anglia that of effecting results by minute continued effort. The poor talk of '***higgling*** up a pig,' i.e., buying and fattening it in that way. A.S., ***higian***, to endeavour, strive. Also to rear an animal that has lost its dam.

HIGGLEDY-PIGGLEDY. All heads and tails, like cuddling pigs. Dan., ***hyggelig***, snug, cosy; ***hyggelighed***, cosiness.

HIKE. To go away. Used also as an angry mandate. 'Come yo' ***hike*** off.' Isl., ***hika***, recedere. *Jam.* A.S., ***higan***, to hie. See ***pike***.

Hike and ***hipe***, to push with the horns, Craven. Dorset, ***hook***; Somerset, ***hoke***; Heref., ***hile***. – ***Hike***, to swing, as a nurse does a child. The ***hiking*** of a boat. ***Hipe***, to rip or gore with the horns of cattle. *Brockett's North Country Words.* ***Hike***, to move hastily; ***hikey***, a swing, Northampts.

HILLD, HILLS. Lees, dregs, settlings, heel-taps.

Wilts., ***hill***, to pour out. N. Ang., ***helle***; Isl., ***hella***; Dan., ***helde***. A.S., ***hyldan***, to incline, stoop the cask. Scot., ***hilliegeleerie***, topsy-turvy.

'And by that time his tobacco merchant is made even with, and he hath dined at a tavern, and slept his under-meal at a bawdy-house; his purse is on the ***heild,*** and only forty shillings he hath behind to try his fortune with, at the cards in the Presence.' *Nashe's Lenten Stuff.*

HIMP, to limp.

Poor fulla, 'a go ***himpin*** about.' Scot., ***hamp***, to halt in one's gait. Craven, ***hamlin***, walking lame. Dan., ***hinke*** and ***humpe***, to limp. Isl., ***hinkra***. Pl. Dut., ***humpeln***, to limp. The *Pricke of Conscience*, has ***hypand***, halting; Isl., ***hipp***. 'Hope came ***hippynge*** after.' *Piers Ploughman.*

HINDER. Yonder. '***Hinder*** 'a go.'

HINGIN. A hinge. Sw., ***hänge. Hingle***, a small hinge; a wire snare enclosing like a hinge. Poachers are said to ***hingle*** hares and rabbits. *Forby.* ***Hengall***, a pot hook; ***hingle***, a bottle neck.

Hengyl of a dore or wyndowe, vertebra; ***hengyl***, gymewe, vertinella. *Pr. Pv.* ***Angelheck***, fish-hook, Fris.; ***hengen***, A.S., a prison; Dut., ***henghen***, to hang; ***hengsel***, a hinge.

'It pd for ***hengells***, verdolls and hoks, hespes and staples for ye same berne, vjs. vijd.' *L'Estrange Household Accounts*, 1519.

HIPPANY. Part of an infant's swaddling clothes. Scot., ***hippen***, a cloth for wrapping the hips or buttocks; North., ***hippings***.

HITCH. To change place, make room. ***Hitch***-in, wriggle in; '***hitch*** your chair aside, – make way for another.' '***Hitch*** it this waah.' In Suff., ***hitch*** (Dorset, ***hick***) is also to hop on one foot.

Dut., ***hutselen***, to shake or huddle together. ***Hotch***, to move the body by jerks, Scot. Isl., ***hika***, cedere. '***Hytchyn*** or remevyn, amoveo.' *Pr. Pv.*

HITHE. A small port, a landing place. A.S., ***hyth***.

Occurs on navigable rivers, as the Thames, Yare, Ouse, &c., up the stream.

HOB, HUB. The nave of a wheel; flat top of a kitchen range side; the mark for quoits and similar games; the hilt or guard of a weapon, e.g., 'up to the ***hub***,' as far as possible.

In most of these instances the idea is that of a point, knob, or projection, as ***hob-***

nails. Dut., ***hobbelig***, knobby. Wel., ***hôb***, anything apt to rise or swell out. Dan., ***hob***, heap; N. Ang., ***hub***, a small haystack.

HOBBLE. A doubt, uncertainty, scrape. Belg., ***hobble***, nodus. *Forby*. Sw., ***hoplappa***, to patch. ***Hobble-bobble***, confusion.

HOBBLE-DE-POISE. Balanced in mind like a rocking stone.

HOBBLES. Roughnesses in a road. Ice frozen in ridges is called ***hobbly***. In the U.S. ***hubby***; Dut., ***hobbelig***, rugged, craggy.

HOBBY. A horse of any size, a hack. Dan., ***hoppe***, a mare. Fris., ***hoppe***, a horse in nursery parlance; Craven, ***houpy***, used only by children. O. Fr., ***hobin***, a nag; It., ***ubino***.

HOBBY-LANTHORN. A will-of the-whisp, from its motion.

HOBIDEHOY. A lad approaching manhood.

Ray has ***hober-de-hoy***, half a man and half a boy. Scot. ***Hobble-de-hoy***, a stripling. 'The next keep under Sir ***Hobbard de Hoy***.' *Tusser.*

HOCS and **HOES**. The feet and leg bones of swine.

The A.S. has ***hoc***, a curved stick (whence ***hockey***); ***ho***, the heel. Ger., ***hakse***, the foot joint of a horse's hind leg. In Linc., ***hock***, is to kick.

HODDING-SPADE. One used in the fens, shaped to take up large portions of earth entire. Dan., ***hob***, a heap; Sw., ***hop***, to heap, pile.

HODDY. I. Pretty well in health and spirits. Wel., ***hoedyl***, existence, act of living; ***hoedlog***, enjoying life. *Richards' Wel. Dict.* II. The uppermost width of a net. A.S., ***hod***, the head.

Seems to convey the sense of jogging along all right. ***Hod***, Sc., is to jog.

HODDLE, to waddle.

HODMANDOD. The Suffolk term for a snail, as ***dodman*** is the Norfolk. In Northampts., ***hod-dod***.

Bacon enumerates the ***hodmandod*** or ***dodman*** amongst fish that cast their shells. Nares has ***hoddy-pike***, a snail. The only difference, according to some, between a Norfolk and a Suffolk man is, that one calls a snail, ***dodman***, the other, ***hodmadod***. ***Hodmadod***, Dorset and Northampt., a bunchy, dumpy thing.

'Other spoil or victory, will prove a busy piece of work for the son of a mule, a raw grammarian, a brabbling sophister, a counterfeit crank, a stale rakehell, a piperly rhymer, a stump worn railer, a dodkin author, whose two swords are like the horns of a ***hodmadod***; whose courage like the fury of a gad bee; and whose surmounting bravery like the wings of a butterfly.' *Gab. Harvey's Pierce's Supererogation,* 1593.

HOGGET. HOG. A year-old sheep, after its first shearing. N. Fr., ***hogetz.*** ***Hog-wool***, the first fleece in shearing lambs.

HOGGINS. Sand sifted from gravel before the stones are carted upon the roads.

From the jogging motion of the sieve. Isl., ***hagga***, to jog. *Wedgewood.*

HOG-GRUBBING. Swinishly sordid.

HOGLIN, an apple turnover.

HOG-OVER-HIE. The game of leap-frog.

HOG-WEED, knotgrass.

HOG-SEEL. The thick skin on the neck of a hog. Sw., ***skal***, skin.

HOISE. To heave or raise aloft. Dan., ***heise***.

'To which I resemble poor scullians, that from turning spit in the chimney corner, are on the sodayne ***hoysed up*** from the kitchen into the wayting chamber, or made barons of the beanes and marquesses of the mary-boanes; some by corrupt water, as gnats, to which we may liken Brewers, that, by retayling filthie Thames water, come in few yeres to be worth fortie or fiftie thousand pound.' *Nashe's Pierce Penilesse,* 1592.

HOIST. A cough. A.S., ***hwosta***. Isl., ***hosti. Hoste, huse*** and ***hauste***, N. Ang.; Cumb., ***heuzz***, hoarseness. 'Hoose or cowghe.' *Pr. Pv.*

HOIT-A-POIT. Assuming unbecoming airs of importance.

Hoit, Craven dialect, is an ill taught, spoilt child. ***Poit***, in East Anglian, is extremely pert. The Fr. has ***haute tête***.

HOLL. I. A ditch, a dry ditch. To clean out or fey a ditch, is called out-***holling*** it. A.S., ***holh***, a ditch. II. Also hollow. A.S., ***hol***.

HOLLOW-MEAT. Poultry, rabbits, game, not sold by butchers.

HOME-DONE. Said of meat fully cooked, well roasted.

'Do you love your meat ***home***-done or rear?' ***Reer***-meat, in Suffolk, is said to be 'too much under-done.' *Moor.*

HONEY-CRACH. A small plum of great sweetness, but little flavour.

Croch, Gael., red; also to hang, suspend. ***Croic***, a skin; Wel., ***crac***, puny.

HOOVERS, HUVVERS. Dried flags for fuel. Differing from turves in being the upper cut, with the grass, reeds, etc. A.S., ***hof***, lifted; Su.-Goth., ***hæfwa***, to raise up.

HOP-CREASE. Hop-scotch. A ***Scotch*** is a cut or ***crease***.

HOPPING-GILES. One who limps, a cripple, of whom St. Giles was patron saint.

HOPPLE. A tether to confine the legs of beasts, leaving them only a ***hobbling***, limping movement. (N. Ang., ***hoffle***; U.S., ***hobble***.) Also a place for hogs. ***Hoppling***, tottering, applied to children.

Analogous are the Sc., ***habble***; Swed., ***happla***, to stutter; Dut., ***hobbelen***, to rock in motion. See also der. of ***himp. Hobble*** is a dimin. of the A.S., ***hoppan***; Swed., ***hoppa***, to hop.

Hobblers, men employed in towing vessels by a rope on the land, Somerset.

'Superstitiously ***hoppled*** in the nets of superfluous opinions.' *Henry More, on Godliness.*

HOP-TO. A grasping fellow.

HOPPET. A small close nigh home.

HORNER-SCORNER. The game of prison bars.

HORN-PIE. The lap wing. ***Horn*** from its tuft, ***pie***, its plumage.

HORNS. The ***awns*** of barley. Not an unmeaning corruption.

HORSE-MA-GOG. Boisterously frolicksome; a large coarse person.

Dan., ***horsegiög***, whinnying, neighing.

HOSE. The sheath or spathe of an ear of corn. In severe drought, when barley should come into ear, it is apt 'to stick in the ***hose***' and perish.

Dan., ***hase***, husk; Wel., ***yd yn ei'hosan***, corn before the ears burst out. *Owen's Wel. Dict.* In Suffolk, fleas are said to be particularly brisk thrice a year, at oat-sahwen, oat-***hahwen*** or hosing, and oat-mahwen.

HOST, HOSTELER. A name formerly given by the buyers to the fish sellers at the Yarmouth Free Fairs, who also lodged their customers.

'***Host*** is still used at Hastings for a vendor of articles out of shops or houses.' *Cooper's Sussex Gloss.*

'Every person not lotting or shotting to the common charge of the Corporation, who should be a common ***hoste*** in the fish-market.' *Hastings Corporation Records,* 1604.

HOT POT. Warmed ale and spirits. Norf. and Sussex coast.

HOUNCE. The leather ornament fastened across the shoulders or ***wallis*** of horses in a team, trimmed with red or yellow worsted fringe. Teams carrying corn to market, or on any public display, were ***hounced***. Hence the Essex phrase ***behounched***, tricked up, made fine. Northampt., ***houzen***; Fr., ***houssé***. *Cotgr.* Wel., ***hws***. '***Hawncyn*** or ***heynyn***, exalto.' *Pr. Pv.*

Richardson derives ***enhance*** from the Fr., ***hausser***, to hoise, raise aloft, and ***haunce*** would seem to proceed from the same.

'He doth no pastour's office that robeth Christen kinges of their princely power and autorite to ***enhance*** the tyrrannous vsurpacyons of Antichrist.' *Bale.*

> 'The spokes were all of silver bright; the chrysolites and gems
> That stood upon their collars, trace, and ***hounces***, in their hems
> Did cast a sheer and glimmering light.' *Golding's Ovid's Metam, b. 5.*

HOUSE. To grow thick and compact as corn does.

A 'mouton ***houssu***,' Fr., a sheep well woolled, of great burthen. *Cotgr.*

HOUSS, HOUGHTS. A contemptuous name for large, coarse feet, as being like a beast's hoofs. A.S., ***hos***, heel; Dan., ***houg***, hoof.

HOVEN. Blown out, swollen, as cattle by eating too much green clover; or as turnips, by a rank growth in strong wet soil. Dan. and N. Ang., ***hoven***, swollen; Wal., ***houzé***.

> 'Tom Piper hath ***hoven*** and puffed-up cheeks.' *Tusser.*

HUB. The projecting nave of a wheel. Dut., ***hobbelig***, knoppy, craggy. See ***Hob***.

HUCKLES. The hips, ***huckle*** bone, the hip bone. N. Ang., ***huggan***.

The Wel., has ***hwca***, hooked, crooked; A.S., ***hoc***. The Dut. has ***huck***, to crouch; Dan., ***huk***, nook, angle; Sw., ***huka***, to squat down.

'A rybbe of seynt Rabarts, with the ***huckyll*** bone of a Jewe.' *Bale.*

> 'The bones of her ***huckels*** Lyke as they were with buckles
> Together made fast.' *Skelton's Elynor Rummyng.*
> 'For getting up on stump and ***huckle***,
> He with his foe began to buckle.' *Hudibras.*

HUCKSTER. A hawker. Ger., ***hökern***, to higgle, sell victuals, etc., in small quantities. L. Ger., ***hucker***, a forestaller, regrater, retailer. Two der. occur. I. L. Ger., ***hucke***, the back, ***hucken***, to bend under a load. II.

Dut., ***hoecker woecker***, usury, interest, Su.-Goth., and Isl., ***okr***, gain, profit. A.S., ***eacan***, Lat., ***augere***. Wedgewood inclines to the latter, as does Ihre, under Su.-Goth., ***hökare***, a retailer of salt fish.

HUDDERIN. A well-grown lad, a ***hobbity***.

The Wel. has ***hurt*** and ***hurtan***, a stupid fellow; the Gael., ***ludragan***, a lout, awkward, and shambling; ***luid earra***, is ragged, slovenly – whence the Scot. ***hutherim***, slovenly. *Brockett's North Country Glos.* has ***hutherikin*** lad, a ragged youth, a sort of ***hobbletehoy***. Bret., ***hudur***, vilain, sordide.

HUFF. A dry, scurfy, scaly incrustation of the skin. Isl., ***yfa***, to irritate; Wel., ***wf***, an expelling out. ***Huffle***, to rumple.

HUFF, to scold, rate, bluster. Wel., ***wft***, a scorning; Isl., ***yfa***.

HUFF-CAP, HUF-SNUP. A swaggering blusterer.

'To all Whip Johns and Whip Jackes, not forgetting the Cavaliero Pasquill, or the Cooke Ruffian, that drest a dish for Martin's diet. Marforms, and all Cutting ***Hufsnufs***, Roisters, and the residew of light fingred younkers, which make euery word a blow and every booke a bobb.' *Nashe's Plaine Percevall.*

HUFFLES, HUFFLINS. A rattling in the throat in breathing. 'The death ***huffle***.' Walloon, ***hufle***, to hiss, whizz.

HUGGY-ME-CLOSE. The merry thought of a fowl.

HULK, HULKIN. A lout, lubber, an overgrown fat fellow like a huge unwieldy tub. Norse, ***holk***, a tub. N. Ang., ***helk***. 'The ***hulk***, Sir John.' *Shaks., 2 Hen. IV.* To go ***hulking*** about; said of a lazy lout, loitering for a chance of pilfering. ***Hulk***, a heavy fall. Essex. To ***hulk***, is to take the inwards out of a hare or rabbit. Sw., ***urhälka,*** to excavate; N. Ang., ***howk***. Goth., ***halks***, empty; Sp., ***hueco***, hollow.

'I could ***hulk*** your grace, and hang you up cross leg'd
Like a hare at a poulter's.' *B. and Fl. Philaster, v.*

HULL. To throw, ***hurl*** (Mid. Ang., ***holl***); of which it seems a cor. Said of a ship carried helplessly along by wind and waves.

'No, no,' said Mr. Peggotty. 'You doen't ought – a married man like you – or what's as good – to take and ***hull*** away a day's work.' *David Copperfield.* Dut., ***hollen***, to run.

'Much the case of people at the seaside, that see something come ***hulling*** towards them, a great way off at sea.' *L'Estrange's Æsop.*

HULLUP. To vomit.

HULVER, HULVA. Holly. Fris., ***hulver***; A.S., ***holegn***. N. Ang., ***hollyn***; Dorset, ***holm***. '***Hulwur tre***.' *Pr. Pv.* Dut., ***hulst.***

Chaucer has ***hulfere***; *Cotgr.*, '***houx,*** the hollie or ***hulver*** tree.'

'Save ***hulver*** and thorn, thereof flail to make.' *Tusser.*

Huel-var, Bret., is the mistletoe.

HULVER-HEADED. Stupid, muddled, hard-skulled.

HUME. A hymn. In common use, say both Forby and Moor.

HUMMER. The well-pleased sound a horse emits when he hears or sees the bait of corn shaken in the sieve by his attendant. Also a falsehood.

HUMMOCK. A lump, hillock, or heap, as of straw. Su.-Goth., ***hump*** and

ock; Ger., ***humpel***, a heap.

HUMP. A contemptible quantity, mere pittance. Dut., ***hompe***, a lump, of which

HUNCH, HULCHIN, a thick slice or lump of food is a var.

Richardson has '***hunch*** or ***bunch***, a lump or bump occasioned by pressure.'

HUNCH. A lift or shove. ' "Give me a ***hunch***, Tom," said a fat East Anglian dame to her grinning footman, after vainly endeavouring to climb unaided into her carriage.' *Forby.*

'***Hunch***, to give a thrust with the (crook'd) elbow.' *Bailey.*

HUNCH-WEATHER. Cold weather, causing the limbs to contract. Dut., ***huck,*** to crouch.

All these appear to be cognates derivable from the roots already given under ***huckle***.

HUNGER-POISONED. Famished, unhealthy for want of proper nutriment.

In Suffolk applied to misers.

HUNKERS. Said of persons squatted down on their haunches, or hind quarters. 'To sit down on one's ***hunkers***, is to sit with the hips hanging downwards. *Jam. Sc. Dict.* Old High Ger., ***hlancha***, the flank.

HURRY. A small load of hay or corn. *Grose.* A drawing or dragging. *Pegge.* To lead or carry anything, N. Ang.

HURRY-CARRIERS, HARRY-CARRIERS. The early name of the Yarmouth trolly carts.

'The Sun was so in his mumps upon it, that it was almost noon before he could go to cart that day, and then with so ill a will he went, that he had thought to have toppled his burning car, or ***Hurry-Curry***, into the sea (as Phæton did) to scorch it and dry it up.' *Nashe's Lenten Stuff.*

Hurry, Sw. and Dan., ***hurlig***, rapid, fleet. Junius explains ***hurry***, 'violenter dejicere, raptim propellere'. It had a stronger meaning, remarks Wedgewood, than that in which it is now commonly used. 'The origin is a representation of the sound made by something rapidly whirled through the air. O.H.G., ***hursc***, quick; ***hurscjan***, to hasten; ***huri***, a cry to urge on horses.' O. Fr., ***harry***, a carterly voice of exciting, ***hay ree***. ***Harry bourriquet***, rudely, confusedly braying out in a loud and harsh accent, such as the French millers use in the driving of their asses; ***bourriquet***, a kind of tombrell; ***harié***, ***hurried***, turmoiled. *Cotgr.* ***Arriero***, Sp., a driver of mules; ***harrer***, quicker, an exclamation to a horse, appears in the Townly Mysteries. The term is now obsolete in Yarmouth, but might with great propriety be re-bestowed upon its rapid, rattling fish conveyances.

Su.-Goth., ***hurra***, cum impetu circum-agi, ***hurra kring***. So the Lat., ***erro***, ***curro, verro***. *Ihre's Su.-Goth. Lex.*, 1769. Ihre recalls to mind a passage in the *Cratylus*; the dialogue in which Plato, broaching his ideas on the origin of language, dwells on the remarkable manner in which certain letters appear by subtle associations of sound with sense, indissolubly connected with the vocal interpretation of the latter, in particular classes of words. The subject is full of interest.

HUTCH. A chest or large coffer. Fr., ***huche;*** Dut., ***hok***; Norse, ***hokk***;

A.S., ***hwæcca***; '***Hoche*** or ***whyche***.' *Pr. Pv.* Fr., ***bahut***; Mid. High Ger., ***behut*** (used by Luther); ***behüten***, to cover, keep.

'A gret summe of money which was gadered for him in a ***hucch*** at Poules, was taken oute.' *Capgrave.*

'Heape up bothe golde and silver, safe in ***hooches***.' *Gascoigne.*

'The eye of the master enricheth the ***hutch***.' *Tusser.*

'An old usurer that hath not an heir, rakes up thirty or forty thousand pounds together in a ***hutch***.' *Nashe's Christ's Tears.*

'As the best pastures are hedged in, the best orchards walled about, the best metals ***hutch'd*** up.' *Id.*

HUTKIN. A case or sheath for a sore finger. Suff., ***hatkin***.

I

ICE-BONE. Aitch-bone of beef, E. and N. Ang.; Dut., ***ischbean.***

ICHON. Each one. '***Ichon*** on em.'

IFE. The yew tree, Suff. Fr., ***if***; Sw., ***idgran***.

ILLEGIBLE. 'A bastard child is sometimes called an ***illegible child***, corruption of illegitimate.' *Spurdens.*

IMP. A shoot, a graft, used by Bp. Hall. Dan., ***ympe***; Wel., ***impiaw***; A.S., ***impan.*** '***Impe*** or graffe.' *Pr. Pv.*

'Worthy Jonathan, which sprang from Saul, as some sweet ***imp*** grows out of a crabstick.' *Bp. Hall's Contemplations.*

'God never did more for the natural olive than for that wild ***imp*** which he grafted in.' *Id.*

I'M SEWER. I'm sure. One of the many expletives common to all colloquialism. 'What's a clock?' – 'I don't know, ***I'm sewer***.'

INDER. A great quantity. 'He's worth an ***inder*** of money.' – 'We av sitch an ***inder*** of poor.'

Forby, Moor, and Grose derive from India. Quite as likely to be a cor. of 'no end of.'

INQUIRATION. Enquiry. 'Ha' yeow made ***inquiration.***'

INWARDS-MAID. A farm-house maid, not employed in the dairy.

IRON-SIDED. Hardy, rough, fearless. Also unruly.

'There's a man ashore there, ***iron-true*** to my little Emily; God bless her, and no wrong can touch my Emily while so be as that man lives.' *David Copperfield.*

IVVA. Ever. So ***nivva*** for never. A Norse hardening.

IZZARD. The last letter of the alphabet.

J

JACKS. The turnip fly. Fr., ***jacquet***, parasite. ***Jecton***, swarm of bees.

JADDER. Infirm. Gael., ***lagaich***, infirm; ***gadhar***, pain; Sw., ***svagha***.

JAGG. An indefinite quantity, but less than a load of hay, or corn in the straw; called also a bargain. Teut., ***sagen***; Dut., ***zaeghen,*** to cut, saw off. In Northampt. ***jog***; Heref. and Chesh., ***jag***.

'He has got his ***jag***.' Not so much drink as he could have swallowed, but as much as he can fairly carry. *Local Saw*. Gael., ***daghdag***, a portion, a little.

JAHNEY. Journey. A day's work in agriculture. Scot., ***jorneye***, from the Fr. ***journée***; Lat. ***diurnus***.

Used chiefly in ploughing. One ***jahney*** a day, is when the horses do their whole day's ploughing (about six hours) at once. Two ***jahneys***, the old East Anglian practice, would be nine hours or more, with an interval. '***Journau***' in Champagne, as much land as a yoke of oxen can plough in one day.' *Cotgr.*

Journey, also formerly included in the exploits of a day, as an engagement, foray, or of an enterprise, &c.; thus, 'The godes, that tham gan falle geten at that ***jorne***.' *Robert de Brunne*. In a letter to *William of Worcester*, in the Paston Letters it is said of the Yorkist victory at St. Albans, 1455, 'All the Lords that died at the ***jorney*** are buried at St. Albans.' At the siege of Berwick by Ed. II, *Capgrave* writes, 'the Kyng lay stille at the sege; and happed for to say a word which was confusion of that ***journey***.'

JAM. A vein or bed of marl or clay ***jammed*** between other strata.

JAMMOCK. To beat, squeeze, crush, or trample into a small mass. Intens. of to ***jam***; also, a soft, pulpy substance.

Applied to fish or ripe fruit squeezed by the pressure of others above.

JATTER. To split into shivers; to shake violently. Old Fr., ***jecter, jatter***; It., ***giattere***; Norse, ***detta***, to shiver.

JERK, YERK. A smart blow. Wel., ***terc***, a jerk or jolt.

Wel., ***iarth***, a rod, goad. 'To yerke or ***jerke***.' *Cotgr.*

'And in her hande, she had a knotted whippe,
At euery ***yerke***, she made Godfrey to skipe.' *Hawes' Pastime of Pleasure.*
'Last that he never his young master beat,
But he must ask his mother to define,
How many ***jerks*** she would his breech should line.' *Bp. Hall's Satires.*

'When children play with their meate, 'tis a sign their bellies are full, and it must be taken from them; but if they tread it vnder their feete, they ought to be ***jerk'd***.' *Pap with a Hatchet*, 1589.

JEROBOAM. A capacious bowl or goblet, a ***jorum***. Isl., ***jord***, earth.

JET. To strut, swagger, bustle about; obsolete. Fr., ***jecter***.

'More than to ride with pomp and pride,
Or for to ***jet*** in others debt.' *Tusser.*

'And yet in towne, he ***jetteth*** every streete.' *Gascoigne.*

JET. A large ladle for raising or emptying water. Fr., ***jetter***.

JETTY. Aught projecting, as into deep water, or from upper stories.

Fr., ***jettée*** a bearing out or leaning over; the bank of a ditch, or the earth cast out of it when made. *Cotgr.*

'Jawed like a ***jetty***; A man would have pytty,
To see how she is gumbed Fyngered and thumbed.' *Skelton.*

JEWS-EARS. *Auricula Judæ*. A beautiful bright red fungus resembling the human ear, found on the elder trunk, the tree on which Judas is said to have hung himself.

JIB. The under-lip. A whimpering child is said 'to hang his ***jib***.'

O. Fr., ***gibbe***, a hulch, anything that stands poking out. *Cotgr.*

JIBE. To fit, agree, Essex. Common in U.S. See ***Gibe***.

JIBBY, A. A frisky, gadding, flaunting wench. In Scot. a ***jinker***. ***Jibby horse***, a showman's horse tricked out.

Gael., ***gibeach***, neat, spruce; ***gibeagach***, abounding with rags or bunches. O. Fr., ***gibbeux***, hunched, (much swelling) embossed. *Cotgr.*

JIECE. A small quantity; a pinch of snuff; a chaw of tobacco, &c. In Essex, ***chice***.

A.S., ***cicel***, a morsel; O. Fr., ***chiche***, niggard, pinching. It., ***cica***, a trifle.

JIFFLE. Quick, bustling, unsettled movement. 'Don't ***jiffle*** about so,' said to a restless child whilst being dressed. To shuffle. – Perthshire. See ***Giffle***.

JIG-BY-JOWL. A local cor. of cheek-by-jowl.

JIGGS. Dregs, sediment as of coffee, physic, &c. N. Ang., ***laggs***.

Sw., ***tjoek***, sediment, also ***diger***, thick. Manx, ***jiughey***, thickened. The Eng. ***d*** interchanges with the Norse ***j***; see under ***jot*** and ***jounce*** a little later on; or the word may be a cor. of the A.S., ***drigan***, to dry up.

JIGS. The carriages belonging to a Norfolk plough.

Gig jeeg, Sc., to work so as to make a creaking noise; ***jiggetting***, jolting. Fr., *Pat. de Champ.* ***jiguer***, to throw the legs about. Hence vulg. ***gigues***, the legs. *Wedgewood.* ***Gigots***, Walloon, a horse's hind legs.

JILLY-HOOTER. An owl. Also called Madge and Billy-wix. A.S. ***jil***. N. Ang., ***Jinny-Hullett***. ***Hullott***, Walloon.

JIM. Suff., Nor., ***jill***. A machine, with two wheels, axle, and pole, for carting timber underneath. On a ***drag*** it is laid above.

Is the der., hence derivable from the carriage being above its load, from It., Fr., Sp., ***cime***, top? ***Jill***, O. Fr. ***jouëlle***, a yoke. Both are probably from the Gael., ***giul-an***, to bear, carry; ***iom-chair***, to carry, support.

JIMMERS. See ***Gimmels***.

JINK. To sprain the loins or back of an animal. See ***Chink***.

JIP. To cheat, impose, trick. See ***Gip***.

JOAN'S SILVER PIN. A single article of finery, displayed amid dirt and sluttery.

JOB. To strike with a pointed instrument. To peck with a strong sharp beak. Ger., ***hieb***, a blow, stroke; Gael., ***gob***, a bird's bill or beak. ***Jobber-nowl***, a fool, simpleton.

'If peacock and turkey leave ***jobbing*** their ***bex***' *Tusser.*

'Have with them for a Riddle or two, only to set their wits a nibbling, and their ***Jobber-nowls*** a working.' *Nashe's Lenten Stuff.*

'As an ass with a gall'd back was feeding in a meadow, a raven pitched upon him and there sate ***jobbing*** of the sore.' *L'Estrange's Æsop.*

JOE-BEN. The great titmouse, Suff.

JOGGING. A protuberance in sawn wood, where the saw was ***joggled*** out of line.

JOGGLE. To push, shake. Dimin. of ***jog***. 'Haaow yeow dew joggle me.' L. Scot., ***schoggle***; Ger., ***schockeln***, to rock, toss. Wel., ***gogi***.

JOLL. To job with the beak, as rooks for worms.

'Joll or heed.' *Pr. Pv.* A.S., ***ceolas***; Gael., ***giall***, the jaws, hence pig's ***chaule***.

JOLLACKS. An irreverent appellation, bestowed on clergymen, says Moor.
From the Gael. ***iolach***, a shouting, a crying aloud.

JOLLICK. All right. Not ***jollick***, not on the square. Fr., ***joliet***.
Gael., ***jollagach***, gay, merry.

JOSS. A command to a horse to sidle up to a block or gate, where the rider may mount. ***Jossen-blocks*** were formerly to be seen near the doors of most farm houses. Fr., ***jouste***, near to, beside.
Chaucer makes the two scholars in the Reeve's Tale call to their runaway horses:
'These sely clerkes rennen up and down,
With kepe, kepe, stand, stand, ***jossa***, wardere.'

JOSS, JOSTLE. To make room by standing or sitting close. *Forby.* Fr., ***jouste***, near to.

JOT. Plump, downright. 'He came down ***jot*** upon his rump.' ***Jot, jotter***, is to jolt roughly; to jog, nudge. ***Jot-cart***, one with the body set flat on the axle, giving it a jolting movement. ***Jottee***, a small conveyance; var. of ***jolt***.
Isl., ***detta***, to stumble; ***dotten***, fallen. Fr., ***jaeter***, to tumble; It., ***játo***, an abyss, gulf.

JOUNCE. To bounce, thump, and jolt, as a vehicle in deep ruts. ***Houncy-jouncy***, in a clumsy, jumbling manner.
Dan., ***dundse***, to thump; Sw., ***dunsa***, to plump down; Fr., ***jancer un cheval***, 'to stirre a horse in the stable till hee sweat withall, or (as our) to ***jaunt***, (an old word).' *Cotgr.* '***Jowncynge***, or grete vngentylle mevynge.' *Pr. Pv.* Manx, ***jonse***, a jolt or wince; ***jonseragh***, wild, untamely; said of a horse that winces.
'And now I bear a burden like an ass,
Spur-gall'd and tired by ***jauncing*** Bolingbroke.' *Rich. II, v. 5.*

JOWER. To exhaust with fatigue; 'right on ***jowered*** out.'
'As from a day's labour or travel.' *Forby.* O. Fr. ***gourd***, stiff, benumbed.

JUB. A sluggish horse's up and down, heavy trot.

JUG. To squat and nestle close together, like partridges at night.
O. Fr., ***jucher***, to roost or pearch as pulleine do. *Cotgr.*
'Should they have liv'd and ***jugg'd*** together to this day.' *Fairfax.*

JULK or **YULK.** To give a sound like liquor shaken in a cask; an onomatopœia. In Suffolk, also, a hard blow. 'Ta give em sich a ***julk*** ta kill'd em stone dead,' said of a child struck by a windmill sail. ***Jaup***, to shake liquid. N. Ang.
Gael., ***glug***, noise of a shaken vessel of liquid not quite full. ***Julk*** is one of the very few East Anglian words, Sir Thomas Browne is found using. In a letter to his son Edward, he writes, 'There was a woeman or mayd in Suffolk, who had a ***julking*** and fluctuation in her chest and somewhat upwardly, so that when she stood and stroked her chest it might be heard by the standers by. *Works, Vol. I, p. 273.*

JUM. A sudden jolt or concussion; injury from a fall. ' A's hoss fell upon em an 'a got a sad ***jum***.' *Moor.* Fris., ***shumpeln***, to jolt.

JUMP. A petticoat. It., ***giuppa***; Fr., ***jupe***; Wal., ***jubea***; Sp., ***al-juben***; Arabic, ***al-jubbah***, a woollen petticoat.

JUMP-SHORT. Mutton from sheep drowned in the fen drains.

JUNCKER. A contrivance for drawing off superfluous water from a pond or moat. Dan., ***gienkrav***, to reclaim.

JUNKETS. Dainties, delicacies. 'Rare deewins! nawn but ***Junketten.***' Also pronounced ***sunket*** as in Scot.

It., ***giuncata***; Old Fr., ***joncade***, *Cotgr.*, dainties of cream and sugar blended. In Devonshire restricted to its famous curds and clouted cream.

'Men's cellars and garrets for meat they searched. If there were but the blood of anything spilt on the ground, like hungry dogs they would lick it up. Rats, mice, weasels, scorpion were no common men's ***junkets***.' *Nashe's Christ's Tears over Jerusalem.*

'They cannot eat of any dish; nothing will downe, unless it be now and then a plumb or some sweet ***junket*** to sweeten the mouth of their consciences.' *N. Rogers' Lost Groat.*

K

KA. Quoth. ***Katha***, quoth he; ***ka,*** here, look here; ***ka***-inda, look yonder; ***'k'*** there now – 'a what hae yeeow done?' *Moor.*

KAIL. To fling stones awkwardly. See ***Cale***.

KEDGE. Brisk, active, hearty. 'How d' ye fare?' – 'Thanky, kiender ***kedgy***.' – 'A fare kiender ***kedge*** still.' Scot., ***kedgie***, applied to the old; Isl., ***kátr***, glad, lusty; Sw., ***kaxe***; Gael., ***cridheach***; hearty. Used in New England. Ex., 'pretty ***kedge***.'

Kygge, or joly, ***kydge***. *Pr. Pv.* Mr. Way in his Notes compares it with the Ger., ***keck***, lively, hardy, nimble, saucy. Isl., ***kiaekr***.

KEEL or **WHERRY**. A flat-bottomed barge or sailing boat, largely used on the East Anglian rivers in transporting produce to and from the seaports. Isl., ***kiol***; O. Fr., ***quille***; A.S., ***ceol***. So named from its keel or backbone.

'Item j ship. Item j Pece with j ***keil***.' *Inventory of Fastolf's Silver Plate.*

'It pd to a ***kele*** for caryage hom of ye beddyng and ye leveryes from Styrbych feyer to Hunstanton, ij*s.* vj*d.*' *L'Estrange's Household Accounts.*

KELL. The cawl of a slaughtered beast; the membranous skin which wraps over part of the loin. Isl., ***skel***, rind, peel, shell. Also a kiln, a brick-kell, a malt-kell. Wel., ***cyl***; Dan., ***kölle***; Isl., ***kylna***. ***Kellen***, a batch of bricks.

'Take heed to the ***kell***, Sing out as a bell.' *Tusser.*

KELTER. Condition, fettle. In good ***kelter***, said of a farm. 'The mauther have slumped into the slush, and is in a nasty forlorn ***kelter***.' Applied also to a plough said to ***kelter*** well or ill, as it works in the proper slope or curve. 'Ta oont ***kilta***.' Suff.

'If the organs of prayer be out of ***kelter***, how can we pray, if we be not ***accincte*** (girt up)?' *Barrow.*

Dan., ***kilte***, to gird, truss up for work. *Elwyn Glos. of Americanisms* der. from Ger., ***kelter***, a press; out of ***kelter***, out of order; or else from ***culter***, the coulter of a plough. ***Kelter***, a cant term for money, N. Ang.

KENCH. That part of a hay stack in cut. See ***Canch.***

Sw., ***kant***, border, edge, corner. '***Kank*** and bro.' *R. de Brunne.*

KETT. Carrion, garbage. 'A ***ketty*** cur.' A nasty stinking fellow. Suff., ***kit***; Su. Goth., ***koett***; Isl., ***kaet***, carrion.

KEYS. The spaces between the upright timbers of the hanging houses for smoking herrings, are called '***quarter keys***.'

Horne Tooke derives key from A.S., ***cægian***, to shut in, confine, which in the present instance expresses the purpose designed. Hence ***quay***, defined by Spelman, ***caia***, a space in the shore compacted by beams and planks, as it were by keys. The Wel. has ***cae***; Bret., ***kae***, enclosure. 'Key or knyttynge of ij wallys, or trees yn an vnstable grownde.' *Pr. Pv.*

KIBBAGE. Small refuse and rubbish, riff-raff. Flem., ***kibbeling***, refuse of fish.

Kæppisch, worthless, is Rothwelsch or German-Jew argot.

KIBBLE. To walk lamely, to creep or hobble limpingly and painfully along.

Common in this sense in Beds. and Cambridge. The Walloon, ***kibalanss***, to totter, sway, balance one's self carefully; ***kibbelen***, Dut., is to nibble, strive, cavil.

KICHEL. A flat Christmas cake, triangular, with sugar and currants strewed over. A.S., ***cicel***, a morsel, little mouthful.

'***Kichel*** is Saxon, a kind of a cake or God's ***kichel***, given to children by their godfathers.' *Cocker.*

KICK. A novelty, dash; ***kicky,*** showy. In Lanc., the fashion, mode. 'Aw th' kick.' Isl., ***skick***, mode, custom. Dan., ***skik***, fashion; ***skikke,*** becoming. 'He's i' heigh ***kick***.' Craven. Devon, ***kicking***, high-***kicked***, smart, shewy.

'With eight score more galliard cross-points, and ***kickshi-winshes***, of giddy ear-wig brains.' *Nashe's Lenten Stuff.*

KID. A small cask or keg for flour. A pannier. Gael., ***cliabh***, a creel, pannier; ***caiteag***, a basket. Also a flattish keg for sprats and herrings. Lat., ***cadus***; Dut., ***kit***, a wooden can. Also faggots, bavins, '***kyde***, fagot, fassis.' *Pr. Pv.* Wel., ***cidysen***.

Kid, New Eng., a large box in which fish are flung as caught. ***Kids***, the husks of beans or pease. *Bachelor's Beds. Dial.* A.S., ***cod.*** Wel., ***cyb***.

KIDDIER. A higgler who buys up fowls, eggs, poultry, &c., at farm-houses, to carry to market. A butcher and dealer in small animals, as lambs, pigs, calves, &c.

'A ***kidder*** is a badger, huckster, a carrier of goods on horseback.' *Ray's Ess. and Suff. Words.* 'A seller of corn, victuals, &c.' *Bailey.* In the North, a ***Cadger***, applied also to those who convey fish from the coast to Newcastle market. As pedlar proceeds from the peds he carries, so probably does ***kiddier*** from his ***kids***. Called also ***kidgier*** from his kegs; Isl., ***kaggje***, a small keg; hence ***cadger***.

KIDDLE. To embrace, caress, fondle; var. of ***cuddle***. N. Ang., ***huddle***. Sc., ***kid***, to toy; ***kiddy***, wanton; Sw., ***kaet***, lewd. To rear young animals by hand. Flem., ***kudde***, a brood.

KIENDA. Kind o'. A qualifying expression. '***Kienda*** snaggy,' rather cross. 'She made game on it, ***kind o'***.' Fris., ***kanda***; Dan., ***kiende***, slightly, rather; ***kiende for stort***, a trifle too large.

Kind of, or resemblance, used in the northern sense of the A.S., like; A.S., ***cyn***, kin, kind; Isl., ***kyn***; Gael., ***cine***, race, family. '***Kynd***, natural; ***kyndely***, naturally.' *Pr. of Consc.* Common Americanisms are ***kinder, kinder, sorter***.

'You han't no call to be afeerd of me; but I'm ***kiender*** muddled; I doen't feel to fare no matters.' *David Copperfield.*

KILLER or **KELLER**. A shallow tub or cooler, a wash killer, milk killer. A.S., ***cœlan***, to cool, chill; Sw., ***kyla***. Ir., ***cilier***.

KILTERS. Tools, instruments, component parts. See ***Kelter***. Also to dawdle. Ir., ***ceilidh,*** a lounge. Sw., ***kel***, to cocker up.

KINDIFUL. Used in the senses of things of every manner or kind. 'Neither chair nor table, nor bed, nor no ***kindiful*** thing.'

KINER. A flannel wrap used by nurses for infants. Lat., ***cingo***. Gael., ***ceangal***; Wel., ***cin***, a wrap, ligament.

KING HARRY BLACKCAP. The Blackcap.

KING HARRY REDCAP. The Goldfinch.

KINK. A rabble, entanglement of a skein. Yarn ***kinks*** in winding. Children are said to ***kink*** their breath in violent crying, i.e. have a stoppage of it. Swed., ***kikna***. Also used in the contrary sense of recovery. A patient, very ill, 'will ***kink*** up again,' as will a nearly moribund fire.

Lanc., ***kench***, a twist; Old Norse, ***kringia***, to twist; Dut., ***krinkel***, to wrinkle; ***kink***, a twist in a cable. In the U.S., odd people are said to have a ***kink.*** A ***kink*** in one's neck is a common phrase there. So is ***kink,*** a crotchet; ***kinky***, queer. The N. Ang. has ***kink***, convulsed breathing from crying or laughter, from A.S., ***cincgung,*** great laughter.

KINSMAN. Specially applied to cousins in Norfolk, and nephews in Suffolk. See under ***nephew***.

KIPLIN. The palate, gullet, sounds and other perishable parts of the codfish, cut away and separate from the body. Flem. and Dut., ***kibbeling***, cod sounds and clippings; ***kibbelen***, to nibble.

Dried cod are called in Norway ***klipfisk***, from ***klippe***, to split open. Of this latter ***kiplin*** seems a metathesis. ***Kiblings***, bait of small pieces of fish used on the Newfoundland Bank. *Bartlett's Americanisms.* N. Ang., ***gubbins***.

KISKY. Dry, thirsty, from fever or dust, Essex; a simile possibly borrowed from the dried ***kisks*** or ***kecksies*** of the hedges, or from the Lat., ***hisco***, to gape; ***hask***, parched; ***hisk***, to breathe with difficulty; ***kizzen***, to parch, dry up, N. Ang. Isl., ***quec***, touchwood.

Bret., ***hesk***, said of a dried up spring; breast of milk, &c. See ***Cambuck***.

KISS-ME-AT-THE-GARDEN-GATE. The pansy.

KIT. A rush basket for herrings or sprats. Gael., ***caiteach***, basket, rush mat. 'The fish is brought ashore again to the cooper's offices, boiled, pickled, and ***kitted***.' *Pennant, – the Salmon.*

KIT-CARL. Careless. *Moor.*

KIT-CAT-ROLL. A bellied roller for land, the horse moving in the furrow, the roller acting on the ridges. Isl., ***quidr***, the womb; Ger., ***dick***, swollen, corpulent. ***Kite***, the belly; ***pod-kite***, pot-bellied. N. Ang. Su. Goth, ***gwed***.

KITTLE, KITTLISH. Ticklish. Isl., ***kitla***; A.S., ***kittelan***, to tickle; Fr., ***chatouiller***, from ***catullire***.

KITTLE-REAP. Old or unskilled hands engaged at harvest.

Kit, brood, flock; Dut., ***kudde***; Swiss, ***kütt***, crew, assemblage. *Wedgewood*; or it may be the Sc. sense of ***kittle***, awkward, untrustworthy.

KITTY-WITCH. A small cancer on the coast, with fringed claws. A small gull, the ***kitty-wake*** of Pennant. A woman grotesquely dressed; called also a ***kitch-witch***. 'Years ago, troops of women, with men's shirts over their dress, and their faces smeared with blood, perambulated Yarmouth at certain seasons, levying contributions.' *Forby*. ***Kitoir***, Walloon, is contorted, crooked, said of the legs, gait, &c. ***Kittie***, Sc., ***cuttie***, wanton. See ***kiddle*** above.

KIVER. Cover, lid; an old local form. Chaucer has ***kevere***.

'My maister's helmet in the ***kever***.' *Inventory of Fastolfe*, 1460.

KNAB. To gnaw, nibble. Dut. and Ger., ***knappen***. See ***nabble***.

'I'll e'en back to my cottage and my mouldy cheese again, for I had much rather lie ***knabbing*** of crusts, without either fear or danger in my own hole.' *L'Estrange's Æsop*.

'An ass was wishing in a hard winter for a little warm weather, and a mouthful of fresh grass to ***knab*** upon.' *Id.*

KNACKER. 'Cart collar and harness marker.' *Ray*. Sw., ***knacka***, to knock gently. ***Knacker's-brandy***, a sound strappado.

From the sound of their tools. O. Fr., ***naquer***, to gnaw with a harsh sound.

'One part for ploughwright, cartwright, ***knacker***, and smith.' *Tusser*.

KNACKS. Knick-knacks, toys, pretty trifles, playthings. Dut., ***knappe***, fine, pretty; ***knap***, nimbly, handsomely.

'Whose states when I looke vpon, I am ready to crie at as a countrey man of mine did, when trauersing London streets, he spide a ***Iacke an apes***, in a gale cote, sit mooing on a marchant's bulke: 'Good Lord! what knacks are made for money, now adaies?' *Nashe's Plain Percevall*.

'***Nique***, a nicke, clicke, snap with the teeth or fingers, a trifle; ***nifle***, bable, matter of small value.' *Cotgr*. Sw., ***nyck***, a whim.

KNAP. A thump, slight knock. A rap on the knuckles. Gael, ***cnap***.

'***Knap*** boy on the thumbs, And save him his crumbs.' *Tusser*.

KNAP-KNEES. Knock-knees.

KNOBBLE TREE. The head. Pl. Dut., ***knobbe***, anything thick and round.

KNOCK. To stir or to work briskly. '***Knock*** away, my lads.'

'Let the music ***knock*** it.' *Shaks. Hen. VIII*. Dan., ***knubbe***, to bang, thrash.

Kindred phrase, used by a Yankee in London – 'I have been smashing round considerable to-day.' *Elwyn*.

KNOCK-SALT. A fool.

KNOP. To bud. Ger., ***knospe***. Dan., ***knoop***. Flem., ***knoppen***. '***Knoppe*** or bud of a tre.' *Pr. Pv.*

'Bunches found upon the common small thistle, running into ***knops*** without flower or seed.' *Sir T. Browne.*

KNOPPET. A little clod or lump of anything. Isl., ***gnupr***.

'***Knoppy-road***,' as the man said when he stumbled over a cow. *Anderson's Cumb. Dialect.*

KNOW. Knowledge. Poor fellow, he has but little ***know***. A ***know-nothing***, utterly ignorant, a wretched ignoramus.

KNUB. A knob. ***Knubble***, a small knob. ***Knubble***, to handle clumsily. See ***Nub***.

L

LADLE. To dawdle. Fr., '***lasdaller***, a lazie draw-latch.' *Cotgr.*

LAD'S-LOVE. The herb southern-wood. *Artemisia atrotanum.*

LADY'S SMOCK. The cuckoo flower. Canterbury bell.

LAGARAG. A lazy bones. In Suff. and Sc., ***lagabag***, the hindmost of a drove. Gael., ***lag***, feeble; Wel., ***llag***, sluggish; Bret., ***lezirek***, idle, nonchalant. Greek, ***lagaros***, slack. Irish, ***ladharnach***, an idler who sits much at the fire.

LAID. Dead, killed, Suff. Sw., ***lugn***. Slightly frozen, Norfolk.

LAID-UP-HER-LATTER. Said of the last laid egg of poultry.

'She's ***laid up her latter*** and she'll sune set.'

'***Laster*** or ***lawter***, thirteen eggs to set a hen.' *Grose.* Sc. ***lachter***; Som., ***laite***; Isl., ***leggia***, to lay; Ger., ***leghtyd***, time of laying. Cumb., ***laghter***; Craven, ***lafter***, a brood of chickens.

LAL. A dawdled, cossetted child. 'It's such a ***lal***,' or ''tis a poor ***lallen*** thing.' Also to lounge, loiter. Dut., ***lollen***, to coddle. Sw., ***lolla***, fool; Sc., ***lall***, useless, inactive person.

LALDRUM. An egregious simpleton; a fool and a half.

Dut. ***lellen***, to tattle, also rif-rafs; Dan., ***lalle***, to prattle; Isl., ***loll***, sloth; Sw., ***lohli***, a booby; ***lallande,*** stammering. Wel., ***llôl***, idle babble.

LAM. To catch eels. ***Lamper-eel***, the lamprey.

Low. Lat., ***lam-petra***, lick-stone, this fish clinging to stones with its mouth; Sp., ***lambriga***, a worm; Bret., ***lampr***, slippery, shining. *Diez.*

LAM, LANNA, LANNER. To beat unmercifully; Fr., ***lanière***, a thong. Isl., ***lemja, lamda***, to thrash; ***hlömm***, a cudgel; Dan., ***lamme***, to paralyse. ***Lamb-pie***, a drubbing. Bret., ***lemm***, sharp, trenchant.

Common in Lanc., Yorks., and in the U.S., where to ***lam***, is 'to give him Jessie.' 'I'd a ***lammed*** him worse than the devil beating tan bark, I know.' *Sam Slick.*

In Norfolk the lash of the whip is called the ***lanner*** or ***lanyer***.

LAMMOCK. To lounge with excessive laziness. ***Lummox***, a fat, stupid person. 'Look o' yin great ***lummox***, lazing and lolloping about.'

Ock is an intensive termination from Su. Goth, ***oka***, to augment. ***Lammock*** would seem to be an intens. of the Dan., ***lömmel***, a lubber, lout; or rather the Sw., ***lam***; Ger., ***lahm***, lame, remiss, wanting in elasticity; the Dorset ***lammocken***, loose-limbed.

In Shrops. dial., ***slammockin***, unwieldy, clumsy; Isl., ***slyma***, to cling idly; Su. Goth., ***slem***, turpis. *Hartshorne's Salopia Antiqua.* The Gael. has ***slamanach***, flabby. *Lummox* is common in the U.S. ***Lammock*** in E. Ang. is also a large quantity, a dollop; intens. of the Devon, ***lamming***, huge, great. ***Lommaking*** is applied to love-making in Heref. dial.

LAND-WHIN. The rest harrow, *Ononis spinosa, Lin.*

LANGLE. To saunter slowly. 'L. Sc., a tether. Sui. Goth., ***lanya***, retardare.' *Jam.*

LAP. Small beer.

LAP-SIDED. An excess of proportion on one side. Var. of ***lob***.

LARGESS. A gift in harvest to the reapers.

'Usually of a shilling,' says Moor. For this the reapers will ask you if you 'chuse to have it hallered?' If answered yes, they assemble in a ring, holding each others hands, and inclining their heads to the centre. One of them detached a few yards apart, calls loudly thrice, 'Holla Lar! – Holla Lar! – Holla Lar! – ***j-e-e-s***.' Those in the ring lengthen out ***o-o-o-o*** with a low sonorous note and inclined heads, and then, throwing the head up, vociferate ***a-a-a-h***! This, thrice repeated for a shilling, is the established exchange in Suffolk. 'There are few rural sounds,' adds Major Moor, 'more poetical, more pleasing, or more affecting.'

'Give gloves to thy reapers A ***largess*** to cry.' *Tusser.*

Fr., '***Largesse***, bounty, handfuls of money cast among the people.' *Cotgr.*

LARRUP. To beat. An East Anglicism. Very common in the U.S. 'May not a man ***larrup*** his own nigger.' Somerset, ***lirrop***; Dut., ***larp***, a lash; Span., ***lariata***, a rope made of thongs of raw hide.

'Just come on an I'll ***larrup*** you till your mammy won't know you from a pile of sausage meat.' *Southern Fun, p. 34.*

LASHY. Soft, watery. Applied to pasture of wet land. Also to a watery flavour in fruit. Fr., ***lasche***, flabby, weak; Bret., ***laosk***; Gael., ***leasg***; Wel., ***llesg***; Sw., ***lossa***, languid. ***Lache***, a bog, mud-hole, N. Ang.

Young clover, or wet pasture, is said to be 'tew lash' for cattle. Autumn grass is said to be ***lashy*** for horses, i.e., relaxing. In the North, ***lask*** is purging; and ***lasche***, cold and moist; ***lash-egg***, one without a full-formed shell. Sw., ***laska***, to refresh, quench; (hence perhaps our ***lushy***,). Dan., ***lös***, lax.

'The aer nebulous, grosse, and full of harres; the water, putrid and muddy, yea, full of loathsome vertmeyne; the earth, spaing, vafast, and boggie; the fire noisome, turfe and ***lassocks*** – such are the inconveniences of the drownings.' *A Discourse concerning the Fennes*, 1629.

'***Lasche*** or to fresche and vnsavery, vapidus... ***Lusch*** or slak.' *Pr. Pv.*

'How ***lush*** and lusty the grass looks.' *Tempest, ii., 1.*

LAST OF HERRINGS. Nominally ten thousand fish; but being counted in long hundreds of 132 amount actually to 13,200.

Dan. and Sw., ***last***, a cargo, bulk, lading; Ger., ***last***, freight, load, tonnage; Fris., ***hlest***; Isl., ***hlass***. Dut., ***last***, a load; ***last*** of wheat, 108 bushels; ***last*** of herrings, 14 barrels; ***last*** of tar, 12 barrels; a ***last*** of ship's stowage, 4000 pounds weight, and a tun at 200 pounds. *Sewel's Dut. Dict.*, 1708.

It., ***lasto***; Fr., ***laste***, ***lest***, a ship's burden; O.H. Ger., ***hlast***; O. Fris., ***hlest***; Norse, ***lest***; A.S., ***last*** (Eng., ***last***, boat load); Fr., ***balast***; Dut., Ger., and Eng.,

ballast is a compound of ***last*** and ***bal.*** Ir., ***beal,*** sand; ***(garbheal)*** gravel, *Diez.* Cel. Bret., ***bili,*** callou rond, plat et poli que la mer pousse sur quelques rivages. *Gonidec's Dict. Celto Breton.*

A.S., ***hlæst,*** a load; ***plœstan,*** to freight. Whence., ***lastage,*** a toll on ships of burthen and ballast. By 31, Ed. I., a ***last*** of herrings was to contain 10,000, at six score to the hundred. A ***last*** of wool, 12 sacks of two weights of wool, a weight to be 14 stones. '***Leste,*** nowmbyr as heryngys, and other lyke –legio' *Pr. Pv.*

'A ***last*** of white herrings is 12 barrels; of red, 20 cades or thousands; and of pilchards, 10,000; of corn, 10 quarters, and in some parts of England, 21 quarters; of wool, 12 sacks; of leather, 20 dickers, or ten score; of hides or skins, 12 dozen; of pitch, tar, or ashes, 14 barrels; of gunpowder, 24 firkins, weighing a hundred pounds each.' *Tomlins' Law Dict.,* 1835.

'Item pd to Shabyngton of Lyn, for a ***last*** of barrels to tun bere in, that is to sey a disen barrells, xjs.' *L'Estrange Accounts,* 1530.

LATCH. I. To catch what falls. Also to alight. A cat is said proverbially 'to allus ***latch*** on her legs.' II. The falling catch of a door or gate. A ***latch-***pan is a dripping-pan.

Gael., ***glac,*** to catch, receive. A.S., ***laccan.*** '***Latchyd,***...or cawtht.' *Pr. Pv.* ***Latch*** is Gypsy dial. for to light upon, to find.

> 'A flight of little angels that did wait
> Upon their glittering wings to ***latch*** him straight,
> And longed on their backs to feel his glorious weight.'
>
> *Giles Fletcher's Christ's Triumph.*

'Some are yet worse, and will sit at table and heare godly ministers and others depraved by vile tongues, and scarce give them their breath to ***latch*** the blow, lest themselves should be thought too forward.' *D. Rogers' Naaman.*

LATCH-ON. To put more water on the mash when the first wort has run off. Craven, ***leck-on; leck-off,*** is to draw off; Dut., ***lekken.*** The Bret. has ***lec'hid,*** sediment of water or other liquid. See ***leech.***

LAUNCH. A long stride. 'That long-legg'd fellow comes launching along.' In the North, ***lainch;*** Fr., ***se lancer.*** *Cotgr.* Gael., ***glamhaich,*** wide-gapped. '***Lawnche*** or skyppe...***Lawnchyn,*** or skyppn over a dyke.' *Pr. Pv.* It., ***lanciarsi,*** to rush upon. ***Lans,*** to spring forward, Sc.

LAY. A large pond. Also to intend. 'I ***lay*** to plough to-morrow.' To profit. 'What sort of a ***lay*** did you make of that there horse?'

LAYER. Soil, manure, &c., brought on the land, Essex.

Basque***, laya,*** a spade; Sp., ***laya,*** a pronged digging fork. Prov. Dan., ***lei,*** fallow; A.S., ***leah,*** untilled land; Dut., ***laag,*** a stratum; Manx, ***laare,*** a floor. ***Layer*** seems to be used in a similar sense to our lay, a bed of mortar.

LAYER-OF-WIND. A dead calm; when mills will not grind.

LAYER-OVER. A gentle term for an instrument of punishment. ***Lay-over*** for medlars, a reproving reply to check curiosity.

LEA, or **LA-A.** In Norfolk forty threads of hemp-yarn.

Wel., ***llian,*** a web of linen, from root ***lli.*** The A.S. has ***læe,*** a bush of hair.

Lea, seventh part of a skein or hank of worsted, containing 80 threads, N. Ang. 'At Kidderminster, every such ***lea*** to contain 200 threads, reeled on a reel four yards about.' *Bailey's Dict.*

LEASTY. Dull, dark, dirty weather, cor. of ***lashy*** above. Compare O. Fr., ***lascheté***. ***Laisti***, Ir., is heavy, stupid.

LECK. To pour. ***Lecking-time***, rainy weather. See ***Leech***.

LEDGER. The thatcher's tool for driving or cleaning reed.

Ledgers, Dorset, the rods fastened down by spars on the thatch of a rick. A.S., ***leger***, a lying down. '***Legge*** ouer twarte byndynge, ***ligatorium***.' *Pr. Pv.*

LEECH or **LETCH**. A wooden vessel, pierced with holes for filtering lye through wood ashes. Dut., ***lekken***, to leak, to draw off, or it may be lye-***latch***. Ger., ***ablassen*** to let off; Swed., ***laka***, to distill. See ***Latch.***

Leck, to leak, Teesdale. ***Leck-on***, to mash in brewing, Craven. ***Lecks***, droppings. '***Lecking*** t' floor,' sprinkling it, Leeds.

LEP, LEPE. A large, deep, basket. A.S., ***leap***. Isl., ***laupur***.

Leap, Yorks., a large osier basket borne between two men to carry corn to be winnowed, called a ***wheat-leap***. A seed leap or seed lip, Wilts. A leap, a weel to catch fish, Lanc. An osier basket borne between two men for carrying chaff out of a barn, called in Northampts. and Bucks., a bear-***leap***. A ***leap*** or ***lip***, half a bushel, Sussex. A seed ***leap*** or ***lib***, a basket to carry corn on the arm to sow, Essex. *Bp. Kennett's Gloss. Coll., Lands, M.S.* ***Lep***, a bundle of straw, Cumb. '***Leep*** or basket.' *Pr. Pv.*

'***Lep*** or ***lepe***, a large, deep basket, and ***seed lep***, a basket for the use of the sower, or for carrying chaff to feed horses.' *Forby.*

LESTLY, LISTLY. Hearing freely. 'I hard 'em as ***lestly*** as I hare yeow speak.' Ger., ***los***, free; Old Fr., ***lissé***, glib, pat.

Leise, Ger., is low, softly; Dut., ***luysteren***, to whisper.

LEWCOME, LUCAM. A window in the roof of a house. Fr., ***lucarne***.

'About eight o'clock an *ignis fulmineus*, or fire-ball, hit against the little wooden pinacle of the high ***leucome*** window of my house.' *Sir T. Browne, vol. iv., 353.* **LOUKE,** a window-lattice, Suff. Ir., ***luacharn***; Wel., ***llygorn***, a dormer-window. ***Lucarne***, is also Fr., argot, for a bonnet.

LEWER. A handspike, ***lever***. Called also a ***lower***.

LIFT. A rough hurdle-gate, not hung on hinges, but raised to pass through. Common in New England. In Suffolk a ***lift*** is a gate not hinged, but with projecting bars let into mortice holes in the posts, in and out of which they must be ***lifted***.

LIG. Lift, lug, pull. 'A good tidy ***lig***' of water, raised from a well. Dut. ***ligten***, to uplift, heave; Pl. D., ***lichter***.

The Northern provincial sense of ***lig*** is to lie, lay down; Fris., ***liga***; A.S., ***ligan***; Isl., ***liggia***. ***Liggers***, Cumb., growing wood notched and laid along a hedge. Dorset, ***ledgers***.

LIGGER. I. A rude footbridge; a plank thrown across a ditch. Fris., a ***legger***; A.S., ***liggan***, to lie down. II. A local trimmer for pike fishing, used in the Broads.

'It is formed of flag or rushes over a foot long, lightly rolled up and tied the thickness of a man's arm. To the centre a stout cord is fastened, 8 to 15 feet long. Most of this is wound round and secured from unwinding by inserting the end among the flags. The baited hook hangs down from one end of the ligger; when a pike snaps the bait, the jerk sets free the cord to unwind from the flags. The ligger now lies flat on the water, instead of endwise, indicating the capture of the fish.'

LIGGLE. To lumber about with something too heavy to carry with ease – as a child ***liggles*** a puppy. Dimin. of ***lig***.

LIKE. The A.S. ***lic***, used as a similitude after nouns and adjectives, – in a passion like, angry like. ***Like of***, to approve.

LIMB, LIMM. Expressing strong propensity. 'I am a ***limm*** for roast beef.' 'She is sich a ***limm*** for gin!' A.S., ***lim***.

N. Ang., ***limmer***, a female of manners. ***Liminish***, inclined to mischief, Cumb. Fr., ***limer***, to scrape, lick, look askew. *Cotgr.* Isl., ***lim***, glue; Dut., ***leem***, tenacious, sticky.

LIMPSY. Flaccid, ***limp***. ***Limmock***, intens. of the latter. Wel., ***llibin***. '***Limsy***, weak, flexible, New England.' *Webster.* Isl., ***limpiaz***, to become slack. ***Lenzare***, Ital-Fourbesque argot.

'When the flesh wants firmness of tone or feeling from feverish symptoms, a person is said, in Norfolk, to feel ***limick***.' *Wright's Prov. Dict.*

LIN. To cease, desist, stop. Isl., ***lina***; Dan., ***linde***, to loosen, slacken; A.S., ***be-linnan***.

'Even as the ivy creepes out of the earth upon the silly stocke of the tree, but never ***lins*** till it have over-topped it, and suckt out the sap and so destroied it.' *D. Rogers' Naaman.*

'Oh! you would never ***lin*** with your owne soules till you had cast it out.' *Id.*

LINE. To beat – from the weapon, a rope's end. Also a place to lie down. ***Lining***, coarse yarn put across fields to prevent birds picking up the seed.

LINTS. A term applied by fishermen to old nets. A.S., ***linet***, Wel. and Ir. ***llim***, flax, hemp, a net. Also a slang term for a halter.

LITHE. To soften, alleviate, render tractable, incline. A.S., ***ge-lithian***.

'And if ge wille lithe, I salle telle it you.' *R. D. Brunne.*

'If they knew whom to trust for amends, or could believe that hundred fold requitall for God and his Gospel, which is promised to all that lose anything for Him; Oh! it would ***lithe*** their hearts exceedingly to suffer anything for Him!' *D. Rogers' Naaman, p. 185.*

'Thou canst remove that utter unwillingnesse and uncouthnesse of the soule to this work, and cause ***lythenesse*** and complying therewith.' *Id.*

LITTLE-SILVER. A low price. 'The stover in my low meadows have been so nationly damnified by this slattering weather (said an old farmer), that 't won't be worth but ***little-šilver***.' *Forby.*

See also under ***Silver***.

LITTLE-STANDS. A shady lane.

LOAMY. Damp. ***Loomy***, rancid and mouldy, applied to meat.

In other dialects as N. and Mid. Ang., ***oamy***, is applied to land as being mellow; Sc., ***oam***, steam, vapour. *Jam.* A.S., ***lam***, mud.

It may be Keltic; the Manx, ***loauey***; Gael., ***lobhta***, putrid; Wel., ***ul***, damp, or from the Old Belg. ***lome***, tardus, piger; ***loomy***, Sc., covered with mist.

LOB. A lout; a tall ungainly lad. Also a ***lobcock, lubbock, lubber***. ***Lob,*** v.

to kick. ***Lob's pound***, the bridewell, E. and N. Ang.

Wel. ***llob***, a heavy lump, a dull fellow; ***llabi***, a looby; Gael., ***leobhair***, a lubber; Dut., ***lobbes*** and ***laboor***. Isl., ***labbaz***, to loiter lazily; Wall., ***loubrere***, vagabondage. *Wedgewood.* Common in Lanc. From this and the following cor. the nautical variations, **LUBBER** and **LUBBERLY**. ***Lob***, to run heavily, Cumb.

'But as the drone the honey hive doth rob,
With worthy books so deals this idle ***lob***.' *Gascoigne.*

'With the draff of the carterly ***Hob-lobs*** thereabouts.' *Nashe's Lenten Stuff.*

'And seeing a stranger in the church put on his hat in sermon time, he openly then called him sawcy, unmannerly clowne, and bid the churchwardens take notice of him, and the next Lord's day took occasion in his sermon again to speak of him, being then absent, and to call him ***lobb***, sawcy goose, ideot, a wigeon, cuckoe.' *White's Century of Scandalous Priests, 1643. (Kettleburrugh, Suffolk.)*

'The Dominican Friars were the next he contested with, whose vitiousness lay pat enough for his hand, but such foul ***lubbers*** fell heavy on all which found fault with them.' *Fuller's Worthies. – Norfolk.*

LOBLOLLY. Any odd mixture of spoon meat; a slabby mixture. Dut., ***slobberen***, to slop up liquids; Wel., ***llabio***.

'***Loblolly***, a slovenly out of the way pottage, whole grists of oatmeal boiled till they burst and then buttered.' *Bailey's Dict.*

LOBSTER, LOP-START. I. The smallest of the weasel tribe, the stoat or mouse-hunt. II. A young sole. Gael., ***leobag***, a small sole, a flounder; Ir., ***leabog-chearr***, a sole; Manx, ***liehbage***, a flat fish.

'A Middlesex man would probably be much surprised to hear a Norfolk farmer talk of the havoc made among game and poultry by ***lobsters***, and on the matter being explained would doubtless think ***lobster*** a mighty absurd appellation for the common stoat. But in Katterfeltos' phrase there is reason for everything if people only knew it. The same in Yorkshire is called a ***clubster*** or ***clubstart***, i.e., ***clubtail***. The Norfolk and Yorkshire terms are evidently allied in origin, and both express the idea meant to be conveyed, viz., an animal with a thick tuft on its tail, which is a true description as far as it goes.' *Garnet's Philosophical Essays.*

Sw., ***löpa***, to leap, run; Sw. and Dan., ***stjert***, a tail. The Dan. has also ***lœp***, a pendulous, fleshy part; Wel., ***llob***, a lump.

L. Ger., ***wip steerten***, agitare caudam. ***Kilian***, Dut., to fisk the tail, as a dog.

LOCK-SPIT. A spade-cut marking out the direction of a fence. A.S., ***loe***, enclosure; ***spœd***, spade.

'Sets out the circuit with a plough, which we call ***lock-spitting***.' *Ogilby's Virgil,* 1688, p. 313.

LODE. An artificial watercourse made in the fens to aid the drainage. A.S., ***lodan***, to draw water; Irish, ***lod***; Gael., ***lad***, a water-course.

LOGGER. A loose irregular action of a wheel on its axle.

Dut., ***log***, unwieldy; Dan., ***logre***, to wag the tail; 'O. Fr., ***locher***, to shog, wag, make a noise like aught that is loose.' *Cotgr.*

LOITER-PIN. A practice of ploughmen of halting at the ridge ends for gossip.

LOKE. A blind alley, shaded lane, narrow pass, a private road closed with gates, or through which there is no thoroughfare. ***Loke***, past part. of locked. Also a door hatch. A.S., ***locen***, an enclosure, boundary; Isl., ***loka***, to shut.

Lonk, a dingle which is not very steep, a hollow. ***Lagger***, a broad green lane not used as a road. Heref. dial. ***Link***, Sussex, a green or wooded bank.

An enclosure, a private road; der. immediately from the Dan., ***lökke***, an enclosure. The word seems also to be used in the sense of a grassy footpath or bridle-way. This may derive from the Su.-Goth., ***lök***, turf, herbage.

LOLLOP. To lounge. Isl., ***loll***, sloth. ***Loll-poop***, a lounger.

LONDES. Desert strips of land. Fr., ***Landes***, plains, heaths.

Bret., ***lann***, a thorny bush; Fr., ***brandes***, heaths. ***Lann*** is pure Celtic, vide *Diez*. and *Zeuss*.

LONDS. I. Old sub-divisions of uninclosed lands or fields. A.S., ***lond***. II. To clog with mire. '***Londed*** up to the knees.'

LONG. Great. Also tough to the palate. ***Short*** is its opposite, easy to masticate, friable, ex. the Sc., ***short bread***. Also to reach, toss.

LONG-LADY. A farthing candle.

LOOK AT THE NOSE. To seem out of temper, to frown, Essex.

LOPE. To take long strides. L. Sc., ***loap***; Isl., ***hlaupa***; Dan., ***lobe***; Dut., ***loopen***, to run. Common, says Bartlett, in the Western States for ***gallop***.

Lope-staff, a leaping-pole. ***Lope-way***, a foot and bridle path. ***Lowpynge*** or skyppynge. *Pr. Pv.*

'Such as in Fens and Marsh-Lands us'd to trade,
The doubtful fords and passages to try,
With stilts and ***lope-staves*** that do aptliest wade.'

Drayton's Barons' Wars, I, 43.

'But not by such large strides as he made in getting money, and ***loping*** into preferments.' *North's Lives, i., 12.*

LOPPER. To turn sour and coagulate. Isl., ***hlaup***, curdled milk.

LORDS AND LADIES. The early species of the *Arum maculatum*.

LOVES. The wood splines in a ventilating loft, across which the steeped and salted herrings are hung to smoke and dry them. Dan. ***lufte***, to air; Ger., ***luften***, to lift, raise, so as to expose to air.

LOVIER. A lover. A vulgarism but no corruption. A.S., ***lufian***.

LOW. A loch left by the tide in hollows of the shore. Sc., ***lowe***.

LUBBER, **LUBBERLY**. See ***Lob*** and ***Loblolly***.

'Some litherly ***lubber*** more eateth than two.' *Tusser.*

LUCK. The yellow flower of the kidney vetch.

LUCKS. Small portions of wool twisted on the fingers of a spinner at the wheel or distaff. A.S., ***alucan***, to pull about.

Leawks, tufts of barren, dry grass, locks of hair, Lanc. ***Locks***, clotted wisps of hay. An ostler is told to give the horse 'just a ***lock*** of hay,' Northampts.; an armful of hay, Dorset. '***Lok*** of hey, ***Lok*** of here, ***Lok*** of wulle, Floccus.' *Pr. Pv.* ***Lucks*** in the E. Ang. sense is common in New England. Isl., ***lokr***, a tress; Fr., ***loque***, shred, tatter. Sc., ***lochter***, and ***lucht***; Su-Goth., ***lugg***.

LUFF. To bring a vessel close to the wind. Fris. and Dut., ***loeven***.

LUM. The handle of an oar. Isl., ***hlumm***. To ***lum*** the oars; to let the handles down into the boat without unshipping them.

Ir., ***leamh***, an oar, a rower.

LUMP. To drub with heavy blows. Dan., ***lumpe***, to treat scurvily.

LUNT. Short, crusty in speech or manner. Ger., ***lumpicht***, stingy; Dan., ***lune***, mood, caprice.

LUNTY, LUNY. Surly, waspish. Su.-Goth., ***luna***; Isl., ***lund***, mood, temper; Isl., ***olund***, ill tempers.

LURDAN. A drone, sluggard.

'***Lourdant***, a dullard, grotnoll, jobernoll, lowte, lob, luske, clusterfist, churl,' &c. *Cotgr.* Old It., ***lordo***. Hence N. Ang. ***lurdy***, lazy dirty. Fr., ***lourd***, (Eng. ***lout***.)

> 'I say lyeutenaunt of the Toure   Make this ***lurdeyne*** for to loure;
> Lodge hym in Lytell Ease,   Fede hym with beanes and pease!' *Skelton.*

LURRIED. Daubed as by rolling in mire. 'His clothes were ***lurried*** all over.' Gael. and Ir., ***luiriste***, slovenly, untidy. See ***Slar***.

N. Ang., ***lair***, mire, dirt; ***laired***, stuck in the mire, from Isl., ***leir***; Dan., ***leer***, clay.

LUSK. To lounge, dawdle. ***Luskish***, lazy; Prov. Ger., ***luschen***, to lounge; Dan., ***luske***, to skulk; Isl., ***loskr***, idle.

> 'Sibright that schrew as a ***lordan*** gan ***lusk***,
> A suynhird smote he to dede under a thorn busk.' *R. de Brunne.*

'Such an old custome of formality in Religion, ease, sloath, restinesse and ***luskishnesse*** of spirit.' *D. Rogers' Naaman.*

LUST. To incline. 'This wall ***lust*** o' one side,' – 'the ship ***lusts***.' A stack out of the perpendicular is said 'ta ***lust*** lamentably.'

Wel., ***ystlysu***, to tend to one side, go sideways; Sc., ***leist***, to incline.

LUTHA. Leather. According to Moor, a binding formula in school boy bargains is

> 'Wha's yar shews made on? ***Lutha***,
> Bahn, bahn for ivva, nivver no change no more!'

M

MAAMBLE. Soil is said to, when adhering to the spade or to the dabs in seed dibbling, causing irregular holes. ***Malmy***, sticky, adhesive, soft. ***Maul***, clay or marl adhering to the spade. ***Mamble*** implies also to eat with disrelish, trifle with food.

Prov.-Ger., ***malmen***, to rub, grind to powder; Wel., ***mall***, sodden, soft, crumbling; Goth., ***malwjan***; Isl., ***mölva***, to break small. N. Ang., ***maumy***, from Sa. Goth. ***mogna***, to mellow, says Brockett; Cumb., ***moam***, mellow; It., ***melma***, mud, from O.H.G. ***melm***, dust. Manx, ***mholmey***, mellow; ***mholmeyder***, a crumbler. See under ***mulder***, &c.

'And the word was no sooner out, but a matter of three-and-twenty whores went to pot, but the flesh was so cursedly ***mawmish*** and rotten that they soon gave over the thought of that projection.' *L'Estrange's Quevedo.*

MAIN. Under-roasted meat is said to be 'i' the ***main***.' Home-done is sufficiently roasted.

May imply, as Forby suggests, the thickest, most substantial part, and the longest in roasting, or be the Wel., ***main***, slight; ***mainly***, meanly, N. Ang.

MAKE. 'To make count,' to intend, reckon on – 'to make a hand on,' to waste, destroy, ex., 'that dog is mad, I must make a hand on him.' – 'to make on,' to caress, make much of – 'to make a noise,' to scold, rate soundly – 'to make ready,' to dress provisions – 'to make bold,' to presume – 'to make a die on't;' to die after a long sickness or decline. *Forby.*

MAKE. A long handled crook, used chiefly for gathering pease.

'A ***meak*** for the pease and to swinge up the brake.' *Tusser.*

A ***meag*** or ***meak***, a pease-book, Essex. *Ray.* Bailey also has it.

Maké Walloon, is to strike, upset, cause to tumble down. O. Fr., ***mackles***, pot-hangers or hooks.

MAMMOCKS. Leavings, wasted fragments. 'Eat up your ***mammocks***, child.' A thing is torn 'all to ***mammocks***.' Wel., ***mam***, a handful.

Also ***mummocks***, used in America. In *Baker's Northampts. Glossary*, ***mommock***, to maul, mangle; also a dirty mess. Cocker, Kersey, and others define it, a fragment, scrap. It occurs in *Florio's World of Words*, 1598, and is used by Shakspere.

'Whan ***mammockes*** was your meate, With mould bread to eat.' *Skelton.*

'Where you were wonte to have cawdels for your hede,
Nowe must you monche ***mammockes*** and lumpes of brede.' *Id.*

'And then so sliced and slashed them, and tore their planks to ***mammocks***, and their lean guts to kites' meat.' *Nashe's Lenten Stuff.*

MANNA. The local term for the sand and shingle thrown into Yarmouth Haven by the wind or tides.

O. Fr., ***maune***, a vein of earth or sand. *Cotgr.*

MANNER. Rich mould of any kind, collected for mixing with dung, cor. of ***manure***. 'Aw've manner'd the land.' N. Ang. To ***manner***, to throw up brows of ditches, or banks for mixing with dung as manure.

MARA-BALK, MERE-BALK. A ***balk*** or narrow slip of unploughed land, separating properties in a common field. A.S., ***mære***. Fris., ***mara***, a mark, boundary; Wel., ***balc***; Mid. Ang., ***meerbalk***.

MARCH-BIRD. A frog. Also a ***fen-nightingale***.

MARDLE. I. A pond, near the house, in the yard or on a green or roadside. Old Fr., ***mardelle***, brink of a well. II. Any gossiping, drawling talk.

II. ***Merdaille***, Walloon, is an importunate, noisy troop of little children. ***Meirdel,*** Sc. a confused crowd; also a huddle of small animals; Gael., ***mordhail***, an assemblage.

III. A jolly meeting, a drinking bout, and to indulge in such jollifications. ***Maudle***, to gossip. 'Tom and I stood ***maudling*** by the stile.' 'Several narbors stood ***mawdling*** together in the road, beside the jossing block.' *Spurdens.*

MARE'S TAILS. Long narrow clouds, floating below the mass, of a darker hue, and indicating continued rain.

'Water dogs and ***mare's tails***

Make lofty ships have low sails.'

MARL. Denoting in East Anglia the clays and soft chalks, spread on the surface of its sandy soils to stiffen and enrich them, pron., ***maul***.

From the Wel., ***mêr***, marrow, and ***llith***, to lubricate, soak in water, assert some philologists; the Wel. has also ***mar***, what is laid flat down. A.S., ***merg***, marrow; Dut., ***marghel***, marl, a sort of fat clay; Dan., ***mergel***.

From the Kymric it seems to have found its way into Gallic and Latin. Lat., ***marga***, a manure; Old Fr., ***marle***; ***(margula)*** Fr., ***marne***, marl, clay, chalk, see *Diez, Introd. to Gram. of Romance Languages.*

'The lean and hungry earth, the fat and ***marly*** mould.
Where sands be always hot, and where the clays be cold.'
Drayton's Polyolbion.

MARRAMS. The *Arundo arenaria*; Gael., ***muran***, sea reed; Dut., ***marren***, to bind. Isl., ***marhalmr***, sea-grass.

MARRISHES. Marshes, lands liable to be flooded. Ang. Nor., ***mareis***.

'***Maryce*** of a fen (or ***myre*** or ***moore***), ***mariscus***,' *Pr. Pv.* ***Moore*** is the O. Fr., ***mare***, any collection of water, a pond; Dut. ***maar***, hence Dut. ***maerasch***, A.S. ***mersc***; L. Ger. ***marsch***; O. Fr. ***maresq***; Fr. ***marais***; Isl., ***myri***, a fen; ***mor***, peat.

'When he cam into that bond, the Scottes fled onto wodes and ***marices***, and other straunge place.' *Capgrave.*

MARSHAL-SEA MONEY. A Norfolk name for the County Rate.

Originating, says Forby, in the new purposes to which the rate was applied by 43, Eliz., c. 2, where payments were directed to be made out of it to 'hospitals, shipwrecked mariners, sufferers by fire, and prisoners in the ***Marshalsea***.' Hence applied generally, to the county prison charges, which forms the largest item of county rate expenditure.

MARSHLANDERS. Cattle of the marshland or short-horned breed.

MARTLEMAS-BEEF. 'Biefe salted, dried up the chimney.' *Hollyband's Dict.*, 1593.

Martlemas, a cor. of ***Martinmas***, or the Feast of St. Martin, falling Nov. 11. It was the customary time for hanging up to dry the salted winter provision, winter fed cattle being too lean for killing. In Essex it was dried in the chimney like bacon. ***Mart*** in the Keltic dialects, a beef or cow.

'For Easter at ***Martilmas*** hang up a beefe;
With that and the like, yer (ere) grasse beef come in,
Thy folke shall look cheerely when others look thin.' *Tusser.*

'And warn him not to cast his wanton eyne,
On grosser bacon or salt haberdine;
Or dried flitches of some smoken beeve,
Hang'd on a wrythen wythe since ***Martin's Eve***.' *Hall's Satires.*

MASH, a vulgarism for marsh. Common also in the U.S.

MASH, MASK. The mesh of a net. Dan., ***maske***; Dut., ***mash***; Wel., ***masg***; A.S., ***maesce***. '***Maske*** of a nette.' *Pr. Pv.* O.H.Ger., ***mascû***, a net; Ger., ***masche***; O. Fr., ***macle***, in Blazon, a ***mascle***. At Hastings, ***mokes***, the Isl., ***möskvi***. The Sw. has ***mocka***, a salmon net. Lat.,

macula.

> 'What wanton, wanton nowe well ymet!
> What! Margery Mylke Ducke, mermoset!
> It wolde be ***masked*** in my net.' *Skelton.*

MATCHLY. Exactly alike, fitting nicely, pronounced ***mackly***; A.S., ***macalic***; Flem. ***makkelyk***, easy, meet, fit; '***makly*** or esyly.' *Pr. Pv.*; Sw., ***maklig***. In Linc. ***matley***.

MAUKIN. A ragged, blowzy wench; a scare-crow; a coarse rag mop. '***Malkyne***, mappyl or oven swepare.' *Pr. Pv.*

Old Eng., ***mawk***, a maggot; Isl., ***makk***, a grub. Possibly as Nares conjectures ***malkin*** a dimin. of Mary. The Gael. has ***moibeal***, a mop. Old Wel. Dictionaries have ***maban***, a puppet. ***Maukin***, Sc., a half-grown female, a lass and a ***maukin***, a female servant and a girl to assist her. See ***mawther*** below. Jamieson derives from Ger. ***maeghdeken***, a little maid. The Isl., has ***morkinn***; Sw., ***murkenn***, to rot. '***Morking***, a deer or other wild beast that dies by sickness.' *Kersey.*

'A sixth sweeps behind the door all earthly felicities, and makes Baker's ***Maulkins*** of them.' *Nashe's Lenten Stuff.*

> 'Could he not sacrifice
> Some sorry ***morkin*** that unbidden dies.' *Hall's Satires, B. III.*

MAUND. A large, open, wicker basket, used in the fisheries and for sowing seed broadcast.

Fr., ***mande***, ***manne***, an open basket or pannier having handles. *Cotgr.* Dut., ***maud***; A.S., ***mand***. Spelman, Nares, and others have derived ***Maundy Thursday*** from the ***maunds*** or baskets in which the royal alms are contained, but Mr. Wedgewood has shewn that the ***Maundye***, the Catholic ceremonial of washing the feet of poor persons, in imitation of our Lord's example at the institution of the Last Supper, when after it he washed his disciples' feet, saying 'Mandatum povum de vobis,' &c., is a cor. of the ***mandatum***, or in Fr. ***mandé***, the office appointed to be read during the ceremony. Dorset, ***man*** or ***mawn***, a large withy two-handled basket for apples, potatoes, &c. At Yarmouth, says *Wright's Prov. Dict.*, the term ***maund*** is given to a basket containing 500 herrings. '***Maund***, skype.' *Pr. Pv.*

> 'So rides he mounted on the market day,
> Upon a straw stuff'd pannel all the way,
> With a ***maund*** charged with household merchandize,
> With eggs or white meat from both dairies.' *Hall's Satires. B. IV, 2.*

MAVIS. A thrush; the *Turdus musicus*, *Lin.* Fr., ***mauvis***.

Of Celtic origin, like so many other names of birds, writes Diez in his *Dict. of the Romance Languages.* Breton, ***milvid***; Cornish ***melhuez,*** (sweet breath).

MAWBLED. Said of beer turning sour.

O. Fr. ***mau***, ill, bad, ***maudolé***, ill favoured, luskish. Ir., ***marbhla***, Wel., ***marwawl***, to deaden, grow numb. Sc., ***marbel***, sluggish; Gael., ***meirbhe***.

MAWSKIN. The stomach, or rather paunch of a calf, which is cleaned and salted to procure rennet used in cheese making.

Dan., ***mave***; Swed., ***mage***; Ger., ***magen***; Dut., ***maag***, stomach.

MAWTHER, MOTHER and **MAU'R.** A girl. The most curious word in the East Anglian vocabulary. A woman and her ***mawther*** means a woman and her daughter.

At a trial in Norwich, when it was asked who was the evidence of what had been stated, the reply '***a mather playing on the planchard***' completely nonplussed the judge, until the phrase was interpreted to him as 'a girl playing on the floor.' The word occurs frequently in Tusser. Ben Jonson uses it in his Alchymist – 'Away, you talk like a foolish ***mauther***!' says Restive to Dame Pliant, Act iv, 7. His servitor and pupil, Richard Brome, makes a more felicitous use of the word.

'P. I am a ***mother*** that do want a service.
Qu. O, thou'rt a Norfolk woman (cry thee mercy),
Where maids are ***mothers*** and ***mothers*** are maids.' *Eng. Moor, III, 1.*

'A sling for a ***mother***, a bow for a boy.' *Tusser.*

'No sooner a sowing, but out by and by,
With ***mother*** or boy, that alarum can cry.' *Tusser.*

'What? will Phillis then consume her youth as an ankresse,
Scorning daintie Venus? will Phillis still be a ***modder***,
And not care to be called by the deare-sweete name of a mother?'
A. Fraunce's Ivy-church, a. 4.

Bloomfield also employs the term in his Suffolk Ballad:—

When once a gigling ***mauther*** you,
And I a red-faced chubby boy.

Sir H. Spelman, seeking to rescue the word from ridicule, asserts that it was applied by our Danish ancestors to the noble virgins, selected to sing the praise of heroes. They were called ***scald-moers, singing mauthers***, and he complains that the Danish word ***moer***, an unmarried girl, had become corrupted to mother. The two words are effectually distinguished in the local pronounciation, ***mauther*** being also usually abridged to ***mau'r***. In Essex it is applied contemptuously to describe a great awkward girl.

'***Moder***, servaunte or wenche.' *Pr. Pv.*, 1440. ***Puera***, a woman chylde, callyd in Cambrydgeshyre a ***modder***. ***Papa***, a yonge wenche, a gyrle, a ***modder***. Elyot, author of the first *Eng. Lat. Dict.*, 1538. ***Fille***, a maid, girle, ***modder***, lasse. *Cotgr. Fr. Dic.*, 1634. Dut., ***moeder***, the womb; Belg. and Fl., ***modde***, a girl; Fris., ***moder***; Dan., ***maar***, maid; ***möbarn***, female child; Sw., ***mö***. Bailey has ***mother***, a young girl, North Country word. It., ***matta***, girl, especially in N. Italy and Rhœtia, says *Diez*, from O.H.G., ***magat***; Ger., ***magd***. Jamieson has Sc. ***may***, a maid; Moes. Goes., ***mawi***. The Isl. has ***maer***, a maid.

The A.S. has ***mœth***, a virgin; ***mœithad***, puberty; the Wel. ***morwyn*** and ***mor***, maid, damsel, which seem the most obvious, immediate derivations.

MAZY. Sickly, unwholesome, spawned, applied to shotten and inferior herrings. ***Masled, mesled***, said of diseased hogs.

'***Masyl*** or ***mazil***, sekenesse.' *Pr. Pv.* ***Meseau*** a meselled, scurvy, leaporous, lazarous person. *Cotgr.* Robert de Brunne calls the leprous Baldwin, King of Jerusalem, 'the ***meselle***,' as does Wycliffe Naaman, and also the four lepers of Samaria. See *Way's Notes to Pr. Pv.* Su. Goth., ***maslig***; Bret., ***mezell***; Ger., ***mesel***; Dut., ***maselen***, from ***maes***, a spot. ***Maised***, Sc., is mellow, spoiled from over-keeping.

'He kissed a ***mysel*** and sodenely the ***mysel*** was hol.' *Capgrave.*

'It was told me by the vndaunted pursevants of your sonnes, and credibly beleeved in regard of your sinnes; that your grout-headed holinesse had turned vppe your heeles like a tired iade in a medow and snorted out your scornefull soule like a ***mesled*** hogge on a mucke-hill.' *Nashe's Almond for a Parrot,* 1589.

MEALS. The sand hills of the East Anglian Coast.

The Isl., ***möl,*** strand-sands, strand-stones, a place piled up with such stones or sand. Ir., ***maol,*** a headland, hillock, heap.

MEAL. As much milk as is taken from the cow at a milking.

A.S., ***mæl,*** a measure of aught, space of time. Hence the deriv. of ***meals, meal-***times, piece-***meal,*** &c. Ger., ***ein-mal,*** once; Isl., ***mál,*** a time of taking food, &c.; Fris., ***en miel molke fenne kou.***

MEASE. 'An old E. Ang. word denoting five hundred herrings in a net. Isl., ***meis,*** a basket to carry fish.' *Wright's Prov. Dict.*

A.S., ***maesce,*** a mesh; Gael., ***meas,*** a measure; ***measg,*** a cask, kit.

'***Meiss,*** a case, box, coffer, specially of the smaller sort, wherein hay is carried for cattle.' *Jonson's Old Nordisk Ordbog,* 1863.

Mease, a measure of herrings, is purely Keltic, and hardly known on the East Ang. coast. It is used in the Irish and West Scotland fisheries. Wel., ***mwys,*** a kind of covered basket, pannier, or hamper, also the quantity contained in such a vessel. ***Mwys o ysgadain,*** five score or 630 of herrings. *Owen's Wel. Dict.* Gael., ***miosar,*** a measure; Irish, ***maois-eisg,*** a maise, 500 fishes; Manx, ***meaish,*** 500 herrings. Sc. ***maze, meze,*** 500 herrings; ***maes,*** a bushel, Roquefort.

Mase, a net with wide meshes of twisted straw ropes – Orkney Islands. ***Mazie,*** a straw net – Shetlands. See under ***Mask.***

MELL. To swing or wheel round anything; a large iron hammer or ***mawl.*** Wel., ***melin,*** a mill. Isl., ***melja,*** to bruise.

MENTLE. A woman's coarse woollen apron. A.S., ***mentel.***

MESLIN. A mixture of flour and meal of different grain.

'Years ago in Norfolk thousands of acres yielded no better grain crop than rye, of which the bread of farm households was made. ***Meslin*** bread made of wheat and rye in equal quantity was for the master's table only.' *Forby.* Fr., ***mesler,*** to mingle. Still used for farm labourers' diet in N. Anglia. See *Dr. E. Smith's Report to Board of Health,* 1864. Called there also ***masselgem,*** from the Dut., ***mastelyn,*** meslin. In Yorks. and Norf. the two kinds of grain are sown together, requiring light land. '***Mestlyone,*** or monge corne or dragge.' *Pr. Pv.*

'And there at the manor of Marlingford, and at the mill loaded both carts with ***mestlyon*** and wheat.' *Paston Letter,* 1482.

'Item, four bushels ***mixtelyn*** of store.' *L'Estrange House Accounts,* 1519.

> 'The tone is commended for grain,
> Yet bread made of beans they do eat
> The tother for one loaf hath twain,
> Of ***mastline,*** of rie and of wheat.' *Tusser, c. liii.*

'For they were neither hogs nor devils, no devilish hogs, nor hoggish devils, but a ***mesling*** of two.' *Fairfax.*

MEVE. To move. ***Meving,*** moving, so also ***preve,*** for prove.

> 'The bestial ***mevyng*** of the body.' *Capgrave.*

MICHAELMAS FLAWS. Bad weather common in the autumn equinox.

MIDDLE STEAD. The central and thrashing compartment of barns.

MILLER. A moth, 'probably from its mealy appearance.' *Forby.*

Dan., ***mol***, a moth; Sw., ***möll***; Irish, ***miol-crion***.

MILLION. A pumpkin. From ***melon***, says Forby; if so, the Gael. form, ***meallain***. Pies pumpkin shape are called ***milgin-pies***. 'A ***million***, une gourde.' *French Schoolemaster*, 1636. It., ***melo***, apple.

MINE. Possessive pronouns are used in a peculiar manner in Norfolk, ex., 'I wish you would come to ***mine***.' 'I shall go to-morrow to ***yours***.' 'We are invited to ***his***.'

MING. To knead, mix as bread; perfect tense, ***mung***. 'She ***mung*** up that bread.' Isl. and A.S., ***mengan***, to mix. ***Minkmeat***, for fowls, mixed with bran or barley meal.

'With the Scottes gan he ***menge***, and stifly stode in stoure.' *Robert de Brunne.*

'The busy bee her honey now she ***mings***.' *Surrey.*

MING. To mention, recall to mind. N. Ang., ***mounge***, to fret over.

Isl., ***minjar***, to call to remembrance; Sw., ***minnas***; Dan., ***mindegave***. Sc., ***munge***, to grumble; Shropsh., to mutter, murmur, from the Wel., ***mwngial***, to murmur.

'Could never man work thee a worser shame,
Than once to ***minge*** thy father's odious name.' *Hall's Satires, B, IV.*
'Ay ***ming'd***, ay mourn'd, and wished oft in wast.'
Bp. Hall's Elegy on Dr. Whittaker.

MINIFER. The white stoat or ermine, the smallest of its species. ***Minifer-pin***, the tiniest pin.

Old Fr., ***menuver***, *Cotgr.* ***Menu***, little; ***feurre***, fur, the latter from ***fourrer***, to case, sheathe, fur; Isl., ***fodr***, sheath.

MINK, MINT. To attempt, aim at. Flem., ***min***, love, liking; Ger., ***meinen***, to intend.

MINNOCK. One who affects over much delicacy. To play the fribble. Also Mid. Ang.

Johnson conjectures it to be ***minnick***, from ***minnix, minx***, and Richardson refers ***minx*** to ***miniken***, without supplying deriv. to either. It is clearly an intensive, as finnickin is of fine; winnicking of whine, and other words ending in ***ock***, from the Su. Goth. ***oka***, to increase. Probably its root is the Gael. ***min***, soft, delicate, tender, as finnicking, from the Gael., ***fiorin***, white, fair, fine, also little. Isl., ***fina***, to polish up, cleanse. The Wel. has ***main***, slender, thin. Or it may be a cor. of ***mannikin***; Dut., ***mande-ken***, a little man; ***kinde-ken***, a little child. Miss Baker conjectures it a cor. of ***mimicking***.

'And forth my ***minnock*** comes.' *Mid. N. Dream, 1st Quarto ed.*

The Fr. has ***mine***, visage, cheer, posture, favour, outward shew; ***mignon***, daintie, spruce; the Ir. ***mineachd***, delicacy, fineness. Sc., ***mim-moued***, affected.

'Their words are common! for euery cut purse vseth them at the Old Bayly, that hath had any skill in his ***miniken*** hand-saw.' *Nashe's Plaine Percevall.*

MIS-BEHOLDING. Offensive, affronting. Applied to words. 'I never gave her one ***misbeholding*** word.'

MISCASUALTY. An unlucky accident. ***Miscomfortune, miscomhap***, mishap.

MISERY. Acute pain in any part of the body. ***Misery-in-the-head***, means a violent head-ache. *Forby.*

'***Misery***, pain; as "They say John Soaker never gets drunk, but he often has a ***misery-in-his-head***," Southern States' *Bartlett's Americanisms.*

MISLEN-BUSH. The mistletoe.

Forby derives from ***mæslen***, brass from its yellow colour; much too far fetched. It is the East Anglian ***meslin***, *i.e.* mixed, from its parasitical growth upon the oak.

MOFFLE, MUFFLE. To speak thick and inarticulate. Dut., ***moffelen***; N. Ang., ***maffle***.

Maflin, a simpleton. ***Mafted***, stifled, – Whitby; ***maffling***, trifling – Craven. In Linc. applied to a small eater.

MOKE. To pull wenches about at fairs.

MOKY. Misty, cloudy, foggy; Irish, ***muich***, a mist; Sw., ***mörk***, obscure; Sc., ***mirky***.

MOLE. An abortion; a slink or castling, dead ere brought forth.

'Otherwise as the unhappy woman who carries a ***mole*** or abortive in her, hath many feares, and saith either I goe with child, or with my death, so shall it fare with you.' *D. Rogers' Naaman.*

Mole-day, a day of burials; a feast made at a burial. West Dial.

MOLE-COUNTRY. The grave or churchyard. 'He's gone to the ***mole-country***, bless his bones.'

MOLT. A profuse perspiration.

Var. of moist. Fr., ***moite***, damp; Wel., ***mwyd***, soaked, damp. Forby regards it as an intens. of ***melt***. ***Molt-water***, clean exudation; a discharge from a blister is also so called.

MORFRY. A four-wheel'd cart, usually two-horse, of peculiar construction, common round Yarmouth.

A cor. of ***hermaphrodite***, from its construction being half cart, half waggon; to the eye, a waggon razé. The class of vessel now called brigantine, half brig half schooner, was until lately also so called on this coast by sailors.

In the autumn of 1863 the writer, struck by the odd appearance of a vehicle in Yarmouth market, went up to the driver and accosted him, asking the name of his conveyance. 'A ***morfry***, master.' – 'How do you spell it?' – 'Bless yo', yo' maun't ax me, I've ollis heerd it cau'd so.' He pointed out the peculiarities. Where the shaft horse or thiller is usually placed, ***foresummers*** (see ante) or ***croulters*** (in Linc., ***waggon shelves***; N. Ang., ***skelvings***) supported permanently upon the shafts by upright wooden bars, occupy the space, leaving a latticed vacuum beneath the front, into which sacks of produce can be stowed, as in the boot of a coach. By this arrangement no weight is borne by the horse, it is all draught. 'I've bin a trading voyage this morning, master,' he added. – 'How's that,' said I. – 'Why, I've brought a load o' taters, and now I'm goin whom wi' this heer jag o' stra.' – 'Well, and suppose you'd gone back empty, what then?' – 'Why that ad a bin gooin back in ballast like.' – 'Well, you've a goodish load.' – 'Ay, bor, a brimming load.' Clearly I ejaculated mentally as I left him, my waggoner, with his salt-water similes as great a ***morfry*** as his very odd looking conveyance.

Croulters, (Mid. Ang., ***copses***) like other E. Ang. names pertaining to waggons, appears to be Keltic. Wel., ***crothell***, a bulging or widening out.

MORK-SHRIEK. A mockery, a humbug, a foolish old wives' tale. From Dan., ***morck***, vapour. *Forby*. Dan., ***skrœk***, terror, fright.

MORT. A great number or quantity. Isl., ***morgt***, much. ***Mortal*** is the adjective. 'I'm ***mortal*** hungry' – 'there was a ***mortashus*** sight a people at the fair.' An old Norfolk saw is – 'One is none – tew is some – three is a sort – four is a mort.' ***Mortling***, a poor wretched mortal.

MOSY. Shaggy, covered with hair. Old Fr., ***moisi***, hoary, mouldy, fusty. *Cotgr*. Isl., ***mosi***, moss; Gael., ***mogach***, hirsute, bristly. ***Moosy***-faced, down-chinned, Whitby and Essex.

Mosy is also verging on rottenness, as ***mosy*** apples. Ger., ***moes***? C. Brit., ***mwydo***, humectari.' *Hartshorne's Salopia*. In Yorkshire, ***moskered***. From the Gael. and Ir., ***mosgain***, musty, rotten.

MOTHER. The thick skum on vinegar or beer in bottles.

Lees, thickening, mouldiness, or dregs of wine, beer, oil, &c. *Bailey*. Dut., ***modder***, puddle; Dan., ***mudder***; Fin., ***muta***, Wel., ***mwydaw***, soaked, pithy. See **CALMY**.

MOUSE-HUNT. The stoat, smallest of the weasel tribe.

MOYLE. A mule, a labouring beast. To drudge, also to be stubborn. Dut., ***muyl***. Gypsy, ***moila***, a mule.

'Theyr styrops of myxt gold begared, There may no cost be spared,
Theyr ***moyles*** golde dothe eate Theyr neyghbours dye for meate.' *Skelton*.

'Should we see a child to cark and care for a livelihood, droyl and ***moyl*** for a poor living; we presently conclude that he is friendless and fatherless, and left to the wide world to shift for himself.' *Roger's Rich Fool*.

'Dost thou give stubborne or ***moyling*** answers to thy master or mistresse, as Hagar to Sara; or sleevelesse answers, as Gehezi to Elisha?' *Rogers' Lost Sonne*.

MOYSE. To thrive, spoken of crops and stock. Also generally, as 'He muddles on but does not ***moyse***.' Gael., ***measach***, abounding in fruit; Fr., ***moisson***, harvest.

MUCK. A coarse term for money, 'where there's ***muck***, there's money.' *Norfolk Proverb*. ***Mucketty***, dirty. Isl., ***mok***; Fris., ***mjuk***.

MUCKINGA, MOCKADOUR. A handkerchief, especially a child's.

Johnson has in this sense ***muckender***. Gael., ***smuig-eudach***, a snot wiper; Span., ***mocadero***, a handkerchief; ***moco***, muck; ***mugack***, snuffling; ***smuc***, a snivel; Fr., ***mouchoire***, a handkerchief; It., ***moccare***, to wipe the nose; Lat., ***mucare***, from ***mucus***, snot; ***emungere***, to blow the nose. Used by the Elizabethan dramatists. Cotgr. has baverette a ***mocketer***, to put before the bosom of a slavering child. Ray has ***muckender***, a cloth hung at children's girdles to wipe their noses on.

'For eyen and nose the nedeth a ***mokadour*** or sudary.'

Lydgate's Advice to an Old Gentleman who wished for a young Wife.

MUCK-SPOUT. One very loquacious and foul-mouthed.

MUDGIN, also **MERGIN.** I. The rubbish of old walls and ruined buildings mixed with clay, straw, &c., and used for building hovels, low walls, &c.

Also mixed with manure as a compost. II. Also a white sort of marl, the refuse of lime pits; chalky clay used for daubing.

I. Old Fr., ***murgé***, heaps of stones, picked out of vineyards, gardens, &c. *Cotgr.* Wel., ***murzyn***, ruins of a building; Lat., ***murus***, wall. Sw., ***mörga***, embers. Ir., ***muirgin***, dung, muck. II. For this see derivations under ***Marl***.

Nares has ***murgion***, soil from the bed of a river, with the following illustration: 'Many fetch ***moore*** earth or ***murgion*** from the river betweene Colebrooke and Uxbridge, and carry it to their barren groundes, 8 or 10 miles off. And the grounds whereupon this kind of soile is emploied, wil indure tilth above a dozen yeeres after'. *Norden's Surveior's Dialogue*, 1610.

MUGGY. Gloomy, damp, murky weather, but neither rain nor fog. A ***roke*** is a fog; a ***smur***, a drizzling rain.

Wel., ***mwci***, fog, from the root ***mwg***, smoke; Gael., ***muig***, misty, vapoury. Breton, ***mouga***, stifling; Isl., ***mugga***, thick, obscure weather.

MULCH. A compost of rotten leaves, litter, road scrapings, &c. In Suff. a thick mixture of earth and water for moistening roots of transplanted shrubs. Also applied to anything thick, slabby, semi-liquid. N. Ang., ***mush***. ***Mulch***, Essex, is half-rotted straw.

A.S., ***molsnad***, rotten; Pl. Dut., ***molsch***, soft, mellow; Wel., ***mallu***, to sodden; Ir., ***malcadh***, rotting; North Ital., ***molla***, slime. ***Melsh***, said of weather mild and warm, inclined to moisture, Leeds.

MULDERY, MULTERY, MULLY. Soft, crumbling, mellow. Dut., ***mullen***, to crumble; Isl., ***molna***, to moulder.

N. Ang., ***murl***; Leeds, ***merl***; Cumb., ***mul***, the dust of peats, 'as ***murly*** as a short cake.' Dorset, ***mullum***, 'as soft as a ***mullum*** cheese.'

MULL. Soft, breaking soil; Su. Goth., ***mull***; A.S., ***myl***, dust; Ger., ***molt***; Lanc., ***mullock***, dirt; Wel., ***mwlwc***, refuse, sweepings. Ir., ***mulach***, puddle-water, mud.

'The ***mullocke*** on an hepe ysweped was.' *Chaucer.*

MULTER or **MULTA**. Land, laid in ridges, exposed to air and frost to pulverise is said when next ploughed to ***multer***, i.e., become friable, mellow.

Dut., ***mullen***, to crumble. Goth., ***mulda***, dust. Isl., ***mölva***, to break small; Wel., ***mallu***, to break into fine particles; It., ***mollare***; Fr., ***mouiller***, to yield, soften; Ger., ***molt***, garden mould. See ***mulch, mulder***, and ***mull*** above.

MUMPER. A beggar. Dut., ***mompen***, to trick, deceive.

MUNG. A mixture of coarse meal with milk, for the food of dogs, pigs, or poultry. N. Ang., ***mang***. See ***ming***.

MURE-HEARTED. Soft-hearted, meek. Sw., ***mör***, tender, soft. Wel., ***mwr***, friable, crumbling.

MUSE. The hole in a hedge through which hares and rabbits pass as a common track.

Trouée, a gap or ***muset*** in a hedge. *Cotgr.* ***Mesh***, the run or lair of hares. Dorset, ''Tis as hard to find a hare without a ***muse*** as a woman without a ***scuse***.' *Green's Thieves Falling Out.* O. Fr., ***musse***, secret corner, hiding hole.

MUSH. Guardedly silent, mum. Fr., ***musser***, to hide; Ger., ***sich maussen***, to hide like a mouse. 'Neither ***mush*** na ***hush***!' Sc.

N

NABBITY, NOBBLETY. Short in stature, but full grown; said of a diminutive female. Gael. and Wel., ***cnap,*** a knob, round body; Isl., ***nabb***; Dut., ***knobbel. Nap***, (A.S., ***cnæp***,) a small rising, Somerset.

NABBLE. To gnaw; a stronger term than ***nibble***. Hares are said to ***nabble*** growing corn. Mice ***nibble*** and rats ***nabble*** our provisions.

Dut., ***knabbelen***, to gnaw; Pl. Dut., ***knappern***, to munch dry hard food with a crunching noise; ***knabbeln***, to gnaw audibly; when the noise is somewhat finer, replaced by ***knibbeln***. *Danneil.*

Barnes in his *Dorset Glossary* has ***snabble***, to eat up greedily or hastily.

'Where the hay-meäkers put all their picks and their reäkes,
An' did squat down to ***snabble*** their cheese an' their ceäkes.'

Vellen the Tree, Barnes' Poems, vol. I.

NAB-NANNY. A louse.

NAKED-BOYS. The autumn crocuses, which flower without leaves.

NANCY. A small lobster. At Whitby a ***ninny-cock***.

NARROW-WRIGGLE. See ***erri-wiggle***.

NASHUN and **NA-TIVE**. One's own town or neighbourhood. 'I fare to be out of my ***nashun***.' Plaint of homesick E. Ang. servant. 'Beccles is my ***native***.' Common amongst uneducated people in the Southern States.

NATTER-JACK. A species of toad – the *Bufo calamita*.

Common in the district of the Broads. Distinguishable by its short hind legs, prominent eyes, yellow lines along the back and black bands on the legs. ***Natter***, to chatter; Wel., ***nadwr***, one who utters shrill cries; Flem., ***knoter***, to chirp; ***nyatrie***, peevish, Aberdeen.

NATTLE. To bustle and stir over trifles. Wel., ***nazial***, to be cutting or chipping continually.

The Wel. ***z*** is a mutation of ***d***, and has the soft or flat sound of ***th***.

Nattle, N. Ang., to hit one hard substance against another, gently quick; to make a noise like a mouse gnawing a board. *Brockett.* ***Nattering***, Whitby. ***Nattelen***, Flem., to tell over again; Gael., ***gnath***, unremitting; ***nattle***, to tap at or rattle lightly, as at a door or window, Lake dial.

NAY-SAY. The right or opportunity of refusal. 'Give me the ***nay-say*** of it.' Mid Ang., ***no-say-nay***, no refusal.

NAZZLE. A diminutive of ass. Forby calls it a ludicrous one, but why? It is the Gael. ***asal***, ass; Wel., ***asyn***; D. and Fl., ***ezel***.

NEAR. The fat of the kidneys. In Suffolk called ***aiyah, ear***, and ***hiyah***. *Moor.*

From A.S., ***nyre***, very tender, conjectures Forby. Rather from the Gael., ***ara***, pl., ***airnean***, Wel., ***aren***, kidneys; Dan., ***nyren***; Isl., ***nyra***; Fris., ***nier***.

NECKING, NECKINGER. A cravat or neckerchief. See ***muckinger***.

NECKUM, SINKUM, SWANKUM. The three draughts into which a jug of beer is divided.

NEEDLE. A piece of wood put down by a post to strengthen it.

NEEDLES. A common weed among corn; the *Scandix pectin, Lin.*

NEEST-GULP. The weakest and smallest bird of a brood. A.S., ***nesc***, tender.

Possibly from ***gulp***, a mouthful; its sense in several dialects.

Niscal, the smallest of a brood, Heref.; ***nestling***, Grose; ***nestlecock***, N. Ang. In Somerset, ***nestle tripe***; in Devonsh., ***nestledrait***; Pl. Dut., ***nestkiken***.

NEMIS. Lest, for fear that, Suff. Lat., ***ne***.

'Mauther gang the grizen into the vaunce-roof, bring my hat from off the spurket, ding the door after you ***nemis*** the cat should get in and eat the suncate.' *Grose's Specimen of Suffolk Dialect.*

NEP, NIP. The herb cat-mint. *Nepeta cetaria.* Its white down has given rise to the simile, 'as white as ***nip***.' A.S., ***nepte***.

NEPHEW, NEVVY. Applied to grandsons in Norfolk.

'***Neve***, sonys sone.' *Pr. Pv.* 'Heber was ***neve*** onto Sem.' *Capgrave.*

'Restrained in our present use to the son of a brother or sister; but formerly of much laxer use, a grandson, or even a remote lineal descendant. ***Nephew*** in fact has undergone exactly the same change that ***nepos*** in Latin underwent, which in the Augustan age meaning grandson, in the post-Augustan age acquired the signification of ***nephew*** in our present acceptation of that word. ***Niece*** has undergone the same limitation, but applied to the female sex alone, being once used as ***neptis*** was at first, for children's children, male and female alike.' *Archbp. Trench's Select Glossary.* ***Nephew*** and ***niece*** are O. Fr., cor. of the Lat. ***nepos*** and ***neptis***, into ***neveu, nieps*** and ***niece.*** See *Cotgr.*

NET-BRAIDING. Net weaving. See ***braid***. Irish, ***lion-obraidhe***, a lint or net-maker.

'Yarmouth, if the like occasion were, could clap up as good a shew of ***net-braiders***, or those that have no clothes to wrap their hides in, or bread to put in their mouths, but what they earn and get by ***braiding*** of nets.' *Nashe's Lenten Stuff.*

NETTUS. The ***neat-house*** where cows are milked.

NEWDICLE. Something new; ***newelty***, novelty.

NEXTING. Very near. A.S., ***nextan***.

NICKLED. Said of crops beaten down by wind, hail, rain.

Dan., ***knygge***, to blow a storm; ***knœkke***, to crack, snap, to humble, bring down; Dut., ***knikken***, to bruise, bend; Fris., ***knuke***, to beat, press down; Ger., ***nicken***, to nod; Fr., ***nique***.

NIDGET. To assist a woman in travail. A.S., ***nid***, need; Dan., ***knide***, dilemma, hobble.

Nares has 'to go a ***nigiling***,' to go to fetch mid-wives, nurses, and gossips. A ***nidgel*** is said also of an amateur mid-wife's services. ***Nidulate*** (from Lat.) to make or build a nest. *Bailey.*

NIFFLE-NAFFLE. To trifle; play with one's work.

Nifle, trifle. *Kelham's Norm. Dict. Cotgr.* has ***nipes***, trifles, ***nifles***. ***Niff-naffs***, trifles, knick-knacks. The radical idea, says Wedgewood, 'is a snap with the finger.' Fr., ***niquet***; Ger., ***knipp***, a snap or fillip. N. Ang., ***niffle***, to steal; Whitby, ***naffling*** and ***shaffling***, trifling about. ***Niffle***, to swallow hastily,

Northampts. ***Niffle***, a thing of little or no value. Old Law Term. *Bailey*. ***Neaphle***, a trifle, Sc. Su. Goth., ***nipp***.

> 'Yes, yes, I am yet as full of game
> As ever I was, and as full of tryfyls,
> Nil, nihilum, nihil, Anglice, ***nyfyls***.' *Skelton*.

NIFFLING. Whining, unhappy; said of a child.

From the Isl. and Teut. root ***neb***, the nose, 'softened in the Romance languages to It., ***niffolo***. Hence Limousin, ***niflà***; Picardian, ***nifler***; Fr., ***renifler***, to sniff; Bav., ***niffeln***; Ger., ***s-nuffeln***; Eng., ***snuffle***.' *Diez*.

Cotgr. has ***nifler***, to snifter, or snuffe up, snivel. Wel., ***gnif***, pain, anxiety.

NIGGER. The E.A. form of snigger. A.S., ***hnægan***; Swed., ***gnagga***; Isl., ***kneggia***, to neigh, laugh coarsely; N. Ang., ***nicker***.

NIGGLING. Careful, laborious, working out by patient detail.

Used here in vulgar but cognate senses, ex., 'He ***niggled*** him of his money.' Said of an affected, mincing gait – ex., ''Ka there how she ***niggle*** along' – of a pinching existence, 'We make but poor outs of our lowans, we ***niggle*** it out as well as we can.' ***Nigler***, an industrious person, Cumb.; ***nigg***, a small piece, Essex.

Possibly a dimin. of ***niggardly***. The Isl. has ***nagga*** and ***gnaga***, to gnaw, nibble; deriv. of our Eng. ***naggle***; Dan., ***gnidst***; Sw., ***njugg***, niggardly. The Wel. has ***nig***, narrow, strait, ***gnif***, trouble, toil, anxiety.

NILDY-WILDY. Whether he would or no. A.S., ***nillan, willan***.

NIP. A near split-farthing housewife. Also a turnip, Ir., ***neip***; A.S., ***naep***; Sc., ***neep***. Its old name.

NISY. A poor simpleton, an ass, a perpetrator of ***niaiseries***. See ***Nazle***. Common in our Eliz. writers.

Niais, a ninnie, fop, noddie, cockney, dotterell, peagoose, &c. *Cotgr.*

NITTLE. Neat, pretty, tidy, shining. Lat., ***nitidus***.

NITTY. Applied to the hair, when filthy and covered with the eggs of lice.

A.S., ***hnitu***; Dut., ***neet***; Isl., ***nyt***.– 'It is an illustration of the dirty habits of people in former times that this insignificant object, the ***nit***, has the same name, allowing for dialect, in all Ger. and Scand. languages, in Welsh, Bohemian, Polish, Greek, having accompanied our race from its first Asiatic home.' *Dr. R. C. Prior*.

'Then begins hee to take his sissars in his hand, and his comb, and so to snap with them, as if he meant to give a warning to all the lice in his ***nitty*** locks for to prepare themselves.' *Greene's Quip for an Upstart Courtier*.

'Although he goes vngartred like a malecontent cut-pursse, and weares his hat over his eyes lyke one of the cursed crue, yet cannot his stabbing dagger, or his ***nittie*** loue-locke, keepe him out of the legend of fantasticall cockscombes'. *Nashe's Pierce Penilesse*.

NOAH'S ARKS. Clouds resembling the conventional form of the ark, turned bottom upwards, and which are supposed to predict rain.

NOBBLE. A bit off a loaf, &c. 'I cut her a great ***nobble*** off the loaf, and she ax'd me if we'ed any warmin that ad eat it, for she wouldn't,' said of a sturdy beggar. *Moor*. Gael., ***cnap***, a lump; Pl. Dut., ***knobbe***.

NOBBY. A very young foal. Wel., ***ebawl***. ***Nob*** and ***nobby***, Heref. and Glouc., common for a young colt.

NOBLE. The navel. Isl., ***nabli***. *Forby*. Ger., ***nabel***.

NOBSTICK-WEDDING. A compulsory one by the parish officers, the woman being pregnant and likely to be chargeable, Norfolk. *Wright's Prov. Dict.*

NOG. A sort of strong heady ale, peculiar to Norwich, says Forby.

'Walpole laid a quart of ***nog*** on't,' *Swift*. Of all the innumerable compounds for which Uncle Sam is famous, none surpass his ***egg-nog***, when deftly compounded and swallowed slick off.

The der. opens an unlimited field of conjecture. Sw., ***nocka***, to beat up; ***nog***, nice; Wall., ***nog,*** encore; Wel., ***nug***; Gael., ***gnog***, a shaking up; Wel., ***cynghogi***, to blend together; ***egg-nog***, to be properly made, requiring to be long and unweariedly kept stirring. '***Noggin***, a little piggen of about a pint. *Ray's North Country Words*. ***Nogan***, Gael., is a wooden cup.

NOGGING. Courses of brick-work between stout studs or upright and diagonal timbers, coloured in white and black chequer or ***pane*** work.

An old and most picturesque mode of building. Numerous fine existing examples occur to the writer, in the streets of Chester, Stafford, Bristol, and, in the ancient, manorial granges of the Midland Counties. Moor remarks, 'the wood seems to outlast the interstitial masonry. As the chalets of Switzerland and the Tyrol harmonize with their Alpine backgrounds, so do these grand old timbered "houses of seven gables," so rich in colour and contrast, in their many-peaked roofs and pinnacles, their barge-boards and dormer windows; their sunny, honey-suckled casements and porches glisten in the rich verdure of our noble English woodland scenery, true and genuine embodiments of the *genius loci*. Why cannot the broad affluence of this once peculiarly English construction be revived? It is sorely needed in this age of mean, pretentious, architectural shams, of cold, staring, shadowless, unsubstantial glass and iron, of perky Italian villas, and pinched up railway-station Gothic; or are these old abodes, decaying memorials of a vanished age, of a squirearchy and yeomanry, whose types have perished from the land?'

Of obscure etymology. The root may possibly be the Wel. ***cyn***, a wedge; ***cynaiz***, wedge-like; ***cynhor***, a door-frame; ***cynhugyl***, plaited or matted work; ***cyngogwz***, a bending together; ***cynghogi***, to blend, bind together. This last appears the immediate derivation.

NO'HN. Syncopated form of nothing.

NOILS. Coarse, refuse locks of wool, of which mops and dwiles are made.

Never applied, says *Miss Baker's Northampts. Gloss.*, to any wool in its natural state, but that in the process of combing the short wool which will not pull out to any length, and is left on the comb, after the slither is drawn, is called ***Noils***. Query from the A.S., ***nyllan***, to be unwilling, or the Wel. ***cynnull***, to collect. The Wel. has ***wlân***, wool; Gael., ***olann***; Gr., ***mallos***.

NO'MATTERS. Not very well. 'I don't fare ***no matters***.' 'A don't behave to me ***no*** great ***matters***.'

NONNACKS. Light, irregular work, idle whims. ***Nonnaken***, idling, dawdling. Possibly a cor. of ***no maks***, do nothing.

NONNY. To trifle, play the fool.

Applied chiefly, says Forby, 'to the fondling and toying of sweet-hearts, and when the fair one is coy, and cries, "be quiet," "you shan't," &c. He derives from the Low Fr., ***nenni***, no. The Isl. has ***nenning***, brisk, sprightly; the Wel. ***nynnu***, to inflame; ***ennynfa***, an ardour, heat; ***cynhenu***, to wrangle; ***nantle***, to fondle, Lake dial.

NOONINGS. The dinner of reapers. A.S., ***non-mete***, cor. in var. dialects to ***nommet***, as in the Gower Peninsula, '***Nunmete***,' *Pr. Pv.* ***Nummet***, Somerset.

'***Nooning***, beavre, drinking or repast, ***ad nonam***, three in the afternoon, called by the Saxons ***non-mœte***, in ye North parts a ***noonchion***, an afternoon's ***nunchion***.' *Bp. Kennett's Gloss. Coll.* In Lanc. ***noon-scape***, and in Norfolk ***noon-miss***, the time when labourers rest after dinner.

'Yet I see he that was cooke and eater thought to feed Martin with these ***nuncheons***, as men feed apes, with a bit and a boxe on the eare!' *Nashe's Plaine Percevall.*

'On sheafes of corne were at their ***noonshuns*** close.' *Browne's Brit. Past.*

NOPPET. A bunch of wood or straw, Norf.; dimin. of Dut. ***knop***.

NORFOLK CHURCHES.

'This county hath the most Churches of any in England, (six hundred and sixty,) and though the poorest livings, (by some occult quality of their good husbandry and God's blessing thereon,) the richest clergymen.' *Fuller's Worthies,* 1662.

NORFOLK DUMPLINGS. Globular, made of dough and yeast, and boiled for twenty minutes; light ones are called pot-cakes. Applied sometimes to the Natives by 'foreigners' from the 'sheers.'

'This cannot be verified of any dwarfish or diminutive stature of people in this county, being as tall of their bodies, and as tall of their arms too, I assure you, as any in England. But it relates to the fare they commonly feed on, so generally called. I wish much good may it do them, and that their bodies thereby may be enabled for all natural, civil and spiritual performances.' *Fuller's Worthies.*

NORFOLK WILES.

'For Norfolk wiles, so full of guiles,
Have caught my toe by wrong so,
That out to thee (Suffolk) I see for me
No way to creep.' *Tusser.*

'Such the skill of the common people hereof in our Common Law, wherein they are so versed, *ut si nihil sit litium lites tamen ex juris apicebus serere callent.* If I must go to law I wish them rather of my counsel than my adversaries. For whereas *pedibus ambulando* is accounted but a vexatious suit in other counties, here, (where men are said to study law as following the plough-tail) some would persuade us that they will enter an action for their neighbours horse but looking over their hedge.' *Fuller's Worthies.*

To check the litigiousness of the district an Act was passed, A.D., 1455, 33, Hen. VI., c. 7: 'Whereas, of time not long past, within the city of Norwich and the counties of Norfolk and Suffolk, there were no more but six or eight attornies at the most that resorted to the King's Courts, in which time great tranquility reigned in the said city and counties, and little trouble or vexation was made by untrue and foreign suits: And now so it is, that in the said city and counties, there be fourscore attornies or more, the more part of them having no other thing to live upon but only his gain by the practise of attorneyship, and also the more part of them not being of sufficient knowledge to be an attorney, which come to every fair, market and other places where is any assembly of people; exhorting, procuring, moving and inciting the people to attempt untrue foreign suits for small trespasses, little offences and small sums of debt, whose actions be triable and determinable in Court Barons; whereby proceed many suits, more of evil will and malice than of the truth of the thing to the manifold vexation and no little damage of the inhabitants of the said city and counties, and also to the perpetual destruction of all the Court Barons in the said counties, unless convenient remedy be provided in this behalf: the foresaid Lord the King considering the premises, by the advice, assent and authority aforesaid, hath ordained and established, that at all times from henceforth there shall be but six common attornies in the said county of Norfolk, and six common attornies in the said county of Suffolk, and two common attornies in the said city of Norwich, to be attornies in the Courts of Record; and that all the said fourteen attornies shall be elected and admitted by the two Chief Justices of our Lord the King for the time being, of the most sufficient and best instructed, by their discretions.'

Many ludicrous illustrations of the local propensity 'to law each other,' on the most trivial pretexts, might be gathered up in the district, – as also of 'that sharpness of wit' in the practitioners, of which Camden made mention centuries ago. Of one departed Yarmouth worthy, it is related that a man, walking in advance of him in the street, stooped down and picked up a small gold coin. Rubbing the treasure trove he turned round and handed it to the lawyer, exclaiming interrogatively – 'Master, isn't this a seven-shilling piece?' – 'Quite right, my good man,' he replied, 'you are perfectly correct in your supposition,' and pocketing the coin brought out another. 'My fee for consultation is 6s. 8d., your change will be a groat, and here it is.' On another occasion a friend bargaining at one of the market peds for poultry, turned to him and sportively asked his opinion on the choice displayed before them. A few days after a bill came in –'To advising with you on the purchase of a goose, 6s. 8d.'

'Tacitus praises the taste and quickness of the Britons. Juvenal notices their capacity for pleading causes. Horace speaks of the Britons as untamed, and Cicero in writing to Atticus advises him to prefer any slave he might find in the Mart to the Briton, as he was so void of mind, and unsusceptible of improvement.' *Hamilton's Yorksh. Dialect.*

NORSELS. The short lines supporting, at 6-in. intervals, herring nets on their ropes. A.S., ***nosle***, a point to tie with, a strap string; Dut., ***nestel***. '***Nostylle*** of nettys.' *Pr. Pv.* Prov., ***noscla***, buckle; O. Fr., ***nassel***, the 'chinne-band of a helmet.' *Cotgr.*

NOSLE. The handle of a cup, &c. The ***nosle*** of a candlestick; that part which holds the end of a candle. *Halliwell.*

'Item, j candylstyk of sylver percell gylt, dowble ***noslyd***.' *Fastolfe's Inventory.*

NOTTAMY. A skeleton; cor. of anatomy.

'He's wasted to a ***nottamy***.'

NOUZLE, NUZZLE. To nestle, snuggle. Dut., ***neuselen***, to search with the nose.

'An hypocrite sees not such mercy from God, or else vanishes in the fruit of them, lets all goe, and ***nouzles*** himselfe in a blinde hope all shall be well; whiles yet old sinnes and dallyings are upon the score, unrepented of and unforgiven.' *D. Rogers' Naaman.*

'When a poore soule falls on meditating of what he hath heard at such a sermon, what doth it, but with the childe in the night, ***nuzzle*** for the mother's breast and missing the nipple, laies hold on the flesh and sucks the breast black, but hath no nourishment?' *N. Rogers' Lost Sonne.*

NUB. The nape of the neck. Ger., ***nap***; Fr., ***nucque***. Also ***nuddle***.

'Cut a lock of hair from the ***nuddle*** of the neck, and hang it in the doke of the stummuck.' *Old Suffolk Charm.*

'***Nuddlin*** is used in the sense of wearisome stooping. Whilst reaping wheat which was ***walted*** or laid, I lately heard a man say, " 'twas sich ***nuddlin*** work."' *Moor.*

In other dial. ***noddle***. Dut., ***knodde***; Dan., ***knude***, a bump, protuberance.

'He used at the Temple to be described by his hatchet face and shoulder of mutton hand, and he walked splay, stooping and ***noddling***.' *North's Lives, i. 144.*

NUMPOST. An imposthume.

NUNTY. Very plain and old-fashioned, applied to dress: stunted.

Nunty, Mid. Ang., is old-fashioned, shabby, scanty; ***nunting***, curtailed in dimensions. Perhaps from Wel. ***hynaint***, antiquated, or Wel. ***dynan***, a little woman.

NUSHED. Starved, ill fed. Gael., ***aognaich***, to emaciate.

NUTCROME. A crook for pulling down filberts or hazels. Walnuts are dashed or brushed with a long pole.

O

OAMY. Light, porous, floury, spoken of plowed land. See ***Loamy***.

OAT-FLIGHT. The chaff of oats, lighter than that of any other grain, and used by the poor for stuffing of beds.

OFF-CORN. Light, refuse grain, given to poultry or stock.

'Such ***off-corn*** as cometh, give wife to her fee.' *Tusser.*

OLD. A redundant adjective of perpetual occurrence in East Anglian dialogue, and used like ***bor*** without the least reference to the age of the objects. 'Look at yinder ***old*** hare in that there ***old*** pitle.'

OLD NOLPE. See ***Alp.*** In Dorset, a bull-finch is a ***mwope***.

OLD SARAH. A hare, Suff.

OLD-SHOCK or **SHUCK.** A spectre dog, much connected with the Danes; walks the Cromer Coast Road, last seen at North Repps, 1853. A.S., ***scucca***, Satan. *Miss Gurney.*

OLD-SOWS. Mille-pedes, woodlice. 'The species which roll up on being touched are believed, if swallowed, to have medicinal virtue in the ague and in scrofulous cases, specially if gathered from the roots of aromatic potherbs.' *Forby.*

OLD-WITCH. The cock-chafer, called also ***buzzard*** and ***daw***.

OLLANDS. (Old Land.) Lay ground, old land that has lain untilled, and is newly ploughed, Suff. In Essex called New Land.

ONTO. Upon. 'I'll lay my stick ***onto*** you.' Common in U.S.

ORATION. Used in the sense of narration, public talk.

ORRUCK HOLES. Oar-drawing holes, as distinct from thole pins which are less used in the Cromer boats. Dan., ***rykke***, to draw, comp. with ***rullocks***. *A. Gurney.*

ORTS. Broken fragments, over-eatings of victual or of cattle-food.

Frisic, ***orten***, to leave something over in eating; Dan., ***ovred***, over, past; ***ort***, ***öret***, is stale, musty; Dut., ***oor-aete***; Pl. Dut., ***ortels***. 'In Sc. a cow ***orts*** her provender when she tosses it aside; a child ***orts*** it when he crumbles it; a father marrying his daughters without regard to seniority, is said to ***ort*** them. Leeds, ***oits*** and ***otts***; A.S., ***orettan***, to spoil, defile.

The liberal housekeeper of the world will not allow the loss of his ***orts***, the children's bread may not be given to dogs. *Bishop Hall's Contemplations.*

OUT-A-HEART. Worn out; applied to land over-cropped.

OUT-A-WAH. Out of joint, as the shoulder, ankle, wrist, &c. 'A put a's sheowda out o' the wah.'

OUT-SHIFTS. Out-skirts, borders and extremities.

OVEN-BIRD. The long-tailed titmouse. *Parus caudatus, Lin.*

So called from its nest, which is also termed a pudding poke. The bird itself is more commonly called the long-tailed ***pick-cheese***.

OVER-GIVE. To thaw, exude or ferment.

OVER-HEW. Said of plants growing too luxuriantly.

OVER-LASH. To exceed. Frequently used by Bp. Hall.

OVER-WORN. Said of old clothes given away.

OWE. To own, possess. 'Mr. Brown ***owes*** that farm.'

Its original sense; very common in Shakspere. Not changed to ***own*** in the Bible until the last century. Goth., ***aigan***; A.S., ***agan***; Isl., ***eiga***, to possess, own.

OWLEN, OWLGULLEREN. To pry, examine. ***Owly*** is to feel half stupid. After 'rousing the night owl with a catch,' to feel like that 'moping' fowl next morning.

P

PACK-GATE. A gate on a packway, often lying through inclosed lands. Many such ways and gates retain their names and uses in High Suffolk. *Forby.*

PACK-RAG-DAY. Old Michaelmas day, when servants change their situations. In Yorks. dial. ***pack-bag-day***; Su. Goth., ***pack-a***, to bind together; ***packa***, baggage.

PACK-STAFF. Plain as a. In other dial. ***pike-staff***.

'Not riddle-like obscuring their intent;
But, ***pack-staff*** plain, utt'ring what things they meant!' *Hall's Satires, B. III.*

PADDUCK. A toad. Isl. and Sw., ***padda***; Dut., ***padde***; A.S., ***pad***, a toad. In Essex also a frog. '***Paddok***, toode.' *Pr. Pv.*

Brockett, in his *North Country Words* writes '***paddick*** or ***paddock***, a frog, never a toad.' Danish and Ger. prov. Glossaries give to ***padde*** the meaning of both frog and toad.

PAGE. The lad attending on a shepherd. Fr. ***page,*** a serving boy; '***page*** de navire, a ship boy.' *Cotgr.*

PAIGLE, PEGYLL, PYGIL. A cowslip, whence ***paigle*** wine and tea are made. Also in Suffolk applied to the crowfoot, the cuckoo-flower. *Ranunculus bulbosus, Lin.*

Forby derives from A.S. ***pæll***, 'a die-plant, a purple robe.' Dr. R. C. A. Prior, in his *Pop. Names of Brit. Plants*, has a long passage upon it; remarking that the name is now scarcely heard, except in the Eastern Counties.

He adds 'it is a word of extremely obscure and disputed origin.Dictionaries derive it from ***paralysis***. Foster, in his *Perennial Calendar*, says that it 'evidently signifieth ***pratingale***, from ***prata***, meadows, where it delighteth to grow. It were easy to speculate upon possible sources of the name, as Fr., ***epingle***, from its pin-shaped pistil; ***speckle***, in allusion to the cinq-spotted corolla, or it may be a cor. of its Mid Lat. name *verbasculum*.' At the close of other and more remote conjectures he concludes – 'it is for East Anglians to follow up the enquiry. There may be some very common words in their dialect which would explain it.'

Its probable root is derivable from its yellow colour; Isl., ***gulr***; Dan., ***guul,*** yellow, with the preposition prefixed to so many Danish words, ***paa***, on, upon, in, – ***paa-guul***, of a yellow surface.

The Gael. has ***buidhe***, yellow; ***buidheag***, any yellow flower. The metathesis of ***b*** into ***p*** from Keltic to English is common, *vide* Parson Sir Hugh Evans, in the *Merry Wives of Windsor*, and the Gael. ***dh*** has our sound of ***gh***. Gr. ***poikilis***, a bird, like a gold-finch, *Lid. and Scott*, but the Gr. root has the sense of varied, broidered colour.

Tusser, among his strewing herbs, has cowslips and ***paggles***; and for windows and pots – '***paggles***, green and yellow.' Ital., ***giallo***; Old High German, ***gelo***; Dut., ***geel***; A.S. ***gelew***.

> 'The yellow marigold, the sunne's own flower,
> ***Pagle*** and pinke that decke faire Flora's bower.'
>
> *Heywood's Marriage Triumphe*, 1613.
>
> '***Blake*** (yellow) as a ***paigle***,' Yorksh. Proverb. *Ray*.
>
> 'Hero, for that she was ***pagled*** and tympanised.' *Nashe's Lenten Stuff.*

PAJ or **PAHJ**. A purge. 'A'v taken a ***paj*** this maurun, an' a fare but kiender tuly.'

'The following is a wholesome piece of advice as to fallowing a field. "Ta owt to be stored ahly an then late ta ***paj***." I do not know if this requires translation; but if ***ta dew***, the following is the same in common English, with an interpolated gloss – "It ought to be stirred (ploughed) early, and then lay to purge' (itself of weeds, to be ploughed in at the second ploughing)." '*Moor.*

PALTRY. Rubbish, refuse, or trash of any sort. N. Ang., ***paltery***.

Isl., ***paltra***; Dan., ***pialt***; Prov. Ger., ***palter***, rags, tatters, ***palterig***, paltry; Old Fr., ***peautraille***, scurvy old stuff, scrapings of skins or leather.

'The date of idle vanities is expired, away with these scribbling ***paltries***.' *Gabriel Harvey's Pierce's Supererogation*, 1593.

'I little delight in such ***paltry***.' *G. Harvey's Foure Letters*, 1592.

PAMMENTS. Square paving bricks. Cor. of ***pavements***.

PAMPLE. To trample lightly. 'A child ***pamples*** about a walk or garden bed newly raked, or a floor new washed, and a slight raking or washing effaces the traces, but if a heavy-heeled fellow ***slods*** over either, the work must be all done again.' *Forby.* Also to walk as if the feet were tender.

The strong sense of trample (foot-stamp) softened into ***pample***. The Dan. has ***pampusse***, a list shoe; Ger., ***pampeln***, to bob, dangle; 'O. Eng., ***pomple***, to stumble, from O.N. ***pompa***,' writes H. Coleridge, in *Dict. of O.E. Words.*

PAN. The crust of hard earth below that moved by the plough.

Wel., ***panu***, to beat, bang, give a thick surface, ***paniad***, matted together, thickened by beating, pressure. Forby derives from A.S. ***panna***, scull.

PAN. To be hardened, as the surface of soil by hot sun following heavy rain. To bind firmly, as a clay floor or gravel road.

PAN. 'A fire-shovel is called in Norfolk a ***fire-pan***.' *Amyot.* A.S., ***panna***, an iron pan.

'Item j ***Firepanne***, item j payre of Tonges.' *Inventory of Fastolfe's Effects.*

PANE. A counterpane.

'Item j Rede ***Pane*** furryd with connyngs (rabbit-skins)' *Inventory of Fastolfe.*

O. Span., ***pena***, fur. A.S., ***pan***, a piece, patch; O. Fr., ***pan***, a piece of cloth, a skirt.

PANE. A regular portion or division of field labour, as sowing, digging, weeding, &c. The quantity of clay or brick noggin between the wooden studs. ***Paned***, striped, mottled, speckled.

Of the bigness of a thrush, coloured and ***paned*** like a hawk. *Sir T. Browne.*

A.S., ***pan***, a hem, plait. '***Pane*** or part of a thynge, pagina.' *Pr. Pv.* Fr., ***pan***, a pane, piece, pannel, or skirt. *Cotgr.*

PANEL, PARNEL. An unchaste woman. O. Fr., ***paneau***. *Cotgr.*

PANNIKIN. Fretting. Dut. and Flem., ***pynighen***, to pain, torment.

The N. Ang. ***peenging***, uttering peevish plaints, may be the A.S., ***pyngan***.

PAR-YARD. An enclosed straw yard for cattle. ***Par***, a beast pen.

Wel., ***parc*** and ***parwg***; Gael., ***pâirc***; A.S., ***pearruc,*** enclosure. From the Keltic, Diez remarks the Lat. and Romance var. ***parcus, parque***, &c. are derived. Languedoc, ***parghe,*** a cattle fold; ***paigha***, to fold cattle; N. Ang., ***parruck***; Dorset, ***parrick***; ***partles***, sheep's-dung, Cumb.

In Norfolk, an enclosed place for domestic animals as calves, is called a ***par***, and the farm-yard containing ***pars*** for the various stock is called a ***par***-yard. *Forby.*

In 1616 a fenced enclosure of nine acres at Hawsted, Suff., in which deer were kept in pens for the course, was termed the ***Parrock***. The spot was a mile long and a quarter broad, and narrower at one end than the other. In 1581 it was called ***le Pok***, perhaps from its shape. *Cullum's Hawsted.*

PASH. To beat anything brittle into small fragments, to dash, bruise. N. Ang., to bruise, crush; aught decayed.

Ajax. 'If I go to him, with my armed fist,
I'll ***pash*** him o'er the face,' *Shakspere, Troilus and Cressida.*

'Beaten down with clubs, and their heads ***pashed*** in pieces.' *North's Plutarch.*

Wel., ***baezu;*** Bret., ***basa***; to bruise, pound; Dan., ***baske***, to thwack; Sw., ***basa*** and ***piska***, to beat. In Lanc. ***pash*** is a sudden gust, an outbreak; Wel., ***pas***, that is expulsive.

N. Ang., ***pash***, a fall of rain or snow. Dut., ***plas***, a deluge; ***pash***, to trudge about; ***pashy***, slushy, Craven; N. Ang., ***poss***, to dash violently in water. ***Poss***, a waterfall, Craven; ***polssen***, Flem., to agitate water, to pump; Dan., ***pladskrega***, a heavy shower; Sw., ***plaska***; Ger., ***patschen***; to splash.

There is a distinction between a '***pash***' and a '***splash***' of rain. 'Here's a wet day, John! Ey, it dizzels and dozzels and duz. Will it continue? Nay, it may be a bit of a splash, but it willent be a girt ***pash***.' *Anderson's Cumb. Dial.*

'But now the rain will rough enter through the crannies of their wavering, the winds will blow and batter open wide passages for the ***pashing*** showers.' *Nashe's Christ's Tears,* 1593.

PATCH-UPON. To impute blame rashly or wrongfully. 'He ***patch'd*** it upon me.' A.S., ***pæcan***, to deceive, bear false witness.

PAUPUSSES. Paupers. Suff.

PAVED. Turned hard, – in the sense of ***pan***.

PAWK. To act secretly, to prowl about for wreck. ***Pawky-bag***, one for collecting fragments from a wreck.

Gael., ***beachdair***, a spy, explorer; ***beachd***, observation; Manx, ***peeikear***, prying, descrying.

PAWKY. An awkward, gawky, tall, two-left-legged lad or man.

In Scot., cunning, sly. In Cumb., too familiar, sly; A.S., ***pæc-an***, to deceive. In the North, saucy, squeamish, proud, insolent. In Craven, proud. The Gael., ***beachd***, with its compounds yields most of the above senses. Wel., ***balc***, proud, arrogant. Flem., ***pochen***, to boast.

PAWTS. Flat boards fastened on the feet to enable men to walk on mud, ooze.

From Fr., ***patte***, says Forby. Rather a cor. of ***sup-ports***. ***Paut,*** N. Ang., to walk heavily or awkwardly, a stroke on the ground with the foot. ***Pawt***, to potter about, Linc.; Craven, ***pause, pote***, and ***pawt***, to kick with the foot. To ***pote*** the clothes off – to kick all off. *Ray's N. C. Words*. ***Paut***, a puny kick, Leeds; Sp., ***pata***; Fr., ***patte***, a foot, ***paw*** or possibly from the Wel. ***paw*** that spreads, extends round.

PAX-WAX. The strong tendon in the neck of animals.

One of Sir T. Browne's words, and said by Forby to be in quite general use. Ray gives it in his *N.C. Words*, but of its derivation remarks he has 'nothing to say to it.' Forby calls it a 'crux etymologorum' which etymologists very reasonably do not care to come near. He adds Linnæus uses it in a passage of his writings which he has failed to trace.

The *Pr. Pv.* gives the right clue to the derivation '***Pax-wax***, synewe'; Ger., ***flechse***, a tendon, nerve, sinew; ***wacks***, in its sense of pliability, or of large growth. ***Fax-wax*** is the name in our North dialects. Old Fr., ***fex-wex***; Gael., ***feich***, sinew; ***feitheach***, tendinous. In Sussex the tough tendinous strip attaching to the neck of veal is termed the ***kaxy-waxy***. Barnes, in his Dorset dialect, has ***keake-horn***, the windpipe, particularly of slaughtered animals. Brocket, in *North Country Words*, has ***fix-fax***, the gristle or tendon of the neck. In Lanc. called ***peawsweawse***; Fris., ***pähs, peez***, sinew; Isl., ***wax***, said of bulk, bigness.

PEAGOOSE. Applied to one of an aspect both sickly and silly.

PECURIOUS. Minutely and scrupulously exact. Lat., ***peculiaris***.

PED. I. A pannier, a large capacious wicker basket with a lid. A pair of peds is commonly used swung one on each side of a horse, in which pork, fowls, butter and eggs are carried to market, and fish hawked about the country. II. An osier basket with lid, containing 125 herrings and upwards. A size of package largely used in the Yarmouth fish trade. A 'pot' is a similar basket, but smaller.

I. Formerly, in the days of small holdings, in very common use by East Anglian farmers and their wives. Numbers may still be seen in the markets of Norwich and Yarmouth. A ***pedler*** or ***pedder*** carrying his wares in peds answered to the pack-man of the North. In the minute roll of husbandry furniture given by Tusser – 'A pannell and wanty, pack-saddle and ***ped***' occur. ***Peder***, a small farmer, Linc.

In old maps of Norfolk, and still traceable in the ordnance maps, occurs the ancient Roman way, leading from the N.W. of Norfolk to Ixworth in Suffolk, known as the ***Peddar's Way***, so named from its use by those itinerant traders. In the *Pr. Pv.* '***pedde***, idem quod panere, calathus; (an osier basket), ***peddare***, calatharius. A ***Pedder*** 'revolus, negociator.– *Cath. Ang.' Way.*

The deriv. may be from Lat. ***pedes***, foot; Fr., ***pied***, borrowed by the Wel. and A.S. In the South ***peds*** are called ***dorsers***, from being carried on the backs of horses. ***Ped-bellied***, pot-bellied, 'podge-guts;' forcible phrases, of which Shakspeare's – 'A fair round belly, with good capon lined,' is a pleasant euphuism. See ***Pod.***

II. The hampers in which herrings are exposed for sale in our markets are always termed ***peds***, and fishmongers frequently say, 'I've got a fine ***ped*** of herrings today!' *Baker's Northampt. Gloss.*

'A haske is a wicker ***ped*** wherein they use to carrie fish.' *Original Gloss. to Spenser's Shepherd's Kalendar.*

'I mvst have myn instruments hyddur, whyche are in the chyst in my chamber at Norwyche, whyche I praye you and Berney togedre joyntly, but not severally to trusse in a ***pedde***, and sent them hyddur in hast.' *Paston Letters.*

'It. pd to the ***pedders*** of Norwyche for bryngyng of the seid spices hom to Hunstanton, ijs. viij*d*.' *L'Estrange Household Accounts*, 1530.

PEE-WEE. Peaking and whining. ***Pee-wic***, to peak and pine. Sc., ***pees-weepy***, puny, whining. See ***Pie-wipe***.

O. Fr., ***piauler***, to cheepe as a young bird, to pule, as a whelpe. *Cotgr.*

PEG. To thump with sharp knuckles. A.S., ***pyc-an***.

PEGGY. A slender poker, bent for raking fires. *Wright's Prov. Dict.* Wel., ***pig***; Sw., ***pigg***, a spike, pike.

PEG-TRANTUM. A great galloping, rantipole girl; a hoydenish mauther.

'Why called Peg, it is impossible to conjecture.' *Forby.* Verstegan, among his ancient English words, 1628, has '***Piga***, a girle, a little wench, so yet used in the Danish, – heerof commeth our Northerne name of Peg, mismeant for Margaret.'

'The Dan., ***pige***, a lass, (Sw., ***piga***,) has suffered that startling change in the sign of the Pig and Whistle, once the ***Pige Washael*** (the Maiden's Greeting) i.e., the Salutation of the Blessed Virgin! *Miss Yonge's Christian Names.* ***Trantum*** may be a cor. of tantrums, (see ***antrums***,) or of ***rantum***. Dut., ***ranken***, pranks, tricks; Ger., ***trandeln***, to toy, trifle. A slang phrase is – Gone to ***Peg Trantum's***, i.e., dead.

PELTING. I. Plucking the feathers from live geese, done in some parts of East Anglia, four times during spring and autumn. ***Ploat,*** to pluck feathers, Lake dial. Dut., ***bloot,*** naked, bare. II. Petty, ***paltry,*** which see above. Gab. Harvey uses ***paulting.***

Lat., ***pellis,*** Ger., ***pelz,*** a skin; ***pelzen,*** to peel.

Pelt, a word used in falconry for the skin of a fowl stuft, or the carcase itself of a dead fowl, to throw out to a hawk. *Ray's North Country Words.*

'A man took an eagle, ***pelted*** her wings and put her among his hens. Somebody came and bought this, and presently new feather'd her.' *L'Estrange's Æsop.*

'But for thee to tender a trade of so invaluable a commodity to these ***pelting,*** petty chapmen for thirty poor silverings, it was no less base than wicked.' *Bp. Hall.*

PEND. To press or pinch, as 'the shoe ***pends*** here.' (Lat., ***pondus.***) To incline or lean. (Lat. ***pendere.***)

PENNY-WAGTAIL. The Water Wagtail.

PENSE. To be fretful. ***Pensy,*** uneasy, fretful; applied chiefly to children.

Probably derived, as Forby and Moor believe, from Fr., ***pensif,*** in its stronger sense of 'heavy, carking, sorrowful.' *Cotgr.* The Gael. has ***pian,*** causing pain or vexation.

PERRY, wind, a. Half a gale. Fris., ***perre,*** a slight stir; Dan., ***pirre,*** to stimulate, urge forward.

PETER FISH. The John Dory.

'We often meet with it in these seas, commonly called a ***Peter-fish,*** having one black spot on either side of the body, conceived the perpetual signature, from the impression of "St. Peter's fingers," or to resemble the two pieces of money which St. Peter took out of this fish.' *Sir T. Browne.*

PETERMAN. A fisherman. Applied in Suffolk to the crews of the Dutch fishing vessels, or Peter-boats; followers of the calling of St. Peter. ***Peter-boat,*** one built sharp at both ends.

PETMAN. The smallest pig in the litter. In Suffolk, a ***rackling.***

O. Fr., ***petit,*** the whelpe, cub, or puppie, the little one. ***Raclures,*** scrapings, remnants. *Cotgr.*

PHEEZY, FEEZY. I. Fretful, querulous, irritable, sore. *Forby.* II. ***Pheese, feize,*** to scare, fright, fill with alarm. III. ***Fease,*** (sea term) to ravel out rope ends, &c. Some minor senses are given below.

Mr. Forby seems to be the only English glossarist who has fully given the four first meanings above. He adds no deriv. The term is not in *Moor's Suffolk Words.* The word is remarkable for the many aspects it wears in our dialects and dictionaries; for the conflicting interpretations attached to it, and for the neglect its etymology has experienced. It is a Shakesperian word moreover, one on which the commentators are at loggerheads. It may be worth while therefore to attempt to define its several meanings, and draw out their etymologies direct and cognate. These latter under heads I. and II. merge so into each other that it is difficult to draw any sharp line of partition.

Deriv. I. Breton, ***fae,*** disdain, scorn; ***faé-uz,*** disdainful. Wel., ***fiaiz,*** loathsome, hateful; ***fieiziaw,*** to detest, be disgusted at. Su. Goth., ***fasa,*** abhorrence, horror.

Sw., ***faslig***, hideous. Isl., ***fussa***, to express antipathy. Dut., ***vies***, nice, dainty, squeamish. ***Viesheyd***, morositas. *Kilian*. Fris., ***piesig***, peevish *(Hettema)*. Fr., ***fâcher; fâcheux***, fastidious. O.F., ***fasti***. It., ***fastio***. Sp. and P., ***hastio***, from Lat. ***fastidiosus***.

II. A.S., ***fus***, ready, prompt; ***fesian***, to drive away; ***fysan, fysian***; ***p***, ede; ***pp***, ed, to drive, expel, send forth (arrows), send away, hasten; ***fysan***, to rush, (***fuse***, will drive away. *Thorpe's An Ang.-Sax.*) Dan., ***fuse***, to rush, be precipitate. Sw., ***fösa***, to drive, push. Wel., ***frwysaw***, to act violently; ***fysg***, impetuous; ***fest***, speedy, hurried. Cornish, ***fest***, quickly; ***fye***, to drive away; ***fys***, scattered; ***fyas***, fled; ***fysta***, to thresh. Isl., ***fysa***, to stir up, excite; to work into a passion. Prov. Ger., ***filzen***. O.H.Ger., ***fillan***, to rebuke, reprimand, scold; ***fillen***, to flay, curry. From Ger., ***filzen***, to press (rather to comb out, to scold) says Diez, (under It., ***feltro***,) 'comes the O. Fr., ***fautrer***, to thrash, and perhaps the It., ***ferzare***,' to whip, lash, flog, spur on, chastise. Ger., ***fetser***, a rod, sword. ***Filz***, Ger., apart from its sense of coarse, matted wool, has secondary ones of rough, rude, stingy, hence occurs ***filz***-geben, to give a good scolding (employed by Luther), and some of the illustrations cited by Grimm, appear to include a drubbing.

III. Dut., ***vese***, fibres, threads. Ger., ***fitsen***, to disentangle. Fr., ***ficelle***, packthread. It., ***filza***, a string of aught. Lat. ***filus***, thread. See also Mr. Wedgewood's der. below.

Veze has a Scandinavian sense of hissing sound. Sue-Goth., ***hwæsa***, sibilare. *Ihre*. Isl., ***hvæsa***. Serenius in his *Ang.-Sueth. Dict.*, Hamburgh, 1734, has '***Veze***, ex. "it came down with a ***veze"*** cum sibilo.' A.S., ***hweosan***, Sui-Goth., ***hwisla***, whence Eng. ***hiss, whistle, wheeze***.

Michel in his *Etudes Philol. sur l'Argot* has a long article on ***Vesse*** (avoir la) to be affrighted. In the xv and the xvi centuries he writes, 'on disait dans le meme sens *avoir* ***vezée*** *de paour*.' He cites illustrations from Prov. Old French verse. Later the word ***vesarde, vezarde*** took rank beside ***vezée***, which he adds continues to exist in the patois of Normandy. ***Vezard*** occurs in Brantôme and Rabelais as a great fear, apprehension. Michel remarks the occurrence in *Oudin's Seconde Partie des Recherches Italiennes et Francoises,* p. 577, of ***Le Vezon***, 'il culo,' the buttock, with a mark noting its rare use. ***Vesse, vessic***, fille de joie, terme d' injure, is the next article in *Michel*. The phrase 'une bonne ***vesse***' occurs repeatedly in Brantôme. Rabelais applies the epithet 'ceste ***vessaille*** de deesses' to the goddesses of Egypt. *Cotgrave's Fr. Dict.*, 1632, has ***fesse***, a buttock, haunch (from Lat., ***fissus, fissa***, cloven) and ***fessé***, breeched, scutched, jerked, whipt, or beaten on the buttock; ***veze***, a bagpipe; jouer de la, to fizzle, the Dan. ***fise***.

The *Dict. d'Academie Francaise*, 6th and last ed. has ***fesse*** (buttock) fig et pop, 'avoir chaud aux ***fesses***,' etre saisi d'une grande peur – 'il en a eu dans les ***fesses***, qui à recu quelque grand dommage, * * * ***fessée***, coups de main ou de verges donnés sur les fesses, 'il a eu la ***fessée***,' ce mot est familier. ***Fesser***, fouetter un enfant. ***Vesse***, vent d'une odeur desagreeable qui sort sans bruit par derriere.

Le Roux's Dict. Comique, ed. de Pampelune, 1786, has ***Fesses***, dans le discours libre, pour deux grosses joues bouffies, ou pour de gros tettons, qui excedent la grosseur des tettons ordinaires. Qui diable a donc placé votre nez emtre deuz ***fesses? Fessier***, pour le derriere, le cul. (***Fetzer***, Ger., has the same meaning.) ***Vessé***, pour membre viril. ***Vezez***, in the Romance dialect is 'Le dieu des jardins',

Priape.—See *Roquefort.*

Florio's Italian Dict. (quoting from Torriano's ed., folio, 1688) has ***fesso***, cleft, and (by metaphor) fem. pud. ***vezzo, vezze***, any kind of wantonness, mignardizing, dandling, dalliance, toying, merry jesting, squeamish simpring, &c.; ***vezzoso***, bucksom, gamesome, coy, pert, squeamish; ***vescia***, a fysty fizzle.

Compare with the above the Arabic ***faiz***, flying, escaping; ***faz-gn, fiz-gn***, fear, flying in terror; ***fasa***, a slight wind from the belly; ***fasad***, violence, horror; ***fasw***, breaking wind gently. The Sanscrit has ***bhai, bhi, bishan***, fear, horror. Under ***fesse*** in Heraldry a Lat. ***fascia***, cingulum, scutum, Minsheu derives vel ab, Hebrew, ***phasa***, quod nates, pudenda, significat. In Sanscrit ***bhasad*** has a similar meaning. *Grimm's Deutsches Wort.* has ***fisel***, penis, virga, Bremen ***pesel***.

OCCURRENCE of FEAZE, or PHEEZE, in ENG. DICTIONARIES. It is absent from *Sherwood's Eng.-Fr. Dict.*, 1632. ***Feazing*** (Sea Term) the ravelling out of a cable or any great rope at the ends. *Phillips' World of Words*, 1678. Copied lit., in *Bailey's Dict.*, 1735. ***Feaze***, perhaps from the Sax., ***fax***, hair; to untwist the end of a rope, to reduce anything that has been twisted or woven to its first stamina, to beat, to whip with rods. *Ash's Dict.*, 1775. This last, Ash seems to have derived from *Skinner's Etymol. Ling., Angl.*, 1671, who says ***fease*** or ***feag*** is to lash, to beat with rods, from Ger., ***fegen***, to sweep, to cleanse, or from ***fricken***, to rub. Dr. Johnson gives the meanings of Phillips, (adding from ***faiser***, Fr.) and of Ash, and gives, moreover, 'to comb, to fleece, to curry.' *Ainsworth's Lat. Dict.*, ed., Morell, 4to., 1808, has to ***pheese*** or ***fease***, pecto, tondeo. *Webster*, 1848, has ***feese***, a race – not in use – Barret. (This rare and extinct meaning may be from the Bret. ***faeza***, to surpass, outstrip, vanquish, particularly in argument.) Also ***phease***, to comb; ***Feaze***, to untwist the ends of a rope. *Jamieson's Sc. Dict.* has ***feeze***, to twist, turn round, hang off and on, also to work into a passion. Both words occur in Richardson, but with Skinner's etymol. given below.

'***Fess***, terminus fœcialium a Fr. G. ***fesse***, idem signante. ***Fease***, flagellare, verges cœdere, parum deflexo sensu a Teut. ***fegen***, verrere, pugnare, vel ***fricken***, fricare, vel scabere ubi purit, item prurire.' *Skinner's Etymol., ffo.* 1671.

[***Fese***, Chaucero est fugare, ab. A.S. ***fesian***, idem notante *Lye*.] *Junius and Lye*, Oxford, 1743.

ILLUSTRATIONS IN ENGLISH LITERATURE.—

'And thereout came a rage and swiche a ***vise***,
That it made all the gates for to rise.' *Chaucer's Knight's Tale.*
'This Sarazins were so ***fesid*** that fled was Saladyn.' *R. de Brunne*, p. 192.
'She for awhile was well sore ***affesed***.' *Browne, Shepheard's Pipe, Eclogue I.*
'Ile ***pheeze*** you in faith.' *Shakspeare's Tam. of Shrew, Line 1.*

[In the older play of 1594, written or adapted by Shakespeare, the word occurs in line 4 '*Slie*. Tilly, vally, by crisee Tapster Ile ***fese*** you anon.']

'*Ag.* O no, you shall not goe.
Ajax. And a be proud with me, Ile ***phese*** his pride, let me go to him.
Id. Troil. and Cress., Act 2, Sc. 3.

Host. 'Thou'rt an emperor, Cæsar, keisar, and ***Pheezar,*** &c.'
Id. Merry Wives, Act I, Sc. 3.

'Italis longè disjungimur oris.'
We are touzed, and from Italy ***feased***,
'Ignavum, fucos, pecus a præsepibus arcent.'

Feaze away the drone bees.'

Stanyhurst's Translation of Virgil, 1583.

'O peerless you or els no one alive,
Your pride serves you to ***feaze*** them all alone.'

Partheniade apud Puttenham, p. 180.

Come will you quarrel? I'll ***feize*** you, sirrah.
'Marry, sweet love, e'en here, lie down; I'll ***feese*** thee.'

Beaumont and Fletcher, the Coxcomb, Act I., sc. 6.

'But Bishop Turbervil recovered some lost lands, which Bishop Voysey had ***vezed***; and particularly obtained of Queen Mary the restitution of the fair Manor of Crediton.' *Fuller's Worthies, Dorset* (a side note in the first ed., folio 1662, to ***vezed***, explains it 'driven away,' in the dialect of the West.)

DIALECTIC OCCURRENCE OF PHEEZE, FEAZE, &c. I. *West of Eng. Dial. Gloss.*, Miss Palmer, in her *Devon dial.*, has to ***veass*** away, to drive or frighten away, ***vease***, to thrust, squeeze; ***veaking***, fretful, peevish. Barnes, in his *Dorset dial.* has ***veath***, funk; ***veze***, to fidget about; ***fess***, fussy, meddling. *Jennings' Somerset Dial.*, to ***vaze,*** to move about a room or house so as to agitate the air. Ray in his *Proverbs*, ed. 1737, p. 269, has 'I'll ***vease*** thee,' (*i.e.* hunt, drive thee) as communicated by a Somersetshire man. *Cooper's Sussex dial.*, ***peeze***, to ooze out, as from a leaking cask, (this is the Wel., ***pyz***, a state of running out.) Halliwell, has the following *West of Eng.* terms:– ***Feage***, to whip or beat; ***feaze***, to harass, worry, tease, dawdle, loiter, ***feak***; a sharp twitch or pull; ***feize***, to drive away; ***pheeze***, to beat, chastise, humble; to ***phease***, to pay a person off for any injury; ***vaze***, to flutter about; ***veze***, to run up and down, Glouc.; also to drive away, to fly. [The common West Country phrase, '***pise***' (plague) take thee, is probably but a var. of ***fease; pize***, West of Eng., is fretful, peevish.] '***Veag***, a paroxysm of anger. He went off in such a ***veag***.' *Barnes' Dorset Dialect.*

II. In **EAST** and **NORTH ANGLIA**. In Pr. Pv., 1440, '***Fesyn***, idem quod ***feryn***, supra; ***feryn***, or make a-ferde; ***terreo, perterreo***.' For Forby, see ante. Grose has ***fessing***, forcing a thing on one, Essex. *Dickinson's Cumb. dial.* ***fizzer***, to punish, give pain, to put in a fix, (imported seemingly by its Irish settlers, the Ir., ***paisighim***, I torment, cause to suffer.) *Whitby dial.*, ***fezzon***, to work up to the pitch of fighting, to get to blows, (from Isl., ***fysa***, ante). N. Ang. and Sc., Jamieson has ***fash*** to tease, be weary of; ***fasheous***, meddlesome, inquisitive, (from O.F., ***fascher***, to displease, irk, disgust, molest, hurry, cloy, bring to a loathing. *Cotgr.*) ***Fasart***, coward, (from the Su.-Goth., ***fasa***, ante). Halliwell has ***feague***, to be perplexed, Linc. ***Feak***, to fidget, be restless, Yorks. A flutter, said of lovers' anxieties, Linc. (the Ger., ***feig***, faint-hearted.) To sneeze, Linc. ***Frawzy***, frisk, pettish, Linc. (the Wel., ***frawzawl***, full of motion.) ***Fese*** to frighten, make afraid. '***Fese*** the cat away.' *Urry*, p. 597.

'When he had etyn, and made hym at ese,
He thought Gye for to ***fese***.' *M.S. Cantab. ff ii, 38, f. 171. [Hal.]*

At this stage ***feage*** and ***feak***, which we have seen to be confounded by Skinner and Ash with ***Feaze***, and of which we have therefore raked together all dialectic occurrence, may as well be ***feased***, i.e., 'scared' out of our way. ***Feige*** occurs also in *Bailey's Dict.*, 1735, as 'to carp at'; and Ash in his Dict., 1775, gives as obsolete, '***feige***, to censure, carp at' (used by Gower). The deriv. of the two words are A.S., ***figan***, to be at enmity, A.S., ***feogan***, to persecute, hate; Ger.,

feige, (Anglice ***feak***) a blow; ***fegen***, vulg. to chastise, rebuke. *Jam. Sc. Dict.* has ***feyk***, restlessness, the fidgets; ***fyke,*** to vex, to dawdle about, make a fuss, (the Irish ***feicam***, to be in continual motion, to fidget).

Turn we next to the Commentators on the English Dramatists, when the word ***feize*** comes across their path.

Whalley's Notes to Ben Jonson, ed. 1811, has '***feize***, I'll drive you'; the word is common in our old authors, and as Mr. Upton adds, 'still used in the west of England.' *Dr. Grey.*

Gifford in his *Notes to Ben Jonson, Vol. IV*, 188, writes, 'This word does not mean to drive, but to beat, chastise, to humble, &c., in which sense (in the West of England) it may be heard every day.' This dictum of Gifford's, a Devonshire man, has been adopted by most of the later commentators, Collier, Singer, Knight, &c., until the recent publication of the *Cambridge* and *Globe Shakspeares*, whose editors falling back on Dr. Johnson, render in their glossaries ***pheeze***, to comb, fleece, curry. Dyce takes no notice of the word. Knight quotes Gifford, and also Johnson – 'To ***pheese*** or ***fease*** is to separate a twist into single threads.' He derived this from *Sir T. Smith's de Sermone Anglico,* 1568, who gives 'to ***feize***, in filâ deducere.'

Staunton, in his note *b* to *Taming of the Shrew*, disposes of ***pheeze*** in very summary fashion – 'This phrase has been much discussed, but never satisfactorily explained. It was equivalent exactly to our figurative saying – 'I'll tickle you', and had a meaning amorous or villainous, according to the circumstances under which it was uttered.'

The standard American ed. of Shakspeare, that by R. G. White, 12 vols., Boston, 1863, has the note:–'It is hardly necessary to remark "***pheese***" means "worry." Sly means to tell the Hostess he will pay her off.'

We close with a recent Eng. etymol. dictionary, that by Wedgewood, a work of extreme value to all present and future students of our language. He gives to ***fease, feize, pheeze*** two main senses: I. To whip, chastise, harass. *Halliwell*, and II. to ravel out the ends of a rope. Deriv. I. Fr., ***fesser***, to whip; Prov. Dan., ***fikke***; Ger., ***fitzen***; Dut., ***veselen***, to whip a child; Dan., ***fijcken***. *Kilian*. Prov. Eng., ***feak***, a sharp twitch; Swiss, ***fausen, fitzen***, to switch; ***fitzer***, rods for children; ***fiseln***, to switch to and fro. *Stalder*. II. Bav., ***fiseln***, to fiddle or twiddle with the fingers. *Schmeller*. Pl. Dut., ***fisseln***, to ravel out threads; ***fiss, fissle***, a thread, fibre. *Danneil*. Swiss, ***fisel***, loose threads; Dut., ***vese, vesel***, fibres, threads; Prov. Eng., ***fassings***, any hanging fibres of roots. *Halliwell*. '***Fasylle*** of a cloth, fractillus.' *Pr. Pv.* Ger., ***fasel,*** to ravel. To ***fease***, also to incite, from O.N., ***fysa***, to instigate.

In the latest Dictionary of the English language, and the one apparently destined to supersede in general acceptance all its predecessors, that of the American Worcester, the word is thus given:–

FEAZE. (Fr., ***fesser***) 1. To untwist as the end of a rope. *Johnson*. 2. To beat, to whip with rods. *Ainsworth*. **PHEESE.** 1. To comb, to fleece, to curry. *Johnson*. 2. To beat, to chastise, to humble. ***Wright.*** **PHEESE,** a fit of fretfulness, peevishness [colloquial and vulgar, U.S.]

A collation of the foregoing definitions, derivations, and illustrations may, to borrow Fuller's humorous vein, render ***feasible*** an attempt to ***feaze***, (in its sense of unravel) the Protean phases of this curious word, which has hitherto eluded the firm grasp of the philologist.

I. ***Feaze***, has the clear, distinctive, East Anglian dialectic senses, given by Forby, possibly originally Keltic, but more immediately borrowed from the Scandinavian and Frisic settlers. Almost obsolete in England, the word is still flourishing in a soil where so many other East Anglicisms have taken deep root, amongst our trans-Atlantic kindred. Bartlett in his *Dict. of Americanisms* has the following illustrations of the word in its irritable, apprehensive senses, and he gives no others:–

FEEZE. 'To be in a ***feeze***,' is to be in a state of excitement.

'Larcenie is the felonious taking away of another man's personal goods without his knowledge or insight, yet without making any assault upon his person or putting him into a ***fease***.' *Code of Laws of Rhode Island*, 1647.

'Some years ago, we remember, New York was in its annual ***feeze*** about mad dogs.' *N.Y. Commercial Advertiser*, Oct. 16, 1848.

'When a man's in a ***feeze***, there's no more sleep that hitch.' *Sam Slick in England, ch. 2.*

II. It had a Wessex dialectic sense of 'scaring away,' which was also widely diffused in the Anglian districts. But it is by no means clear that this involved the additional meanings of 'to beat, humble, chastise.' None of the West of England glossarists, as we have seen above, either give or imply these senses. Nor do any of our old writers who employ the term, suit the action to the word. The old N. Ang. chronicler, Robert de Brunne, says expressly that 'thise Sarazins were so ***fesid*** that fled was Saladin.' Fear is the only sense given by the E. Ang. compiler of the *Pr. Pv.* (we may note here that the word does not appear in Hearne's index to the West of Eng. chronicler, Robert of Gloucester). With this sense tallies the old Scottish word, ***fasart***, cowardly. In this sense Chaucer uses it. Scare is the only sense in ***affezed***, as employed by Browne, a Devonshire man, and by Stanihurst, a writer also from the west. Shakspeare only places the word in the mouths of the pot-valiant tinker, Christopher Sly; of the vain-glorious boaster, Ajax, the butt of Ulysses, Nestor and the other Grecian chiefs; and of that good fellow, mine Host of the Garter, in a 'huff-cap' scene with bully Hercules Falstaff, and his swash-buckler followers, Nym and Pistol. In all three instances there is a broad burlesque latent in Shakspeare's employment of the term, a running riot in those quibbling conceits to which our great poet was addicted.

What then was the sense in which ***feaze*** or ***pheese*** was used by the Elizabethan dramatists, whose hastily dashed off pages received so freely, and now yield back so vivid a reflex of the foreign influences, which in that era flooded the atmosphere of English literature and society? We conceive in that of *double entendre*, that beneath the Wessex ***feaze*** lurked but half concealed either the old French '***vezée***' of Brantôme and Rabelais, or uttered with a very slightly modified inflection of voice, broader allusions, such as – the '***fessé***,' 'breech-jerked, scutched and whipt' of that coarse but racy dictionary of Cotgrave, which has made so many covert allusions of the play wrights of that age intelligible to ours. By the 'civet-wits, the travelled gallants and sweet bloods,' who thronged the pit and tiring rooms, or sat upon the stage 'prompting us aloud,' growls out surly Ben, such new-minted phrases, 'choice remnants of French and Italian' would be eagerly affected as of 'the most received and gentle fashion.' 'Pick me out more of these play-particles,' cries out in ecstasy Amorphus in *Cynthia's Revels*, 'and (as occasion shall salute you) embroider or damask your discourse with them, persuade your soul, it would most judiciously commend you.'

The currency of the word upon our stage was but of brief duration. Like the dreary, far-fetched puns of modern burlesque, as the newly caught up allusions it enwrapped grew stale, it wore out. Had, however, the word ***fease***, uttered in the ears of a London audience, ever embodied an understood, legitimate, and recognised sense of 'to beat, chastise, and humble,' it is hard to see why a term describing menace, or assault and battery, 'stage business' of such incessant occurrence, alike in tragedy, comedy, and farce, deadly rapier fence, terrific broad-sword combat, or oak towelling should have been so abruptly and peremptorily discarded.

III. Of ***fease*** in its sense of to unravel, it is note-worthy that it has never found its way into our provincial glossaries, merely enjoying a traditional and galvanised existence in the pages of our dictionaries, each copying its predecessor. There are copious articles under ***filz*** and ***filzen*** in *Grimm's Deutsches Worterbuch*, which shew the terms to be of very early Teut. usage.

In conclusion, it is somewhat singular that the vitality of a word of such varied and distinct meanings, inheriting so many vigorous strains of etymological blood, should have become so feeble and attenuated in the English language. Under every heading given above, it seems to be nearly obsolete.

PHIZ-GIG. A wizened old woman, tricked out, 'like an old ewe dressed lamb-fashion.'

PICK CHEESE. The titmouse.

PICKLE. To glean a field a second time.

Sc., ***pickle***, to pick up as a fowl, from Sw. ***picka-ell***; Dut., ***pikken***, to peck. ***Pickle***, Sc., is also a grain of corn. ***Pedgel***, Northampts. dial. is to pick and eat corn in the fields, ***picking***, re-gleaning a field.

Pickling, in its sense of curing herrings, Mr. Wedgewood remarks, has the radical meaning of gutting or cleaning of the fish, with which the operation begins. The *Pr. Pv.* has '***pykyd***, purged fro filthe or other thynge grevows, ***pykyn*** or clensyn, or cullyn owte the on-clene.' A.S., ***pyc-an***, to pick out. In the same way to ***cure*** fish is from Fr. ***ecurer***, to scour, cleanse.

PICKLIN. Coarse linen used for seed bags, aprons, &c., from refuse pickings of flax.

PIE. The barrow or mound raised over pitted potatoes to protect from frost. In Suff. also called a ***clam***. In Chesh. a ***hog***.

PIE-WIPE. The pee-wit or lapwing. In Sc., ***pee-wipe*** and ***pease-weep***, *vide* a memorable passage in Christopher North. Swed., ***vipa***; O. Fr., ***dixhuict***, lapwing. *Cotgr.* Ger., ***kiebitz***; Dut., ***kiewit***.

PIGGLE, PINGLE. To be dainty over one's food, turning it over and over as a pig does with its snout. To boggle over. Cumb., ***pyfle***, to pick delicately. Su. Goth., ***pick-a***; Isl., ***pikka***, to strike lightly, peck at.

Pingle, Sc., to labour assiduously without making progress. Northampts., to root up potatoes by the hand; Dan., ***punge***, to fork out; Sc., ***pike***, to cull, select, poke cautiously with the fingers; Wel., ***pigiad***, a culling; A.S., ***pycan***, to peck.

'Judging all to be clownes which be not courtiers, and all to be ***pinglers*** that be not coursers.' *Lyly's Euphues*.

'He filleth his mouth well, and is no ***pingler*** at his meate.' *Topsell's Beasts*, 1607. *(Halliwell.)*

PIGHTLE, PICLE. A small angular enclosure of land.

Apparently from its ***piked*** or pointed shape, of which the Wel. root is ***pig***. A.S., ***pycan***. Used in Mid Anglia. N. Ang., ***pingle***.

Mr. Spurdens derives from the old law Latin phrase ***pictellum***, the root being the It., ***piccolo***, little. ***Pichel*** is given in *Ducange*, as a measure of land, occurring in *Charta Lusitan*, A.D., 1313. ***Pichea***, a Norman measure of land, ***bichetus*** apud Burgundos.

PIKE-OFF. Begone, move off. Lanc., ***pick***, to push sharply; Wel., ***pigaw***, to prick, sting.

Isl., ***pikka***, to rap; Sw., ***picka***, to beat. N. Ang., ***pouk***, to strike, push.

'Nay, quod the Byshop, I defy the and thy fesauntys also, and wrech as thou art, ***pyke*** the out of my howse.' *Merie Tales of Skelton.*

'Ye, but I bade hym ***pyke*** out of the gate,
By Goddes body, so dyd I.' *Skelton.*

PILCH. A flannel wrapper for a child, a skin coat, saddle cover. A.S., ***pylce***, a skin or fur garment; Isl., ***pilz***, a shirt. '***Pylche***, pellicium.' *Pr. Pv.*

'A carman in a lether ***pilche*** that had whipt out a thousand pound out of his horse-taile.' *Nashe's Pierce Penilesse.*

PILGER. A fish spear. O. Fr., ***pille***, a javelin or dart, steel-headed.

It., ***pigliare***, to catch, take hold of; Dan., ***pigge***, a pike; Wel., ***pill***, a shaft, stake; the Gael. has ***spealg***, to split, break with violence, ***spealgair***, one who splinters; ***tilg***, to cast, throw; Ger., ***pfeil***, an arrow; Sw. and Dan., ***pil***, dart, shaft; Isl., ***pill, pilar***.

PIN-BASKET. The youngest child in a family. Sc., ***pock-shakings***.

PIN-FEATHERS. The incipient feathers before the birds are fledged, the roots. Fr., ***penne***, a quill; Wel. and Bret. ***pen***, a beginning. 'He's only ***pen-feathered,'*** *i.e.* shabby. Fris., ***pinnig***, slim, weak, lank.

'A Metaphor (saith Aretius) taken from young birds, which offering to fly before the time, being but ***pin-feathered*** and not well fledged, fall down to the ground.' *Rogers' Rich Fool.*

'The Irish Hobbie is a pretty fine horse, having a good head and bodie, indifferently well proportioned, saving that many of them be slender and ***pin-buttocked***.' *Blundeville's (a Norfolk Squire) Horsemanship*, 1558.

PIN-PATCHES. ***Pin-paunches***, the common periwinkle, shell-fish.

'By some called ***pin-patches***, because the pin meat thereof is taken out with a pin or needle.' *Sir T. Browne.*

PIPPERIDGE. The barberry tree. Fr., ***pepin***, a pip and ***rouge*** red.

PITTER. To grieve piteously. '***Pittering*** and pining.' To make a low shrill noise. O. Fr., ***pituitaire***, snivelling.

'And when his ***pittering*** streames are lowe and thin.' *R. Greene.*

PLANCHER, PLANSHARD. A boarded floor. Fr., ***plancher***.

'Ye holys yat ben made for hand gunnys ben scarse kne hey fro ye ***plawncher***.' *Paston Letters.*

'Pursuing my journey I saw a good way before me a large building, that look't (methought) like some enchanted Castle, or the picture of ill-luck. It was all ruinous, the chimneys down, the ***planchers*** all to pieces, only the bars of the windows standing. *L'Estrange's Quevedo.*

PLATE. The mould-board of a plough, Norfolk. Ger. ***platt***.

PLASH. I. A shallow pool. II. To cut down an old and stubby quick fence, intertwining the lower branches. N. Ang., ***pleach***, to bind a hedge. III. To splash; Whitby, ***plosh***.

I. '***Plasche*** or ***flasche***, where reyne watyr stondythe.' *Pr. Pv.* Dut., ***plas*** or ***plasch***, a puddle, a hole full of standing water. Hence ***plashet*** in the Essex Marshes, Plaistow, Pleshey, &c. *Way.* ***Ploshet***, a water meadow, Devon. Dut., ***vlacke***, a lagoon; ***flaque***, a puddle.

'If thee drynks the halfe, thee shalt fynde it no scoff.
Of terryble deathe thee wylt stacker in the ***plashes***.' *Bp. Bale's King Johan.*
When making for the brook the falconer doth espy
One river ***plash*** or mere where store of fowl doth lie,' *Drayton.*

II. Fr., ***plesser***, to plash or plait young branches. *Cotgr.* III. Sw., ***plaska***.

'Cut vines and osiers, ***Plash*** hedge of enclosure.' *Tusser.*

'One Cerdicus, a ***plashing*** Saxon, that had revelled here and there with his battle-axe.' *Nashe's Lenten Stuff.*

'***Plesh, plush***, to cut the larger sticks or ***plashers*** of a quickset hedge, nearly but not quite off, so that the sap may come up over the cut and throw out perpendicular shoots.' *Barnes' Dorset Dial.*

PLAW. To parboil; a boiling or bubbling up.

Pr. Pv., '***plaw*** or ***plawynge***, bullicio' a boiling; ***plawn***, as pottys, bullio, ferveo. Ray, in his *S. and East County words*, has 'To ***play***, spoken of a pot, kettle, or other vessel full of liquor, i.e., to boil, ***playing*** hot, boiling hot.' The Wel. has ***pludaw***, to make soft, tender; the Fl., ***blaes***, a bubbling, blistering, boiling; ***plooyen***, to wrinkle, curl up; Dut., ***blaas***, bubbles.

PLENNY. To complain fretfully, said of sick children. N. Ang., ***plean***, ***pleenin***. ***Pleany-pye***, a prating gossip. Fr., ***plaindre***.

PLOUNCE. To plunge with a loud noise. N. Ang., ***plodge***; Dut., ***plotsen***, to plunge; Sw., ***plumsa***; Ger., ***plätsen***. See ***pash***.

PLOW-JOGGER. A common term applied to the Norfolk ploughmen.

'And in his catechising and preaching calls his parishioners ***plow joggers***, bawling doggs, weaverly Jacks, and church robbers (the Parson of Hepworth, Suffolk).' *White's Century of Scandalous Priests*, 1643.

'At the rate of this thick-skull'd blunder-head, every ***plow jobber*** shall take upon him to read upon Divinity, law, and politiques, as well as physick.' *L'Estrange's Æsop.*

PLUGGY. Short, thick, and sturdy.

Gael., ***plub*** and ***pluc***, a bump, knot, bunch. Hence N. Ang., ***plooky***, pimpled. Dut., ***plukk*** and ***plug***. A ***plonker,*** aught unusually thick, Leeds dial.

PLUMPANDIKALLA. Perpendicular.

PLUNKY. Thick, short, and heavy. Gael., ***pocanta***, squat, thick; Ger., ***plumpheit***, unwieldy, awkward.

POD. A fat protuberant belly. 'I'm a gitten kienda ***poddy***.' ***Podgel*** is dimin. of ***pod*** in Suff., where a man is said to run to ***pod***.

Poddit, plump, ***pud***, the belly, ***pudgetty***, fat-bellied, Sc.; ***pook***, the belly, Somerset; ***pod***, the belly of a cart, Sussex.

Wel., ***bog***, a swelling, rising up; Gael., ***bronn.*** Dan., ***pude***, a pillow.

'By God ye be a praty ***pode***.
And I love you an hole cart lode,
Gup, Cristian Clowte, gup Jak of the Vale!
With Manerly Margery, mylk and ale!' *Skelton.*

PODGE. To stir and mix together – a hodge-podge. ***Podge***, confusion, Perths. Fr., ***pocher***, to thrust, dig about with the fingers. *Cotgr.*

'And with their fingers ***poched*** out his eyes.' *Du Bartas.*

'To ***poche*** ground, to tread it when wet: gate-ways where cattle stand in winter, are said to be ***poched***.' *Sir G. C. Lewis' Heref. Dial.*

'To ***poach***, to tread soft ground or snow, as cattle leaving deep tracks.' *Bartlett's Americanisms.*

POGRIM. A fanatic, canter, affecting over much sanctimony.

Fogram is an old cant word for the same. Fr., ***foigner***, to dissemble. The Dan. has ***frog***, a dolt, booby, our ***fogy***.

POIT. An intens. of pert. Gael. has ***bead***, forward, impudent.

POKE. A bag, sack, pouch, Isl., ***poki***; A.S., ***pocca***; Dut., ***poke***.

'Found in the egg-***poke*** or lower part of the matrix.' *Sir T. Browne.*

POKE-CART, POKER. A miller's cart; ***poke-day***, that on which labourers receive their allowance of corn.

POKE-SHAKKENS. The youngest pig of a litter. ***Pokey***, very small.

Gael., ***beag***, little; Wel., ***bycan***, diminutive; ***pokey***, N. Ang., saucy, inquisitive, from Gael., ***puichean***, a little impudent fellow.

'Recd. of Thoms. Hewer for lxj of ***poke*** lambis xxxv*s.* vij*d.*' *L'Estrange's Household Accounts.*

'Item pd for a ***poke*** of canvass to put in all the seed stuffe, iiij*d.*' *Id.*

POLLAIN, PULLEN. Applied in E.A. to poultry in general, says Moor. ***Poller***, a hen roost.

Sw., ***pulla***; Fr., ***poule***, a hen; ***poulaille***, poultry.

'The sleihty fox small ***polayl*** doth opprese.' *Lydgate.*

'Where ***pullen*** use nightly to perch in the yard.' *Tusser.*

'A pearle to one that findes it is both house and ground, sheep, cattell, ***pullen*** and all.' *D. Rogers' Naaman.*

'Shall the great Housekeeper of the world provide for all his ***pullen*** and poultry in the yard; and is it likely that he will suffer his servants and children that are within doors in the meantime to starve? Who can imagine it?' *N. Rogers' Rich Fool.*

POLLENGERS, POLLENS. Pollard trees. Isl., ***kollr***; Dut., ***pol***, head, top.

POLLIWIGGLE, PURWIGGY, the tadpole, a little frog; also called from their shape pot-ladles. N. Ang., ***pow-head***; Sc., ***podle***; Northampts., ***pollard.*** Isl., ***pöddu***, frog; Wel., ***broga***, frog; Fris., ***podd***; ***Pol***, in A.S. and Gael., is marsh, pool; A.S., ***wickga***, worm – pool-worm – frog. ***Pol*** or ***poly*** is the second element in ***tad-pole***. It occurs also in the old legendary '***Rowly-Poly.***' ***Tad*** is A.S. toad; Gael., ***poll-cean***, tad-pole; A.S., ***pol-***

yke, marsh-frog.

'In that black and round substance, in a few day began to dilate and grow longer, after awhile the head, the eyes, the tail to be discernible, and at last to become that which the ancients called *gyrinus,* we a ***porwigle*** or tadpole.' *Sir T. Browne.*

POLT. A hard driving blow. Manx, ***polt***, a blow, stroke.

Gael., ***buail,*** to strike; Ir., ***pall-tog***, a thump, blow; Fr., ***poulser***, to jostle, jolt, thrust; Sw., ***bulta***, to beat; Old Eng., ***pulte***, to push. The Lat. has cata-***pult***, from ***pulsare***.

POPLER, POPELER. '***Popelere***, byrd or schovelerd' (schoveler-duck, *Anas clypeata, Lin.*) *Pr. Pv.* The shoveler though widely distributed is by no means common in any part of England; a few, however, are known to breed regularly in Norfolk.

Amyot the antiquary, editor of the 'Inventory of Sir John Fastolfe's Effects,' seems to have been perplexed by the following entry –

'Item ij clothes portrayed full of ***popelers***.' He interpreted it to be ***poplar*** trees.

In the entries of provisions of ***gyste*** or in store, which appear in the *L'Estrange Household Accounts of 1533*, amongst pigeons, spowys, rabbetts, pygges, &c., occurs – 'Item iij ***popelers*** of store.'

POPPLE. To tumble about with a quick motion, as dumplings play about when the pot boils briskly. Ger., ***poppelen***, to bubble; ***popeln***, to play.

Possibly provides derivation for the above, ***Popler***.

POSE. A cold in the head, applied commonly to horses. A.S., ***ge-pose***. '***Pose*** or sneke, catarrus.' *Pr. Pv.* Corn., ***pâz,*** a cough; Wel., ***pas***.

'Snevelyng in her nose, As though she had the ***pose***.' *Skelton.*

POT-DAYS. It was the custom formerly, even among very substantial farmers, to cook but three days a week, Sunday being one; on these, which were called ***pot-days***, visitors were received. *Wright's Prov. Dict.*

POTTENS. Crutches. ***Pattens***, stilts, from Fr. ***patin***. '***Potent*** or crotche.' *Pr. Pv.*

Fr., ***potence***, a gibbet, also a crutch for a lame man. *Cotgr.*

POULTER-KNOTS. ***Pull-tow-knots***, the knotty parts of cord.

PRALING. Tying a bladder with pease, or a tin kettle to a dog's tail, and then chivvying him off.

Fris., ***praal, prâl***, a loud clamour, report, scream.

PRESBYTERIAN TRICK. A dishonest bargain, a knavish turn, Essex.

PREY. The herd of cattle driven from the common pasture and impounded. A fine is levied on those belonging to a neighbouring hamlets to redeem them. *Wright's Prov. Dict.*

Wel., ***praidd***; Corn. ***praed***, a flock or herd, booty of cattle.

PRIG, PRIGSTER. Pert, coxcomb; ***priggish***, conceited; from Dut. ***priiken,*** dare se spectandum, says Richardson.

Dan., ***pragt***, parade, show; Sw., ***pryda***, to adorn, set off, ***prydlig***, elegant, ***prœgtig***, splendid, ***prœg***, balderdash, gammon.

For deriv. of ***prig***, to steal, see under ***proctor*** and ***prog***.

Cheatly. 'Thou shalt not see the ***Prigg***, thy brother, till thou shalt out jingle him.' *Shadwell's Squire of Alsatia.*

PRIM. Very small smelts. Smelt fry, so called at Lynn.

Probably derived metaphorically from the Dan. and Su. Goth., ***prein***; Isl., ***prionn***, any sharp point, a needle, &c.; Fris., ***prieme***, a stickle-back, a point.

'***Spirinches*** or smelt, in great plenty about Lynn; but where they have also a small fish, called a ***priame***, answering in taste and shape a smelt, and perhaps are but the younger sort thereof'. *Sir T. Browne.*

PRITCH. A sharp pointed iron instrument. A ***fold-pritch*** is for making holes to receive the toes of hurdles. An ***eel-pritch***, an eel-spear. A.S., ***pricean***, to prick; also the sensation of throbbing in a sore. 'Ta boolk, an ta itch and ta ***pritch***,' said of the irritation of a push or boil.

'The least word uttered awry, the least conceit taken or ***pritch***, the breaking in of a cow into their grounds, yea, sheep or pigs is enough to make suits, and they will be revenged.' *Rogers' Naaman the Syrian.*

'Christians in generall will professe self-denial, yet take ***pritches***, discontents.' *Id.*

PROCTOR. To hector, swagger, or bully. Lat., ***procurator***.

From the ***proctors*** or sturdy beggars allowed by 1 Ed. VI. to travel round the country, gathering alms for the sick and lame in hospitals, &c. They became so great a nuisance as to render it necessary to put them down by stat. 39 Eliz., c. 4., which makes them rogues and vagabonds. *Forby.*

PROG. To pry or poke into holes and corners. Abr. of ***proctor***.

'***Prokkyn*** or ***styfly askyn***. ***Procor***.' *Pr. Pv.* Isl., ***prokka***, to scrape; Dan., ***prakkeri***, beggary; Sw., ***prackere***; Dut., ***prakker***, a beggar, vagabond; Sc., ***prig***, to importune, haggle, cheapen.

PROG. A curved spike or prog put forward to seize aught. N. Ang., ***prod***.

Isl., ***brydda***; Dan., ***brodde***, to stab, prick, skewer; Wel., ***proc***, a thrust; Gael., ***brog***, to goad; Ir., ***prioca***, a goad; Northampts., ***proggle***.

Also a cant term for food – 'I get my ***prog*** found.'

PUCKETS. Caterpillar nests, Suffolk. Wel., ***bwcai, bwceiod***, a maggot.

PUDDER. Pother, bother, fuss, worry. Dan., ***puddre***, to powder; Sw., ***puder***; Dut., ***poeder***.

Wedgewood derives from ***puddle*** in the sense of troubled water mixed with dirt, preventing one from seeing through. Is it not rather a sense of clouds of dust smothering and choaking alike the nostrils, throat and vision?

'Oh, yes, those were his own, this is God's; those he made no bones of, but this was that which he had made all this ***pudder***.' *D. Rogers' Naaman.*

'What a ***pudder*** have those Estonists and Pointers (as they call them) made in Norfolke of late.' *Id.*

'So long as he who has but a teeming brain, may have leave to lay his eggs in his own nest, which is built beyond the reach of every man's ***puddering*** pole, why should the ears of all the neighbourhood be dinn'd and grated with the cackle, as if the whole world besides were all weasils and polecats, vermine and lurchers?' *Fairfax.*

'In the sermons of Barrow, who certainly intended to write an elevated style, and did not seek familiar, still less vulgar expressions, we constantly meet such terms as to rate, to snub, to gull, to ***pudder***, dumpish, and the like, which we may confidently affirm were not vulgar when he used them.' *Archbp. Trench's English, Past and Present.*

PUDDING. A stuffed cushion placed round a child's forehead when first trusted to walk alone. Fr., ***boudin.*** Dan. has ***bude***, pillow.

Examples may be seen in Rubens' charming pictures of his children.

PUDDING-PYE-DOLL. The dish called toad in the hole, meat boiled or baked in a crust.

PUGGLE. To stir the fire, Essex. Ger., ***puken***, to poke; Dan., ***pukke***, to stamp; Lat., ***pugio***, a dagger.

PUGGY. I. Thick, warm weather. II. Muggy weather preceding a tempest. ***Puggy*** hands, dirty, clammy. I. Pl. Dut., ***puddig***, thick, and see ***Podge***. II. Dan., ***pukke***, to threaten.

PULK. A small pool, a muddy pond; the sea-water lakelets left on the beach by the ebbing tide. A.S., ***pul***; Gael., ***pollag***, a little pool; Wel., ***plwca***; Isl., ***pollr***. '***Polke*** of watyr, vortex.' *Pr. Pv.*

'It is easy for a woman to go to a pond or ***pulke*** standing near her door, (though the water be not so good) rather than to go to a fountain of living water further off.' *Rogers' Naaman the Syrian.*

Congers ** in frosty weather left in ***pulks*** and plashes upon the ebb of the sea. *Sir T. Browne.*

PULKY. Thick, fat, chubby, short. Dan., ***pludsfed***, chubby. Gael., ***pollach***, lumpish.

PULTHY. Dirty, muddy. Gael., ***poll***, mire; Wel., ***bawlydd***, filthy.

PUMMACE. The mass of apples mashed under a stone roller, before placing between layers of straw on the cyder press. Fr., ***pommé***, cyder.

Pummy, the dry substance of apples, after the cider is expressed. Dorset.

PUNDER. To be on an exact equipoise. ***Pundle-tree***, the cross-bar to which horses are fastened to draw ploughs or harrows. Isl., ***pundari***; A.S., ***pundern***, a balance. '***Punder***, librilla.' *Pr. Pv.* Sw., ***pyndare***, steelyard.

Punder, a cross-bar attached to cart shafts, to keep it when loaded horizontal. To unload, the word is given '***unpunder***,' when the bar is withdrawn and the cart falls backwards. ***Pundle-tree***, the cross bar to which horses are attached to draw ploughs or harrows.

PUNGLED, PINGLED. Shrivelled as wheat from mildew, heat, &c.

In the sense of pricked, collapsed. Lat., ***pungere***. See under ***piggle***.

PUR, PROTER. A poker. '***Pur*** the fire.' N. Ang. ***por***. Sc., a ***purring*** iron; Gr., ***pur***, fire; Dan., ***purre***; Fris., ***porre***, to poke or stir up the fire; Dut., ***porren***.

PURDY. Surly, ill-humoured, self-important. 'A fare so big and so ***purdy*** tha's no speaken tew em.'

Dan., ***pur***, crisp, ruffled, curled up; Scot., ***pirlie***, crisp; '***pirlie*** fellow,' one who is very difficult to please; Wel., ***pyr***, a crest. '***Pyry***, or storme.' *Pr. Pv.*

PUSH. A boil, swelling, inflammation.

Lat., ***pustula***; Dan., ***puse***, to swell up; Wel., ***pws***, that is expelled.

'But at length, in the place where the sore had been, which had dispersed, there arose a sort of ***push*** like what boys sometimes have. It had a black head, and was so angry that looking upon it almost hurt it.' *North's Lives, iii.* 57.

PUSSLE, PUZZLE. A very dirty drab, a filthy slut.

Fr. ***pucelle***; Grisons, ***purscella***, a damsel; It., ***puzza***, stink; ***puzzola***, polecat; or rather from the Wel., ***bawzyn***, a dirty, nasty creature; from ***bawaiz***, the probable root of the Lanc., ***pousement***; Corn. Brit., ***pwyo***, refuse.

PUTS. Mole-warps or hills. Wel., ***pwtiaw***, to push forth.

PUTTOCK. A kite, a cormorant, ravenous fellow. Lat., ***buteo***; Wel., ***barcut***. '***Puttok***, bryd, milvus.' *Pr. Pv.*

'A ***puttocke*** set on a pearch, fast by a falcon's side.' *Gascoigne.*

'Such ravening ***puttocks*** for victuals so trim.' *Tusser.*

'The hen clocketh her chickens, I would have clocked and called them by my preaching, the hen shieldeth them and fighteth for them against the ***puttock***.' *Nashe's Christ's Tears.*

PUY. A pew, the front of an edifice.

Its proper form from the Dut. ***puye***, a pulpit, reading desk, or praying-***puye***, (hence our Eng. ***pews***, copied from the Dutch,) the place at Town-halls whence proclamations are read. Lat., ***podium***, a balcony; O. Fr., ***puy,*** an elevation; ***pue***-fellow, a school comrade at the same desk. Fl., ***puy***, the lower part of a front.

'He hired a desperate knave to laye stones of great wayghte vpon the roufe beames of the temple, ryght over his prayenge ***pewe***, and to lete them fall upon hym to hys vtter destruccyon'. *Bale's Eng. Votaries, p. II.*

'What carking care goeth with riches! A poore cobler very merry in his song, while poore, having a bag of money cast into his ***puy***, ceased to sing. At last he that threw it him in came and askt him why he was so sad all on the sudden? He suspecting who it was, threw him back his bagge, and bid him take it, for he could never bee merry with it.' *D. Rogers' Naaman.*

Q

QUACKLE, QUAGGLE. To suffocate or choke. Dan., ***qværk***, throat. ***Querkened***, suffocated. Craven. ***Quocken'd***, Northamp. ***Querking***, grunting. Exmoor. Dut., ***quaaken***, to croak.

'He yoxeth, and he speketh thurgh the nose,
As he were on the ***quakke***, or on the pose.' *Chaucer's Norfolk Reve's Tale.*

QUADDLE, QUODDLE. To coddle, to boil gently. Sw., ***quabblig***, squeamish.

QUADDY. Very broad, short and thick in person. Ger., ***quader***, broad, square-hewn, ***quab***, squab.

QUAIL. I. To curdle, said of milk, custards, &c. II. To ail.

I. Ger., ***quark***, curds; Dan., ***quarre***, crusting of small pieces of ice on water; It., ***quagliare***, and Fr. ***cailler***, to curdle. II. N. Ang., ***quail***, to sicken, faint, to ***queal*** away, to die away, Devon; Ger. ***quelen***, to languish; ***qual***, pain; Dut., ***quaal***, amiss, gone wrong; Dan., ***qvæle***, to choke; also to torment.

'They yelleden as fendes don in helle;
The dokes crieden as men wold hem ***quelle***.' *Chaucer's Nonnes' Tale.*

'Then, I say, you shall be sicke at the stomacke of all these, and vomit your sweet morsels, and all your ***quailes*** and objects of sufficiency shall come out at your nostrills, yea, vanish before the sufficiency of Christ.' *D. Rogers' Naaman.*

QUAIRE. A quire of paper. Old Fr., ***cayer***. Isl., ***kver***, a little book.

QUAVERY-MAVERY. Undecided, hesitating. '***Quavyn***, as myre, tremo.' *Pr. Pv.* Quagmire in O.E. is ***quavemire.***

'Somme peple calle an earthe-***quave***, by cause they fele ther the meve and ***quave*** vnder their feet.' *Caxton's Mirrour of the World.*

'Some loke strawry, Some ***cawry mawry***.' *Skelton.*

'But it was a great deepe marrish or ***quavemyre***.' *North's Plutarch, 411.*

QUEACH or **SQUEACH.** A rough, bushy plot left untilled, full of ***quicks***, shrubs or brambles. ***Queachy***, wet, boggy. A.S. ***cuacian***.

Ger., ***queck***; Dan., ***quik***; and ***quas***, brushwood; Dut., ***queek***.

'Which in flat Holland lurk among the ***queachy*** plashes.' *Drayton's Polyolbion.*

QUEEZEN, QUIZZLE. To smother or choke. Dan., ***quœle***; Sw., ***quäfia***, to choke; Prov. Dan. ***quase***, to smother with mud. '***Quellyn*** or ***querkyn***, suffoco' *Pr. Pv.* Fris., ***querdzed***, choked. ***Quisey***, confounded, N. Ang. L. Ger., ***quetsen***, to shake violently.

'The spirable odour and pestilent steam ascending from it put him out of his bias of congruity, and as true as the truest Latin of Priscian would have ***queazened*** him.' *Nashe's Lenten Stuff.*

QUICKLINGS. Young insects.

QUINNY. Not quite, not just yet.

QUONT. A pole to push a boat or barge forwards, used by the wherrymen in the inland navigation. Lat., ***contus***.

R

RAB. A wooden beater to bray the ingredients of mortar.

Fr., ***rabat***, the staffe wherwith plaisterers beat their mortar. *Cotgr.*

RACK. A rut, the channel made by a cart-wheel. Isl., ***rak***, furrow, streak; ***reika***, to roam, stroll. Dut. ***rakje***, part of the road; Gael., ***rathad***, a road.

Dan., ***rat***, a wheel, whence Sw., ***ratta***, a path; Ger., ***rutteln***, jolting of a vehicle. ***Rack***, in Mid. Ang. and Wessex dial., a narrow path in woods for rabbit shooting. ***Rake***, Cumb., a mountain track across a steep; to follow in line, as sheep do. ***Rack-hurry***, the track or rail for unloading coals at a wharf, N. Ang. ***Rake***, a streak, Craven. ***Rack-cutting***, trimming the underwood in forest bye-paths, Northampts. A sheep-***raik*** or walk, a cattle ***raik***, Scot. ***Een rak wegs***, part of the way, Dut. ***Raik***, the direction the clouds are driven by the wind. Ettr. Forest.

RACK. Driving mist. Craven, ***rag***; A.S., ***reac***; Isl., ***hregg***, vapour. Also A.S., ***racu***; Isl., ***rekia***, rain, damp. See ***roke*** and ***rafty***. ***Rag-ryme***, hoar frost, Linc.

'As Phebas doeth, at mydday in the southe,
Whan every *rak*, and every cloudy sky
Is voide clene.' *Lydgate.*

RACK. Weeds, refuse, sea-weed flung ashore.

Sw. ***Vrak***; Dan. ***Vrag***, wreck, refuse; Dut. ***rak***, water-weeds. Isl., ***hraki***, vomit.

RACKLE. I. Rash, hasty. II. Noisy talk.

Rackle, rude and disorderly, N. Ang.; ***rackle-deed***, loose conduct, Cumb.;

rachlin, hare-brained; ***rackel***, rash, Sc.; Isl., ***rakkliga***, quick, bold. II. Gael., ***racail***, noise like that of geese and ducks; Fr., ***raclure***, a rasping, grating; Su.-Goth., ***racla***; Ger., ***rockeln***.

'And then to wyving be thou nat ***racle***.' *Lydgate.*

'He came in at the chrych dore, as the dyrge was doo,
Rynnyng, roryng, wythe hys ***rakyls***, as devilles semyd to doo.' *Lydgate.*

'The ***rakell*** life, that longs to love's disport.' *Surrey.*

RACKS. A kitchen fire-place, Essex. A.S., ***reac-an***, to smoke.

RAFF. Refuse, rubbish. **RAFFMEN.** Chandlers. The term grocers and ***raffemen***, occurs in old Norwich records. – See *Nares.*

Old Fr. Proverb, '***Il ne luy lairra rif ne raf, rifle ne rafle***.' He will strip, reave, or deprive him of all. *Cotgr.* Dan., ***rips-raps***, tag-rag.

'To rumble rime in ***raffe*** and ***ruffe***, yet all not worth an hawe.' *Gascoigne.*

Raff, literally, is what is swept up; Ger. ***raffen***; Isl., ***hrafla.***

'Fleand fast thei thrist, and fled bothe ***rif and raf***.' *Robert de Brunne.*

RAFFLIN or **RASSLIN-POLE.** I. The baker's pole with which the embers are spread to all parts of the oven. In the North a ***fruggen***. II. Brushing walnuts off the trees is called ***raffling*** or ***resselling*** them. See ***ressle***.

I. Wel., ***rhavu***, to spread out; ***rhaw***, a shovel; ***rhaviaw***, to spread with a shovel. II. A.S., ***reaflac;*** Isl., ***hrifling***, spoil, booty. See also under ***Raffling***.

RAFFLING. Idle, unsteady.

Raffertory, masterful. ***Rafle***, to play with dice, N. Ang. ***Raffle***, to dissipate intemperately, talk confusedly, Whitby.

Ger., ***raffeln***, to snatch away; Isl., ***hraffi***, rapacious; ***raf***, to roam about. A.S. ***reafl***; Sw. ***raffel***, to gamble; Dut., ***raffen***, to rive, rob.

RAFTY. I. Fusty, stale. ***Raffiness***, staleness. II. Misty and damp, 'raw and ***rafty***.' 'Ta fare kienda ***rafty*** this morning.' Dan., ***rag***, sea vapour; Dut., ***rag***, cobweb. Sc. ***raf***, a flying shower.

I. ***Rafty***, rancid, Dorset; ***rasty***, Somerset; ***raisty*** and ***reasty***, in other dial. ***Raffie***, rank, Sc.; Ger., ***reiftig***, ripe, mature; Wel., ***rhyfaeth***, over-ripe.

RAKE. To gad or ramble in mere idleness, without any immoral implication. Applied often to truant children. *Forby.*

'***Reyke***, or ***royt***, ydylle walkynge abowt.' *Pr. Pv.*

Rake, to walk, to range or rove about, N. Ang.; Su. Goth., ***reka***, to roam.

RALLY. I. A projecting ledge in a wall built thicker below than above, serving the purpose of a shelf. II. A coarse sieve for peas or horse beans. Sc., ***ralis***, nets; Fr., ***raiz***, nets; Wel., ***rhwyll***, lattice-work.

I. Ger. ***rille***, a chamfer, small furrow; Wel., ***rhwyll***, a mortise, fretwork; Dut., ***rillen***, to shiver. II. Dan., ***ralle***; Fr., ***raller***, to rattle; ***rallar***, Sp., to grate; Lat., ***radiculare***.

RAMP. I. To prance, romp. II. To grow rapidly and luxuriantly. III. To bend, crook a piece of iron to adapt it to the wood work of a gate. 'Ta oont dew sooin, yo' must ***ramp*** it.'

To ***ramp and reave***, to get by fair or foul means. Rampantous, overbearing, Linc., ***rampage***, to be riotous. ***Ramp***, to sprain; Cumb.

I and II. Su.-Goth., ***ram***; Isl., ***rammr***, stout; Dan., ***ram***, rank; A.S. ***rempend***, rampant, headlong; Wel., ***rhamant***, a rising, soaring up. III. It., ***rampa***, a claw; Ger., ***krampf***; Eng. ***cramp***.

'Although she were a lusty bouncing ***rampe***, somewhat like Gallimeta or Maid Marian.' *Gabriel Harvey*.

RANCH. To scratch deeply and severely, as with a nail.

Dut., ***wrongk***, distortion; Bav., ***renken***, to tear; It., ***dirancare***, to tear out.

'Not a weed sprung up but ere it aspired half to his growth, by them it was weeded and ravenously ***raunchte*** up.' *Nash's Christ's Tears*.

'Griffade, a ***ranche*** or clinch with a beast's paw.' *Cotgr.*

RAND. I. A fleshy piece of beef cut from the rump, loin, or leg. II. A strip of leather in the heel of the shoe, turned over and seamed to strengthen it.– See ***rond***.

A.S., ***rand***, margin, edge, round; Isl., ***rond, raund***; Su.-Goth., ***rand***; Sp., ***randa***, rim. See quotation from Fuller under ***Weaver's Beef***.

RANDAN. The yield of a second sifting of meal.

Possibly from the Fl., ***rondom***, roundabout, an old mode of sifting the bran, the first quality of which is the ***randan***, being the working it round and round in large sieves; or it may be the A.S., ***randun***, running down.

RANNY. The shrew mouse. *Sorex araneus, Lin.* Fr., ***musaraigne***; Isl., ***rani***, snout.

RANTER. I. A tin or copper can in which beer is brought from the cellar, and poured into drinking vessels. II. To sew up a rent in a garment, Fr., ***rentraire***.

Rant, to drink, Craven; ***ranty***, tipsy, Sc.

I. The Wel. has ***rhanitor***, to distribute, to dispense. The der. seems rather the O. Fr., ***rentonner***, to tun the second time.

RAP AND REND. 'A spend everything 'a can ***rap and rend***,' *i.e.*, all he can seize and lay hands on.

Dan., ***rapse***, to pilfer, filch; Ger., ***rappen***, to snatch up; Sp., ***rapar***, to plunder; A.S., ***rendan***, to tear; Fris., ***renda***.

'Whatsoever he could ***rap or rend***, he confiscated to his covetous gut.' *Nash's Pierce Penilesse*.

'Though he should set all to saile which he could ***rappe and rend***.' *D. Rogers' Naaman*.

'For many years of his life all that he could (as they say) ***rap or run*** went the same way.' *North's Lives, iii, 291*.

RAPE AND SCRAPE. Synonyms of the last. ***Rape***, haste, Old Eng. – See *Coleridge's Dict. O. Norse*, ***rápa***, cursitare.

RASP, RESP. To belch. '***Rospynge*** or bolkynge, ***eructatio***.' *Pr. Pv.* O.S. ***ropizon***; Dut., ***rispen***; Su.-Goth., ***rapa***. O. Fr., ***respirer***, to vent, gasp. *Cotgr.*

RASSELS. The land-whin, Suff. '***Rastylbow wede***, resta bovis.' *Pr. Pv.* Gael., ***ras***, a shrub.

'The petty whinne or ***rest-harrow*** is commonly called *aresta bovis* and *remora aratri*; in Fr., ***areste bœuf***.' *Gerarde's Herbal*, 1633.

Rest-Harrow, arrest harrow; Fr., ***arrete-bœuf***, from its strong matted roots impeding the progress of plough and harrow. *Ononis arvensis, Lin.–Prior's Pop. Brit. Plants.*

RATHE-RIPE. Coming early to maturity. A.S. ***rath***, quickly.

'Let me mention another real loss ** the comparative ***rather*** stands alone, having dropped on one side its positive ***rathe***, and on the other its superlative ***rathest***. ***Rathe*** having the sense of early, though a graceful word ** embalmed in the *Lycidas* of Milton –

'And the ***rathe*** primrose, which forsaken dies'

might still be suffered, without remark, to share the common lot of so many words which have perished, though worthy to have lived; but the disuse of ***rathest*** has left a real gap in the language, and the more so seeing that liefest is gone too.' *Archbp. Trench.*

'He regned fifteen yere, and died alle to ***rathe***.' *Robert de Brunne.*

'Open your eyes, ye ***rathe-ripe*** invaders of God's chair, and see your Saviour in his younger years, not sitting in the eminent pulpit of the doctors, but in the lowly floors of the auditors.' *Bp. Hall.*

RATHER OF THE RATHEREST. A very little too much or too little. Applied to insufficient cooking of meat; sometimes to one half drunk.

RATTOCK. A great noise. Ger. ***rattern***, to crash, make a noise.

RAUM. To sprawl. Ger. ***raumlich***, filling space, wide.

RAVARY. A violent raving fit of passion.

RAWINGS. After grass, eddish, the coarse feed of the marsh lands.

Wel., ***rhw, rhwawg***, abounding with growth, what grows out; ***rhws***, rank, fertile; or it may be a cor. of ***roughings***. '***Raweyne***, hey, (***rawen***)' *Pr. Pv.* Fenum serotinum. *Cath. Ang.* – See ***rowén***.

RAZOR, RIZZER. A small pole, used to confine faggots.

Gael., ***ras***, a rod or twig; Dan., ***riis***, faggots, rods; A.S., ***hris***; Isl., ***hriis***; Ger., ***reis***; Sw., ***ris***; Wel., ***gwyrsg***. ***Ryse***, brushwood used in hedging, N. Ang.; ***stake and rice***, a wattled fence. ***Rice***, pease, straw, Norf. ***Pea-rice***, pea-sticks, Chesh.

REAVE. To unroof a house, to blow the thatch off. A.S., ***reafian***.

Reuvv, to unroof, Cumb.

RED-INKLE. Red tape; Fr., ***lignel***.

Inkle, an inferior kind of tape. *Brocket's N. Ang. Words.* 'Thick as ***inkle***-weavers' – very intimate, Cumb.

RED-ROW. Barley just before it is ripe for cutting.

REE. A river or flood. 'All is in a ***ree***,' i.e. overflowed, Essex.

Ree, Sc., is half drunk; Wel., ***rhe***, a swift motion, current; O. Fr., ***riu***, a deep rain, gullet of water.

REED ROLL. A thicket of reeds on the brink of a broad. ***Reed***, Suff., a wood, or a woody piece or strip of land. Squeech, shaw, dingle, 'mean nearly the same thing.' *Moor.* '***Reed Pytte***, or fenne.' *Pr. Pv.*

REEN, REIN. To drop the head as ripe corn.

Gael., ***crion***, to droop, ***crom***, to bend down; Wel., ***crym***, to stoop, bend; if from the action of ***reining*** in; Lat., ***retinere***; Fr., ***rêne***.

'Crist himself for sothe bygan.
He may ***rene*** both boure and halle.' *Lydgate.*

REER, RERE. Meat, 'too much underdone.' When cooked enough 'it is home-done.' A.S., ***hrere***, raw. '***Rere*** or nesche, as eggys, mollis.' *Pr. Pv.*

REESTIE. Rancid, rusty. '***Reest***, as flesche, rancidus.' *Pr. Pv.*

May be a cor. of the L. Ger., ***roestigh***, rusty, or the quot. from Bp. Hall may supply a clue to the der. ***Reest*** is the skin of bacon, possibly from the Isl., ***hreistr***, a scale.

'He was of an adust swarth choleric dye, like ***restie*** bacon, or a dried scate fish.' *Nash's Have with you to Saffron Walden.*

'So I could pluck a crow with Poet Martial for calling it putire halec, the scauld rotten herring; but he meant that of the fat, ***reasty*** Scottish herrings, which will endure no salt, and in one month (bestow what cost on them you will) wax rammish if they be kept.' *Nashe's Lenten Stuff.*

'Or once a week, perhaps for novelty,
Reez'd bacon-soords shall feast his family.' *Hall's Satires, b. iv.*

REFFEJ. Refuse. Picking out sheep is in Suffolk to ***reffej*** 'em.

RELEET. A meeting of three or four different roads

Isl., ***leita***, to guide, direct, resort to; A.S., ***lædan***.

'**REMEMBER** Parson Melham – and pray Sir, drink about,' a Norfolk phrase. *Bailey's Dict. of Cant Words,* 1776.

RENDER. To give a finishing coat of plaster to a wall, Fr., ***rendurcir***, to re-harden, ***renduire***, to smear afresh.

RENNIBLE, RANNILY. Fluent, voluble. Used by Bishop Hall. A.S., ***rynan***, to roar; Isl., ***hrina***, to cry out. The A.S. has also ***rennan***, to run, flow.

RESH. Fresh, recent. Carrots just pulled up and moist are said to be too ***resh*** for cattle, and more wholesome when a little ***clung***.

Ger., ***resche***; Fr., ***rèche***, harsh, rough, sour; Isl., ***hress***, fresh, recent.

RESSLE. Ripe walnuts are brushed off the tree with a long ***resselling*** pole.

A.S., ***hris***, tops of trees, ***hrisciun***, to shake, vibrate, rustle; Pl. D., ***russeln***; Dut., ***ritselen***; Prov. Ger., ***rasseln***, to shake; Scot., ***reissil***, a loud clattering noise, a blow, stroke; Su.-Goth., ***ris-a***, to beat with rods.

RESTIE, REASTY. East Anglian forms of ***restive***. Lat., ***re-stare***.

A horse is said to run ***rusty***, i.e., restive. ***Reast***, to take offence, Linc.

'If their Masters see them, how nimble at a start are they, but if their backes bee turned, how ***resty*** and lazy?' *D. Rogers' Naaman.*

'Now, sirs, knowing your bellies full of Bishops bobbs, I am sure your bones would be at rest: but, wee'le set vp all our ***rests***, to make you all ***restie***.'

Nashe's Pap with a Hatchet, 1589.

RET. To soak, macerate in water. ***Retting*** pit, a pond or ditch for soaking hemp; Su., ***röta***, to soak, steep; Fl., ***reeten***, to hickle or bruise flax. ***Ret***, a wart, Norf.; Dut., ***vvrat***.

Retting is the process of steeping flax in water to separate the fibres. 'Rettyn tymbyr, hempe, or other lyke, rigo, infundo.' *Pr. Pv.*

RHENOISTER. A rhinoceros, 'called by the Dutch settlers at the Cape, ***rhenoster***.' *Forby.*

RIB-WORT. The common water-cress, *Coronopus Ruellii.*

Ribe, A.S., is hound's tongue.

RICKY. Masterful. Lanc., ***rick***, to scold; Wel., ***rhoci***, to grunt, growl; Isl., ***rikr***, imperious; Dut., ***ryk***; Swed., ***rik***; Plat. D., ***riek***, dominion.

RIDE. To '***ride*** grub,' is to be out of humour, sulky.

RIE. The raised border on a stocking top.

RIFLE. A strop used after the whetstone for sharpening a scythe. Generally hung on the sned of the scythe. *Moor's Suf. Words*; Ger., ***riffeln***, to polish; Su.-Goth., ***rifwa***, to rub.

'A brusk sythe and grass sythe with ***rifle*** to stand.' *Tusser.*

In other Eng. dial. a ***rifle*** seems to be a bent stick attached to the butt of the scythe handle, to collect the corn or grass into the swathe, and is called a bale. See *Halliwell* and *Wright.*

RIG. A ridge in ploughed land, a stocking rib. A.S., ***rig***, the back. Isl., ***hriggr***, Sue-Goth, ***rygg***. ***Riggish***, wanton; Fr., ***rigoler***.

A sheep laid on its back and unable to turn itself, is said to be ***rigg'd***.

RIG, RIDGIL. ***Ridjillon***, an animal half castrated. Gael., ***ruig***; Isl., ***rog***.

RIGHT. Obligation. 'I've no ***right*** to pay so much.' 'He have a ***right*** to pay his debts.' 'He have a ***right*** to be hung, and don't ought to be pardoned.' ***Right***, very, as ***right*** rotten. ***Right***-down, down-right; ***right-on***, positively, straight-forward. ***Right-up***, upright; ***right-away***, straight off, directly. The three latter have been transplanted to the United States. ***Right-out***, directly, completely; ***right-up-eared***, prick-eared, pert, saucy.

RILE, ROIL. To stir up liquor and make it turbid by moving the sediment; hence to irritate and rouse to anger – 'dont you ***rile*** the water.' ''A was lamentably ***riled***.' Common in America.

Isl., ***rugl***, to stir up, ruffle, discompose; Su.-Goth., ***rulla***; C. Brit., ***ruila***; '***Ryall*** of foom or berme, spuma.' *Pr. Pv.* '***Riall*** of wyne, fome, brouée, fleur.' *Palsg.* A ***riled*** complexion is one coarsely ruddy.

Rile, to vex, annoy, Cumb.; ***roil***, to play the romps, frolic, Whitby. ***Rile***, to render turbid, disturb, vex. *Brockett's North Country Words.* ***Rool***, to ruffle, rumple clothes, Craven. ***Reul***, to be rude, unmannerly. *Ray.* ***Roil***, to perplex, to muddy, make turbid, *Grose.* ***Rile***, to ruffle; ***roiling***, fidgetting, climbing about, said of children, Northampts.; ***rile***, to reach as a restless child, Dorset; ***roil***, an abusive female; ***roily***, to scold, Devon; ***roily***, to traduce, to backbite, West of Eng.; ***roil***, a great awkward hoyden, a big, ungainly slammakin. *MS., Devon. Gloss.* ***Roil***, to rove about, from O. Norse, ***hrolla***. *Coleridge's Dict. of 13th cent., English.* '***Roytyn*** or ***roylyn***, or gone ydyl abowte.' *Pr. Pv.*

> 'Maydes myxte with men in company,
> Let them in solempne flockes goe ***royle***.'
>
> *Seneca's Tenne Tragedies*, 1581.

'Were woont to roam and *roile* in clusters.' *Stanihurst's Ireland, 1584.*

'Sathan is now in his passions; he feeles his passion approaching, he loves to fish in ***royled*** waters.' *The Simple Cobbler of Aggadam, p. 2*, 1647.

'He took a turn or two in his dining-room, and said nothing, by which I perceived his spirits were very much ***roiled***; therefore I kept silence also, expecting what would follow. There was no need of asking what news, when the purse, with the great seal, lay upon the table. At last his lordship's discourses and actions discovered that he was in a very great passion, such as may be termed agony, of which I never saw in him any like appearance since I first knew him.' *North's Lives, i.,* 415.

'But that his friends, intelligent persons ** should believe it, was what ***roiled*** him exceedingly.' *Id. ii.,* 168.

'But although his fears of the law, or rather of my Lord Jeffries were removed, yet his spirits were so ***roiled*** with this expedition, that he never heartily enjoyed himself after.' *Id. iii.,* 140.

'And King William, having secured his own game, would not ***roil*** it to gratify them.' *Id. iii.,* 183.

'As surely as wormwood shall still and heal such ***roilings***.' *Fairfax.*

RILLY. The dado or moulding round the base of a room. 'Dust the ***rilly***.' *Moor.* See under *Rally.*

RIM of the Body, the membrane lining the abdomen and covering the bowels.

Old Eng., ***rim*** or ***rymme***. Bishop Wilkins defines it the membrane of the belly 'Omentum, a fat pannicle, caule sewet, ***rim***, or kell, wherein the bowels are lapt.' *Florio.* A.S., ***rima***, an edge; Wel., ***rhim***. Pistol, at Agincourt, threatens Monsieur ler Fer –

'For I will fetch thy ***rim*** out at thy throat,
In drops of crimson blood.' *Hen. 5, Act 4.*

RIM. To shoe a horse; a bill sent to a Norfolk clergyman ran – 'To ***rimming*** your ass.' ***Rere and rym***, back and edge.

'Bot non stode Harald dynt, that bifore him kam
The rought of thare rascaile he did it ***rere and ryme***.' *Robert de Brunne.*

RIMPLE. A wrinkle, pucker. A.S., ***hrimple***.

RINGE. The border of a cap or kerchief, a row of plants. 'Plant em in ***ringes***.' A.S., ***hringe***. '***Reenge*** or rowe.' *Pr. Pv.*

RINGLED. Married.

RINGLENS. Coarse flour.

Ring is Sc. for the meal falling between the millstone and the case. ***Renge***, a hair sieve for flour, Dorset; in Somerset, a ***range***.

RINKIN. A fox, Suff.; Ger., ***reineke***.

RIPPIER. One who brings fish from the coast to sell inland. Lat., ***ripa***, a sea shore.

Cowell, in his *Law Dict.* calling them ***reparii***, derives á fiscella qua in devehendis piscibus utuntur; in Eng., a ***ripp***, basket. Isl., ***hripp***.

'It appeareth on record, that in the yere 1522, the ***rippars*** of Rie and other places solde their fresh fish in Leadenhall market.' *Stowe's London,* 1599.

In Suffolk, Moor states the word is used, pronounced ***rib***, for open work hen cages, and baskets in which oranges, &c. are hawked about.

'Where tis to be noted that they come in with a sleeueless conscience, and thinke it no good doctrine which is not preached with the cloak cast over each shoulder like a ***rippier***.' *Pap with a Hatchet,* 1589.

RIPPLE. A Norfolk mode of ploughing; laying the land two furrows together.

RISPS. Stems or stalks of climbing plants, the fruit-bearing stems of raspberries. In Suff. the green straw or runners of growing peas and potatoes.

It., ***raspo***; Span., ***raspa***, a stalk of grapes, beard of corn. Hence ***rape*** tabac; Eng., ***rappee***.

'Strabery rype, and cherryes in the ***ryse***.' *Lydgate.*

RIST. A rising ground; advance of prices; an origin. Ger., ***rist***.

'And the rather, for that the words thus foisted in are of such a sort trust and end, that if you look but to their ***rists*** and lay their betokenings to the things whose names they bear, I dare undertake twenty for one, that even the slighted and off-cast words in the mouths of handy-crafts-men and earth-tillers shall be better drawn and more patly brought in.' *Fairfax.*

RIVERS. The women in the herring curing houses who string the fish upon spits for smoking. Dan., ***rive***, to lacerate, pierce. Isl., ***ryf***. '***Ryvyn*** or ***reendyn***.' *Pr. Pv.*

'Little knocks ***rive*** great blocks.' *Local Proverb.*

ROARERS. The men who spread and turn over the herrings on the floor of the curing houses. Dan., ***röre***, to stir about. Su.-Goth., ***röra***; Isl., ***hrœra***. '***Rooryn***, or ruffelyn amonge dyverse thyngys.' *Pr. Pv.*

ROB. Jam, thick jelly made from fruit.

Fr., ***rob de ribes***, the preserved juice of gooseberries or currants; It., ***rob***; Pers., ***rubb***.

ROBBLE. A rake, used by bakers in stirring bread in the oven. O. Fr., ***roable***, an oven-rake; Wel., ***rhawbal***, a shovel.

Hartshorne in his *Salop. Ant.* remarks, 'I never heard it but once, and then it was used at a mill under the south side of the Wrekin, to describe an instrument with which oats are stirred in an oven.'

ROBLET. A large chicken or young cock. A var. seemingly of ***gobbler***, the local term for a turkey-cock; Sc., ***bubbly-jock***.

The Dut. has ***robbenol***, a nickname for a lusty boy, or plump child.

Roblet occurs in East Anglian literature, with the meaning apparently of the Low Ger. ***rabbelen***, garrire, mugari, blaterare, precipitare, sive confundere verba. *Kilian.*

'But if the man who is so all to benighted, will needs be setting up a Will-in-the-Wisp no wonder if the glare of it sometimes ***roblet*** him into bogs and marl pits.' *Fairfax.*

'But now one reason at least why the understanding has been ***robletted*** into these wastes and wildernesses is, the forefearing that if emptiness far and wide were not granted, the world would not be bounded.' *Fairfax.*

ROCKET. A row of holes made by dibbles; the length of the stetch.

ROCK-STAFF. A distaff. An 'old woman's ***rock-staff***' is a contemptuous expression for a silly superstitious fancy.

Swed., ***rock***; Ger., ***rocken***, a distaff; ***rocken-weisheit***, old woman's philosophy. '***Rokke*** of spynnynge. Colus.' *Pr. Pv.*

RODE. To spawn. – E. Ang.; Wel., ***rhid***, spawn; ***rownd***, fish roe, N. Ang., from Dan., ***raun***. Ger., ***rogen***. Su.-Goth. ***rok***. Isl., ***hrogn***.

Rid, a hollow place in gravel where salmon deposit their roe, from Sc., ***redd***, spawn. *Jam.*

ROGER'S BLAST. A sudden local motion of air, perceptible only by its whirling up the dust on a dry road in perfectly calm weather, somewhat in the manner of a water spout. It is reckoned a sign of approaching rain. *Forby.*

Gael., ***ruidheas***, a blast, agitated movement; Wel., ***rhuadaiz***, blustering, roaring. '***Rowdyonys***, blaste or qwyrlwynd, turbo.' *Pr. Pv.*

ROGGE. To shake roughly. Su.-Goth. ***rycka***. Isl., ***hröcka***, cum impetu ferri; Sc. ***rug***, to tear in pieces. ***Roggle***, N. Ang.; Wel., ***rhuglaw***, to move about briskly; Prov. Ger., ***rogel***, loose, unfixed.

'He romede, he rarede, that ***roggede*** all the erthe.' *Morte Arthure M. S. Linc.*

'She ***rogged*** on hym, and was nothing a-dradde.' *Lydgate.*

ROKE. A fog. ***Roky***, foggy. Sea ***roke*** is a cold fog or thick mist spreading rapidly along our eastern shores, sometimes to a distance of eight or ten miles inland. Mid Ang., ***rawk***.

Isl., ***rok***; Dan., ***ryger***, a steaming, reeking exhalation; A.S., ***reac***. In Sussex, ***roke*** is the steam from boiling water. '***Roke***, myste.' *Pr. Pv.*

'Her lewde lyppes twayne. They slaver men sayne – Lyke a ***roky*** rayne.' *Skelton.*

ROLLIKY. Uneven, rough. **ROLLIPOKE.** Hempen cloth of coarse texture. A.S., ***hreog***, rough.

ROMMOCK. To romp or gamble boisterously.

Old High Ger., ***hromjan***, to bustle, make a noise; Ger., ***rammeln***, to tumble, romp; Su.-Goth., ***ram***, stout, robust; Isl., ***rammaukinn***, sturdy, of overflowing energy and spirits.

> 'And yet she's a ***rommaking***, slommaking thing,
> And as wild as a filly let loose in the spring.' *Clare's M. S. Poems.*

RONDS, or RANDS. Terms applied to the unembanked margins of the East Norfolk rivers. O. Norse, ***rönd***, margin, edge. Scc ***Rand***.

ROOKER. Refuse broken fish. Sw., ***râk***, fish guts.

ROOMS. The spaces between the thwarts of a boat. Isl., ***rummr***. Used in this sense only.

ROOZLY or **RAWSLEY.** Gravelly subsoil, thin-skinned with mould. A.S., ***hruse***, a rock, hill, earth. ***Ros-land***, heathy land; Wel., ***rhos***, a moor, peat land.

Rosil or ***rosily*** soil, land between sand and clay, neither light nor heavy. *Ray's Eastern Words.* ***Russell'd***, withered as an apple, Whitby. Wel., ***rhuzawl***, ruddy, russetty; ***rosel,*** to crisp with heat, Teesdale; to ***rossel*** his shins, to kick the skin from the legs, Salop; Gael., ***rusal***, to scrape, scratch.

ROUNE. To whisper, A.S., ***runian***. '***Rownyn*** to-geder. Susurro.' *Pr. Pv.* O.H.G., ***rûnen***, hence Gothic ***runa***, mystery; ***runic***, &c.

'Were I but to whisper to him of whom so many talk aloud, I should ***rown*** him thus much in the ear.' *Fairfax.*

ROUT. To snore, to roar, bellow, like animals, to holla.

Sax., ***hrutan***; Isl., ***rauta, hriota***. ***Rute***, to cry with vehemence. Chesh. ***Rout***, the bray of an ass, Leeds. '***Rowtare*** yn slepe, ***stertor***.' *Pr. Pv.*

ROUT, ROATING. Coarse grass, which looks brown and sere in the meadows in spring. 'It differs from ***fog***, in that the latter is green and sour.' *Moor*. See der. under ***rowen***.

'The Good Shepherd will not let his sheep feed in hurtful and ***roating*** pastures, but will remove them to good feeding grounds.' *Pilkington*.

Rowty, applied to rank grass, occurs in an old Essex writer, *Harrison's Britaine*, prefixed to *Holinshed's Chronicle*, 1577.

ROVE. A scab. ***Rovy***, scabby. A.S., ***hreof***. Also a mode of ploughing, similar to ***baulking***. 'Three clean earths and a ***rove***,' is a stipulation to an out-going tenant, dated 1740. *Cullum's Hawsted*, p.217. Su.-Goth., ***rifwa***. Isl., ***riufa***, to cleave.

ROVING WEATHER. Uncertain weather.

ROWEN, ROUGHINGS, or **ROWINS**. The after-math of mown meadows. See ***Rawings***.

Roughings, latter grass, after mathes. *Ray's S. and E. Words*.

'Which ever ye sow That first eat low,
The other forbear For ***rowen*** to spare.' *Tusser*.

A.S., ***hruh***; Ger., ***rauh***; Dan., ***ru***, rough, coarse; Ger., ***raugh-gras***, small meadow grass.

'Rowen is a field kept up till after Michaelmas, that the corn left on the ground may sprout into green.' *Bailey's Dict*.

ROWS. The names given to the blocks of narrow streets, running east to west, which constitute Old Yarmouth.

N. Ang., ***raw***, as ***Pether-Raw***, ***Shiney-Raw***; Sax., ***ræwa***; Old Eng. and Sc. ***rew***, a street; Lat., ***ruga***; Sp., ***rua***; Fr., ***rue***.

ROWY, ROWNY. Of uneven texture. Cor. of ***rough***. A.S., ***ruh***.

ROYNISH. Scabby, mangy, mean, base. Fr., ***rogneux***. It., ***rógna***.

'The sloven and the careless man, the ***roynish*** nothing nice.' *Tusser*.

'She was not such a ***roinish rannell***, (strumpet) or such a dissolute gillian-flurtes, as this wainscot-faced Tomrig.' *Gab. Harvey's Pierce's Supererogation*, 1600.

RUCK. I. A wrinkle, crease, plait or fold. Isl., ***hrukka***, a wrinkle. II. To cower, to huddle together. Isl., ***hruku***; Dut., ***hurken***.

In the same sense a ***ruck*** is a heap, N. Ang.; Isl., ***hraukr***; Sue-Goth, ***ruka***; Fris., ***ruk***. '***Rukkun***, or cowre down.' *Pr. Pv.* Dan., ***ruge***, to brood, hatch.

Reawking, idling in neighbours' houses. *Tim Bobbin*.

'The wolfe in fieldis the shepe dothe grete duresse,
Rukking in foldis for fere dar nat arise.' *Lydgate*.

RUDLE. A beverage composed of warm beer and gin, with sugar and a slice of lemon peel. *Moor*.

The Ger. has ***rudeln***, to stir about.

RUFFATORY. A rude, boisterous lad, fond of horse-play.

It., ***ruffa***, a scrambling, pulling; ***arruffare***, to dishevel; ***baruffa***, a fray; Prov., ***barrufaut***, fighter, brawler, from Old H. Ger., ***bi-roufan***. *Diez*.

RUMBUSTICAL. Boisterous, bustling, shoving.

Scot., ***rambaskuns***. Possibly from the Su.-Goth. ***ram***, robust, and ***busa***, cum impetu ferri, irruere, ***basa***, ferire. In some Eng. dial. ***robustical***, of which it may be a var.

RUMGUMSHUS. Opinionated, rough and surly, quarrelsome.

The Moes. Goth. has ***raum***, stout, sturdy; ***gaum-jan***, to perceive, estimate. Scot., ***ramgunshock***, coarse, unpolished. ***Rumgumption***, rough sense.

RUMMER. A large, strapping lass. ***Rumpkin***, a large drinking glass.

'A ***ramman*** girt an' a very large one', Cumb. Isl., ***rumr***; Su-Goth., ***rum***, bulky, large.

RUNDESCANT. To enlarge on, used by Bp. Hall. Sw., ***rundiscanten***.

RUNNABLY. Currently, smoothly, without hesitation. 'The boy reads pretty ***runnably***.' In Suff., ***renably***. See ***rennible***.

RUNT. An obstinate old cow, or ill-conditioned woman; ***runty***, crusty, surly. Ger., ***rind***; Dut., ***rund***, a cow, heifer; Isl., ***hrund***, a woman. (*Mulier libertina*, says Jamieson.)

Runt, an aged ox, Cumb. ***Runty***, thick short-set, red faced, Whitby.

RUSNS or **REWSNS**. The splints or narrow bands of wood running inside a boat by which it is raised. Sw., ***resa***, to raise up.

RUTTLE. To make a rough noise in breathing, as when there is an obstruction in the throat or lungs. Dut., ***reutelen***.

S

SAD-BAD, *sadly-bad, sadly-badly,* very ill, sadly-poorly.

Sir G. C. Lewis in his *Herefordshire Dialect* notices the propensity in the poor for using qualifying diminutives, specially conversing with those better off. He attributes the habit to a desire to excite compassion, by making themselves appear ill off. Ask 'what sort of crop of potatoes have you?' 'I think I shall have a few taters.' They would say no more if they expected the best possible crop. 'How are you?' 'Middling, or indifferent well,' would be the answer, though the person was not ill, and had not had an ailing for years. Though a man said, 'we do rent a little house and bit of garden of Mr. Jones,' his cottage and garden might be the largest in the district. 'I did take the man his bit o' victuals' would mean his ordinary dinner, and perhaps a large one too. So 'he do get a drop of drink,' might mean six quarts of cider a day. Ask a woman, staggering under a load of wood which she has got on her head, she will answer, 'I ha just been picking a few chats.' On the same principle the cottagers amplify, when talking of those objects which are expensive to them. 'How many children have you?' *Woman* – 'a large family, I ha had ten.' You do not discover until you ask a second question, 'but I had buried six when they were babies.' The habit of farmers and gardeners, in speaking of their crops, is precisely analogous. They will neither admit times to be good, or weather to be altogether favourable.

SAFER or **SEA-FARE.** A voyage. 'What sort of ***safir*** have you made?'

SAG. To bend, give way, decline from weakness or over-loading, as gate bars, beams, rafters, &c. Applied to health also. 'How is your neighbour?' 'Why 'a fare kedgy – but 'a begin to ***sag***, kiender.' To decline in health.

'Nature hath lent him a flabberkin face like one of the foure windes, and cheekes that ***sagge*** like a woman's dugges over his chin-bone'. *Nash's Pierce Penilesse.*

'Next, the Norfolk Hog, or Swine-worrier who had got him a ***sagging*** pair of cheeks, like a sow's paps that gives suck with the plentiful Maste before him, came lazily waddling in, and puffed out Pork, Pork, Pork.' *Nash's Lenten Stuff.*

'The mind I sway by and the heart I bear,
Shall never ***sagg*** with doubt, nor shake with fear.' *Macbeth, v. 3.*

A.S., ***sigan***, to sink, fall; Ger., ***sakken***; Fris., Isl., and Goth., ***siga***; L. Ger., ***sijgen***.

'What a ***segging*** gait he has,' said of the heavy labouring walk of a corpulent man, N. Ang. ***Sagg'd***, bulged out. Whitby. '***Saggyn***, or ***satlyn***. Basso.' *Pr. Pv.*

SAG-LEDGES. Cross-bars or braces, to prevent gate ledges ***sagging***.

SALE. The iron or wooden part of a cart horse's collar.

A.S., ***sæl***, harness for a draught horse, a fetter, chain; ***sol, sal,*** a wooden hoop, to put round the neck of an ox. Su-Goth., ***sele***, a horse's draught collar. '***Sele***, horsys harneys,' *Pr. Pv.*, and *Palsg.* ***Arquillus***, an oxe bowe. *Ortus Vocabulorum*, 1500. '***Sole***, a bowe about a beestes necke,' *Palsg.*, 'Restis a ***Sole*** to tie beasts.' *Gouldman's Dict.*, 1664. A.S., ***Sælan,*** to bind, unite.

Sahl, sole, sow, an ox yoke. Chesh. ***Sole***, a collar of wood put round the neck of cattle to confine them to the stelch (upright stake), Heref. '***Soole***, beestys teyynge,... ligaculum.' *Pr. Pv.* Fris., ***säle***, horse collar.

SALLY. To pitch forward.

To run from side to side as at a ship launch, N. Ang. ***Sally*** and back stroke, a term among ringers; Northampts. ***Sally***, a tottering situation, Sussex. Fr., ***sailler***, to issue forth, leap, spring out; ***saillie***, a quick egress.

'The horse, when he found himself clear of pursuers, stopped his course by degrees and went with his rider (fast asleep upon his back) into a pond to drink, and there sat his lordship upon the ***sally***.' *North's Lives, i. 92.*

SAM. Anything heated for a long time in a low heat so as to be in part spoiled, is said to be ***zamzodden***. *Somerset Dialect.*

SAMMEN-BRICKS. Bricks insufficiently burned, soft, and friable. Ger., ***samisch***, soft. The A.S. has ***sam***, half.

Sammy, is a term for any soft half-baked individual, applied to both sexes, common to most of our Eng. dial. Gael., ***samh,*** rustic, clownish. ***Sammy, clammy***, sticky, ***sammy*** bread. Salop. Moist, sweaty, Northants.; watery, soft, Beds. The Scand. ***sammen*** has the sense of sticky, coherent.

SAMMODITHEE. A word noted by Sir Thomas Browne. He left it unelucidated, and it has remained until our day a puzzle to philologists. Hickes interpreted it 'Say me how dost thou.' Lately it has been unriddled by Mr. Spurdens, as a corruption of 'Sam onto thee,' the constant response to the toast 'Here's t'ye!'

Syncopated phrases were common in O. Eng. colloquialisms. Two are instanced in the Gram. to *Cotgrave's Fr. Dict.*, 1650, ***Muskiditti***, much good may it doe to you; and ***Godigodin***, God give you good evening..

SANNY. To utter a whining, wailing cry, without apparent cause.

Possibly a cor. of the Fr. ***s'ennuyer,*** or from ***sangloter***, to sob, or a var. of

SANNYKING. Lasting, said of wind. Isl., ***seinka***, to linger; ***seinn***, slow, late; Su.-Goth., ***sinka***; Old Fr., ***senis***, late. A 'pining, sannying wind,' is a common phrase; ***sannyking***, lingering.

SAPPY. Silly, shallow-pated. ***Sap-scull***, a half-witted fellow.

Derived, says Moor, from the outer timber next the bark being less solid and weaker than the inner. The weak unsolid part is called the ***sap***. A.S., ***sæp***; Dut., ***sap***.

SAPY. Pallid, sickly. Meat when moist on the surface, in the first state of putridity, is said to be ***sapy***. A person also will say, 'I fare ***sapy***,' if exhausted and about to faint. Gr., ***sepein***, moistness, wetness, damp, such as causes putrefaction. *Spurdens*. A.S., ***sipan***, to steep.

SARNICK. Inanimate. A small quantity. Wel., ***swrn***, a little.

Ger., ***saumig***, slack, slow, backward.

SAUCE. I. Insolence of speech. II. Any sort of vegetable eaten with flesh meat.

Sauce, vegetables on the table. Hallamshire dial. 'Long ***sarse*** and short ***sarse***, and round ***sarse***, are not unfrequently applied to different vegetables; carrots, beets, and potatoes are so called, according to their respective dimensions.' *Elwyn's Americanisms*.

SAY. A taste or trial, a sample. 'Now the sheep have got a ***say*** of this grass they cannot keep out of it.' Fr., ***essayer***. ***Say-nay***, to refuse, forbid.

'The medling ape, that like a tall wood-cleauer assaying to rend a twopenny billet in two pieces, did wedge in his pettitoes so fast between the two clefts that he stucke by the feete for a ***saic***.' *Nash's Plaine Percivall*.

SCAITHFUL. Given to breaking from pasture. Said of open fields liable to be overrun by stock. A.S., ***scethan***, to spoil, damage. Fris., ***scatha***, Su-Goth., ***skada***.

SCALD. I. A multitude, said in a depreciating sense. 'I found the whole ***scald*** on em, as of boys robbing an orchard or hen-roost.' Su-Goth., ***Skall***, a noisy crowd; a general hunt. A.S., ***sceol***, a gang. II. A patch in a barley field, scorched and withered by the sun in a hot season, and on a light soil. To scorch, make bare; Isl., ***skalladur***, bare, bald; Su.-Goth., ***skallog***; Dan., ***skold-corn***, blighted corn. Scabby, scurfy, also mean, disgusting.

'Other news I am advertised of, that a ***scald*** trivial lying pamphlet, is given out to be of my doing.' *Nashe's Pierce Penilesse*.

'And safely covered from the ***scalding*** shine.' *Phineas Fletcher*.

Scald, equivalent to the whole ***boiling***. *Miss Baker*. ***Schald***, shallow, Sc. '***Scholde*** or ***schalowe***, not depe, bassus,' *Pr. Pv.*, hence shoal.

SCAMBLE. To scramble, to shift. '***Scamblingly***, griffe-graffe, by hooke or by crooke, squimble-squamble, catch that catch may.' *Cotgr.* Isl., ***skalma***, to take long strides. Su.-Goth., ***skamma***, to despoil; Dan., ***skæmme***. See ***shamble***.

'And somewhat to ***scamble*** for hog and for hen.' *Tusser*.

Scambler, a bold intruder at other people's dinner tables, Sc. ***Scamble***, to rove about, climb, scramble, obtain by struggling with others. Also to mangle, maul. *Bailey*. ***Scambling***, sprawling, Heref.

'Yea, but it is a harder, and not so easie for an old man, since the cushion was taken away from it'; meaning 'Since Dr. Scambler had ***scambled*** away the revenues thereof.' *Fuller's Worthies*, London.

SCARE. To spend, Suff. A cur to drive away pigs and poultry.

SCATCH-PAWED. Left-handed, Essex. N. Ang., ***skiff-handed***.
Ger., ***schicht***, unable, disabled.

SCHISMS. Frivolous excuses, whimsies, fancies, and fooleries in general. Ex. 'Come, come, let us have no more of your ***schisms***.' 'That man have always one ***schism*** or another in his head.'

SCHOOL. A shoal; a ***school*** of whales or herrings are common phrases. A.S., ***sceol***, a multitude; ***scolu***, a shoal. '***Sculle*** of a fysshe, examen,' *Pr. Pv.*
'The youth in ***sculs*** flocke and runne together.' *Foxe's Acts and Monuments.*

SCHRAIL. A light rail or fence.

SCOCKER'D, or COCKERED. ***Rifted***, as a tree blasted by lightning; said also of sappy timber.
A var. of ***cockle***, a term applied to any surface rendered uneven by shrinking or expansion after wet. Der., Lat., ***cochlea***, a snail, from what Sir T. Browne describes as the wreathy spires and ***chocleary*** turnings of its shell.

SCOOT. An irregular angular projection in a field, garden, &c. Su.-Goth., ***skoet***, an angle. A.S., ***sceat***. Isl., ***skeyt***.

SCOOTER. To run like ***scooter***, i.e., be very nimble, a simile borrowed from the rapid flight of the scoter duck. *Anas nigra, Lin.* ***Scuty***, smart, clean, brisk; ***scooter***, a squirt.
Scote, to shoot along in running, Dorset. A.S., ***sceotan***. Su-Goth, ***skutta***.

SCOPPET. To lade, empty. ***Skuppet***, a scooping implement used in embanking, having its sides turned a little in, and the handle with no eye-tiller or perforator, as the common spade has. It is intended for turning over ***muckles*** or midden heaps rather than for digging. Su-Goth., ***skopa***. L. Ger., ***schuppe***.

'Sharp cutting spade for dividing of mow,
With ***skuppet*** and skavell that marshmen allow.' *Tusser.*

'Though he puts them to their trumps other times, and ***scuppets*** not his beneficence into their mouths with such fresh water facility.' *Nash's Lenten Stuff.*
Scuppit, a small scoop used by maltsters. Sussex.

SCORE OUT TO. To scour as the tide scores out the beach. In Suffolk the gangways to the sea are called ***scores***. At Lowestoft the very steep lanes running down to the shore are termed ***scores***.
Score, a deep narrow indentation on a hill side, Sc.; Isl., ***skir***, a fissure, cleft. Su.-Goth., ***skora***; Wel., ***ysgar***, to cleave. A.S., ***scoren***, cleft. The A.S. has also ***score***, the shore, Su.-Goth., ***skär***.

SCOTCH. To spare, to refrain. 'I did not ***scotch*** to tell him my mind,' i.e., I did not mince the matter with him.
Sw., ***skiuta***, to break the matter to; to hint at an affair. In the Su-Goth it has similar senses, the root being to thrust at, push at. A.S., ***sceothan***.

SCOVE. To run swiftly, to ***scour*** along. A.S., ***scyfe***, precipitation.

SCRAB, SCRAP. To scratch or claw; dimin., ***scrabble***; Dan., ***skrabe***, to scrape; Isl., ***skrapa***; Dut., ***schrap***. Scrabbled eggs are a Lenten dish of eggs boiled hard, chipped and mixed with butter, salt and pepper. Su.-Goth., ***skrada***, to cut small.

'As when David, fearing the Philistines and distrusting God's protection, let his spittle fall downe upon his beard, and ***scrabbled*** upon the doores.' *Rogers' Naaman.*

SCRADGE. To dress and trim the slope of a fen bank, to strengthen it from an apprehended overflow. Dan., ***skred***, slope; ***skraane***, to slant. A.S., ***screadian***; L. Ger., ***schraden***, to cut in slanting pieces.

SCRANCH, SCRANGE. A deep scratch. Dut., ***schrammen***, to scratch with a nail. Dan., ***skramme***, to scar.

SCRAPE. A scrape, or scrap, a Norfolk term for a quantity of chaff mixed with grain, and laid as a decoy to attract small birds within range.

'Making a ***scrape*** for sparrows and small birds.' *Sir T. Browne.*

A term applied also, says the same writer, by seamen to the *Canis carcharias*, or other members of the shark species, sometimes taken entangled in herring nets.

SCREET. Half a quarter of a sheet of paper. Low Sc., ***scread***. A.S., ***screadian***, to cut in pieces, divide, shred. See ***vessel***.

SCRIGGLE, SKRUGGLE. To writhe, struggle, twist about. 'A ketched an arrawiggle, an ta ***skriggled*** an got awah'; 'a ***skrigglen*** eel.' Dut., ***stribbelen***, to struggle; ***schrikkig***, skittish.

'They ***skriggled*** and began to scold,
But laughing got the master,
Some ***quackling*** cried, "Let go your hold";
The farmers held the faster.' *Bloomfield's Horkey.*

SCRIMMAGE, SCRUMMAGE. To skirmish. A.S., ***scrimbre***, a sword-player. O.H.G., ***skirm***, shield. Bav., ***schremen***, to fence. Fr., ***escrimer***. Isl., ***skylma***.

One of the numerous words pertaining to arms, which the Romance nations received from their Gothic conquerors. *Diez.*

SCRINGE. To shrink, or shrivel, as with sharp cold or dry heat. A.S., ***scrincan***.

SCROGGY. Twisted, stunted; ***scrog legs***, bandy legs. Ger., ***schrag***, awry. ***Scrog***, a stunted bush or shrub, N. Ang.

SCRUMTIOUS. Stingy, screwy. ***Scrimpie***, niggardly, Sc.; ***scrinch***, a small bit, Mid Ang.; Ger., ***schrumpen***; Su.-Goth., ***skrumpen***.

SCUD. To shake herrings out of the nets. Dut., ***schudden***. Su.-Goth., ***skudd-a***.

SCUM. To mow.

Probably a vulgarism, although the Wel. ***ysgawm*** and the Gael. ***sgud*** have meanings akin, and the Su.-Goth. has ***skämma***, to crop, cut short.

SCUMMER. To foul with dirty liquid, to defame.

'He and his brother ***scummered*** out betwixt them an epistle to the readers against all poets and writers.' *Nash's Have with you to Saffron Walden.*

Su.-Goth., ***skæmma***, to load with opprobrium.

SCURF, SKRUFF. A thin crust, as of a wound healing; impure remains, filthy, scabby matter, &c. Su.-Goth., ***rufwa***, crusta vulneris. Also the back part of the neck.

Su.-Goth., ***skrof***; Ger., ***schorf***; A.S., ***sceorfa***; Isl., ***skurfur***.

'And so lickes up ***scurfe*** as the spider doth venom, or the sinke gathers dregges daily.' *D. Rogers' Naaman.*

'If such ***scurfe*** were only coloured with base Popish varnish, it were a lesse evill: but to set such base wares forth upon God's stall, which were too base to be vended upon the basest stall in a market, how odious is it?' *Id.*

SEA-PYE. The oyster catcher.

'It., pd. To Nicholas Grey for a ***sepye***, a red shancke and a stynte, ij*d*.' *L'Estrange Household Accounts.*

SEAL. Time, season, as hay ***seal***, barley ***seal***, wheat ***seal***, &c.

Of an idle fellow it is said, he 'keeps bad seals'; of poachers, 'that they are out at all ***seals*** of the night'; of an industrious man, that he keeps 'good ***seals*** and meals'. A.S., ***sæl***, time, occasion. '***Seel***, tyme.' *Pr. Pv.*

'To give one the ***seal*** of the day', i.e. to be ordinary civil to him but nothing more. Local Saw.

SEED-LEP. The basket carried by the sower. A.S., ***sæd-leap***.

SEGS. Rushes, reeds, sedges; a ***seggen***-bottom'd chair, a ***seggen*** collar. A.S., ***secg***. Wel., ***hesgen***.

'***Sedge***-collars for plough-horses, for lightness of neck.' *Tusser.*

'Sche took a ***leep*** of ***segg'***, i.e., a basket of rush. *Exod. ii., 3. Wycliffite Version.*

SEISINGS, or **NOSSELLS.** The short lines by which, at 6-inch intervals, herring nets are attached to their supporting rope. Dan., ***seisings***, seizings, ***seise***, to seize.

SEKETTA. An executor.

SENCION. Common groundsel, *Senecio vulg, Lin.* '***Synchone***, herbe' *Pr. Pv.*

SET. A game, as whist; a rubber consisting of two or three ***sets***.

'When we have matcht our rackets to these balles,
We will in France (by God's grace) play a ***set***
Shall strike his father's crowne into the hazard.' *Hen. V., i., 2.*

Also used for sit. 'Dew that there owd hin ***set***?' 'No, she lah.' A place in a river where fixed nets are set.

SET-FAST. In use, not at liberty. 'Retch me the black jack.' 'You can't het, 'tis set-fast; s' full a burgad.' *Moor.*

SEW. To ooze out, as water from wet land, blood from a wound. To ***sew*** out stammingly, to flow out surprisingly. Cor. of ***issue***.

SHACK. I. *v.* To rove about as a stroller or mendicant; *s.* a shabby fellow, lurking and prowling about, a ***shackaback***. A.S., ***sceacere***, L. Ger., ***schœcke***. II. *v.* To turn pigs or poultry into the stubble to feed on the scattered grain; *s.* the shaken-out grain remaining on the ground after harvest and gleaning. In woodlands, the acorns or mast.

'Yoke seldom thy swine, While ***shack*** time doth last.' *Tusser.*

'Like a broad ***shak***-fork with a slender steale.' *Hall's Satires.*

'Or that none of those rayes of other atoms, that are ***shacking*** all over the world's wastes come riding or drilling through both.' *Fairfax.*

Shack, to shake out or shed as corn at harvest. ***Shak-fork***, a hay fork, N. Ang.; ***shack-ripe***, fruit ready to fall with a touch. Whitby. ***Shack***, offal corn, the refuse of the ***tailings***, Northants. Su-Goth, ***skaka***. A.S., ***scacan***, to shake.

'***Shack***, (in Norfolk and Suffolk) the liberty of winter pasturage; the Lords of Manours having the privilege to feed their flocks of sheep at pleasure, upon their tenants' land during the six winter months. Also a custom in Norfolk to have common for hogs, from the end of harvest till seed time in all men's grounds; whence ***to go at shack*** in that country, signifies as much as, to go at large.' *Phillips' World of Words*, 1706.

'***Common at Shack***. (Eng. Law) a species of common by Vicinage in Norfolk, Lincoln, and York, being the right of persons occupying lands lying together in the same common field, to turn out their cattle after harvest, to feed promiscuously in that field.' *Burrill's Law Dict.* 1850.

'***Shack*** is in several places the term which expresses a general right. There is a piece of common; each inhabitant of that district claims a portion or use of it. This is denominated the right of ***shack***. The lawyers have been greatly puzzled with it. Perhaps the difficulty will vanish if we remember the French *chacun*, each.' *Rev. R. W. Hamilton's Yorks. Dial.*

Miss Gurney der. from the Ger., ***zeche***, a club, *zur zeche gehen*, to go shares. Possibly from the Ger. ***schicht***, share, portion; ***schichtung***, division of property. The Su.-Goth. and Dan. have ***skick***, order, custom, usage.

SHACKY. Shabby, ragged, shiftless, shirtless, at a loose end.

SHAGGY. Morose, coarse, and ill-tempered. A.S., ***sceacged***.

SHAIL. To run ***shailing*** about, to move as if the bones were loose in their sockets (like a ripe nut in its ***shale*** or shell. *Forby*.)

'Our Thomasen she doth trip, our Jenet she doth ***shayle***.' *Skelton*.

Shale, to drag the feet so as to scrape the ground, Teesdale. ***Shawl,*** to walk badly, or with the legs crooked, Cumb.; Fr., ***aller eschais***. ***Shallock***, to trail the feet from sheer laziness, Leeds. Su.-Goth., ***skælg***, oblique, crooked. '***Schaylyn***, disgredior,' *Pr. Pv.* '***Shayler***, that gothe awrie with his fete, boyteux. I ***shayle*** as a man or horse dothe that gothe croked with his legges. *Ie vas eschays.*' *Palsg.*, 1530.

SHALE. The mesh of a net, from the ***shale*** or netting-pin thrust in to tighten and gauge it. A.S., ***scylan***.

SHALM, SHARM. To scream shrilly and vociferously. Dut., ***schroom***, fright. Su.-Goth., ***skerma***, to vociferate, lament loudly. Wel., ***ysgarm***. See ***sharming***.

SHAMBLE. To drive away, disperse, make away with. Dut., ***schampen***, to slip aside; Dan., ***skæmme***, to despoil, cause to fall off. Su.-Goth., ***skamma***, to diminish, lose, spoil.

SHANNY. Harum-scarum, scatter-brained, frolicksome, unruly (not from vice), high-spirited, romping, head-strong. N. Ang., ***shandy***.

In N. Ang. and Sc. ***shanny*** has the stronger senses of silly, worthless. Su.-Goth., ***skamm***, Isl., ***skömm***, dishonour, ill-doing. A.S., ***scande***. In Linc. and Mid Ang. ***shanny*** has the sense of shame-faced.

> 'And out ran every soul beside
> A ***shanny-pated*** crew.' *Bloomfield's Horkey.*

SHARMING. A confused noise, din, or buzzing, such as is made by disorderly children. 'What a ***sharmin*** them there children dew keep.' *Moor*, who considers it a cor. of ***swarming***, and borrowed from the confused noise of bees.

Ger., ***schaere***, a multitude, crowd. Su.-Goth., ***skerma***; Wel., ***ysgarm***, a shouting, screaming.

'Whence would arise what I am not forward at all to speak of; an harshness in these things not being so harmless as the cutting of cork, whereby, though you saw and wring the ears with the ***sharm***, yet still 'tis but a light business you have to deal with.' *Fairfax*.

SHAUNTY. Shewy, flashy. Cor. of Fr., ***gentil***, or of jaunty.

SHEATH. The handle of a long pitch-fork. A.S., ***sceat***, partition.

SHEEPED. Disgraced. Used by Bp. Hall.

SHEER. I. Brittle. Su.-Goth., ***skör***, fragile; '***Spere***, britill or brekyll,' *Pr. Pv.* II. Bright red, shining with inflammation. Gael., ***cear***, blood-coloured, red.

SHELLED, SHALED. Pie-bald. Su.-Goth., ***skildra***, Ger., ***schildern***, to paint in diversified colour. Ger., ***schecken***, to dapple, streak. Used in ***shell-***duck, ***shell-***drake, &c.

Shell-apple, the chaffinch; ***sheld***, flecked, speckled, N. Ang., ***shell-***cock, the missel thrush, Cumb.

SHELDRAKE. Or burrow-duck; *Anas tadorna, Lin.*

'***Burganders***, a noble coloured fowl which herd in coney-burrows.' *Sir T. Browne.* ***Burganders***, the name given this species by Dr. Browne, may, writes his editor, Mr. Simon Wilkin, be a cor. of ***burrow-ganders***.

Berg, Isl. and Teut. is a rock, hill, mountain. Ger., ***berg-huhn***, a wild hen; ***berg-enterich***, a wild drake.

SHELVE or **SHOLVE.** To remove the surface of land with a shovel. 'We say ***sheow*** for shove, and ***showl*** for shovel,' in Suffolk, remarks Moor. ***Show***, pronounced like ***cow***, to push or thrust with force. *Forby.*

Ger., ***schaufeln***, to shovel out; A.S., ***scufan***.

A calf or colt is said to be ***shoovin*** when parting with its early teeth; trees putting forth their leaves are also ***shoovin***. *Moor.* ***Shove*** is also used in East Anglia in the sense of to germinate, to shoot. Dut., ***schuyven***, to push forth; ***shoovly*** is Gypsy for pregnant.

SHEPHERD'S SUNDIAL. The scarlet Pimpernel.

SHERE-MAN. One not enjoying the good fortune to be born in one of 'the three counties.'

'He is a sort of foreigner to us; and to our ears, which are acutely sensible of any violation of the beauty of our phraseology, and the music of our pronunciation, his speech soon bewrays him. Aye, I knew he must be a ***shereman*** by his tongue.' *Forby.*

SHERES. A term applied disparagingly to all the counties in England, except Norfolk, Suffolk, and Essex, which are called by the natives, 'the three counties.' A.S., ***scyr***, from ***scyran*** to divide.

'A'v a touch a' the ***sheers*** in 'em,' is a very malevolent character to give of a horse, and is not safely to be uttered loud enough to be heard by a Suffolk owner.' *Moor.*

SHET. To shoot. Also to shut. E. Ang. Vulgarisms.

'Item, j clothe of arras, with iij archowrys on, ***scheting*** a doke in the water withe a crosse bowe.' *Inventory of Sir J. Fastolfe's Effects.*

SHIM. A narrow stripe of white, or blaze, or star on a horse's face. In Essex the Jack o' Lantern is called ***shim***. A.S., ***sciman***, to glitter. '***Schymmid***, as hors. Scutilatus,' *Pr. Pv.*

SHIVE, SHIVER. ***Skiver, slivva***, a slice; A.S., ***scyftan***, to divide. L. Ger., ***schiefferen***; Dut., ***schyf***, a round slice; Dan., ***skiæve***.

Also the small iron wedge into which the bolt of a window shutter is fastened. In Suffolk called a ***sheer***.

'***Schyvere*** of brede or other lyke.' *Pr. Pv.*

'To toste white ***shevers*** and to make prophit roles.' *Barklay's Egloges*, 1514.

SHOAF, SHOOF. A sheaf of wheat; pl., ***shoves***; Dut., ***schoof***.

'***Schoof*** or ***scheef***.' *Pr. Pv.*

SHOES AND STOCKINGS. The varieties of primrose and polyanthus which have one flower sheathed in another.

'***Pattens and clogs***' is the Sussex phrase for a like form in the *genus cypripedium.*

SHOO. To scare birds; Ger., ***scheuchen***, to scare birds.

'***Chou***, a voice wherewith we drive away pulleine.' *Cotgr.* Sc., ***shue***; Lanc., ***shu***, Tim Bobbin. In our 13th cent. lit. ***shawel*** occurs as a scarecrow. Ger., ***scheusal***, object of fear.

'So are these bugbears of opinion brought by great clerks into the world to serve as ***shewels***, to keep them from those faults whereto else the vanity of the world, and weakness of senses might pull them.' *Sir Philip Sidney's Arcadia, 1674, p. 263.*

SHOOL, SHULVE. To saunter along with extreme laziness, as if shovelling up the dust with the feet. Ger., ***schollicht***, cloddy; Dut., ***schoor***, to trail along.

SHOOT. To throw in, contribute. 'We ***shot*** a shilling piece tow'rds the frocks.' A.S., ***scot***; Ger., ***schiessen***. *Miss Gurney.*

From the A.S. ***sceotan*** in its sense of to expend, pay; hence our modern ***shot***, contribution.

SHOSHINS. Aslant, sloping. 'Dew yeeow cut that there dreen ***shoshins*** athelse t'al keeve.' *Anglice.* 'Do you cut that drain sloping, or else it will cave in.' *Moor.* See ***Ashosh***.

SHOT, or **SHOAT.** A young pig. In Suffolk, ***sheat***; in Essex, ***shote***; U.S., ***shote***, where 'A poor ***shote***' is said of one contemptuously; Dut., ***schots***, sorry, base.

Sc., ***shets***, three months' old pigs; ***shott***, an ill-grown ewe. In New England, a young hog between a sucker and porker. Dut., ***schot***, a hogsty.

SHOT-SELE. Eventide, when wild fowl and twilight birds come forth to feed and fly about.

A term applied to it by gunners on the Norfolk Ouse. *Wright.*

SHOTTEN-HERRINGS. Herrings which have recently discharged their spawn.

Applied also to gutted herrings.

'Alas, good gentleman! his mandillion was over-cupped, his wit paunched like his wife's spindle, his art shanked like a lath, his conceit as lank as a ***shotten*** herring.' *Gab. Harvey's Pierce's Supererogation*, 1593. A.S., ***sceotan***.

SHOVELARD. *Platalea leucorodia*; white Spoonbill. See ***popler***.

'***Schovelerd*** or popelore, byrd ***scholarde*** or poplerd, schoues, (shovel) bec or popler byrd.' *Pr. Pv.*

'The platea or ***shovelard*** which build upon the tops of high trees.' *Sir T. Browne.* Formerly a regular summer visitor to this county; still met with on the Norfolk coast.

SHOWL. A shovel. N. Ang., ***shull***; Dan., ***skovl***.

SHRAGS. Ends of sticks, as of broken twigs in a broom, or of whins and furze. 'Yar brum owt ta ha' fine ***shrags***,' said to a man about to dress recently thrashed barley for market; the clippings of live fences. *Moor.* Ger., ***schrag***, crooked, awry; ***schragen***, a stack of wood. ***Scrog***, a stunted bush, N. Ang. Gael. ***sgrog***; A.S. ***scrob***. ***Shrog***, a person of low stature.

'***Shragge*** trees, schredynge, of trees and other lyke. Sarmentacio.' *Pr. Pv.* 'To ***shrag***, castro, *vide*, to lop.' *Gouldman's Dict.*, 1664.

'Sleiden reports of a souldier cast out of the top of a castle, yet by miraculous providence catching hold on the ***shrags*** of a mulberry tree saved his life.' *D. Rogers' Naaman.*

'They consider not that they fish with a golden hooke for minums, (minnows) if they loose their hooke upon a ***shrag*** of triall and temptation they can never make amends againe for it.' *D. Rogers' Naaman.*

SHRAVEL and **SHROUGH**. Dry sare faggot-wood, fragments of sticks, reeds, &c., bits of coal, cinders, &c., picked up by the poor for fuel, and called ***shruff-stuff***. Applied also to other refuse and scrapings. ***Shrovy***, shabby, ragged, squalid.

Ger., ***schropfen***, to cut; ***schroff***, rough, rugged; ***schrot***, of refuse quality, applied to wood, grain, &c.; ***schuftig***, ragamuffin, squalid, rascally.

SHREEP. Thin. A.S., ***screpan***, to pine away.

SHREEVE. The sheriff, ***shere-reeve***. A.S., ***sur-geref***.

SHREPE. To clear. 'The fog begins to ***shrepe*** yonder,' i.e. to lift, move off. Isl., ***skreppa***.

SHRIMP. Any thing very small; ***shrimpshin***, a tiny bit.

SHROWD. To lop the branches of pollard trees. A.S., ***screadian***, to prune, lop away; ***shrowds***, the loppings so cut away.

SHROWDY. Said to showery weather, causing people to ***shrowd*** or take shelter; ***shrowds***, underground caves, dens of wild beasts.

Sw., ***skygd***, shade, shelter, ***skydda***, to shield; Wel., ***ysgodi***, to take shelter. Isl., ***skygga***. Usually derived from A.S., ***scrydan***, to clothe. Isl., ***skrud,*** a garment. See art. in *Nares*.

SHUCK. Var. of ***shack***, which see. To shed, strip off. Applied to the shelling out of over-ripe corn, and to the scattered ears of wheat shed in harvesting. Pea ***shucks***, pea husks.

Shuck is the form which has naturalised and widely prevails in the U.S. In the South the Indian corn husks are corn ***shucks***. Corn ***shucking*** or husking, a gathering of the young people in a farmer's house or barn to aid him in stripping the husks from the corn. To ***shuck*** off one's coat, to strip or peel it off. ***Chuck***, a shell, North Ang. dial., an egg shell. Gael., ***cochull***, a husk. Fr., ***coque***; It., ***guscio***.

SHUG and **SHUCK**. To shake, a shaking. 'Give the tree a good ***shug***.' 'A gon it a good ***shuck***.' 'A ***shuck*** 'a's hid.' Growing beans are said to be ***shuckl'd*** when beat down by wind or hail; ***hickled*** is said of corn root fallen; ***walted*** of it when beat down on its side. ***Shuck-trot***, a jog trot. ***Shuggins***, that which is shed or scattered, as corn at harvest. '***Schoggyn*** or roggyn. Agito. ***Schakyn*** or waveryn. Vacillo.' *Pr. Pv.*

Su.-Goth., ***skudda***, Dut., ***schudden***, to shake, ***schok***, a shake; Ger., ***schutteln***. 'And the boot in the myddil of the see was ***schoggid*** with wavis, for the wynd was contrarie to 'hem.' *Wickliffe. Matthew, c. 14.*

SHUTTLE. Slippery, sliding hither and thither. Ger., ***schütteln***, to shake, joggle; Wel., ***sitellu***, to whisk round. (Wel. ***si*** is pron. ***shi***.)

'***Schyttylle***, styrtyl, or hasty. Preceps.' *Pr. Pv.*

'I am aferd that Jon of Sp'h'm is so ***schyttyl*** wyttyd that he wyl sett hys gode to morgage.' *Paston Letters.*

'The rest was at my fingers' end; but farewell it since it is gone. Beare with my ***shittle*** remembrance.' *Nash's Plaine Percevall.*

'You know this well, that if you put a good sure horse in a teame amongst a sort of jades, he will ***shuttle*** and soon become untoward.' *Rogers' Lost Sheep.*

SHY. Wild in conduct (not in the sense of bashful). 'A ***shy*** boy, or a ***shy*** girl, is wanton, unsteady, amorous.' *Spurdens.* L. Ger., ***scheue***, Fris., and Dut., ***scheuh***, a trollop, trull, meretrix.

SIBRIT. See under ***Sybrit***.

SIDE. Long, as applied to dress. A.S., ***sid***. Used in East Anglia, says Forby, in the contrary sense of straight, as 'this sleeve is too ***side***, it must be let out,' or 'it is too loose, it must be made ***sider***.' A confusion which may have arisen from the equal inconvenience of movement felt in wearing a garment too long or too straight.

Old Fris. and Dan., ***sid***, deep. Su.-Goth., ***sid***; Isl., ***sidr***. Used also in Lanc. A.S., ***wide*** and ***side***, the Norfolk sense; or as Lanc. people say 'the width and the ***sith***'. In Linc. and in the North Bp. Kennett remarks the usage of a ***side*** field, i.e. long, a ***side*** house or mountain, i.e. high and ***side***. Used also to describe a high, i.e. a haughty person.

> 'Sumtyme I can be a monke in a long ***syd*** cowle,
> Sumtyme I can be a none and loke lyke an owle;
> I am ower Syre John sumtyme with a new shaven crowne,
> Sumtyme the person and swepe the stretes with a ***syd*** gowne.'
>
> *Bale's King Johan.*

> 'Seest thou how ***side*** it hangs beneath his hip?
> Hunger and heavy iron make girdles slip.' *Hall's Satires.*

SIDUS and **SIDLINGS.** Sideways. 'Kiender ***sidous***,' crooked.

SIGHT. A great number, so as to attract observation. 'What a sight of fine folks at the races!' Common in New England where the phrase 'by a long ***sight***,' is also prevalent.

'If youth could know what age do crave,
Sights of pennies youth would save.' *Norfolk Proverb.*

SILE. To strain as milk, to set down a turbid fluid to deposit its sediment. Whence ***silt, silth***.

'Thus stode I in the frytthy forest of Galtres
Ensowked with ***sylt*** of the myry mose.' *Skelton.*

'One would think so large a sea should in time sand or ***sylth*** up.' *North's Lives, iii, 78.*

Isl., ***sila***; Dan., ***sil***, to strain, filter; Ger., ***seihen***; Ir., ***silim***, to distil.

Sile, filth, because it subsides to the bottom. *Ray's E. Ang. Words.*

SILE. The fry of fish; Icel., ***sil***, a long, narrow herring, ***sile***, a sprat; Dan., ***silder***; Scot., ***sillock***; Wel., ***sil***, spawn or fry of fish. 'The sile of herrings and sprats cooked like whitebait is scarcely distinguishable.' *Gurney.*

Applied, says Ihre in his *Su.-Goth. Lex.* from the Keltic ***sil***, spawn, to the herring, from the incredibly rapid multiplication of that fish.

SILVER. To lose, to sustain a loss. ***Spend silver***, to lay out money. Common East Anglicisms. See also under ***Little silver***.

'Item, I wil that there be fowunde with my good a priest a yeer to synge in seynt Marie chirche for the soulys whoos bodyes I haue causyd ***to lese sylvir*** in ony vyse in my lyve at ony tyme.' *Bury Wills, (John Baret, 1463).*

'And may well be wondered at, that any should be at cost and paines and ***spend silver***.' *Rogers' Lost Sheep.*

SIMPER. To simmer, bubble, or boil gently. In Linc., ***simber***.

For other instances of this E. Ang. usage see under ***hamber***.

'That their vital heat and moisture may not always onely ***simber*** in one sluggish tenour, but sometimes boil up higher and seethe over.' *Henry More's Antidote against Atheism.*

SIN. A slur of to stand. 'Don't ***sin*** talking, but go to work.'

SINNOWED. Gaily ornamented. ***Sinnow***, a shewily dressed woman.

Of the rarest occurrence in Old Eng. literature. Possibly from the Fr., ***sinueux***, 'bosomy, crooked, full of hollow turnings, windings or crinkle crankles.' *Cotgr.* Or the Wel., ***sidanu***, silky, satiny; ***sidanen***, applied to a fine woman.

'What a prejudice it is to the thrift of a flourishing state to poyson the groth of glory, by giving it nought but the puddle water of penury to drinke; to clippe the wings of a high towring faulcon, who, whereas she wont in her feathered youthfulnesse, to looke with amiable eye on her gray breast, and her speckled syde sayles, all ***sinnowed*** with silver quilles, and to driue whole armies of fearfull foules before her to her master's table; now shee sits sadly on the ground picking of wormes, mourning the cruelty of those vngentlemanlike idle hands that dismembreth the beauty of her trayne.' *Nashe's Pierce Penilesse.*

SISERARA. A hard, cruel blow. A violent scolding, N. Ang.; ***sessarara***, a good beating or scolding, Northants.

Nares calls it a cor. of ***certiorari***, a writ at law.

'As for the matter of that,' returned the hostess, 'gentle or simple, out she shall pack with a ***sassarara***.' *Vicar of Wakefield.*

'That their sins may be removed with a writ of error, and their souls fetched up to heaven with a ***sasarara***.' *Revenger's Tragedy, Old Play.*

SITHE. To sigh. Old Eng., ***sike***; A.S., ***sican***. '***Sythynge***, syynge. Suspiracio.' *Pr. Pv.*

SITHES. Times. A.S., ***sithe***; Moes. Goth., ***siutha***.

'Sex ***sithe*** on is sex (six times one is six.)' *Capgrave*. '***Sithe*** vicis.' *Pr. Pv.*

'Wishes for home a thousand ***sithes*** a day.' *Hall's Satires, Book IV.*

SIZZLE. The half-hiss, half-sigh of an animal, as of an owl; the effervescence of brisk beer; to dry and shrivel up with hissing, by the action of fire on some greasy, or juicy substance. Dut., ***sissen***.

'Yeast is called ***sizzing***, from the sound of working beer.' *Ray.* Gr., ***sizo***.

SKAVELL. A small spade or skuppet used in draining, and in outhawling or feying narrow-bottomed ditches. It differs from a spade in having its sides slightly turned up. See ***Scoppett.***

'With skuppet and ***skavell***, that marsh men allow.' *Tusser.*

Fris., ***skofel***; Su.-Goth., ***skyffel***; Sw., ***skofwel***.

SKELP. In Suffolk, ***skelf***, a blow. 'To kick with violence.' *Forby*. Isl., ***skellr***, a crack, smack; Ger., ***schell***, a box on the ear.

SKEW. To start aside, as scared. Dan., ***skeie***, to swerve; Ger., ***scheu***, timorous, skittish.

'Some wenches come vnlased, Some huswyves come vnbrased,
Wyth theyr naked pappes That flyppes and flappes;
It wygges and it wagges, Lyke tawny saffron bagges;
A sorte of foule drabbes, All scurvy with scabbes;
Some be flybytten, Some ***skewed*** as a kitten.' *Skelton.*

Fable of an old Crab and a Young. 'Child, (says the mother,) you must use yourself to walk strait, without ***skiewing and shailing*** so every step you set.' 'Pray mother, (says the young crab) do but set the example yourself and I'll follow ye.' *L'Estrange's Æsop.*

SKILLET. The thin brass perforated implement used for skimming or fletting (A.S., ***flet***, cream; Isl., ***fleyta***, to skim off) the cream off milk. A small brass saucepan with a long handle. A.S., ***scell***, hollow.

Skeel, N. Ang., is a milk or water pail, contracting upwards and usually borne on the head with a pad.

'Some ran a good trot, With a ***skellet*** or a pot.' *Skelton.*

'Item, I giue to Elizabeth my daughter, my panne, a skommer, a gredyron, a spitte, a ***skillet*** panne.' *Bury Wills, (William Herde, shepherd, 1559.)*

Vessels usually made of bell metal, Gage Rokewode. '***Sceletta***, a little bell for a church steeple, whence our vessels, called ***skillets***, usually made of bell metal.' *Philips' New World of Worlds,* 1678.

SKIMMER. To flutter, gleam, flicker. Isl., ***skima***; Dan., ***skimten***, a glimmering; Ger., ***schimmer***. ***Skime***, to look asquint, N. Ang.

SKINCH. To stint, pinch, give short commons.

Ger., ***schinden***, to exact from, rape and scrape, skin a flint; Dan., ***skinden***, to fleece.

SKINK. I. To serve at table, particularly to serve the guests with drink. A.S., ***scencan***, to give drink; Isl., ***skenkr***, a gift, drink; Dan., ***skienk***, a buffet, ***skienke***; Su.-Goth., ***skaenka***, to pour out liquor. '***Schenkyn drynke***. Propino.' *Pr. Pv.* II. To squint, peer or spy about. Norfolk, ***skime***; Dan., ***skinsyge***, jealous, watchful.

In these, in the two last, and in several previous examples the tendency on the East coast to employ the Norse hardened ***k*** in preference to the Teutonic ***ch*** is noticeable, whilst in others, (as under ***sh***) it is reversed.

SKIP or **SKEP**. A basket. A bee-hive, Sc. Dan., ***skieppe***.

'A pitch-fork, a dung-fork, sieve, ***skep***, and a bin.' *Tusser.*

Gael., ***sgeip***; A.S., ***scep***; Sw., ***skeppa***; '***skeppe***, sporta, a plaited basket.' *Pr. Pv.* Lat., ***scappa***.

SKIP-JACK. A pert whipper-snapper. Merry thought of a fowl.

'Now 'tis but odde to think how such a flicketing, ***skip-jackly*** thing as that is, which is always so much upon the snatches.' *Fairfax.*

SKIRL. To ***shrivel*** up from excessive heat, as parchment, card, or paper before the fire. Isl., ***skraele***, to scorch, wither up; Goth., ***skior***, fire.

SKIWANIKIN, SKIWINCKIN. Awry, crooked, warped. Dan., ***skie***; Dut., ***zwanken***, to distort.

SKIZZLE. A large marble taw rolled at others placed in a ring.

It., ***schizzare***, to spin, squirt forth.

SKOPPOLOIT. Play, romps, frolicking. O. Eng., ***scoppe***, a leap, skip.

'What ha made yeow sa long?' 'Why, I ha bin havin a game a ***skoppoloit*** along i th' man Jenkins i th' chatch yahd.' Much used at Ipswich. ***Scope***, to loiter, has been surmised as its origin. *Halliwell.*

The Gael. has ***sgioball***, quick, active, nimble; the Isl., ***skopa***, to take a run; Sw., ***skutta***, to leap; O. Eng., ***scoppe***. ***Sooperloit***, play time, South Eng.

SKRANSH. To crunch, munch, or grind audibly between the teeth hard fruit or raw vegetables, biscuit, &c. It., ***granciare***.

Sc., ***crinch***; Fr., ***grincer***. ***Skrunchlen***, a small green shrivelled apple.

SKROWJ. To push, squeeze, crowd up. Gael., ***sgrog***, to compress, squeeze. Ger., ***schrauben***.

SKRUSSLE. The hard crackling skin of a roast loin of pork, breast of veal, &c.; Dan., ***kruse, krusul***, crisp.

SKULL. Probably the plaice. Sw., ***skolla***, a plaice.

'Bret., bretcocke and ***skulls***, comparable in taste and delicacy unto the sole.' *Sir T. Browne, IV, 331.* ***Skulls*** may possibly be the ***scald-fish*** or megrim, one of the smallest of the flat-fish tribe.

SKUPPATT. The handle of a spade.

Scuffet, a smith's fire shovel, Sc.; Belg., ***schup***, a spade. ***Shuppick***, a hayfork, Heref. Ger., ***schuppen***, to work with a shovel.

SKUTTLE. A shallow basket like a bowl. ***Skuttles***, a ship's hatches.

Skuttle, a skreen for dressing corn, i.e. a large, broad and shallow shovel for casting threshed corn from one side of the barn to the other, that light grains and dust may fall short. I. Dut., ***schotel, schootel***, an oven peel, a platter; Lat., ***scutella***. II. O. Fr., ***escoutilles***.

'A ***skuttle*** or skreen to rid soil from the corn.' *Tusser.*

'The night was not very dark, and one of the Mariners was gotten into the ***skuttle*** (I think that's the name on't) at the main-mast-top to see if he could make any land.' *L'Estrange's Erasmus' Colloquies.*

SKUTY. In small irregular pieces; A.S., ***scyt***; Su.-Goth., ***skoet***, an angle.

SLAB. I. The outer cut of timber taken off to square it for sawing into planks. Wel., ***llab***, a flag or thin strip, ***yslab***; A.S., ***slaf.*** II. A bricklayer's labourer, a drudge; Wel., ***yslabi***.

'Save ***slab*** of thy timber for stable and stye.' *Tusser.*

SLABBY. Dirty, refuse, pappy, dabby, sloppy, muggy, puggy, miry. Gael., ***slaib***, mire, sediment, filth. Dut., ***slabberen***.

SLADE. A small, open hanging wood, called also a ***shaw***. In Scot. a hollow, dingle; A.S., ***slæd***; Isl., ***slaed***, a valley, also a green road. In Essex applied to a dried water-course.

'***Slade***, ground sloping towards the sea.' *Pen. of Gower.*

'And satyrs that in ***slades*** and gloomy dimbles dwell.' *Drayton.*

Slade, N. Ang., a breadth of green sward in ploughed land, or in plantations.

SLADE. To carry on a sledge, to slide. Dan., ***slæde***, a sledge.

'***Slede***, (instrument) to drawe wythe.' *Pr. Pv.* Su.-Goth., ***slada***; Wel., ***ysled***.

SLAKE. Leisure, opportunity, ***slackness***. Isl., ***slakr***.

SLAM. Lanky and thin. Fr., ***esclam***, gaunt, thin bellied.

'A ***slam***, thin-gutted fox made a hard shift to wriggle his body into a hen-roost.' *L'Estrange's Æsop.*

SLAMMAKEN. A gawky, dawdling, untidy wench. 'A great ***slammakin*** mauther.' Dan., ***slam***, dirty; Su.-Goth., ***slem***, with the augmentative ***ock***. Dut., ***slabbaken***, to dawdle; Isl., ***slyma***.

'A ***slammakin*** lass,' a big, sprawling, untidy trollop. *Lake Dial.*

SLAR, SLARE. To bedaub. Isl., ***slor***, filth, fish refuse; Ger., ***slorig***.

'***Sloor*** or ***sowr***, clay; ***sloryed*** cenosus. (dirty)' *Pr. Pv.* Isl., ***slauka***.

Slairking, daubing with the finger, Whitby. To cleanse carelessly. 'Ti'nt horf weshed; nobbut just ***slared*** ower', Leeds. Fries., ***sloeren***. ***Slurry***, the drip of a grindstone, Salop.

SLATS. Dark blue ooze, left by the ebb of the sea. Dan., ***slat***.

'***Slothe***, where fowle water stondythe aftyr reyne.' *Pr. Pv.*

SLATTER. To wash carelessly, splashing the water about.

Lanc., ***slat***, to spill water about; Wel., ***yslotian***, to paddle, dabble; Dan., ***slatter***, slops; Ger., ***sletse***, a slattern; Prov. Ger., ***schlottern***, to dabble in wet. '***Sloteron***, or defowlyn.' *Pr. Pv.* Fris., ***sladderig***.

SLATTERING WEATHER. ***Slavering***, continuance of slight rain.

'Some go streyght thyder Be it ***slaty*** or slyder;
They hold the hye waye, They care not what men say.' *Skelton.*

SLAYS. Lanes or cuts through woods or coverts for rabbit shooting, netting, hunting, &c. See ***hay-net***.

In other dial. applied to wood cut and laid in rows for tying up.

O. Fr., ***esclayer***, to make a way through; Lapp., ***släwet***, to strike through.

SLAZY. Of loose texture, flimsy, easily torn and worn out.

Cor. of Silesian, whose manufacturers were formerly so stigmatized, says Forby; but the Isl. has ***slasa***, damaged, impaired, come to grief. Su.-Goth., ***slosa***, dilapidare; O. H. Ger., ***sleizen***, to break in pieces.

Sleeze, to separate, come apart easily, applied to badly woven cloth, Somerset.

'I cannot well away with such ***sleazy*** stuff, with such cobweb compositions, where there is no strength of matter!' *Howell's Familiar Letters*, 1650.

SLEEPER. I. The stump or stub of a tree left in the ground. II. The beams under barn and other floors. Hence railway ***sleepers***. A.S., ***slepan***, to put on, to impose. III. A rushlight.

SLENT. A deep puddle, any small pit in a common or plain.

The Scand. senses of ***slent*** are stagnant, torpid.

SLICK, SLICKEN. To make smooth, polish. '***Slyke*** or smothe.' *Pr. Pv.* Ger., ***slichten***. ***Slick***, smooth, shining, clear entirely; ***slick off***, right off. A popular Americanism. ***Slick***, rabbits' down; ***slike***, slippery, Heref.

'***Slekyston***, linitorium.' *Pr. Pv.* In former times polished stones, called ***slick***-stones, were used to smooth linen paper, to finish starching, &c.

'But paint and ***slicke***, til fayrest face be foule.' *Gascoigne.*

Su.-Goth., ***sleka***, to lick; Isl., ***slikja***, to polish, make to glisten. '***Sleker***, homo blandus qui suis blanditiis alios captat.' *Ihre's Su.-Goth. Lex.*

SLIDDER. To slide, slip along. Dut., ***slidderen***. '***Slyderyn***, labo.' *Pr. Pv.* Su.-Goth., ***sliddrig***, slippy; Isl., ***slidrir***, to slide.

'Some go strayghte thyther. Be it slaty or ***slider***.' *Skelton's Elinour Rumming.*

SLIFT, SLIVER. I. The fleshy part of the leg of beef. II. A slip of a growing plant or shrub. A.S., ***slifan***; Wel., ***ysleivyn***.

SLIGHT. To wear and tear, use up. Pret., ***slat***; past., ***slitten***. 'You'll soon ***slight*** up that thin coat.' Dut., ***slighten***, to wear. *Wright.*

SLIMSLACKET. Of very thin texture, loose, and flaccid; ***slimsy***, lazy, dawdling. Dan., ***slattet***, loose, flabby.

Su.-Goth., ***slak***; Wel., ***yslac***; A.S., ***slac***, lax; Isl., ***slæmr***; Dan., ***slem***, bad, ill.

SLINK. I. Lank, slender, gawky. Scot., ***slinkie***; Dan., ***slunken***, gaunt, scraggy. II. To suffer abortion, applied to cows only; Ger., ***schlenken***, to cast out; Su.-Goth., ***slincka; slink***-veal, the flesh of such an abortion, known as ***bobby***. Sw., ***slyna***, carrion.

Staggering Bob, the name given by butchers to very young calves, Chesh. dial.

The cow ***slinks*** her calf, the mare ***slips*** her foal, the ewe ***warps*** her lamb. I. Sc., ***slank***; Eng., ***lank***; Belg., ***slanck***.

SLOB, SLAB. A puddle, wet place. Isl., ***slabb***, mire, mud; Fris., ***slabbe***; L. Ger., ***slabben***, to leak, drip.

SLOD. I. To wade through mire, half-dissolved snow, &c. Isl., ***slod***, a foot-print, rut. ***Slodda***, to trudge through mud. Dan., ***slud***, sleet; Gael. and Wel., ***slod***, a puddle; Isl., ***slödr***. II. A short cake, baked before bread goes into the oven.

Sloods, deep cart ruts, Chesh. '***Slothe***, where fowle water stondythe.' *Pr. Pv.*

SLOFF. To swallow greedily and slovenly. '***Sloffynge*** or on-gentyll etynge.' *Pr. Pv.* Dut., ***sloef***, a sloven; Ger., ***soff***; Sw., ***sluskig***.

SLOON. The sloe. 'I sah, bawh, where ar yeow a gooen?' 'Why, a ***sloonen***.' 'Her eyes are as black as ***sloons***.' A.S., ***slan***; Dan., ***slaaen***.
Mid-Ang., ***slon***; Oxfordsh., ***slags***; in Kent, Salop, Wilts., ***slans***.

SLOP. The white hempen smock-frock, reaching mid-leg, worn for centuries past by farm labourers. A.S., ***slop***, an over-garment. '***Sloppe***, garment.' *Pr. Pv.*

'A slender ***slop***, close crouched to your dock.' *Gascoigne*, 1572.

'Item paid for iij yerds of blankett for a petycott and a peyre of ***slopps*** for the fool of the kechin, ijs., vjd.' *L'Estrange Household Accounts*, 1530.

SLOP. Underwood, ***loppings***. Ger., ***laub***, foliage, ***lauben***, to strip off leaves. Su.-Goth., ***löpa***.

SLOSH-WAYS, also **SWISH**. See ***Asosh***.

SLUB, SLUBBER. Thick, slabby mire. To swallow, making a noise with the throat or lips. Swed., ***slabbra***; Dan., ***slubbre***; Lat., ***labrum***, lip; It., ***labbro***; Teut., ***slabben***.

'Now every trade hath his sleights to ***slubber*** up his worke to the eye, and to make it good to the sale, howsoever it proves in the wearing.' *Greene's Quip for an upstart Courtier.*

'Noble Cæsarean Charlemain Herring! Pliny and Gesner were to blame they ***slubbered*** thee over so negligently.' *Nashe's Lenten Stuff.*

'Professe, some will say it is hypocrisie; walk accurately, and then it is but singularitie; give almes, then see his vaine glory; give not to some, (it may be unworthy) then there is your faith without charity; preach God's Word plainely, and it is but carelesse ***slubbering***; if elaborately, then see his affectation.' *Rogers' Lost Sheep.*

'Some there were (in fine) that would have fetcht a man's guts up at's mouth to see them, with their masques of after-birth, and with their menstruous ***slibber-slobbers***.' *L'Estrange's Quevedo.*

SLUG. Said of heavy surf, tumbling in with an off-shore wind, or a calm.
Slagg. Su.-Goth., Isl., and Teut., has the senses of rough weather, of rude assault, to smite, strike, &c. ***Slagga***, Su.-Goth., to buffet with frequent heavy strokes as on an anvil.

SLUG-HORN. One short and ill-formed, stunted and turned downwards. Also called ***snail***-horned.

SLUMP. To sink suddenly and deep into mud or rotten ground. A ***slumpy*** meadow, wet and boggy. To ***slump***, to slip or fall plump down in a wet or dirty place.

'***Slump*** (having the primary meaning of a shapeless lump), with us and with the Danes and Saxons, is used to denote an accidental fall.' *Ihre's Su.-Goth., Gloss.*, 1769. Dan., ***slumpe***, to stumble; Fris., ***slumpe***, a fall; 'in een ***slump***, or ***rumpsplump***,' all in a heap. Ger., ***sumpf***, a swamp; ***sumpfen***, to sink into a bog. Gael., ***sluib***, a puddle. In use in New England.

'In Susquehanna's woods when timber brash,
Slumps in the flood with many a hideous crash.' *American Pastoral.*

SLUR, SLURRY. Loose, thin, almost fluid mud. See ***Slar***.

SLURRUP. To swallow greedily any liquid. N. Ang., ***slorp***; Dut., ***slurpen***;

Isl., ***slupra***. Also O.H.G., ***slorpe***, a whirlpool; Dan., ***slurk***, a gulp.

SLUSH. I. Loose mud. Dut., ***sluyse***. II. Filthy talk, a ***slushy*** fellow, foul-mouthed. Su.-Goth., ***slask***, humor sordidus.

Under ***fl*** and ***gl*** groups of word have been noticed indicative of the action upon our senses of air and fire in movement. Under ***sl*** occur a number similarly expressive of water, conveying the nicest gradations of its sound, seeming, or sensation, whether ***sl***abbering, ***sl***aking, ***sl***attering, ***sl***eety, ***sl***imy, ***sl***ippery, ***sl***obbery, ***sl***oppy, ***sl***oughy, ***sl***uicing, ***sl***urried, &c., with their numerous dialectic off shoots derived from Scandinavian roots. It is observable that the prefix ***sl*** is foreign to the Romance languages.

SMALE. A hare's form. ***Smile***, the small gap in a fence, made by hares or rabbits. A.S., ***smygela***, a coney hole. *Wright.*

SMART as a carrot, very smart indeed. Essex.

SMASHER. An employer who sends his men to the truck shop.

SMEATH. An open level of considerable extent, as ***Markam Smeath***, the scene of the Swaffham Coursing Meeting, pronounced ***smee***. '***Smethe***, or ***smothe***' *Pr. Pv.* A.S., ***smœthe***, smooth, even.

SMEE. Herring fry, used for bait. Wild ducks of the first year's plumage are called ***smee*** – small things. Su.-Goth., ***smœ***, small; Sw., ***smä-fisk***, fry.

'In Essex is a fysshe, called a ***smie***, which if he be longe kept will turn to water.' *Elyot's Dict.,* 1598.

SMICK, SMICKET. Diminutives of smock or shift.

SMITHER. Light small rain, or smur. A Scotch mist. 'Dew it rain?' 'No, ta ***smither***.' Plat. Dut., ***smetten***; Dut., ***smetje***, a little spot; in E. Anglia, a ***smotch***. ***Smithers***, fragments, atoms, Mid Anglia.

SMOCK MILL. A windmill standing on wooden supports.

'So called from its shape resembling that garment.' *Forby.*

SMOTCH. To stain, defile. 'I have ***smotched*** my fingers with ***crock***' – which see. Sw., ***smutsig***; Ger., ***schmutz***; Fris., ***smodse***. Wel., ***ysmot***.

> 'And eke for she was somdel ***smoterlich***
> She was as digne as water in a ditch.' *Chaucer's Norfolk Reve's Tale.*

SMOUCHER. A smuggler. A.S., ***smuan, smugan***, to creep privily. Old Norse, ***smocka***; Fris., smucken; Eng., ***smuggle***.

SMOULD. *Ammodytes lancea. Lin.* The sand launce.

'The sand-eels, commonly called ***smoulds***, taken out of the sea sand with forks and rakes about Blakeney and Burnham, a small, round, slender fish, about three or four inches long, as big as a small tobacco pipe; a very dainty dish.' *Sir T. Browne.*

A valuable bait for turbot. On some coasts called a wriggle.

SMOUS. A Jew. Suffolk. Fries., ***smous***.

A term which seems to have puzzled Moor. It is an old Dutch name for a German Jew, so called, because many being named Moses, they pronounced it in Holland ***Mousyee***.

SMOUSE, SMEWSE. The track above ground of a hare through a fence or bank. The underground way of a rabbit through a bank is called

throushot. Fr., ***musse***, a secret corner, privie hiding place. *Cotgr.* A hare ***smoot*** or creeping hole, Cumb.

' 'Tis as hard to find a hare without a ***muse***, as a woman without a ***scuse***.' *Greene's Thieves Falling Out.*

SMORE. To abound, swarm. A swarm of bees are said to come ***smoring*** out of the hive; A.S., ***smoran***, to stifle. '***Smore***, wythe smeke,' *Pr. Pv.*

SMOUCH. A coarse kiss. To kiss with a loud smack; Fries., a ***smok***; Ger., ***schmucken***, to kiss; ***schmatz***, a kiss.

'What bussing, what ***smouching*** and slabbering one of another.' *Stubbs' Anatomy of Abuses,* 1583.

SMUG, SMUCK. To dress up neatly, to ***smudge*** or smarten up. Dan., ***smuk***; Dut., ***smuk***, ornament, finery.

'He hath so lick't and ***smug'd*** it up, cast such a gloss and varnish on it.' *Rogers' Lost Sheep.*

'In the craft of catching, or taking and ***smudging*** it, merchant and chapmanable as it should be it sets a work thousands who live gaily well by what in some few weeks they scratch up then, and come to bear office of Questman and Scavenger in the parish where they dwell.' *Nashe's Lenten Stuff.*

SMUR. Fine drizzling rain. Isl., ***smyr***; Dan., ***smyre***, to smear; Belg., ***smoor***.

SNAFFLED. Said of ripe corn beat down by wind or hail, which is also termed nickled, baffled, shuckled, and walted.

Sw., ***snafva***, to stumble, fall; Fl., ***sneuvelen***.

SNAG. A rough knob or gnarl on a tree, the shortened part or stump of pruned boughs; a process called ***snag*** pruning, in distinction from close pruning. Isl., ***snagi***, crooked, gnarled; Dut., ***snoeigen***, to prune.

One of the numerous East Anglicisms which have found wide currency in America. On the Western rivers it marks the great hidden danger of their navigation, the projecting stumps or branches of sunken trees.

Snag, to hew or cut roughly with an axe; N. Ang., to lop off branches. Teesdale. 'I have ***snagged*** my gown,' i.e., caught and torn it against a nail or thorn. Mid. Ang. ***snag***, a tooth; Somerset, ***snaggle***-toothed, or gag-toothed. *Nomenclator,* 1585.

'How much more then should we beware of ***snagging*** and snarling at God's secrets.' *D. Rogers' Naaman.*

'Search them presently, (cry'd the Intermedler) squeeze the balls of their eyes, and let their gums be examined, you'll find ***snaggs***, stumps, or roots, or enough of somewhat or other there to spoil the jest.' *L'Estrange's Quevedo.*

SNAGGY. Morose, snappish, snarly. 'How is a' this morning?' 'Kiender ***snaggy***.' 'Why, he's got the ***snags***.'

Gael., ***enagachd***, knottiness, knobbiness, sternness.

SNAP YOUR EYE. To wink or squint.

SNARL. To twist, entangle, knot together, as a skein in winding off. Isl., ***snarla***, to weave, entwine; Dan., ***snerle***, bind-weed. 'Snarynge, or ***snarlynge***, or rufflynge,' *Pr. Pv.* Ger., ***snarren***.

Snack-snurled, entangled; N. Ang., ***snarrel***, a hard knot; Cumb., ***nurled***, twisted; ***nurly***, ill-tempered; ***narle***, a knot; Mid. Ang. ***norle***. Craven.

'Her black, dangling tresses about her shoulders, with her ivory comb ***in-snarled*** in them'. *Nashe's Lenten Stuff.*

'Till the creature creep in too farre, the heart wax wanton and defiled; yea so ***snarled*** that it must cost her the vomiting of her morsels ere she can recover a cleare appetite again.' *D. Rogers' Naaman.*

'Let Hymen's easy ***snarls*** be quite forgot.' *Quarles.*

'Whence a snail, whose eggs have other kind of foes, besets them with other kind of shield and buckler. Their setting being the casing or housing such a tickleish piece of workmanship that wind and weather may not ruffle and ***snarle*** it, or any stragling bodies clutter up its rooms and stifle it.' *Fairfax.*

'It suits the men of business, whose affairs are getting into what is called a "***snarl***" or entanglement, in consequence of the depreciation of the currency.' *Times New York Correspondent*, Sept. 2, 1864.

SNARSTED. Scorned, defied.

SNAST. The burnt portion of the wick of a candle, the snuff. In Suff. ***sneest***. ***Gnaste***, *Pr. Pv.* Dan., ***snause***, to dirty, soil, ***snuus, snauset***, snuff; Isl., ***snatt***. ***Snaich***, a thief in a candle; ***snace***, candle snuff.

'But of lower consideration is the common fortelling of strangers from the fungous particles about the wicks of candles, which only signifieth a moist and pluvious air about them, hindering the avolation of the light and favillous particles; whereupon they are forced to settle upon the ***snast***.' *Sir T. Browne's Vulgar Errors.*

SNASTY, i.e., to take a thing in snuff, to be angry, captious, passionate. Su.-Goth., ***snäsa***, to huff, snub, upbraid.

SNEATH or **SNAITHE**. The crooked pole or handle of a scythe. A.S., ***snæd*** and ***sneath***, from the root Su.-Goth., ***sned***, oblique; Isl., ***sneida***, to twist, be awry. ***Sned*** is still used in Derbyshire.

Snathe, to prune or lop, N. Ang., from A.S. ***snithan***, to cut.

SNIB. To snub, cut a person short. N. Ang., ***snape***; Isl., ***sneipa***.

'The kyng cleped hem to his presens, and ***snybbed*** hem.' *Capgrave.*

'Others by their ***snibbing*** and chiding, or over-bearing them, doe blast that bud which else would blossome and beare.' *Rogers' Naaman.*

SNICKER-SNEE. A large clasp-knife. Dut., ***snicker-snee***.

Sc., ***snagger-snee***, see ***snag*** above; Dut., ***snee***, knife edge, a gash; Ger., ***schnecken***, to cut. ***Snick***, a cut, notch. Craven.

'I do verily bear myself in hand, that if the humor of huffing be but a little further cocker'd and more warmed, the Leyden gown must needs take place of the long robe at Cambridge and Oxford instead of the side thing, the thing by the side, and ***snicking*** and ***sneeing*** will be nothing else in the world but writing of Book *a la mode d'Angleterre.*' *Fairfax.*

> 'But they'l ere long come to themselves you'l see,
> When we in earnest are at ***snick a snee***.' *Norfolk Drollery*, 1673.

SNICKLE, SNITTLE, SNIDDLE. A slip-knot, a double knot in form of a bow. In Derbyshire to ***snickle*** hares is to snare them.

A.S., ***snicendne***, creeping; Ger., ***schnirkel***, to form into spirals; ***schnicken,*** to move quickly; ***schneide***, a noose, snarl.

SNIDDLE. Mown or cut green rushes, sedges. Su.-Goth., ***snida***, to cut.

Applied also to stubble, adds Pegge.

Sniddle or hassocks, the long grass which grows in marshy places. *Aira cæspitosa, Lin.* – Chesh. Long coarse grass, the *Poa aquatica* of botanists, common in ditches and gutters. Salop.

SNIPPOCK. A very small morsel. L. Ger., ***snippen***, to clip off.

SNOOD. The part of a fishing line to which the hook is tied. Sw., ***snoe***, string, line; Dan., ***snoe***, to twist, twine; Wel., ***ysnoden***, a hair lace, a fillet.

SNOUL. A short, thick cut from the crusty part of a loaf or of a cheese. Ger., ***schneiden***, to cut; L. Ger., ***snoeyen***, to lop off. ***Snoul***, a small quantity, Sussex.

In the vocabulary of dialectic words, found in the little Peninsula of Gower, (quoted in *Latham's Eng. Lang.*, p. 393) believed to have been imported by the East Anglian colonists, temp. Hen. I, occurs, '***soul***, cheese, butter, &c., as eaten with bread.' Is it the above? or is it rather the O. Eng. ***sowel***, and der. either from the O. Fr., ***saoul***, to stuff with food, or the Dan., ***suul***, victual, provisions? ***Sowl***, aught eaten with bread, Lanc. ***Sowle***, any liquid eaten with bread, Craven. See ***soil*** infra.

SNUCK. To smell, snift up. L. Ger., ***snicken***.

The der. may be A.S., ***snuck***, past part. of ***snican***, to sneak, creep. Dan., ***sniger***.

SNUDGE. I. Implies motion, as brisk as an aged person may use. 'The old woman went ***snudging*** along,' i.e. snugly wrapped up – Forby, who, with Miss Gurney, derives from A.S. ***snude***, celeriter. II. To ***snudge*** over the fire, to creep and cower close to it. 'I heent ben out – I ha' bin ***snudging*** over the fire all day.' *Moor.*

Under ***snabb***, celer, agilis, Ihre, in his *Su.-Goth. Gloss.*, has as cognates A.S., ***snude***, celeriter; Sax. ***sneidig***, celer; Isl., ***snudur***, citus.

The der. may be A.S., ***snuck***, past part. of ***snican***, to sneak, creep. Dan., ***sniger***.

The Su.-Goth. has ***snudda***, to handle gently, and the Prov. Ger., ***schnudeln***, to do imperfectly.

SNUDGING. Penurious, greedy, sordid; (Lanc., ***snidgy***,) ***snudge***, shuffling; ***snigging***, sneaking. A.S., ***snid***; Dan., ***snedig***, cunning.

> 'Where if he were a ***snudge*** to spare a groate.' *Gascoigne, Fruites of Warre.*
>
> 'And least esteemes the greedie ***snudge***, which goes
> To gayne good golde, without respect of fame.' *Id.*

'Those grey-beard huddle-duddles and crusty-cum-twangs were struck with such stinging remorse of their miserable Euclionism and ***snudgery***, that he was not yet cold in his grave, but they challenged him to be born amongst them.' *Nashe's Lenten Stuff.*

'Others are so dangerously worldly, ***snigging*** and biting usurers, hard and oppressing, or defrauding the simpler in their bargaines, cannot abide any should go out of their fingers without a nip.' *D. Rogers' Naaman.*

SNUFFS OF WEATHER. Fits of rough gusty squally weather.

'There is light sowne for the righteous, though it lie long in the moulds by reason of cold ***snuffes*** of weather, yet a sweet day at last will come, and a sunshine to fetch it up.' *D. Rogers' Naaman.*

SNURLE. A cold in the head, to snort; to talk through the nose.

Snurl, a nostril, N. Ang. Prov. Ger., ***schnau***, the nose, ***schnüren***, to snuffle; Isl., ***snörla***.

'Item Apollo that whirllid up in his chare,
That made sum to ***snurre*** and snuff in the wynde,' *Skelton.*

SNUSKIN. A nicety, tid bit.

Dan., ***snaske***, to champ one's food with a smacking noise.

SOAK. To bake thoroughly, applied to bread.

SOB. To wipe or suck up any liquid. 'Sob it up.' Cor. of ***absorb***.

'The land is very ***sobby'***, soaked with wet. In Warwick, ***sobbed***. *Miss Baker.*

SOCK. Moist on the surface, socky, soaky. A.S., ***socian***; Wel., ***swg***.

Sock-dyke, a ditch on the inside of a marsh embankment to carry off the water which soaks through. *Wright.* In Dorset, ***sog***; Dut., ***zaght***, washy.

SODGER. The whelk shell-fish. Also a brownish red beetle.

SOE. A large tub carried by two men on a stout staff or stang, passing through two iron rings at the top, for carrying water, grains, hogwash, &c. Fr., ***seau***, a water-pail. O. Fr., ***seille***, Provencal, ***selh***, Portuguese, ***selha.***

SOIL to, **SOILING**. The last fattening given to fowls when taken from the barn door and cooped for a few days. Old Fr., ***saoul***, to glut, stuff full; O. Eng., ***soyled***, pampered, high fed, said of horses.

SOLING. An assault, a beating, and

SOLL, SOWLE. To seize by the ear. Applied chiefly to swine.

'Wool 'a ***sowle*** a hog?' is a frequent enquiry into the qualification of a dog. A low bred mongrel will attack the *porcus a posteriori*; but this is not genuine ***sowleing***, and a boy would blush to own so base an animal. 'He'll go, he says, and ***sowle*** the porter of Rome gates by the ears.' *Coriolanus, iv. 5.* The last three words would be redundant to a Suffolk audience. *Moor.*

Skinner's der. from ***sow*** to pull by the ears as dogs do ***sowen*** (swine), although accepted by lexicographers and Shaksp. commentators, is unsatisfactory. Minsheu's, though copious, are no better.

Gotten a good ***sowling***, been severely dressed down. ***Sowl***, to duck, to plunge in water, rinse well. 'Come goa gie thesen a good ***sowling'***, says a mother to a sooty child, Leeds and Craven dial. ***Sowl***, to agitate in water for cleansing. Whitby.

To take ***soil*** is an old hunting term for taking to the water when the game is driven to that refuge. Fr., ***souiller***, to wallow in the mire; A.S., ***sol***, mire, a place to wallow in.

SOLLER. A loft, upper room, now usually confined to a belfry. Gael., ***solair***; Old Fr., ***solier***. '***Solere*** or lofte,' *Pr. Pv.*

Anything placed in an upper room is said to be laid on the ***soller***. Heref. Dial. Dut., ***zolder***, a garret. ***Soler***, a high seat, Cornwall.

'And namely ther was a gret college,
Me clepe the ***soler*** hall at Cantebrege.' *Chaucer's Norfolk Reve's Tale.*

'The ij chambrys with the ***soler*** above in the end of the balle towards my gardeyn,' Bury Wills (John Baret, 1463).

'Some skilfully drieth their hops on a kell,
And some ***on a soller*** oft turning them well.' *Tusser.*

'At Christmas, good husbands have corn on the ground.
In barn and in ***soller*** worth many a pound.' *Tusser.*

SOLLOP. To lounge, dawdle about; var. of lollop.

SORDS. Filth, washings, off-scourings. Lat., ***sordes***; Sw., ***sörja***, dirt, filth.

SORELY. Exceedingly. 'He'll be sorely pleased.' Ger., ***sehr***, very.

'In this tyme begunne men ***sore*** to multiplie.' *Capgrave.*

SORZLE, SOZZLE. To intermingle confusedly. ***Sorzel***, *s.*, an odd heterogeneous mixture. Var. of ***soss***.

Sw., ***sörja***, to mix cattle food with water or wash.

SOSS, SUSS. I. A jumble, or mixed mess of food; anything fouled or muddied. '***Sos***, howndysmete,' *Pr. Pv.* II. To drink. III. ***Soss*** also means a noise. 'It came down with a ***soss***.'

Soss, to fall with a thud; ***sossing***, heavy, sodden drinking; to be ***sossing*** in bed, to lie lazily stuffing there. Lake Dial.

Soss, 'full sowce' a heavy, clumsy fall, N. Ang.; to lap like a dog, Teesdale; to plunge into water; a boiled mess for a cow, Cumb.; ***sosslings***, tea leaves, Northants.

I. Gael., ***sos***, a mixture of food for dogs, an untidy mess. II. Ger., ***soff***, drinking, guzzling; Gael., ***sas***, to glut. III. Su.-Goth., ***susa***; L. Ger., ***suizzen***; Fl., ***suyzen***, to make a whizzing noise.

SOTTER. To boil gently, simmer, said of thick mixtures; also N. Ang. A.S., ***seothan***; Isl., ***sioda***.

SOUPINGS. Any sort of spoon meat. '***Soup*** it up.' Sw., ***supa***.

'Even as God tried the lappers of water from the ***soopers*** of it, for Gideon, so will he try thee.' *D. Rogers' Naaman.* Dut., ***zuypen***.

SPANK. To move swiftly and stoutly. ***Spanking***, striding along stoutly, moving nimbly. Also 'shewy, conspicuous, specially if large.' *Forby.* Dan., ***spanke***, to strut, stalk. Su.-Goth., ***spinkog***; Isl., ***spinka***, slender.

Spanker, N. Ang. and Sc., is applied to a tall well-made woman. A ***spankering*** hizzie, a tall nimble girl. ***Spankers***, long and thin legs. ***Spanky***, frisking, dashing. Of this ***spunky*** may be a cor. The Wel. has ***ysponc***, a jerk, spirt, a skip, bound; ***ysponciaw***, to bound sharply. ***Spankin***, provoking; also dashing, Lanc. Seldom said in a disrespectful sense, remarks Moor. 'A spankin gal.' 'A spankin hoss.' 'She's a spanker, i' fags.' We have several similar words applicable to our healthy, buxom damsels, he adds – a bonnka, a bouncer, a smashen gal, or smacken, slashen, smashen, swashen, strappen, swingen, swhacken, splashen, dashen, wappen, &c.

These vigorous similes nearly all appear derived from the tingling associations connected with the hearty buffet or loud resounding ***smack*** dealt by these sturdy Phillises, on fit occasion to their too forward Corydons.

Various der. have been suggested, as the Dut., ***spannen***, to stretch out; A.S., ***spannan***; also the Gael., ***spangach***, of metal, anything shining or sparkling; but the original sense seems to be the Scand. one of tall, slender, and long legged.

SPALT, SPARCH. Brittle, said of dry wood, &c., hence careless, heedless, pert, saucy, giddy, and frail. Ger. and Dan., ***spalt***; Dut., ***spalten***; Gael., ***spealt***. ***Spalsky***, snappy, brittle, Northants.

'***Spalle***, or chyppe,...***spelke***, fissula; ***spelte***, broke bonys or other thyngys; ***spelkyn***,' *Pr. Pv.* ***Spalls***, chips, Devon; Su.-Goth., ***spiaell***. ***Spelk***, to set a broken bone, Yorks. Dut., ***spalken***.

SPAT. Oyster spawn. Su.-Goth., ***spad***.

SPATE-BONE, SPAUT-BONE. The shoulder bone. In Suff., ***spade***-bone.

Albanian, ***spate***; Basque, ***izpata***; Wel., ***ysbawd***; O. Fr., ***espalde***; It., ***spalda***, Lat., ***spatha***. *Diez*.

SPAWLE. To spit out with force; spittle, saliva. A.S., ***spaw***.

'Another while the well drenched, smoky Jew,
That stands in his own ***spaul*** above the shoe.' *Bp. Hall.*

'Our Norwich, now vpon her legs was a poor fisher-town, and the sea ***spawled*** and springed (sprinkled) up to her common stairs in Cowper Street.' *Nashe's Lenten Stuff.*

'To spit and ***spawl*** upon his sun bright face.' *Quarles' Emblems.*

SPECK. I. The sole of a shoe, the heel is the heel-***speck***; ***speckings***, large long nails. II. The sole fish, from its resemblance in shape. *Forby.*

'***Spek*** is the name in the Cornish dialect for the ***dorade*** (apparently the sea-bream or gilt-head).' *Gonidec's Bretonne Dict.*

SPECKE. The woodpecker. Ger., ***specht***; Fr., ***spicken***, to peck.

SPENDER. A consumer. 'Small ***spender***,' one with little appetite.

SPERKET. A wooden peg to hang hats, &c., upon an iron hook. Var. of ***perch***.

'High on the ***spirket*** there it hung.' *Bloomfield's Horkey.*

SPILE. A wedge of wood, iron pointed, used in marl pits, &c.

Spile-peg, the wooden peg closing the air hole in barrels. Fris., ***spile***. ***Spelk***, a thatching pin, a splinter, N. Ang.; ***spile***, a stake, Cumb.; Su.-Goth., ***spiale***. Gael., ***spealt***; A.S., ***speld***; It., ***spillo***.

'Their silver spurs, or ***spils*** of broken spears.' *Hall's Satires, B. IV.*

'His fellow went down for a rope to ***spill*** the foot of the sail, which was blown out.' *North's Lives, ii, 317.*

SPLACK-NUCK. A miser. Gael., ***spiocach***.

SPOFFLE. To be over busy about little or nothing.

'***Beffleries***, fooleries, mockeries, gulleries.' *Cotgr.* Ger., ***buffeln***, to drudge.

SPONG. A long narrow slip of enclosed land. If planted called a squeach.

Spong-water is a narrow streamlet. Isl., ***sponn***; Sw., ***spänna***, a stretching out.

Spang is Frisic – a little brook which can be stepped across, or the plank or gangway over it. North Fris., a foot-step or path into a churchyard.

'***Swonge***, smal and long (or gawnte), *gracilis*,' *Pr. Pv.* Su.-Goth., ***spang***; Isl., ***spaung***, a plank, thin slice.

'The tribe of Judah with a narrow ***spong***, confined on the kingdom of Edom.' *Fuller's Pisgah Sight of Palestine.*

In Salop dial. a ***slang***; in Northants. a ***spung***.

Hot-spong, a sudden warmth from the sun breaking through clouds.

SPONG. A calm at sea. ''Twas a perfect ***spong***; not a brabble on the water.'

Su.-Goth., ***spang***, quod laminæ simile est, like a flat plate, Isl., ***spöng***, flat.

SPOUCH. Sappy as wood. Possibly from the Ger. ***speich***, spittle.

SPRAID. To sprinkle, bespatter, to moisten with spray.

SPRAK. Brisk, alert. Isl., ***sprækr***; Sc., ***sprag***; Eng. and Yankee, ***spry***. 'He is a good ***sprag*** memory.' *Merry Wives, IV, 1.*

SPRANK. A crack, flaw, or split in wood. Dan., ***spragen***; Ger., ***sprengen***, to split; ***sprock***, crackling. ***Sprunk***, to split, Essex.

SPRAT-MOWE. Herring gull. Ger., ***mowe***. 'Sea-***mowe*** byrd, or ***semewe***, alcedo.' *Pr. Pv.*

SPRAWLS. Small twigs or branches of trees. A.S., ***sprædan***, to spread; ***spranta***, a twig; Wel., ***ysbrigawl***, full of sprigs.

SPRIT. A pole to push a boat forward. A.S., ***spreot***; Isl., ***sproti***.

'***Sprete*** or qvante, contus,' *Pr. Pv.*

SPRUNNY. Neat, spruce, spry, a sweet-heart. Var. of ***pruning***, the action of hawks and other birds trimming up their feathers. Sc., to ***preen***. '***Sprunt***, lively, brisk.' *Phillips' World of Words.*

Sui.-Goth., ***pren***; Isl., ***prionn***; Ger., ***pfreim***, a large pin, bodkin; Dut., ***krulpriem***, a curling iron.

SPUD. I. A small weeding spade at the end of a stick. Dan., ***spyd***, a lance. '***Spudde***, cultellus vilis,' *Pr. Pv.* Wel., ***yspawd***. II. Any very diminutive person or thing; ***spuddy***, stumpy.

Spuddle, to rake the ground, as chickens in search of food, Devon.

SPUNKY. Brisk, mettlesome; common in U.S. See ***spank***.

SPURGE. To plaster with a thin coat of mortar between the rafters, without laths. A.S., ***spœren***, plaster, ***parget***.

Cor. of ***parget***, the plaister of a wall. '***Pargettynge,*** or ***spargettynge***, ***sparchyn*** of wallis.' *Pr. Pv.* See Way's note upon. 'To ***parget***, quasi ***parietare***, parietes cœmento incrustare.' *Skinner.* Lat., ***paries***, a wall, from Sansk. ***pari***, around. 'It., ***paretonio***, white fatty earth or clay, good for loam or daubing mortar, the name of the colour, houses, doors, or windows are commonly painted.' *Florio,* 1598. O.F., ***pariette*** for walles, blanchissure. 'I ***parget*** or whyte lyme.' *Palsg.*, 1530.

'If ye have bestowed but a little sum in the glazing, paving, ***parieting*** of God's house, you shall find it in the church-window.' *Bp. Hall – of the Vainglorious.*

SPURK. To brisken up. 'Come ***spurk*** up, here's your sweet-heart a comin.' *Moor.* Wel., ***percu***.

To ***spurk*** up, to spring or brisk up. *Ray's S. and E. Words.*

SQUAB. To squeeze down, beat flat. Dan., ***qvab***. Wel., ***yswad***.

'While we lay tumbling and tossing the sea-priest I told you of, ***squabs*** himself down directly upon our shoulders; it was a fat, heavy fellow, and we both of us cry'd out.' *L'Estrange's Erasmus' Colloquies.*

SQUADDY. Thick set. Dan. and Ger., ***qvader***.

'He was a fatte, ***squaddy*** monke that had beene well fedde in some cloister.' *Greene's Newes from Heaven and Hell,* 1593.

SQUAJ. To ***scourge***, whip. 'A gon em a right good ***squajen***, an a desarv'd it.' *Moor.* A whipping top is a ***squajen*** top.

SQUALDERS. *Discophoræ Medusadæ.* Varieties of the jelly-fish.

'*Urtica marina*, of divers kinds, some whereof called ***squalders***.' *Sir T. Browne.*

SQUALLY. Said of corn or root crops broken by vacant, unproductive patches.

SQUAT. To settle, compose, quiet; from the ***squatting*** or settling down of the hare. It., ***quatto***, crouched down; Fr., ***cacher***.

'An old word. Moor gives ***squat*** as meaning to settle; in Suffolk, a squatter is there a settler; but we, though no doubt taking the word from that county, always use it in a bad sense. Its meaning with us is to occupy another's land.' *Elwyn's Americanisms.* Wel., ***yswatiaw***, to squat, lie flat.

SQUATTING PILLS. Opiates or composing pills. ***Squat***, to quiet, M. Ang.

SQUIGGLE. To shake a fluid about the mouth with closed lips. In the U.S. to move about like an eel.

It., ***squizzare***, to slip away like an eel.

SQUINANCY. Quinsey, used by Bp. Hall. '***Sqwynacye***, sekenesse, (sqwynsy)', *Pr. Pv.* O. Fr., ***squinancie***; Lat., ***cynanche***.

'Som for glotoni sal haf thare,
Als the ***swynacy*** that greves ful sare.' *Pricke of Conscience*, 1340.

SQUINDER. To burn and smoulder faintly as damp fuel, or as a candle with bad wick.

Ger., ***schwinden***, to dwindle, decay, waste away; A.S., ***swindon***.

SQUINNY. Lank, thin, narrow, ***squinny***-gutted. Su.-Goth., ***swinna***.

SQUOLK. A draught of liquor. An onomatopœia like ***julk***.

SQUY BOBBLES. Difficulties conjured up, ***quibbles***. 'He'd a bawt the home but for the lawyer's ***squi-bobbles***.' *Moor.*

STADDLE. What anything stands on, as the support of a corn stack, hay rick, &c., a bottom or foundation. Su.-Goth., ***stad***; A.S., ***stathol***. I. Sax., ***stadel***, a foundation; Wel., ***ystadledd***; Dut., ***stathel***. Applied also to young trees left standing in thinning, to grow. ***Stadles***, Lanc. and N. Ang., marks left by the small pox.

'Then see it well ***stadled*** without and within.' *Tusser.*
'The straightest ye know For ***staddles*** let grow.' *Tusser.*
'Leave growing for ***stadles*** the likest and best.' *Id.*

STAG. I. A Wren. II. A Cock-turkey killed for the table in his second year. Isl., ***steggi***, a drake, gander, or male of various birds; A.S., ***steig***.

Steg-month, N. Ang.; or gander-month, E. Ang., the month of a woman's confinement.

STALE. The handle of a rake or long fork. Also the stalk or reed of hemp. A.S., ***stela***; Ger., ***stiel***, a column, boll of a tree; Pl. Dut., ***steel***, a stem, stalk; Dut., ***steel***, a helve, handle.

'Like a broad shack-fork with a slender ***stele***.' *Hall's Satires.*

'***Stele*** or stert of a vesselle, ***ansa***,' (a haft, handle), *Pr. Pv.*

STALE. A decoy, snare. '***Stale*** of fowlynge or byrds takynge.' *Pr. Pv.* Fr., ***estaler***, to display, shew; ***estalon***, a decoy.

Originally the counterfeit of a bird, set up to allure hawks and birds of prey.

'The more holy the person is, the more carefully doth Satan act by him, that by his ***stale*** he may ensnare us.' *Bishop Hall's Contemplations.* (Explained by the commentator of the recent S.P.C.K. ed., ***means.***)

'Neither was Ishbosheth any other than Abner's ***stale***'. *Id.* (***Pretence***, interprets the same commentator.)

STAM. To astonish, overcome with wonder, to fairly stun.

Su.-Goth., ***stimma***, to make an uproar; O. Ger. ***stam***, a stunning noise, report, rumour, filling with surprise and fear. Ger. ***ungestümm***, tempestuous, blustering. Fl. ***stommelen***, to make a loud din; Dan., ***stime***, to make an uproar, hubbub; Wel., ***stamuss,*** astounded; Fr., ***estommi***; Salop, ***stomber***.

'But to break off from this so great a ***stamme*** to the mind.' *Fairfax.*

An Akenham rustic visiting the Suffolk coast for the first time, on his return from Aldborough was asked by his master what he had seen. 'Tha fare a rare lot o' water for a small place like that' was his answer. 'Why John,' was the rejoinder, 'that's the sea.' 'Well I know'd ta war.' 'Well, and what did you think of it?' 'I dun knaw, Sir, ta fared in such ***stammin'*** agonies all th' time I war theer, Sir.'

At the same place, on the first night of the re-appearance of great comet of Donati, a farmer who had just snuggled himself in bed, was abruptly roused by one of his serving men. 'Who's that?' 'Plase Sir, that's me.' 'What do you want?' 'Why, yar must come down, Sir, if yar plase.' 'What's the matter?' 'Yar must come down Sir, if yar plase.' Down came the farmer in sulky mood and was led out into the yard. 'Dew yar but look theer, Sir,' exclaimed the man excited, pointing to the comet, 'I feel wholly ***stammed*** if that theer star dont fare to ha' bust hisself.'

STAND. A flower-stalk. Swed., ***sittande***.

STAND-HOLES TO. To rest content as one is. ***Stated***, suited, Suff.

STANK. A dam, pond. Su.-Goth., ***stäng***, a lake, tank; Bret., ***stank***, a fishpond. Fr., ***étang***, Lat., ***stagnare***, to stop, hinder. Wel., ***ystanc***, that confines, limits. Eng., ***staunch***, watertight. Old Fr. ***estancer***, to stay, stop; N. Ang., a ***tank***. Cornish, ***stanconni***, to prop.

'Item, Sir John Buck, parson of Stratford, fished my ***stanks*** at Dedham and helped to break my dam.' *Sir J. Fastolf, in Paston Letters,* A. D., 1450.

'Thei lighted and abiden beside a water ***stank.***' *Robert de Brunne.*

STAN-STICKLE. The stickle-back; *Gasterosteus aculeatus*, of *Lin.*, from its sharp spiny belly, the Jack Sharp of Cheshire. A.S., ***sticel***, a prick. Su.-Goth., ***stänga***, to prick, sting. '***Stykelynge***, fysche,' *Pr. Pv.* Also called ***stuttle***, and in Suff. ***tantickle***.

'*Pangilius Marinus*, or sea-***banstickle***, having a prickle on each side. The smallest fish of the sea, about an inch long.' *Sir T. Browne, IV, 331.*

Forby mentions their occurrence some years ago in the Ouse above Lynn, in such myriads as to almost choke it up, tainting the air ten miles round with their stench as they were carried away by the farmers for manure.

STAPLER. A settler, a stopper, a floorer, a final upsetting of any further hope. L. Ger., ***stapelen***; Lat., ***stabilire***, to make firm.

STATHE. A term in common use in Norfolk for a wharf or landing place. A.S., ***stath***; Isl., ***stædr***, a shore, bank; in Kent, ***stade***. '***Stathe***, waterys syde,' *Pr. Pv.*

'For caryeng of ye same Lyngs, from ye Bulle to ye Common ***Stath***, iiijd.' *L'Estrange Household Accounts.*

STEAD. To supply a place left vacant; ***stedded***, suited. 'I can't git no work – the farmers are all ***stedded***'. ***Stead***, a place, site, as fair-***stead***, home-***stead***. A.S., ***stede***. '***Stede***, place.' *Pr. Pv.*

'There screeching satyrs fill the people's empty ***steedes***.'
P. Fletcher's Purple Island.

STEEN. Spite, envy. A.S., ***teon***, slander, malice, reproach.

STIANY. 'The ***styanye*** yn the eye.' *Pr. Pv.* A.S., ***stigend***.

STIFLER. A stickler, busy on occasion, raising the dust. 'She was a high ***stifler***.' Also a stunning blow. ***Stifle***, to ruin. See der., under ***tiffling***. ***Stiffle***, to suffocate, stifle.

STILTS. Crutches. A lame man is said to walk with ***stilts***. A.S., ***stealcian***, to go warily, to stalk. Su.-Goth., ***stylta***.

STINCH. To stink. A.S., ***stinc***; so O. Eng., ***slinch***, to slink.

'What a great part of the day is taken up by many in ***pranking*** up the body, lapping up ***stinch*** in silke, in adorning dung, guilding rottennesse, poudring excrements, perfuming putrefaction.' *Rogers' Lost Sheep.*

STINGY. Piercing cold, Norf. In Suffolk, ***stringy***.

Su.-Goth. & L. Ger., ***strenge***, rigorous, severe; ***streng köld***, bitter, biting cold.

STINT. A species of polecat or weasel, Suffolk. ***Stint***, L. Ger. for ***stink***.– *Kilian*. A.S., ***stine***.

STIR-UP-SUNDAY. The last after Trinity. From its collect.

STIVE. To raise dust. 'Go gently, Tom, you ***stive*** the ladies.'

'***Steyyn*** up, scando, ascendo,' *Pr. Pv.* Isl., ***styfa***; Su.-Goth., ***stoft***; Dut., ***stof***, dust; Dan. and Teut., ***stöve***, to be dusty; O. Fr., ***estouffer***, to stifle; It., ***stufa***, a hot-house.

Stive, Somerset, to keep close and warm; Fr., ***estuver***, to warm. Also to tremble. Dut., ***verstuyven***, to shiver with cold.

'***Stive***, dust, Pembroke, where dust implies only sawdust.' *Pegge.*

STOCK. The blackened plate or place at the fire back, or sides; hence the common simile 'As black as the ***stock***.' See ***Crock***. ***Stoker***, which may be a cognate, seems der. from Ger., ***stockern***, to prick, poke; Isl., ***stokkr***; Dan., ***stok***, stick.

Stoke, to stir the fire. Fries. and Dut., ***stooken***, to kindle, stir the fire.

'***Stoaker***, one that looks after the fire in a brew-house.' *Phillips' World of Words*, 1658.

STODGY. Thick, clayey, clogsome. Said in Suff. of a heavy road. More frequently applied to porridge and similar mixtures.

Ger., ***stocken***, to stagnate, stiffen, thicken. Su.-Goth., ***stocka***. Also to oppress, stifle, as ***stodging*** weather; ***stodgy***, said of a fat, clumsy girl, Lake Dial. ***Stodged***, crammed full, Craven.

STOLY. Dirty, disorderly. Dan., ***söle***, to dirty, befoul.

A.S., ***sol***, mirc, dirt, a place to roll in. Dut., ***stollen***, pieces and fragments; Sw., ***ställa***, to disorder.

STONGEY. Hot blistering weather. Cor. of ***stinging***, the Su.-Goth., ***stänga***. Or it may be by one of those curious inversions of meaning common in E. Ang. (vide ***sore*** and ***sweet***); which see ante.

STOOR. To stir; a commotion. 'A ***stoor*** of yeast,' the quantity required for a brewing, is a phrase implying that it is to be ***stoored*** (stirred) into the wort to excite fermentation. Ger., ***storen***, to stir up. Sax., ***styran***.

'The whyche preest I wyll shall calle vpon, ***meve and stoor***, that all thyng in my seyd wyll be pformyd and doon.' *Bury Wills. (Marg. Odeham*, 1492).

STOUR. Stiff, stout, sturdy. Applied in Suff. to stiff land; in Norf. to strong vegetable growth. Pl. Dut. ***stuur***; Su.-Goth., Fris. and A.S. ***stor***, strong, great. '***Stoor***, or hard or boystows,' *Pr. Pv.* Su.-Goth., ***stort***, haughty, proud.

'Tille Uttred his kosyn, a stiffe knight in ***stoure***.
He gaf his kyngdom and died in langoure.' *Robert de Brunne.*

'For body being a ***stour***, unwieldsome thing, or at least, a boaky, unthrough-faresome thing, it cannot stir without asking another bodies leave to crowd by.' *Fairfax.*

STOVER, STUVVA. Winter food for cattle, fodder from thrashed corn, whether straw, chaff, or colder. Clover made into hay, straw, fodder, &c. 'Spend ***stover***,' to consume provisions. *Bp. Hall.*

'Thresh barley as yet but as need shall require,
Fresh threshed for ***stover*** thy cattle desire.' *Tusser.*

'The lean and feeble cattle, that would but spend ***stover***, and die alone, shall perish by the sword of Israel.' *Bishop Hall's Contemplations.*

Old Fr. ***estouvier***, convenance, nécessité, provision de tout ce qui est nécessaire.

STOW. To cut the boughs of a pollard close to the head. Dut., ***stœvne***, to prune, poll; Gael., ***stoth***. The cuttings are called ***stowins***, and if stolen are termed ***brumps***, which see.

STOW. To drive cattle into a corner to catch them. See ***unstowly***.

STOWTER. To struggle along, to walk with a lumbering, heavy gait. Dut., ***stooten***, to push along, thrust, stamp heavily; Su.-Goth., ***stöta***.

'Here greet shulderys, square and brood,
Here breestys up bere, hire bely so large,
For upon hire is a greet carte lood;
She is no bot, she is a barge,
A ***stouhte***, that no man may charge.' *Lydgate.*

STRAFT. A scolding bout, an angry din. Isl., ***straffa***, angry, morose; Su.-Goth., ***stræff***; Ger., ***straffen***, arguere, objurgare.

STRAIK. The iron tire or rim of a cart wheel. ***Strings***, the shafts.

Strake, the iron hoop or band which binds together the fellies of the wheel. It. ***strica***, a long narrow plate of metal; Sp., ***straca***; Ger., ***starken***, to strengthen; L. Ger., ***stricken***, to bind together. ***Strakes***, Suff., boat planks.

Strines, Lanc., are handles of a barrow, sides of a ladder. Wel., ***ystrom***, frame work; Lat., ***stringo***; Fr., ***estreindre***, to bind, keep fast in; L. Ger., ***stringhe***, a chain strap; It. ***strenga***.

STRAM-MALKING. Gadding and loitering; said of a dirty, slovenly female.

See ***maukin.***

Stram and ***stramash***, loud and sudden noise; ***stramming***, noisy, banging; ***stram-bang***, ***stramming***, huge, ***strammer***, a big lie, Devon; ***strammerly***, ungainly, Kent; ***stramash***, to smash, as with a flail amongst china, Whitby. ***Stramp***, to trample upon, N. Ang.; ***strammullion***, a strong masculine woman, Sc.; ***stramash***, a broil, Sc.; Fr., ***estramacon***, a blow, cuff, bang; It., ***strammazone***, a staggering blow or fall, and ***strammazzo***, a wad, a whisp, a swab or maulkin; Ger., ***strampeln***, to kick, stamp. There are two roots, the Su.-Goth., ***ström***, Isl., ***straumr***, œstuans, and the It., ***strame***, straw, conveying the sense of litter, untidiness. From the latter, ***strammalking*** seems derived.

STRAMMEL, STRUMEL. A head of long, dishevelled hair. L. Ger., ***striemelen***, to wave about; Isl., & Dan., ***strimmel***, a shred, tatter.

It may derive in a littery untidy sense, from It., ***strame***, straw. ***Strammel*** and ***strommel*** are N. Ang. cant words for straw; vide *Jamieson* and *Grose.*

STREEK. To iron out clothes. Dut., ***stryken***; Ger., ***striechen***.

Streeking-board, used formerly for composing the limbs of a corpse. A.S., ***streccan***. Now applied to the ironing board.

STREELY. Long and thin. O. Fr., ***estrillé***, thin, slender, lank.

STRINKLE. To sprinkle. Ger., ***strekelen***. Bret., ***strinkella***.

'Men whose brains were seasoned with some ***strinklings*** at least of madness and phrensy.' *Henry More, on Godliness, c. 14.*

STRIPPINGS. The last milk drained from a cow in milking, esteemed richer than the first; Norfolk, ***strockings***; Sc., ***stribbings***.

STRIVE. To rob a bird's nest. Sw., ***ströfva***, to rove about in search of plunder.

STROME. To step out with long strides; Dan., ***ström***, to rush forth.

STRONG-DOCKED. Thick-set, strongly made about the loins and rump.

'Betty is a good shearer (reaper, Su.-Goth., ***skaera***) said an old labourer in commendation of his daughter; she is a fine ***strong-docked*** wench!' *Forby.*

STROOP. Gullet or wind-pipe; Dan., ***strube***, throat; Isl., ***strapa***.

'***Strowpe*** of the throte, epiglotus.' *Pr. Pv.*

STROUT. To strut, also a struggle, bustle, quarrel. Dan., ***stryg***; Isl., ***strokit***. Sc., ***strouth***; A.S., ***struddan***; O. Fr., ***estrois***, to protrude, swell, strut out.

'***Strowtyn***, or bocyn owte, turgeo.' *Pr. Pv.* Ger., ***strotsen***, to be swelled, puffed out; ***stroter***, a robber, highwayman.

'These upstart changelings went ***strouting*** like Philopolimarchides, the Bragart, in Plautus.' *Greene's Quip for an Upstart Courtier.*

'There is a beast in the north part of Suetia which they call a Jerffe, whose property they say is this – having killed his prey and pufft up his belly with feeding, (so that it ***strowteth*** out like a bag-pipe) he getteth presently betwixt two narrow trees and streineth out backward that which it hath eaten, and thus emptying of itself it returns again to the remainder of the carkasse and filleth himself again; and so continueth his former course until it hath devoured all; which being consumed he hunts after more, and after this sort passeth the time.' *Rogers' Rich Fool.*

STRULL. Excellently well. A.S., ***til, tól***; Fl., ***struys***.

STRY. To destroy, waste; ***stry-good***, a spendthrift; ***stryance***, wastefulness; ***stry-goodly***, extravagant; ***stryful***, wasteful, cor. of destroy. '***Stroy*** or ***dystroyare***.' *Pr. Pv.* ***Strushons***, wastefulness, Lanc.

'Lincolne and Lyndeseie thei ***stroied*** and wasted.' *Robert de Brunne.*

STUBBY. Blunt-pointed, short, thick, stunted. ***Stubs***, decayed stumps, broken stakes, props, short nails for heavy shoes.

'And like a ***stubbed*** thorne.' *Gascoigne.*

'An ynche above her kne, Her legges that ye myght see,
But they were sturdy and ***stubbed***.' *Skelton.*

Su.-Goth., ***stubbe***; A.S., ***stybbe***; Isl., ***stubbe***; Sw., ***stubig***. A good ***stub***, a round sum, Devon.

STUGGISH. Stout, strong, sturdy. Dan., ***stug***. '***Stugge***, a hog's trough.' '***Stuk***, short.' *Pr. Pv.*

Strugg'd, stuggy, applied to a broad shouldered, chubby-cheek'd boy, Devon.

STULK-HOLE. A puddle. Su.-Goth., ***sylta***, a bog, swamp.

Stolky, wet and miry, Glouc. A.S., ***sol***, mire, dirt, a place to wallow in; Wel., ***twl***, a hole, pit; Gael., ***tuilc***, an over-flow, flooding with water.

STULL. A luncheon, a lump of bread or other eatable. Gael., ***stiall***, a slice or piece.

STULP. A boundary post, or a support. Su.-G., ***stolpe***, a tree trunk. '***Stulpe*** or stake.' *Pr. Pv.* Dan., ***stolpe***, a post.

STUNTY. Short, stunted. A.S., ***stintan***, to stop in growth; Dut., ***kluntet***. Also crusty, snaggy, runty. In Linc., stubborn, angry; A.S., ***stunt***, foolish, mad.

N. Ang., ***scrunty; strunty***, dwarfish, Cumb.; Fr., ***estreint***, shrunk up. Took ***stunt***, became stupid; ***stuntish***, obstinate. Whitby. ***Stunta***, a fool, ***stunship***, folly. *Verstegan.*

STYE. To soar, ascend. A.S., ***stygan*** and ***stylan***, to mount up.

SUDDED. Soiled, dirtied, defiled. N. Ang., ***suddled***; Ger., ***sudeln***, to daub, defile; Su.-Goth., ***sudda***; ***sulsh***, Wessex.

Meadows are said to be ***sudded*** when covered with drift sand left by the floods, Devon.

'Repent, repent, you ruins of intemperance, recover your souls though you have ***sudded*** your bodies.' ***Nashe's Christ's Tears***.

'And useth in his sermons to raile upon his parishioners, calling them ***sowded*** piggs, bursten rammes, and speckled frogs.' (Vicar of Bedingfield, Suffolk.) *White's Century of Scandalous Priests*, 1642.

SUFFOLK CHEESE. See ***Trip***.

'Having quoted so many hard sayings on Suffolk cheese under ***Bang***, it is but fair to give Fuller's commendation of it. "Most excellent cheese are made here (in Suffolk), whereof the finest are very thin, as intended not for food but digestion. I remember when living in Cambridge, the cheese of this county was preferred as the best. * * * Pantaleon, the learned Dutch physician, counted them equal at least with them of Parma in Italy. Butter, for quantity and quality this county doth excel, and venteth it at London and elsewhere. The child not yet come to, and the old man who is past the use of teeth, eateth no softer, the poor man no cheaper, the rich no wholesomer food. I mean in the morning."'

Fuller's Eulogium stands almost alone. Early in the century following, Ned Ward, in his *Infallible Predictor*, foretells that 'Many London prentices will be forced to eat ***Suffolk cheese***, that their master's daughters may be kept at a boarding school.'

SUFFOLK FAIR MAIDS.

'It seems the God of nature hath been bountiful in giving them beautiful complexions, which I am willing to believe, so far forth as it fixeth not a comparative disparagement of the same sex in other counties. I hope they will labour to joyn gracious hearts to fair faces, otherwise, I am sure there is a Divine proverb of infallible truth –"As a jewel of gold in a swine's snout so is a fair woman which is without discretion."' *Fuller's Worthies.*

SUFFOLK MILK.

'This was one of the staple commodities of the Land of Canaan, and certainly most wholesome for man's body, because of God's own choosing for his own people. No county in England affords better and sweeter of this kind.' *Fuller's Worthies.*

SUFFOLK STILES.

'It is a measuring cast whether this proverb pertaineth to Essex or this county, and I believe it belongeth to both, which, being enclosed countries into petty quillets, abound with high stiles, troublesome to be clambred over, but the owners grudge not the pains in climbing them, sensible that such severals redound much to their own advantage.' *Fuller's Worthies.*

SUKEY. A breeding sow.

SUMP. A dead weight; a blockhead; fossil wood. ***Sumpy***, lumpish.

Su.-Goth., ***sump***, a shapeless lump; Ger., ***sumpfen***, to stagnate, stand still. Dut., ***sompig***, boggy. One of the East Anglian words carried into Gower.

SUNKET. To pamper, cocker. Hence a silly fellow; a sickly child is 'a poor ***sunketing*** thing.' Var. of ***junket***, which see.

Sunkets, Sc., provision of any kind. Also a small quantity of food or drink, specially if given grudgingly. ***Sunkets***, suppers, Cumb.

SUSAN, OLD, or **SUKEY.** A hare.

Gypsy dial., ***shushy***, a rabbit; Gitano, ***jojoy***; Hindostanee, ***susa***.

SUSS. A call to swine; to swill like a hog; an unclean mess. See ***Soss***.

SWACK, SUSSACK. A violent fall; also a blow. 'A gon em a right good ***sussack*** i' the guts.' 'The baw Sparrak shuvv'd the mawther Sal ***swack*** down off a the stule, an crackt ar sconce.' *Moor.* Ger., ***swacken***; Isl., ***svacka***. ***Swak***, to throw or cast with force, N. Ang. Isl., ***svakk***, violence, racketing horse play. ***Swacker***, something huge; 'a ***swacking*** lie.'

SWACKER. A handsome, sprightly, bouncing girl.

Sw., ***vacker***, handsome, beautiful, charming, pretty.

SWAD. A sword. A silly clown or bumpkin.

Swad is a common term of reproach in the Eliz. Drama, see *Nares*, der. uncertain, but supposed to be the N. Ang. ***swad***, a peascod. The Dan. has ***svadse***, to babble, jabber, gabble. Applied in Prov. Dan. to a giddy coquette, or to an impudent forward fellow.

'For so he was a Dutche, a deuill, a ***swadde***.' *Gascoigne.*

'Let country swains and silly ***swads*** be still.' *Id.*

SWAILING. Lounging from side to side in walking. ***Swallop***, a heavy, lounging gait.

Zwail, to move about with arms extended, and up and down, Somerset.

Su.-Goth., ***walla***, used 'de motu inconstante vagantium et erronum.' *Ihre.*

Ger., ***schwallen***, to waver, undulate, sway to and fro.

SWAKE, SWIKE. The handle of a pump.

In other dial. ***swape*** is a long pole for raising a bucket from a well. Isl., ***svipa***, to swing up and down, oscillate. Grose has ***swape*** the handle of a pump, Norfolk. It is rather N. Ang. Sc., ***swap***, to draw. ***Swipe***, a crane or engine to draw up water out of a well. *Nomenclator,* 1585.

SWALE. I. A low place, a hollow. Dan., ***svœlg***, an abyss. II. Shade, in opposition to sunshine: '***Swale*** or shadowe.' *Pr. Pv.* Isl., ***svala***, cool; Su.-Goth., ***swal***. In Suf. a gentle rise of ground. A.S., ***swellan***, to rise.

SWALLOCKY. Applied to the appearance of clouds in hot weather, before a thunderstorm.

Su.-Goth., ***swalla***, æstuare, fervescere, with the intensive ***oka***; A.S., ***swaloth***, heat.

SWAMMOCKS. A slatternly girl. 'As dirty as a ***Moll-swammocks***.'

Ger., ***schwamm***, toadstool, excrescence, proud flesh; ***schwammig***, proud, flaunting. With the Su.-Goth. intensive, ***oka***.

SWANK. To sink in the middle. Dan., ***svang***, hollow of the sole. Ger., ***schwanken***, to waver, fluctuate; ***swinky***, pliant, Devon.

SWAP. Smart and sudden, clean and quickly done. Isl., ***svipa***; A.S., ***swipan***. 'Swap or stroke,' *Pr. Pv.* Dan., ***i et svip***, in a trice.

SWAPER, SWAY. A switch. '***Sweype***, for a top or scoorge.' *Pr. Pv.* A.S., ***swapan***, to sweep; Dut., ***zweep***, a whip. Su.-Goth., ***swepa.***

'***Swap*** of his bed, this is my sentence here.' *Chaucer's II Nunne's Tale.*

'Dastards, why stand you still? he sayth, and straight
Swaps of the head with his presumptuous yron.'

Grimoald's Death of Cicero, 1553.

SWARD-PORK. Bacon cured in large flitches. Su.-Goth., ***sward.***

SWATTOCK. A severe fall. Intensive of ***swack***.

SWEETLY. Excessively. 'How sweetly cold it is!' 'Yes, 'tis bitter cold!'

SWELKING. Sultry. 'A ***swelking*** hot day'; ***Sweldersome, sweltersome, swullocking***, overpoweringly hot. A.S., ***sweltan***, to perish by heat; ***sweltendlic***, ready to die; Isl., ***swaela***, Su.-Goth., ***waella***; L. Ger., ***swelten***, to languish.

Grass cut in wet weather is said to ***swelt***. In a hot, dry season every green thing ***swelts*** for want of rain, Cumb. ***Swelt***, dead, says Verstegan.

'In such a cause in weary woes to ***swelt***.' *Gascoigne.*

'For veray sweme of this swemeful tale;
About his hert he thoughte he gan to ***swelt***.' *Lydgate.*

'And as little able are we (though we should sweat and ***swelt*** our hearts out.)'

Rogers' Rich Fool.

SWERTLE, SERTLE. To startle, surprise.

Swirtle, to move uneasily or in a fidgetty manner, Cumb. dial.

SWIG, SWIDGE. To drain off, swill, guzzle, suck in. A roof leaking is said to be 'all of a ***swidge***.' A puddle or plash of water is called a ***swidge***. ***Swiggle***, a dimin. of ***swig***, means also to shake liquor in an enclosed vessel, to drink greedily. ***Swuggle*** and ***swulk*** are variations.

A.S., ***swilgan***, to swallow; Norse, ***swiga,*** to drink in; Gael., ***suigh***, to drain, suck in; Dut., ***zuigen***, to suck. Richardson is curiously astray here, 'to ***swag*** or weigh down,' his illustration ought to have set him right –

'The flock is drain'd, the lambkins ***swig*** the teat,
But find no moisture and then idly bleat.' *Creech's Virgil.*

SWILL. A basket containing about 500 herrings, made of unpeeled willows. Used for transferring the fish from the boat to the shore. Probably from the Gael., ***suil***, a willow; Fr., ***saule***; Su.-Goth., ***salg***; A.S., ***seal***.

SWINFUL. Sorrowful, wistful, longing. 'Poor thing, ta looked so ***swinful*** aata me,' said by a nurse of a weaned child. A.S., ***swincful***, wretched; ***swincan***, to toil; '***swinkt***, wearied.' *Milton.*

'***Swync***, labour. We say yet, "***swinc*** and sweate."' *Verstegan.*

'For he had ***swanken*** all the longe night.' *Chaucer's Norfolk Reve's Tale.*

'Mary that I wyll and the one half with hym ***swynke***,
To encourage hym to drynke the botome off.' *Bale.*

SWINGE. To cut brambles, &c., from hedges. A leash for hounds.

SWINGEL. That part of a flail which swings. A.S., ***swingl***; Dut., ***swinghelen***, to cut weeds down. In Chesh., ***swippo***.

'She ***swynged*** up a quarte At ones for her parte.' *Skelton.*

'In the ***swindge*** of his Trident he constituted two Lord Admirals over the whole navy of England.' *Nashe's Lenten Stuff.*

'Hwæt tha, tha arleasan Eadmundum bundan, and bysmoreden hyxlice, and beoten mid sahlum, and swa sythan læddon thonne ileaffulne kyng to ane eorthfestum treowe, and tegdon hine thærto, mid hearde bendum, and hiue eft ***swancgon*** longlice mid swipum, and he symle clypode, betweox tham ***swincglum***, mid sothan ileafan to Hælende Criste.' *Homily on Martyrdom of St. Edmund, written in the Ang.-Sax. dialect of East Anglia.*

SWOB. A very awkward fellow, fit only for coarse drudgery. It is our form of the sea term ***swabber***, one who sweeps and cleans the decks with a ***swab*** or mop. *Forby.*

A.S., ***swapan***, to sweep, brush; Dan., ***svaber***, to mop; Swed., ***svabb***; Dut., ***zvabber***, the drudge of a ship; Fr., ***fauberter***.

SWOBBLE. To talk in a noisy, bullying, blackguard manner. Ger., ***schwabbeln***, to roll, shake to and fro; ***schwaddern***, to rattle, boast.

SWOBFULL. Brimful. Prov. Ger., ***schwabbeln***, to drink hard.

SWOTTLING. Corpulent, greasy and sweaty. A.S., ***swat***. Also noisy, chattering; Ger., ***schwatteln***, to prate, babble.

SYBBRIT. The banns of marriage. One of Sir T. Browne's words, and in full use at this day on the East coast.

Cybrede, banna; ***sybrede*** or bane; ***cybbe*** or kyn, skyn, *affinis*. '***Sybbe*** or of kynne, consanguineus, contribulis.' *Pr. Pv.* ***Sibberidge*** or ***sibbered***, the Banes of matrimony, Suff. *Ray's East Country Words*. Way in his note on the word has, 'Affinis viri et uxoris cognati, – alyaunce or ***sybberd***. – *Whitint. Gramm.*, 1520. 'consanguinitas, affinitas, ***Cybrade***. – *Wilbr. Dict.* ***A sybredyne***, consanguinitas.' *Cath. Ang.*, 1483.

Der. by Hickes and Spelman, from A.S., ***syb***, akin, (still in common use in the North) and ***byrht***, to bruit, divulge. This der. after much disputation and conjecture has been accepted by the compilers of our dictionaries and glossaries for the last two centuries.

The term occurs in a curious entry in the old assembly books of the Yarmouth Corporation, Dec. 25th, 1625, Charles I. 'WHEREAS by the marriage of many poor folkes in this town, the increase of poverty and poor people is much augmented, and the great charge of the town being already too much overcharged, it is thought fitting and very requisite to intreat Mr. Brinsley, our minister, to forbear to take any banns, ask any ***CYBREDDS***, or marry any poor persons in this town with license or without, except such couples shall first obtain the handwriting of the aldermen or chief constable of the ward where they inhabit, to signify they be allowed inhabitants of this town, and may fittingly and without exception marry.'

From the Wel. root, ***cyd***, (corresponding with the Lat. ***con, cum:*** Gr., ***sun***; Sansk., ***sam***,) denoting union, joining together, a mutual act, derive hundreds of words with that prefix and added significance in the Kymric language. ***Cydbriodas*** and ***cydbriawd***, intermarriage, from ***cyd*** and ***priodas***, espousals, wedlock; ***cydbriodi***, to inter-marry; ***cydwaed***, consanguinity. ***Sibbril*** appears to be a corruption of the foregoing.

Moor in his Suffolk words has two long articles upon it. He appears to have been put on a red herring trail by 'a learned and reverend' correspondent, on whose authority he sums up, – 'After all the word is deduced from the beginning of the banns, as they used to be published in Latin, ***si quis sciverit***, &c.' Later on, in his appendix, he admits with compunctious visitings, the sad downfall of his exultation over this happy etymology. On consulting the Latin liturgies, no such passage could be found.

SYNNETTS. Cygnets, young swans.

'Item in reward to Arnold's sarvant for bryngyn of ij ***synetts***; xvd.' *L'Estrange Household Accounts*.

T

TA, TE, TO, *art.* or *pron.* The, this, that, it. '***Te*** appears to be the A.S. article ***the***; ***ta***, the Isl., ***thad***, without its final letter; ***to***, the Mæso-Goth. ***tho***; all deprived of the aspirates in accordance with a strongly marked East Anglian propensity.' *Forby*.

'Dew it rain?' 'Is ta dew.' 'Ta crumble all ta pieces.' 'Te frize, te hail?' It freezes, it hails. Isl., ***thad frestur, thad heilar***. 'Ta frize?' 'Yes, and ***that*** hail too.' 'Do it frize?' 'No ***that*** don't frize now, but ***ta*** wull at night.' ***To***-day, ***to***-night, are used for ***this*** day, ***this*** night. ***Tan***, then, 'now and ***tan***.' *Forby* and *Moor*.

Our ***the*** is the old Frisic ***thi***; fem. ***thin***; neut. ***thet***; answering to the Teutonic

der, die, das. In E. Anglia, Scandinavian influences have rejected the aspirate, as in N. Anglian dialectic speech, in which the Norse pronoun *et* to this day holds its ground against the Sax. article ***the***, but shortened by elision to t', as t' house, t' wood.

T and ***th*** are curiously interchanged in the E. Ang. dialectic speech. 'There are tree apples on that three.' 'I went to the shop for tree ha'porth o' tread, and tumbled over the trossold.' ***Th*** also becomes ***f***; e.g. famble for thimble. 'Just yar look here, Mum, I tuk up Miss Fahny's dress, and there fares sumthin like a famble in it.' These peculiarities are noticeable in the Yarmouth dialect, which is said to come all out of the throat.

TAB. A shoe-latchet fastened with a thong. A lace ***tag***.

L. Ger., ***tap***; Ger., ***zapfen***, to cover, pin, peg, fasten. The Gael. has ***taodh***, a chain, binding, fastening.

TACK. A trick or take-up at cards; the handle of a scythe. Dut., ***tacke***. Fr., ***attacher***; Isl., ***taka*** and ***tekia***. Also said of food of cattle and other stock. 'Tough meat has plenty of ***tack*** in it.'

Tak, a trick or lift in card playing, Cumb.

Gael., ***tacar***, provision, plenty; A.S., ***tacan***, to lay hold of; Isl., ***tak***, possessions, means.

TAG, to follow closely, 'He's allways ***taggin*** aater her.' Dan., ***tag***, a grip, grasp. A.S., ***tigan***, to fasten to.

TAHNATION. A modified oath. Also used in the sense of magnitude. 'A ***tahnashun*** sight of folks.' An Essex phrase, transplanted to and widely prevalent in America.

> 'Poor honest John! It is plain he know'd
> But liddle of live's range,
> Or he'd a know'd gals oft, at fust,
> Have ways ***tarnation*** strange.' *John Nokes and Mary Stiles*.

TAINT. I. A very dirty slut; Fr., ***teindre***. A protuberance at the top of a pollard. A.S., ***tanede***, one diseased with a tetter.

TALLET. Any upper room, with an unglazed lath window.

Tallet, a hay loft, West. Wel., ***tal***, a space overhead; ***taflod***, a loft.

TANGLE. Dark, thick-stalked sea weed, beset with little bladders. ***Sea-tang***, ***laminaria digitata***. Isl., ***thöngull***. Su.-Goth., ***tang***.

TANGS. Dirt, disorder. 'Yar in pretty tangs,' – very dirty, Norf.

O. Fr., ***tan***, frenzy, riot; O. It., ***tangari***, a slovenly, filthy, greasy fellow.

TANTABLET, a fruit tart with its surface tricked out with shreds of pastry. O. Fr., ***tabletté***, cut in angles, facets, lozenges.

Tantadlins, apple dumplings, Gloucester; ***tantarrin***, a squab pie, Northants.

Dan., ***tant***, a loy, trifle; Wel., ***tant***, a whim; Ger., ***tandélig***.

TAPPIS. To lie close to the ground. A sportsman's phrase. Ex., 'It is so wet the birds cannot ***tappis***.' Fr., ***se tapir***, to crouch.

Tapished, hidden. To ***tappy*** as a deer, delitesco. *Coles' Dict.*, 1677. ***Tapassant***, lurking or squatting. *Kersey's Dict.*, 1708. (a Suff. writer.)

> 'With joy alle at ons thei went tille Snawdone,
> On Inor and Ini that ***tapised*** by that side,

To purveie tham a skulkyng, on the Englis eft to ride.' *Robert de Brunne.*

TARDRY. Immodest, loose, tawdry.

A vulg. cor. of St. Audrey, or Auldrey, meaning St. Ethelreda; it implied originally that the things so called had been bought at the fair of St. Audrey, once as famous as St. Bartlemy, where gay toys of all sorts were sold. This was held in the Isle of Ely and elsewhere on her name day, Oct. 17. An old chronicler, *Harpsfield, Hist. Eccl. Angl.*, makes St. Audrey die of a swelling in her throat, which she considered as a particular judgment for having been in her youth much addicted to wearing fine necklaces.

'But with white pebbles makes her ***taudries*** for her neck.' *Drayton.*

The O. Fr. has ***taudis***, a fowle, sluttish, unhandsome, undressed room. *Cotgr.*

TASK. A tax. '***Taske*** or talyage...***taxyd***, taskyd.' *Pr. Pv.* Wel., ***tasg***.

Tax is used in U.S. in the sense of charging a price for aught.

'She says, Peacock hath paid for him two ***tasks*** at that time.' *Paston Letters*, A.D. 1475.

'The Kyng's Money. – Item pd. to the constables, Batyley and Thaccar of Ryngsted, for the ***taske*** of Barnard's londs, xxijs.' *L'Estrange Household Accounts*, 1530.

'***Ax*** we all deem low, but we all speak of ***tax*** which is originally ***task***, – the reason probably is task-masters and tax-gatherers closely resemble each other.' *R. Winter Hamilton's Yorkshire Dialect.*

TATTER. To stir actively and laboriously. 'He is a very painstaking man, always ***towing*** (tewing) and ***tattering*** after his business. Whitby, ***tetter***. Fr., ***tâter***. ***Tatterer***, a female scold.

'***Tateryn***, jaueryn, or speke wythe owte resone.' *Pr. Pv.* Fr., ***tatillon***, a meddling busybody; Fl., ***tateren***, to famble, fumble, maffle in the mouth, tattle.

TAWNY. Very small, tiny; ***teyny***, Cumb.

TEATHE, TAD. Manure dropped on the land by the cattle depastured. Isl., ***tad***, excrement; Gael., ***todhar***, land manured by cattle.

Tathy-grass, soft grass grown under trees, Cumb. Grass luxuriant from the use of manure. *Essays Highl. Soc.*

'Tayin londe wythe schepys donge, ***tathyn***, stercoro.' *Pr. Pv.*

TEEN. To trouble, vex; ***teenful***, vexatious. A.S., ***tynan***, to vex.

'With preyerys, fastynge, coold and mekel ***teen.***' *Capgrave.*

TEES. Chains fixed to the ***sales*** of the thill horse. A.S., ***teo***, to pull.

TEEVA, TIVER. Suff., red ochre. A.S., ***teafor***, ruddle.

TENDER. A waiter at a public table or place of entertainment.

This is, we believe, strange to say, almost the only E. Anglicism to be found in the whole range of Crabbe's poetry.

As a naval term it is of old standing. It occurs in *Dampier's Voyages*, 1685.

Forby writes, 'waiters were called ***tenders*** in East Anglia, till recently'. The word is now used to designate the truck that waits on the railway engine with coals.

TERRIFY. To tease, irritate. A blister is said to terrify a patient. Flies tormenting horses and kine, '***terrify*** 'em sadly.' A flea ***terrifies*** a child, and an adult is ***terrified*** with the tooth ache.

'Flies terrify a horse's sore back; stones in the ground ***terrify*** a man digging it, in

Heref. and Glouc.' *Sir G. C. Lewis.* 'I can't ***terrify*** myself with no books; I can't be troubled with any reading.' *Miss Baker,* Northants. Used also in a similar sense in Sussex.

'***Teryare*** or ertare, irritator.' *Pr. Pv.* O. Fr., ***tarier,*** to vex, plague.

TETCHY. ***Touchy,*** peevish, snappish, irritable. Applied also to land difficult to work. It., ***ticcio,*** capricious, skittish.

Fr., ***tache,*** a reproach, disgrace, disreputation, blot to one's good name.

'The soule is full of ***teches*** and pritches against reproof; or it hatcheth some false conceit, that it hath obeyed when it hath not, or puffes and snuffes against some other thing.' *D. Rogers' Naaman.*

TETTER. A pimple. A.S., ***teter.*** Also called a twiddle.

> 'In faythe, Mesure is lyke a ***tetter***
> That ouergroweth a manne's face.' *Skelton.*

TEW, TOW. To pull, tear, ***tousle,*** as hay with a fork, weedy soil, with harrows; to tease flax and wool. A.S., ***teon,*** to tug, pull at, or ***tawian,*** to dress, pull, prepare. Dut., ***touwen.***

Tue, to labour hard, to fatigue by incessant toil, N. Ang.; to ruffle, disturb, 'My gown's sadly ***tewed.***' Teesdale, to ***tew*** (tumble) and toss about in bed; 'a ***tewing*** haytime,' wet and therefore laborious. 'A ***tewing*** bairn,' a restless child, Whitby. ***Tew,*** a rope or chain for dragging vessels along. '***Sare tues,***' great difficulties, N. Ang.; ***teaw,*** a pulley for raising weights, E. Ang.

'***Tewynge,*** of lethyr, frunicio, ***tew*** of fyschynge, piscalia... reciaria.' *Pr. Pv.*

> 'The toiling fisher here is ***tewing*** of his net.' *Drayton.*
> 'Hire skyn is tendyr for to towche
> As of a hound-fyssh or of an hake,
> Whoos ***tewhyng*** hath coost many a crowche,
> Hire pylche simple for to make.' *Lydgate.*

'And lest you that bite and snarle be devoured by others! I have noted it that nothing will coole some men's spirits till they meet with such as tame and ***taw*** them.' *D. Rogers' Naaman.*

'Mines of metal, or layers and veins of barren earths and sapless medlies, we can't tell how far they may be ***tiew'd,*** and drest, and mingled, so as at length to be made fit for the good of body.' *Fairfax.*

TEWELL. A tail, a pipe or funnel. The straight gut, *intestinum rectum.* In Norfolk applied to the fundament of a horse.

O. Fr., ***tuiau,*** a pipe, quill; Lat., ***tubellus;*** Old Fris., ***tülle,*** a pipe, channel. It occurs in *Niebelungen Lied, vv. 38-39.* Wel., ***thwl;*** Bret., ***tuellen*** or ***duellen.***

'For thei put a horne in his ***tewhel,*** and the spete thorw the horne.' *Capgrave. – Murder of Ed. II.*

THACK. To thatch, thatching materials, reeds, &c. A.S., ***theccan.***

'For strawe, for ***thakke,*** for ye same berne – xxs.', *L'Estrange Household Accounts,* 1525. ***Theak,*** Whitby. Isl., ***thekia.*** '***Thak*** for howsys,' *Pr. Pv.*

'Item pd. to Dingle for iiij dayes ***thackinge,*** at iiijd, the daye.' *L'Estrange Household Accounts,* 1547.

> 'Plucke downe lede and ***theke*** with tyle.' *Skelton.*

THAPES. See ***Fapes.***

THARRAGO-NIMBLE. Diarrhœa. In Scot., ***woolly-wombles.***

THEAD. The tall wicker strainer placed in the mash tub to run off the wort clear; more commonly called a ***fead***. A.S., ***thydan***, to strain. '***Thede***, bruarys instrument.' *Pr. Pv.*

THE. It. 'The child will cut theself,' ***them***, those; ***then***, that time; ***there and there-away***, thereabouts; ***the t'one, the t'other***, the one and the other; ***thinder***, yonder; ***thisn's, thusn's, thatn's***, in this or that manner; ***thennum***, at that time; ***thoffer***, because.

THICK-END. The greater part. The ***thick end*** of a mile.

THIGHT. Applied to turnips or other crops, close, ***thick***-set; applied to roofs or vessels, impervious, as opposed to leaky. I. A.S., ***theon***, to flourish, grow thick. II. Dan., ***toette***, to tighten.

Theat, firm, close, staunch, said of barrels that do not run, N. Ang.

'***Thyht***, hool fro brekynge, not brokyn, integer solidus.' *Pr. Pv.* Isl., ***thott***.

THILLER. See ***filla***. A.S., ***thil***, a pole or shaft. '***Thylle*** of a cart, temo; ***thylle*** horse, veredus.' *Pr. Pv.*

In a coal mine the surface on which the tram runs, N. Ang.

THOKISH. Sluggish, slothful. One of Sir T. Browne's words. A.S., ***thac***, slow. ***Thokish***, applied to wet boggy land.

Isl., ***thoka***, musty, foggy. '***Thoke***, as onsadde fysche, humorosus, insolidus.' *Pr. Pv.* '***Thokes***, fish with broken bellies; cowerde,(i.e. silly, foolish). herteles, long-***thoke***, vecors,' Winchester MS. of *Pr. Pv. Way.* Sw., ***tok***, a fool; Dan., ***tokke***, to behave like a fool.

Thokes, an old Eng. term for broken-bellied fish, may perhaps derive from the Prov. Dan. ***tokke*** (*Molbech's Danske Dial. Lex.*), which has the sense of the Dan., ***sönderg***, asunder, e.g. broken, squeezed, crushed, smashed in pieces. ***Tocke***, Fris., to draw, tug, lug, &c.; 'Su.-Goth., ***tokka***; Isl., ***thoka.***' *Ihre's Su.-Goth. Lex.* The ***tokke-net***, a trawl or drag net, would bring up many fish in this damaged condition. The statute, 22 Ed. IV., c. 2, regulating the packing of fish, prohibits the mixing of ***thokes***, broke-bellied fish, with tale fish. ***Thoke*** occurs as a local name in old E. Ang. documents, and is sometimes written ***Toke***.

THONY. Said of damp timber or underdried hay. See ***Dank***.

Thampy and ***thany***, Craven; ***thony, thoan***, Lanc.; A.S., ***than***, moist, wet; Su.-Goth., ***dunken***; Teut., ***tuncken***.

THOWLS. Either the elevations or ***thole*** pegs, or the hollows in a boat's gunwale, to receive the oars. A.S., ***thol***. Dan., ***tol***.

THOWTS. The ***thwarts***, the across seats of the rowers.

THREAP. To dogmatise, beat down in argument; A.S., ***threapian***; O.N., ***threfa***; ***Thrip***, Suff., a clipping stroke. Su.-Goth., ***drapa***.

Threap is a very expressive N. Anglicism. '***Threaping*** agean! when wi' tuh ha' done? ther's nivver noa peace whear he is.' Leeds Dial. Chesh., ***thrippa***, to beat; ***threphel***, a flail, Lanc.

A place is said to be ***thrapt*** full when excessively crowded, Essex.

'My fooes they bray so lowde, and eke ***threpe*** on so fast.' *Ps. 55, Surrey.*

'With eagle-soaring Bullingbrook, that at his removing of household into banishment as Father Froysard ***threaps*** us down, was accompanied with forty thousand men, women, and children weeping, from London to the Land's End, at Dover.' *Nashe's Lenten Stuff.*

'A ghost being in itself not roomthy it cannot bear any roomthy behaviour towards bodies that are so, any more than bodies that are bulky can bear immaterial respects or thoughtsom behaviours towards ghosts that are so; roomthiness being as much nothing to a ghost as thinking is to a body, so that you may as well ***threap*** one down that a ghost is heavier or lighter, colder or hotter, wetter or dryer, harder or softer, whiter or blacker than a body.' *Fairfax.*

'***Threap***, to dogmatise. A man will say of a clamorous talker, he did not convince me, he ***threaped*** me down. ***Threpian***, or ***drepian***, and ***thregan*** are the same in meaning, and both in A.S. mean to inveigh rather than reason.' *R. Winter Hamilton's Yorksh. Dial.*

THRUM. To purr as a cat; also Whitby Dial. Sw., ***drum***.

THUMP. Hard Suffolk cheese. See ***Bang***.

THURCKY. One of the now obsolete words gathered by Sir T. Browne, meaning (say Hickes and Ray), dark. *Forby.* '***Therke***, or dyrk, or myrke.' *Pr. Pv.* A.S., ***theorcung***, twilight.

Tharky, very dark, South. *Grose.* ***Tarky***, dark. *Halliwell.*

THURRUCK. The lower flooring of a boat's stern.

'***Thurrok*** of a schyppe, sentina,' *Pr. Pv.* L. Ger., ***dorck, durck***, sentina -*Kilian.* Sentina, Lat., is the bilge water at a ship's bottom, hence by metaphor the lower part of a ship's hold. Gr., ***thura***, door; A.S., ***thuruk***, through, also a gutter.

'And the same harme do somtime the smal dropes of water that enteren thurgh a litel crevis in the ***thurrok*** and in the botom of the ship'. *Chaucer's Persones Tale.*

'The men that were withen schip thei killed, save a boy that fled to on of the Flemysch schippes and hid him in the ***hurrok***.' *Capgrave.*

THWACK. To thump, lump, whack, or bang together. A ***thwacker***, a big piece. Isl., ***vakr***, full of fire, force, and movement; Prov. Dan., ***vakker***. Hence perhaps also the E. Ang., ***twack***, to change frequently.

'When he comes to describe the office of his imaginary doctor, ***thwacks*** fourteene scriptures into the margent, whereof not any one hath any just claim of inference to his purpose.' *Bp. Hall. An Apologie against Brownists.*

'If Jove speak English, in a thund'ring cloud,
"Thwick-thwack," and "riff-raff," roars he out aloud.' *Bp. Hall's Satires.*

'Which would be a ***thwacker*** as unspeakably big as that is little.' *Fairfax.*

'And now, though the coethy bird should be as much bent upon setting and starving, as it was before upon rising and eating; yet, as then the strength of the law overbound it to set still and hatch, so now the force of the same oversways it to flie away and eat; all this while she plotting no more (without wiser than we) than the shruff, moss, and hair, that the nest was ***thwackt*** together of.' *Fairfax.*

TICK. A gentle touch; to toy. 'Lovers like ***ticking*** and toying.' Ger., ***tick***. Mœs.-Goth., ***tekan***. N. Ang., ***tig***. U.S., ***tag***.

'***Tek*** or lytylle towche,' *Pr. Pv.*

'By slaundrous steppes and stayres of ***tickle*** talke.' *Gascoigne's Steele Glos.*

'Such ***ticking***, such toying, such smiling, such winking, and such manning them home when the sports are ended.' *Gosson's School of Abuse*, 1579.

TIDDIDOLL. A flaunting, over-dressed, affected, young girl.

TIDDLE. To cosset daintily, to tickle. A girl says 'I 'ont be ***tiddled*** by you nor no one.' Ger., ***tippeln***, to touch gently.

Tiddle, to pet, nurse by hand, Hereford; A.S., ***tidder***, tender; ***tyddrian***, to nourish, feed.

TIDDLIN. ***Tittlin***, topmost. 'Lawk! Kienda! dew look at that there bahd.' 'Kthere, on the ***tiddlin*** top, a' that tree.' *Moor.*

TIFFLE. To be very busy over little or nothing. Isl., ***tefia, tifa***. Old Fr., ***tiffer***. ***Tiffed out***, smartened up; O. Fr., ***attiffé***, decked, pranked, tricked out.

'***Tyfflynge*** or unprofytablle werkynge,' *Pr. Pv.*

Tifell, to entangle, mix knots together; standing corn trodden down is ***tifled***; N. Ang., ***taffle***, to perplex, throw in disorder, Cumb. and Devon; ***tifled***, sprained in the back, Craven, ***tifle***, to tire, Leeds. ***Tiffles***, light downy particles, Devon; ***taffling***, idle, trifling, said of servants, Northants. Sc., ***taffle***, to tire, wear out; ***tuffle***, to ruffle, disorder by frequent handling.

Tiffling, faddling, busy with trifles, Northants.

'I ***tyfell*** with my fingers, or busy myself longe aboute a thynge to make it well to the contentynge of my mynde.' *Palsgrave's Fr. Dict.*, 1530.

TIGHT-LOCK. Any coarse sedge used to bind sheaves.

TILD. To incline, to tilt up. Isl., ***tildra***; A.S., ***teáltian***.

Tilled, propped, set up, as a pole ***tilled up*** against a house, a horse ***tilled up*** too high on his legs, Hereford; ***tile***, to set a trap a-tilt, Dorset; to ***teel*** it, Devon.

TILL. The diluvial soil of the coast cliffs, the ***tilth***. A.S., ***tilth***.

That part of the soil loosened by the plough.

'***Tillin***, crops, produce; when the ***tillin***'s ripe; A.S., ***tilda, tylung***.' *Hartshorne's Salop.* Dut., ***teelt***.

TILLER. I. The handle of a shovel or spade; Dut., ***tillen***, to lift, heave. II. The handle of a ship's rudder. III. To throw out many stems from a root. A.S., ***tilia***, a begetter; ***telg***, a shoot, Fr., ***talle***. ***Till***, to urge, *Bp. Hall.* A.S., ***tilian***, to toil, endeavour.

TIPE. To tip up, fall headlong as if topheavy. ***Tippling***, haymaking, from the act of turning it over.

Isl., ***typpi***, summit; Su.-Goth., ***tipp***; L. Ger., ***tip***.

Tipe-trap, for rabbits, mice, &c., on the balance or tilt-up principle, Whitby. ***Tip***, to turn or raise on one side; hence ***tip*** (and ***tipple***) a draught of liquor, Somerset; to ***tip***, to capsize, Devon.

TIPS. Small faggots.

TITTER-CUM-TOTTER. Children see-saw on a plank, singing

> '***Titty-kum-tawtah***, the ducks in the water,
> ***Titty-kum-tahtah***, the geese follow aater.' *Suffolk saw.*

'***Totyr*** or myry ***totyr***, chylderys game,' *Pr. Pv.* See Way's Notes upon.

Tite, to tumble over. An East Ang. importation into Gower, Pembroke. ***Toit***, to tumble over, commonly said of whatever stands on one end; a child falling is said to ***toytle*** over, Cumb. ***Titter-totter***, on the balance, Craven; ***tawtah***, to totter, Suff.; ***täit***, to play at see-saw, Dorset; to ***teeter***, U.S. ***Tite***, to weigh, Somerset; ***tite***, a fall of water, Glouc. ***Baccoler***, to play at titter-totter, *Cotgr.* '***Tytter-totter***, a play for childre, balenchoeres,' *Palsg.*

Isl., ***titra***, to shake, quiver. Wel., ***tityr***, that makes a whirl or spin; Fl., ***touter***, to balance, swing, wag, swag, totter up and down.

TITTLE-MY-FANCY. Pansies. *Viola tricola, Lin.*

TOD. I. The head of a pollard, chump end of a tree; Wel., ***tob***, a summit; Fris., ***dodd***, a clump, lump, stock. II. A bunch or tuft. Hence a bundle of wool. Isl., ***todda***.

Hurdle tods, the upright stakes of wattled hurdles.

TOGETHER. In very common use, addressed to a number of persons, e.g., 'Well, how are ye all ***together***?'

TOLC. To tempt, coax. 'Good sauce ***tolcs*** down the meat.' In Suff., to ***tole*** away. A.S., ***tolcetung***, a tickling pleasant moving.

Toll on, to entice, to draw on, Craven; ***tole-box***, a cheap decoy article, Dorset; ***till***, to tempt on, Northants; ***tole***, to tice, U.S. '***Tollynge***, styrynge or mevynge to good or badde,' Pr. Pv. Su.-Goth., ***taelja***; Isl., ***taela***, to coax, decoy.

'With empty hand men may na haukes ***tull***.' *Chaucer's Norfolk Reve's Tale.*

'Sensualitie ***tollying*** and alluring him again.' *Udall, Marke, c. 9*, 1530.

'Here he was ***tolled*** to land at Moha by the treacherous Aga, and then had eight of his men treacherously slain.' *Fuller's Worthies, Chester.*

TOLERATE. Used by a strange perversion, remarks Forby, for to domineer, to tyrannize over.

TOM BLOWEN. A bloated herring, Suff. See ***Bloat.***

TOMMY. A small spade to excavate narrow drains; ***tom-tommy***, a double-breasted plough to clear out furrows.

Su.-Goth., ***töma***, to empty out, to drain; Isl., ***tomr***; Gr., ***tomé***, a cutting off or down.

TOM POKER. The great bugbear of naughty children, supposed to inhabit the dark closets, cocklofts, &c. From the Sui.-Goth., '***tomte-poeke***, the house ***puck***.' *Forby.*

TONGUES. Small soles, such as though incomparably the best, are like cringled carrots, unfit for the London market. *Moor.*

'In the western parts of India the sole is called the ***tongue*** fish. ***Jib è mutchy***, ***jib*** being the tongue, and the sail so called by us, is there the ***tongue*** sail.' *Moor.*

Sw., ***tunga***, a sole; Dan., ***tunge-fisk***; Dut., ***tong***.

TOPPINGS. The second skimmings of milk, cream being the first.

TOTE. To spy, pry. ***Toot***, to blow a horn, to whistle; Fl., ***toeten***.

'***Tote hylle***, or hey place of lokynge,' *Pr. Pv.*; A.S., ***totian***, to lift up, elevate. Su.-Goth., ***titta***, to spy. ***Teet***, a stolen glance, Sc.

> 'A myrrour of glasse, that I may ***toote*** therein.' *Skelton.*
>
> 'Nor ***toot*** in Cheapside baskets earne and late.' *Hall's Satires, Book IV, 2.*

TOTTY-HEADED. Reeling, dizzy from drink, &c.

Fl., ***touter***, to shake, shog, totter, reel, stagger, waver.

'My hed is ***tottie*** of my swink to-night.' *Chaucer's Norfolk Reve's Tale.*

TOSHY. Muddy, sticky; ***tash***, Craven, to bespatter. Fr., ***taché***, fouled, muddied; Dut., ***taai***, sticky, clammy.

TOW. Necessary tools or apparatus for aught. A.S., ***tawa***, tools, fishing tackle. Dan., ***toi***.

TOWERS, or **TAWERS.** The superintendents of the processes of curing herrings.

A term derived apparently from the ***tanning*** processes, steeping, hanging, &c., which herrings undergo. A.S., ***tawere***. Dut., ***touwer***.

TOWT or **TOUGHT**. To set fast, disorder, as skeins of thread, &c. 'This skein is ***toughted***.' A.S., ***tawain***, to pull; Dut., ***tuyt***, a tress; plaited lock; L. Ger., ***tuyte***, a rabblement of threads.

TOZE. To tease, pull or draw out wool. 'To ***touze*** and ***mouze***,' to pull about roughly. In other Eng. dial. to ***touze***. See ***mosy***.

'***Tosare*** of wulle or other lyke,' *Pr. Pv.*

A.S., ***tæsan, teosu***; Dut., ***teezen***; Ger., ***zausen***; It., ***tozzare***.

'Prophets there were before, who did beat upon him, and ***tozed*** him with rebukes and terrors.' *D. Rogers' Naaman.*

'Grosse sins which are as iron moles, and will hardly be worne out of the flesh, being bred in the bone, save by ***tozing*** and searching the heart thoroughly.' *D. Rogers' Naaman.*

'Starts, tosses, tumbles, strikes, turns, *touses*, spurns, and sprawls.' *Drayton.*

TRADE. Line of conduct, course of action, practice, habit. 'If this is to be your ***trade***.' ***Trad***, Scot., course of travelling or sailing.

Prov. Ger., ***trade***, rut, track; Su.-Goth., ***træda***, to proceed, advance; Lat., ***tractare***.

TRAFFING-DISH. A bowl for straining milk. It., ***straforo***, perforated work; ***trafila***, a tool full of holes.

TRAMMEL. I. A fowling net. A fishing net for trawling. II. A chimney iron to hang pots upon. Prov. Ger., ***tramel***, a lever, cross-bar.

'***Tramayle***, grete nette for fyschynge,' *Pr. Pv.* Fr., ***trameau***, a kind of drag net or draw net for fish, also a trammell net for fowle. *Cotgrave.* It., ***trama***, a weaver's woof. Walloon, ***tramaie***, basket work. From ***tri*** and ***macula***, mesh.

'Poets talk of enticing Syrens in the sea, that on a sunny day lay forth their golden ***trammels***, their ivory necks, and their silver breasts, to entice men; sing sweetly, glance piercingly, play on lutes ravishingly.' *Nash's Christ's Tears.*

> 'Nay, Cupid, pitch thy ***trammel*** where thou please,
> Thou canst not fail to take such fish as these.' *Quarles' Emblems.*

TRAPE. To trail. A young man courting a young woman is said 'to ***trape*** his wing at her.' A metaphor borrowed from the habits of the turkey cock. In other Eng. dial. to ***trapse***.

Ger., ***traben***, to trot; Fl., ***trap***, a step, stride; Isl., ***trappa***; L. Ger., ***trap-wüs***, by degrees, gradually; Sc., to ***traik*** after; Su.-Goth., ***traka***.

TRATTLES. The dung pellets of hares, rabbits, sheep; Craven, ***tridlins***; Sussex, ***trestles***. Other dial., ***tirdles***. '***Tyrdyl***, schepys donge.' *Pr. Pv.*

TRAUL. To trail along. Hence ***trawl***-net. L. Ger., ***treylen***, to tow with a rope; ***treyl***, a tow line.

> 'He that can winke at any foule abuse,
> As longe as gaines come ***trauling*** in therwith.' *Gascoigne's Steele Glos.*

TRAUNT. To traffic in an itinerant manner like a pedlar.

'Men who carry fish from the sea-coast to sell in the inland countries.' *Phillip's World of Words*, 1658.

'And had some ***traunting*** chapman to his sire,
That trafficked both by water and by fire.' *Hall's Satires, B. IV.*

Traunt, the L. Ger., ***trouwant***, a camp follower, satellite, prætorian soldier, and by metaphor a vagabond, parasite, buffoon, deceiver, cheat, idler; Ger., ***trabant***, halberdier, life-guardsman, (Ger., ***traben***, to trot,) Fr., ***truant***. *Kilian.*

Truand, Fr., a common beggar, vagabond, rogue, a lazie rascall, an upright man; also a knave, scowndrell, varlet, filthie and lewd fellow; ***truande***, a filthie beggarlie queane, a doxie or mort; ***truander***, to beg or cant, to play the rogue, to carrie himself most basely, scurvily, to oppress, wrong, abuse; ***truandise***, beggary, roguery, knavery, cousening, villanie; ***truandaille***, a crue of rascallie beggars, a rabble of lewd rogues. *Cotgrave.*

This very curious word would thus seem to reflect primarily the hatred borne by oppressed and plundered continental nations to the thieving marauding soldiery and camp-followers of the middle ages, specially the ***laggers***. Somewhat later in England, happily less familiar with these scourges, the word got transferred and applied with ***fogger*** (which see), ***huckster***, and other opprobrious epithets, to itinerant traders. A collection of the uncomplimentary epithets in various languages, bestowed on this latter class, would open up an hitherto unnoticed chapter in social history, illustrating the rise of prejudices existing in the present day in their almost original intensity.

Ducange's Med.-Lat. Gloss. has several articles under ***Trutanus*** and its cognates, with quotations from many mediæval writers. Some derive from the Lat., ***trado***, some the Keltic ***truan***, wretched, pitiful, others from the O. Fr., ***treu***, toll, taxes, tribute; tax-gatherers (***reuants***) and sinners, continuing to rank together in public esteem. The sense generally applied to ***trutanus*** is that of abandoned and profligate vagrancy, mendicancy and buffooning. An ordinance, A.D. 1340, cites among the most indigent objects of alms ***Trutani et baraterii***. It is noticeable that this word has no meanings akin to any of the above in the copious ed. of *Florio's Old Ital. Dict.*, by Torriano, 1688. From the O. Fr. ***treu*** the ***Trouveres*** of Romance poetry have been traced by some; hence, more probably, may descend the two following:-

'*Qui fit Normand, it fit* ***truand***,' he that a Normand made, a beggar made (for the Normands have been more fleeced and harried than any people subject to the crown of France). *Cotgr.*

Tranterie, an O. Eng. term for money arising from alehouse fines.

TRAVVIS. A smith's shoeing shed. Old Fr., ***travail***, the frame whereinto farmers put unruly horses to shoe them. *Cotgr.*

'***Trawe*** of a smythe, ypodromus,' *Pr. Pv.* Portg., ***trave***, stocks, fetters.

Horses harnessed ready for work are said to be 'in the ***trave***.' '***Traves***, shackles for a horse that is taught to amble or pace.' *Phillips' World of Words.*

TRICKLE, TRITTLE. To bowl. '***Trickle*** me an orange across the table.' Gr., ***trokos***, *Forby.* ***Trickle*** bed, a truckle bed.

Wel., ***treiglaw***, to roll, revolve, circulate; Su.-Goth., ***trilla***, to roll, trundle; Isl., ***tritla***. To ***trinkle round one***, to seek to influence unfairly.

TRICULATE. To adorn, as masons with finishing touches. *Forby.* Used also in gardening, says Miss Gurney, who thinks it a confusion of ***trig up*** and

decorate. To ***trick up***.

Treklen, trekkelen, Dut., has the sense of to ornament with flourishes, &c.

TRIG. To trot gently, or trip, as a child after its nurse.

TRIP. New milk cheese, to be eaten fresh, whilst soft and curdy, as it soon becomes dry, tough, and uneatable. Suffolk.

'A Goddes kichel, or a ***trippe*** of cheese.' *Chaucer's Sempnoure's Tale.*

Several of Chaucer's editors, ignorant of its dialectic significance, render ***trip*** a small piece.

It differs from cream cheeses, as having no cream in, and being thicker.

Flet is another species of Suffolk cheese, made from ***fletted*** or skimmed milk. L. Ger., ***vloten*** (also Holl., Fland., Fris., and Zealand), to skim the cream; ***vlote-melch***, skim milk. ***Wonmil*** is a Suffolk cheese made from *one milking*, and ***Trip*** may derive from the ***strippings***, a Suff. term for the last milk drawn from a cow, and esteemed richer than the first.

TRIP-SKIN. I. Leather worn on the right side of spinners with the rock or distaff, to receive the friction. II. The skinny part of roast meat, which soon becomes tough and dry.

It., ***trippa***; Wel., ***tripa***, a cow's stomach; Ger., ***strippe***, Dan., ***stribe***, a strap; L. Ger., ***stroopen***, to skin, flay.

TROLLY. A market cart. 'Sich roads! we got rarely jounced i' th' trolly.' *Moor.* Wel., ***troell***.

TRUCK. Rubbish, refuse. A field or bank foul with speargrass or weeds is said to be 'full o' ***truck***.' 'Nawn but a bargain o' ***truck***,' applied to a lot of rubbish. *Moor.* ***Truck***, U.S., applied to vegetable stuff.

Ger., ***trug***, deceit, deception; It., ***truccare***; Fr., ***troquer***, to barter, swop, chop, swab, scoorse, *Cotgr.*; or from Ger., ***triegen***, to draw, as goods to market.

TRULLIBUBS. A butcher's term for entrails. 'Tripe and ***trullibubs***'; Suff., N. Ang., ***trolly-bags***; Ger., ***trollen***, to roll, coil round.

TRUNCH-MADE. Short and thick, squab. Dan., ***trunte***, a stub, log. Fr., ***tronché***.

TRY. To purify, melt down by fire, as the suet of hogs.

Specially applied on the E. coast to boiling down whale's blubber; Ger., ***thran***, blubber, train oil; ***thranen***, to distil, drop; Su.-Goth., ***trä***, to waste away; Isl., ***tran***, humorem qui lacrimarum instar guttatim defluit. *Anderssen's Iceland*, quoted by *Ihre*, who objects to its current der. in Skinner, copied by later Eng. lexicographers from Fr., ***trainer***; Lat. ***trahere***, to drag.

Try, a corn sieve; used in some Eng. dialects. An illustration from *Sir T. Elyot's, the Governor*, is given in *Richardson's Dict.*

'They will not pass through the holes of the sieve, ruddle, or ***try***, if they be narrow.' *Holland's Plutarch, p. 26.*

TULY. Poorly. '***Tuly***-stomached.' 'A well naaba, how de yeow fare?' 'Wa' naaba, but ***tuly***.'

A.S., ***twilie***, doubtful, uncertain, anxious; Fris., ***dwaale***; Dan., ***dwale***, mawkish, torpid, sleepy; Moes.-Goth., ***dwala***, dull, foolish. *Schilter's Thesaur. Ant. Teut.* has ***artuaalen***, torpere; the Niebel. Lied. has ***twalm***, a trance.

Twaly, vexed, ill-tempered, Salop; Wel., ***dywalu***, to be enraged; Dut., ***dul***;

twily, restless, wearisome, Somerset; ***tewly***, small and weakly, Dorset. ***Tewly***, qualmish, in delicate health, Essex and Camb. ***Twall***, a whim, Suff.

Tuly appears to imply that languid, doubtful, fluctuating state of health in which there appears no convalescence. Su.-Goth., ***dwala***, a passive state between life and death; ***dwœljas***, morari, cunctari. 'Magnæ Britanniæ nonnulli incolæ ***dwaule*** appellant mentis illam alienationem sub qua ægrotantes deliria proferunt.' *Ihre's Su.-Goth. Lex.*, 1769. '***Dwale***, herbe, morella sompnifera.' *Pr. Pv.* The term is applied by Chaucer and other early writers to the deadly nightshade, *Atropa belladonna*, for its sleeping properties.

A cat. A domestic cat is in the Welsh, ***cath deulu***.

TRUNKING. Lobster and crab catching with conical wicker cages or pots, baited inside, and sunk with lines and weights in the sea.

'***Trunke*** for kepynge of fysche, gurgustium.' *Pr. Pv.* In the *Cath. Ang.*, a N. Ang. Eng. Lat. Lex., 1483, it is ***nassa*** (a wicker basket with narrow neck for catching fish.)

Su.-Goth., ***drunkna***, to submerge; Ger., ***trenken***.

TUNMERE. The line of procession in parochial perambulations. A.S., ***tun***, a town, territory; ***mæra***, boundaries.

TUSSOCKS. Rusty knots of coarse sedgy grass, thick tufts of rank growth in corn. Wel., ***tuswawg***, a tuft.

O. Eng., ***thussock***, a tuft of loose hair, or of any sort. See *Nares*.

TUTSON. The periwinkle flower. *Hypericum androsæmum, Lin.*

In old works ***tutsayne***; Fr., ***toute-sainé***, all wholesome. Some derive from ***tutti santi***, all saints. Rather from its Greek bot. name, *androsæmum*, man's blood, from the claret colour juice of its ripe capsule, thus ***tout sang***, or more probably ***toute saignée***, every bleeding, from its being used, says Duchesne, to stop haemorrhages. *Prior's Pop. Names Brit. Plants.*

TUTTER. Trouble, fuss. 'What a ***tutter*** he makes of it.' Dut., and L. Ger., ***tuyten***, to blow a horn, make a noise, rustling or disturbance.

TUZZY-MUZZY. Rough, dishevelled, ***touzed and mouzed***. See ***toze***.

TWINNY. To rob a cask before it is broached.

Su.-Goth., ***twina***; Isl., ***dwina***; A.S., ***dwinan***, to melt gradually, lessen, dissolve, and dwindle away; Prov. Dan., ***dvine***, a dripping, trickling, leavings or dregs from a cask's bottom. A.S., ***cwanian***, to pine away.

TWITTLE. To prate, ***twittle-twattle, twit-com-twat***, idle gossiping talk. Su.-Goth., ***qwittra***, to chirrup, chatter like a bird. Fl., ***quetteren***; Isl., ***kwittr***; Wel., ***chwitian***.

'First he's subjected to all the pukings, longings, and peevish importunities that a breeding woman gives those about her till she's laid, and then comes the squalling of the child, and the ***twittle-twattle*** gossipings of the nurse and midwife, that must be well treated too, well lodg'd and well paid.' *L'Estrange's Quevedo.*

TWITTY. Cross, snappish, reproachful. A.S., ***ætwitan***, to reproach.

Twit, a fit of hasty ill humour, snappishness, Northants; ***tutty***, sullen, Beds. ***Tuttle***, an awkward ill-tempered fellow, Lanc. Wel., ***cwithawl***, perverse, untoward.

TWIZZLE. To turn in quick rotations. A sheep in the staggers is said 'ta fare dunt an ta ***twizzled*** about stamminly.'

TYE. An extensive common pasture, a word used in central Suffolk and North Essex.

'No researches have hitherto ascertained the derivation of the word' says Forby. Isl., ***teigr***; Su.-Goth., ***teg***, a piece of general public land; Dan., ***tye***, to resort to, have recourse to; Sax., ***teag***, a common.

U

UNDER-DECK. The low broad tub into which wort runs from the mash tub. O.H.G., ***dekjan***; Dut., ***dekken***, to cover, spread out.

UNEATHILY. Unwieldy, hard to put in motion. A.S., ***uneathelic***.

UNFRAW. To thaw, or to ***unfriz***, as a native would say. See ***frawn***.

UNSENSED. Stunned, stupified; also insane.

UNSTOWLY. Unruly, applied to children. Dirty, disorderly. ***Stow***, to confine, as cattle in a pound or yard. Isl. and Fris., ***sto***, a fixed place.

UPPEN. Mention, reveal, disclose. A.S., ***yppan***, to disclose, betray.

UPRIGHT. On his own means. 'A live ***upright*** on 'a's forten.' More ***right upper***, less inclined

UPSTARING. Presuming.

UTIC. The Whinchat, from its note.

V

VAUNCE-ROOF. The garret. Possibly from Fr., ***vanner***, to ventilate. Or ***avancer***, to put forth.

VERGYN. An ancient package of herring.

'Itm pd for a ***virgyn*** of haringe, iijs.' *L'Estrange's Household Accounts*, 1547. In 1549, 200 white herrings are charged in the same account the same amount. In 1547, 2 barrels of white herring are charged at 12s. 8d. per barrl.

Isl., ***verja***, covering, wrapping; ***vergögn***, fishing tackle.

VESSEL, FASSEL. Half a quarter of a sheet of writing paper. A term used in the Bury and other E. Ang. schools. See ***frawl***.

The most probable derivation of this school-boy phrase seems to be that supplied by Lemon, 'Lat., ***fasciculus***, or ***fasciola***; quasi, ***vassiola***, a ***vessel*** or small slip of paper.'

It appears to be a Med.-Lat. corruption. *Ducange's Gloss. ed Adelung* has '***Fesseltus, fasciculus, faissellus***, in alia.' The Arabic however has ***fasl***, a section, article, chapter, or other division of a book.

VICE. A winding stair; the central shaft or stay of a tower stair.

'***Vyce***, rownde grece or steyer, coclea.' *Pr. Pv.* ***Vyce***, a towrnying stayre; ***Vis***, *Palsg.* The ***vyce*** dore of the steeple is mentioned in churchwardens' accounts at Walden, Essex. In Gage's Suffolk, pp. 141-2, among payments for building Little Saxham Hall, 1506, occur disbursements for a ***vice*** of freestone and another of brick, the last called in the context a 'staier.' *Way's Notes to Pr. Pv.*

O. Fr., ***vis, viz***, the spindle of a press; a winding staire. *Cotgr. & Roquefort.*

VIRGIN MARY THISTLE. The *Carduus Marianus*, or blessed thistle.

Tusser includes it in his March abstract of herbs and roots for salads and sauce.

VOIDER. A clothes basket. 'A wooden flasket for linnen cloaths.' *Bp. Kennett.* O. Fr., ***vuyder***, to hollow out.

'Item pd for a payer of ***voyder*** yt my Mr. gaffe ye seid Sir John, xd.' *L'Estrange Household Accounts.*

W

WAD. The edge of grass, hay, or stubble left higher than other parts in mowing a field, between each mower's work. A mark set to guide in ploughing.

'In the Su.-Goth. lang., ***wad, wada***, denotes the given direction of two stakings carried in a straight line, so that each owner might mow his crop of hay. In the same way marshlands admitting of no other demarcation were divided.' *Ihre.* Ger., ***schwad***, a row of mowed corn.

WADMAL. Coarse thick woollen, a great coat of ***duffle***.

'***Woadmel*** is a hairy, coarse stuff, made of Iceland wool, brought thence by our seamen to Norfolk and Suffolk.' *Ray's Eastern Words.* Isl., ***vadmal***. Dan., ***vadmel,*** coarse frieze. Ihre, in his *Su.-Goth. Lex.*, has a long article upon ***wadmal*** cloth, deriving its name from ***wæd***, worth, price, and ***mæla***, to measure; it forming a common standard of value in early times when scarcity of coin necessitated barter.

WAHTS. Any edible greens, as cabbage sprouts, turnip tops, &c. 'What are ye got for dinner?' 'Pork an ***wahts***.' Cor. of ***wort***. A.S., ***wurt***.

WALLIS. The withers of a horse. Wel., ***gwäell ysgwyz***, the shoulder blade. In Teesdale, ***warrish***; Cumb., ***warridge***; Dut., ***gewrichten***; Ger., ***widderist***.

WALLOP. I. To hurry along with violent unwieldy effort. II. To wrap up in clumsy hasty fashion; cor. of ***envelop***. In Heref., to ***wrobble***. Sc., ***wrabil***; L. Ger., ***wurbelen***.

I. Su.-Goth., ***walla***, said de motu inconstante quailis est vagantium et erronum. *Ihre.* L. Ger., ***walop***, to gallop. *Kilian's Appendix.*

WALTER. To cause extreme fatigue and exhaustion. 'I'm right-on ***waltered*** out by my long journey.' A.S., ***wealtian***, to reel, stagger; ***walted***, said of grass or corn beat down by wind, or trampled. Said also of one rolled in the mire. A ship ***walts*** (is cranky, Eng. and U.S.) when her ballast does not suffice to bear her sails to keep her stiff. *Bailey.* ***Walt***, to throw down. A sheep on its back is ***rig-welted***. Leeds.

'***Waltrynge***, or ***welwynge***, ***walowynge***,' *Pr. Pv.* 'O.F., ***voultrant***, ***walterynge*** as a shyppe dothe at the anker, or one yt tourneth from syde to syde.' *Palsg.* ***Welter***, to reel or stagger, N. Ang. Isl., ***valter***; Sw., ***weltra***, to overturn; L. Ger., ***walian***; hence '***weltering*** in blood.' Chest., ***walt***; Lanc., ***wawt***, to upset a carriage. Sc., ***tolter***, to reel; Su.-Goth., ***tulta***.

> 'And some I make in a rope to totter and ***walter***.' *Skelton.*
> 'Whose ***waltring*** tongues did lick their hissing mouths.' *Surrey's Virgil.*
> 'From bottom depth doth ***weltre*** up the seas.' *Id.*

WALTHAM'S CALF. As wise as, that went nine miles to suck a bull! A very old local saw.

> 'As wise as ***Waltom's Calfe***.' *Skelton's Colin Clout.*

'And thinke me as wise as ***Waltam's Calfe***.' *Heywood's Dialogue on Proverbes in the Eng. Language,* 1546.

'As wise as ***Waltham's Calf,*** that ran nine miles to suck a bull.' *Ray's Proverbs.*

'As wise as ***Walton's Calf,*** – is fayne to return home more foole than he come.' *Arthur Hall's Works,* 1579.

'He that shall do it, is himself more akin to ***Waltham's Calf,*** that was to suck part of that Bull's milk that had none at all.' *Fairfax.*

'A fine fetch for a devil this, is it not? cry'd Lucifer. But hell is no more the hell it was when I knew it first than chalk is cheese, and the devils now-a-days are so damnd'ly insipid and dry, they're hardly worth the roasting. A senseless puppy to come back to me with a story of ***Waltham's Calf,*** that went nine miles to suck a bull.' *L'Estrange's Quevedo.*

WAMBLE, WOBBLE. I. To reel, totter along from side to side. To move fast with effort and agitation, as the gallop of a cow or cart-horse. Somerset, to ***wammell***; the L. Ger., ***wummelen***. A cow chewing a turnip awkwardly, is said 'to ***wobble*** or ***wamble*** it about in 'ar mouth.' II. To retch, to feel queasy, to vomit.

I. Isl., ***rambla***; L. Ger., ***wommelen***; Sw., ***wämia*** and ***quabbel***; Fris., ***vamler*** and ***wommelik***; Ger., ***wabbeln*** and ***schwabbeln***; A.S., ***wapelian,*** with senses of to be qualmish, to wabble, shake, waddle.

II. '***Wamelynge*** of the stomake, nausea,' *Pr. Pv.* 'Allecter, to ***wamble*** as a queasie stomacke doth.' *Cotgr.* Su.-Goth., ***wämb,*** the belly; ***wæmjas***; Isl., ***vemuleg,*** inclined to vomit.

'Instead of comfits and sugar to strew him with, take well in worth a farthingworth of flour to whiten him over and ***wamble*** him in.' *Nashe's Lenten Stuff.*

'The sixt is self-slothe, when the soule hath a ***wambling*** and fulsome aime at the promise.' *D. Rogers' Naaman.*

'Upon taking a soup of the same liquor, their stomachs ***wambled,*** and up came the water, frogs and all.' *L'Estrange's Æsop's Fables.*

WANCKLE, WANKY. Weak, pliant; ***winky-wanky***. A.S., ***wancol.*** Isl., ***vanki; wankelly,*** N. Ang.; Su.-Goth., ***wanka***; O.H.G., ***wankel***. Fries. and Dut., ***wankel.***

'As ***wanckle*** as water.' ***Wankle*** weather, changeable, Whitby. ***Wangle,*** Salop and Chesh.; ***wankling,*** weakly, Heref. and Northants.

WANGHER. Large, handsome, strapping, said of a girl especially.

Isl., ***vænnleikr,*** of pretty appearance, beautiful; Su.-Goth., ***wœn***; Wel., ***gwen.*** (Bret., ***gwener,*** Venus.) The Dan. has ***svangher,*** big with child. ***Wanghe,*** Old Sicamb, the calf of the leg; L. Ger. ***wanghe,*** a buffet on the cheek or ears, which is its meaning in Leicestershire; a blow, Somerset.

WANG-TOOTH. A molar tooth or grinder, the jaw or eye-tooth.

A.S., ***wang,*** a jaw-bone, the cheek; Su.-Goth., ***wang***; Isl., ***vangi***; It., ***guancia.*** 'Wange-toothe, molaris.' *Pr. Pv.*

> 'Our manciple I hope he wol be ded,
> Swa werkes ay the ***wanges*** in his hed.' *Chaucer's Norfolk Reve's Tale.*

WANT. A mole. A.S., ***wand,*** a mole; ***wande-weorp,*** a casting up, a mole-hill; ***moldiwarps*** in some dialects; in Wessex ***wont-heaves*** and ***wont-***

hills; Salop, ***wont.***

WANTS TO. Ought to, should do; e.g., 'That little dish ***wants to*** go down into the dairy.'

WANTY. A large girth or surcingle for a packhorse. L. Ger., ***want***, a fillet, binding; Sc., ***wanton***, a girth.

'A pannel and ***wanty***, pack-saddle and ped.' *Tusser.*

WANZE. To waste, pine, wither away. A.S., ***wansian***, to lessen.

'***Wansynge***, ***wasyng***,... decrescencia.' *Pr. Pv.*

'Thenk on Job that was so ryche. He wax pore fro day to day.
His bestys dyeden in yche dyche. His katelle ***wanshed*** alle away.' *Lydgate.*

'So to hold them there, as a naile fastened in a sure place from ***wanzing*** and leaking out.' *D. Rogers' Naaman.*

'Many bewrayed themselves to be time servers and ***wanzed*** away to nothing as fast as ever they seemed to come forward.' *Id.*

'As it was said of Ottoman's horse, that where he had once set his feet, grasse would no more grow after; so where the devotions of these hypocrites takes place, religion and the power of godliness ***wanze*** and perish.' *Id.*

'When the Lord separates the pretious from the vile and shewes them the vanity and ***wanzingnesse*** of their own principle.' *Id.*

WAP. To wrap. Su.-Goth., ***wipa***, involvere. *Forby.*

'Lappyn, whappynge in clothys... happynge, or hyllynge.' *Pr. Pv.* The L. Ger. has ***happen***, to lay hold of, catch up.

Sw., ***vepa***, any kind of cloth for lapping about a thing; Su.-Goth., ***svepa***; Isl., ***rafa***, to wrap up.

WAP, WHAP, WHOP. To beat, thrash. Wel., ***wab***, a slap; ***wabiaw***, to cuff; Su.-Goth., ***wipa***, to beat.

'At this all the company fell in a great laughing, and Sir James was amazed that a woman should so ***wap*** him in a whinyard.' *Merie Tales of Skelton.*

WAPES. Low spirits, nervous, yawning moods; ***wape***, pale, Essex.

The A.S. has ***wepan***, to mourn; the Su.-Goth., ***wäp***, dull, stupid.

WAPPER-JAWS. A wry mouth. L. Ger. and Fl., ***wapperen***, to mumble, waggle about; A.S., ***wapean***, to waver; ***wapper-eyed***, sore-eyed, Devon. ***Wapper***, to flutter, Somerset. ***Wappered***, fatigued, restless, Glouc.

WAPS, WAPSY. A wasp. A.S., ***wæps***.

WARBLE, WARBLET. A hard swelling in cattle hides, produced by the larvæ of the ox-gad fly, which, deposited under the animal's skin, create a protuberance. ***War-beetles***, large maggots bred in the backs of cattle. A.S., ***wear***, Ger., ***weer***, a knot, a knob; in Dorset, a ***wornäil***.

Wards, hardness of skin on hands or feet.

'***Warbote***, wyrme, boa,' *Pr. Pv.* Bibo (bubo) exbane or ***warbodylle***. *Lat. Eng. Vocab. Roy, MS.* ***Warbot***, a worme, escarbot, *Palsg. – Way's Notes to Pr. Pv.*

WARP. Four herrings make a warp. *East and South Coast Fisherman's Tale.* A.S., ***a-worpan***, to throw out.

Der. apparently from the mode of reckoning, the fisherman throwing out two in each hand at every count.

'Paid x*s* for bryngyng of vj ***warpe*** of stockfyshe and vj ***warpe*** of lytill codde callyd habburdyn, iiijd.' *L'Estrange, Household Accounts*, 1522.

'On those imbeached shelves stamped his footing where cods and dog-fish swam not a ***warp*** of weeks fore running.' *Nashe's Lenten Stuff.*

WARPING. Said of a hen laying eggs. Dan., ***værpe***.

WASH. A narrow path through a wood. O.H.G., ***waso***; Ger., ***wasen***, turf.

WASH-BOUGHS. Lower straggling branches and undergrowth of trees. L. Ger., ***wassen***, excrescere; Ger., ***wase***, a bundle of brushwood.

WASH-DISH. The titmouse, a term the East Anglian settlers in Gower, Pembroke, *temp.* Hen. I. carried with them; ***dish-washer***, the wagtail, Dorset and Devon.

'Nay, shall we not be as wise as the unreasonable creatures, the Storke, the Crane, the Turtle, the Swallow, the little ***Wash-dish***?' *Rogers' Lost Sheep.*

WASK. A paviour's rammer; ***wasking***, a beating.

Possibly a corruption from the Dan., ***bask***, to beat, thump; or from the Wel. roots ***gwasg*** and ***gwast***. More probably the Wel. ***pastynew***, to beat with a long staff.

WASTE, WASTER. To bang or cudgel. '***Waster*** and buckler,' an Old Eng. name for cudgel play. Wel., ***pastwyn***, a cudgel; Bret., ***baz;*** Fr., ***baston***; Fl., ***bussato***, cudgelled. ***Buckler*** is also a Keltic word; the Wel. and Corn., ***bwccled***; Ir., ***buicleir***.

Waster, Sc., a trident for striking salmon; Isl., ***vas***, cum impetu ferri. *Jamieson.*

WATER-DOGS. Small, dark, rounded clouds indicating rain.

WATER-SLAIN. Said of weak tea; in Suff., of wet undrained land.

WATER-WHELPS. Dumplings boiled sad, or kneaded without yeast or eggs.

WAVER. A pond, Suff. Dut., ***vyver***.

Lat., ***vivarium***; '***wayowre***, stondynge water,' *Pr. Pv.*; ***wayre***, where water is holde, *Palsg.*

WEAR, KNUR. A knot or protuberance in a tree.

'***Warre*** or knobbe of a tre,' *Pr. Pv.*; *Neu.*, ***warre*** or knobbe, *Palsg.*; ***Noueux***, full of knurres, knottie, knobbie, *Cotgr.* A.S., ***wear***; L. Ger., ***weeren***.

WEATHER-HEAD. The secondary rainbow; above the primary.

Weather-gall; N. Ang., indicating wet weather; Ger., ***wasser-galle***; Wilts., ***water-gall***; ***weather-go***, the end of a rainbow as seen in the morning in showery weather, Cumb.; Wel., ***gwawl***, a reflected light.

WEAVERS' BEEF, of Colchester, – Sprats.

'These are ***sprats***, caught hereabouts and brought hither in incredible abundance, whereon the poor weavers (numerous in this city) make much of their repast, cutting rands, rumps, surloyns, chines, and all joynts of beef out of them, as lasting in season well nigh a quarter of a year. They are the Minums of the sea, and their cheapness is the worst thing (well considered, the best), which can be said of them. Were they as dear, they would be as toothsome (being altogether as wholesome) as Anchovies, for then the price would give a high gust unto them in the judgment of pallat men.' *Fuller's Worthies, Essex.*

WEAZEL-LING. The lamprey, *Gadus mustela, Lin.*

'*Mustela Marina*, called by some a ***weasel ling***, which, salted and dried, becomes a good Lenten dish.' *Sir T. Browne.*

WEEVILS (A.S., ***wifel***; Fris., ***wefel***). A common name for coleopterous insects of genus *curculia*, Lin.

Their larvæ are very destructive in granaries, 'Breeding in Norf. and Suff. they are called ***bowdes***.' *Ray*. (which see, ante.) '***Wevyl***, or malte boode.' *Pr. Pv.*

WELK. I. To give a sound drubbing to. II. To mark with wheals, contusions. I. Ger., ***walken***, act of fulling, milling, hence fig. to cudgel, beat one soundly. II. A.S., ***swelca***, a wheal, pock.

'Her ***wealked*** face with woful tears besprent.' *Sacville's Induction, p. 257.*

WELK, WELT. I. To soak, roll and macerate in a fluid. Fries. and Dut., ***weeken***, to soak; A.S., ***wealwian***, to roll, wallow. II. To expose to sun and air to dry, as seeds, hay, onions, &c. Ger., ***welken***; Dut., ***verwelken***; and from the same A.S. root in its further sense of to dry, ripen.

Welk, to dry, to wither up, N. Ang.; ***welted***, shrivelled, scorched, Northants.; shrunk, wasted, Sc.; to become pale, to fade; A.S., ***wealwian; wilted***, Bucks. and U.S.; ***wilt-down***, to look sheepish, an Americanism.

'***Welkyn***, or seryn,' *Pr. Pv.*

WELT. A border edge or narrow strip of a garment turned over to strengthen the hem stitched. Su.-Goth., ***wœlta***; Isl., ***vellta***.

'I may not dully overpass the gallant beauty of their haven, which having but as it were a ***welt*** of land.' *Nash's Lenten Stuff.*

'*Urtica marina*, * * * often found cast up by shore in great numbers, about the bigness of a button, clear and ***welted***.' *Sir T. Browne.*

WEM. A small fretted place in a garment. A.S., ***wem***, a spot, stain. '***Wemme*** or spotte,' *Pr. Pv.*

'This scuffling or bo-peep in the dark, they had awhile without ***weam*** or brack.' *Nashe's Lenten Stuff.*

WENNEL. A calf just ***weaned***.

'Young colts with thy ***wennels*** together go serve.' *Tusser.*

WENT. The mesh of a net.

Fl., ***want***, filets de pêcheur; Dut., ***want***, rigging, fishing-nets, a mitten; It., ***gant***; Sc., ***wand***, wicker work; Fris., ***wende***; O. Ger., ***unentan***; Moes.-Goth., ***wandjan***, vertere, mutari, revertere, from the act of net braiding.

WESSEL. A vessel, very common. 'Mowthe of a ***wesselle***,' *Pr. Pv.*

WESTY. Dizzy, giddy; O. Ger., ***welzen***, to reel, or the A.S., ***wesan***, to soak, sodden.

'Whiles he lies wallowing with a ***westie*** head,
And palish carcase on his brothel bed.' *Bp. Hall's Satires, b. iv.*

WET ONE'S WHISTLE. To drink. ***Wet the sickle***, drink given as earnest money in engaging reapers at harvest.

'So was hire joly ***whistle wel ywette***.' *Chaucer's Norfolk Reve's Tale.*

WHANG, a thick piece of aught eatable; Wel., ***gwang***, a gorging, glutting; Su.-Goth., ***swanger***, hungry. **WHANG,** a leather thong; to flog with one.

A.S., ***thwang***. A ***whanging*** fellow, a stout lusty body, N. Ang.

WHART-WHARTLE. To tease, irritate, wear out the patience, var. of ***thwart***; ***wartle***, to wrangle, Northants.

Su.-Goth., ***twar***; O. Ger., ***dwerhi***; Fl., ***dwars***, athwart, crooked, cross.

WHEATSEL BIRD. The cock chaffinch. From their congregating in flocks about harvest time.

WHEEL-SPUR. The raised horse path which in ancient roads ran between the two wheel tracks; Ger., ***spur***, a track; A.S., ***spor***. '***Whele spore,*** orbita.' *Pr. Pv.*

WHELM. I. Half a hollow tree placed hollow downwards to form a small watercourse. II. To turn a tub or other vessel upside down to cover anything; L. Ger., ***wemmelen***; circumversare, obversare; Su.-Goth., ***hwimla***. The A.S. has ***helan***, to cover.

Whemmel or ***whammel***, to turn upside down, to tumble over, N. Ang.; ***whummelled***, upset, as a vessel of liquid, Teesdale. '***Wammelan*** like an eel,' Cumb.

Whemmle, to totter and then upset. 'It ***whemmled*** ower.' It is said Sir Walter Scott was so struck with the expressiveness of the term, as used by a labourer, that he presented him with half a crown. Whitby Dialect, 1855.

'***Whelmyn***, a vessel, suppino.' *Pr. Pv.*

WHEWT. To whistle, to squeak as a young bird. ***Whew***, a whistle, N. Ang.; a low whine, Leeds.

WHID, E. Ang., is a quarrel, contention. Isl., ***hvidra***, to attack smartly; Sc., ***whither***, to belabour. Sc., ***witter***, to fight; Fl., ***veter***.

Whitter, Sc., any thing of weak growth is a ***whiter***, Sc. ***Twitter***, slender, is used in the same sense. ***Whitter***, loquacity, prattle, Roxb. A garrulous woman is a perfect ***whiter-whatter***. A struggling poor man is a ***witterin*** body.

WHIFF. Flavourless food. 'Neither ***whiff*** nor ***whaff***,' unmeaning chat. N. Ang., ***waffish***; '***wiffe***, taste,' *Palsg.*; ***weft***, a musty taste, Northants.; Wel., ***chwaeth***, taste; ***chwyth***, a puff, blast, breath; Su.-Goth., ***wefta***; A.S., ***wiffend***.

'I can not awaye with this ale, it hath a ***weffe***, elle est de mauluays goust.' *Palsgr.*

WHIFFLER. One who heads a procession to clear the way.

Whifflers are employed by the Norwich corporation when marching from the Guildhall to church on the Guild-day. Active men, armed like harlequins, with lath or latten swords, which they keep in continued motion ***whiffling*** the air, or bestowing a slap on the shoulders or posteriors of intrusive boys. Anciently they blew horns to clear the way. A.S., ***wæfflere***; Dut., ***weifilen***; Isl., ***vifla***; Wel., ***chwfw***; ***waffle***, to wave, fluctuate, N. Ang.; ***whiffle***, Craven; ***waffler***, an unsteady person not to be depended on, Cumb.; '***wyfle***, wepene, bipennis,' *Pr. Pv.*; to shift, as the wind, Northants.; ***wiffle-waffle***, idle talk, Lanc.; L. Ger., ***weffel***, the mark of a stripe. See also a note in *Nares*.

'***Whiffler***, a meer trifler, a pitiful poor or inconsiderable wretch. ***Whiffler*** is also taken for a piper that plays on a fife in a company of foot-soldiers. Also a young freeman that goes before and waits upon the society or company to which he belongs, on some public solemnity.' *Phillips' World of Words.*

'Item vj ***wifles***.' *Inventory of Sir J. Fastolfe's Armour.* Probably swords of wood for practice, remarks Amyot. He adds, in Elizabeth's time those who taught the soldiers their exercise were called ***wyfflers***.

WHILE. Used for until. A Lincolnshire shibboleth.

WHINNOCK. To sniver, whimper as a child; intensive of ***whine***.

Su.-Goth., ***wenga***; Sw., ***hwina***; Ir., ***cuinim***; Dut., ***winuk***; ***whinge***, to whine, cry, Teesdale.

WHIP-BELLY-VENGEANCE. Poor sour beer, or similar tipple.

WHIP-THE-CAT. I. Said of extreme parsimony, grudging even scraps and shreds to the cat. II. In Suff., applied to the custom of the village tailor going from house to house to work.

In Cumb. the latter is also called 'whipping the cat.'

'Twice a year the tailor came to the house and fabricated the semi-annual stock of clothes for the male members, this being called ***whipping the cat***.' *Goodrich's (Peter Parley) Reminiscences of early New Eng. Customs.*

Su.-Goth., ***wippa***, motitare se, sursum deorsum celeriter ferri, ***wippa-kring***, circumcursitare. *Ihre.* Dut., ***wippen***, to skip about, leap over. Su.-Goth., ***kate***, house, dwelling.

Whip-the-cat, said of a whist-player who wins all the tricks in one deal, Northampts.

WHITTERY. Pale and sickly. Applied to puny children.

Witter, fretful and plaining. 'Tha'll ***witter*** theesen to death!' Leeds Dial. ***Whitter***, to murmur, pine; ***whittering***, tedious; ***whittery***, fretful, Northants. A.S., ***wite***, affliction, torment; ***witan***, to twit, complain; ***wither***, opposed to, contradictory.

WHITTLE. To peel the bark off sticks; to cut away in small slices a stick with a knife. A.S., ***hwitel***, a knife; ***hwitta***, a sharpener.

One of the most famous of modern Americanisms.

Whet, white, to cut with a knife;'***whiting*** sticks'; ***whittle-te-whet***, to sharpen, set an edge on; ***whittle***, a clasp-knife, N. Ang.; Sc., ***thewittel, thewtill***; A.S., ***thwitan***; Sax., ***hwettan***. ***Whittle***, to haggle in cutting, Cumb.; to shave or plane wood with a knife,Whitby. In Salop, to ***swite***, to ***thwite***; ***whittle***, to wear by friction, to chafe, Northants. To whittle sticks, to 'cut off the bark with a knife to make them white.' *Ray's E. Ang. Words.*

'***Telwynge, Thwytynge***, or ***whytynge***. Scissulatus,' *Pr. Pv.* '***Thwyting*** is properly the cutting of little chippes from a stick.' *Carew's Cornwall.*

'I ***thwyte*** a stycke, or I cutt lytell peces from a thynge.' *Palsgr., Fr.-Eng. Dict.*, 1530. ***Whittle***, Sc., applied to the harvest book. L. Ger., ***wette***, edge of a knife.

'The knot, a very dull ***whittle*** may cut asunder.' *Bp. Hall.*

Whittled is also in the U.S., tipsy, drunk, answering to our modern 'cut.'

In this sense ***whittled*** is a very old English slang term, of which we give an East Ang. illustration. See *Nares* for a number of others.

'Skelton did fille all the cuppes in the house and ***whitled*** the frere, that at the last the frere was in myne eames peason.' *Merie Tales of Skelton.*

WHOA, WOOH, WOOE, WO THEN. Stay, stop, the immemorial cry of the waggoner to his team; Wel., ***wo***.

'There's no ***wo*** in him,' and 'he knows no ***wo***,' common expressions for a good workman.

WHOLE-FOOTED. Very intimate, closely confederate.

WHOP, WHAP. A heavy blow; Wel., ***wab***, a slap; ***wabio***, to cuff.

WHYBIBBLE. A whimsy, idle fancy, silly scruple. See ***squibobble***.

WIDDLES. Very young ducks. Young chickens are called ***biddies***.

Widdle, Sc., wriggling, bustling motion; Ger., ***wedeln***, to wag the tail.

WILCH. The wicker strainer set upright in the mash tub to prevent the grains from running off, with the wort. L. Ger., ***weyche***, macerare in aquâ, insuccare liquore. *Kilian*. In Suff. the sediment or lees of beer, wine, &c.

Wel., ***gwaellawd***, dregs, sediment.

WILLOCK. A guillemot, or any sea-bird of the Awk or Diver kind.

Willick, a young heron, Lothians. Also the Puffin or *Alca Arctica*.

WIND-HOVER. The kestrel. *Tinnunculus alaudarius*. From its ***hovering*** movements in quest of mice and other prey.

Stand-gale and crutch-tail are similarly applied to the kite.

'And as a sillie kight (not falcon like that flie,
Nor yet presume to ***hover*** by Mount Hellicon on hie).' *Gascoigne*.

WINGE. To shrivel as fruit overkept. Fris., ***dwinje***; Isl., ***dvina***.

WINNOL-FAR. The great horse-fair now held at Downham Market, and originally granted to St. Winwaloe's Priory, Wereham.

WINNOL WEATHER. The stormy weather common at the beginning of March, the third of which is the anniversary of St. ***Winwaloe***, a British Saint.

'First comes David, Then comes Chad,
Then comes ***Winnol***, Blowing like mad.'

WIPS AND STRAES. Odds and ends, heads and straws of corn; Dan., '***wipper og straae***.'

One of the provincialisms of the Danish island of Zealand.

WISHLY, WISLY. Eagerly, earnestly, wistfully. 'The children eyed the plum pudding ***wishly***.'

'Sike lay the manciple on a maladie
Men wenden ***wisly*** that he should die.' *Chaucer's Norfolk Reve's Tale*.

'This miller hath so ***wisly*** bibbed ale,
That as an hors he snorteth in his slepe.' *Id.*

Dut., ***wis***, certain, sure; L.Ger., ***wislich***.

WONG. An agricultural division or district of some uninclosed parishes. Spelman says of arable rather than pasture land. A.S., ***wong***. A very common name for a field, Northants.

'Wonge of londe.' *Pr. Pv.* Dan., ***vœnger***; Su.-Goth., ***wang***.

WONMIL CHEESE. Made of one meal or milking. See ***bang***.

WOOD-SPRITE. The woodpecker.

WOOSH. The teamster's call to his horses to go to the left. Fr. ***gauche.***

WORK. To ache, to throb; violent head ache. A.S., ***wærc***, pain.

Wark, N. Ang.; ***warch***, Chesh. and Lanc., in common use.

'***Werkynge*** or heed akyn, ***werkyn*** and akyn as a soore lymme.' *Pr. Pv.*

'For those Yrish men are ever good to the Church;
Whan kynges dysobeye yt, than they begynne to ***worch***.' *Bp. Bale*.

WORRELL. The round cap or ferrule of a stick, umbrella, &c. Sc. ***virle***, a small ring put round a body to keep it firm.

Old Eng., ***vyroll***; Fr., ***virolle***; Somerset, ***worral***. ***Vardle***, a common eye or thimble of a gate with a spike only. *Marshall's Rural Economy of Norfolk.*

'***Vyrolfe*** of a knife, spirula,' *Pr. Pv.*; O. Fr., ***virole***, an iron ring put about the end of a staff to strengthen it and keep it from riving; ***vironner***, to veere, wind about; ***virer***, to whirle about. *Cotgr.* See ***vyce***, ante.

WOULDER. To wrap or roll up in a bandage. Ger., ***welteren***.

WOULDERS. Bandages. 'Teent quite well, I'm forced to keep the ***woulders*** on.' '***Wolynge***, (***woldynge***) or stronge byyndynge, provolucio.' *Pr. Pv.*

'***Woulding*** (a sea-term), the winding ropes hard round a yard or mast of a ship after it has been fish'd or strengthened, to make it hold better.' *Phillips's World of Words.* Dut., ***woelen***, to wind about with a cord; Prov. Ger., ***wuhling***.

WRASTLE. To dry or parch. ***Wrastling-pole***, see ***arseling*** and ***ressling***. Wel., ***crasu***, to dry, roast; ***craslyd,*** parched.

WRAWL. To wrangle. '***Wraw***, froward, on-goodly, perversus,... exasperans,' *Pr. Pv.*

O. Eng., ***wrayle***, chatter, abuse. Dut., ***rallen***. Sw., ***ralla***.

'Though ***wrauling*** and rocking be noisome so near.' *Tusser.*

'With brawling fools that ***wraul*** for every wrong.' *Id.*

WRET. A wart. '***Wrette***, or ***werte*** yn, a mannys skynne,' *Pr. Pv.*; L. Ger., ***wratte***.

Wret-weed or wart-weed, sun spurge, *Euphorbia helioscopia.*

WRIGGLER. A term applied to the quick-writhing ***launce***, or sand eel.

WRONGS. The larger boughs of timber trees, the crooked branches.

Wrong, crooked; a ***wrong*** man or woman, Norf., *Grose.* Applied in shipbuilding to the crooked timbers, as distinguished from the body or upright timbers; ***wranglands***, misgrowing trees that will never produce timber. *Bailey.* '***Wronge*** in foorme of werke, curvus.' *Pr. Pv.* Su.-Goth., ***wränga***, to distort.

WRY. To cover close; '***wrie*** him warm.' A.S., ***wrigan***, to clothe; ***wrying***, bed clothes, covering.

'But those which touch their souls, especially to kill their lusts, they care not how narrow they frame them, even as the bed and covering of which Esay speakes, that is so narrow that it will not ***wry*** them warme.' *D. Rogers' Naaman.*

WUNT. To sit as a hen. A.S., ***wunian***, to abide.

WURROW. To burrow, as holes of crabs, &c.

The Ger., ***wehre*** corresponds with the A.S., ***beorgh***, a burrow.

Y

YAFFLE. To snatch or take illicitly, as a poacher's dog a hare; Wel., ***gavael***, to grasp, lay hold of.

Yaffling, eating. *Grose's Cant Words.*

YAG. To irritate by ill-natured remarks or acts, to persist in teasing and provoking. Two female servants who look favourably on the same lad 'are ollost ***yagging*** one another.' *Spurdens.*

Su.-Goth., ***jaga***, to follow after, pursue vehemently; hence applied to the chase. *Ihre.*

YALE. A small quantity. Fr., ***gale***, a measure.

YANGLE. To tether a horse by fastening a fore and hind leg.

Ger., ***hangen***; Prov. Ger., ***hangelen***, to fasten, attach to, or the Su.-Goth., and Isl., ***hank***, a chain, fetter. See under ***hingin***.

YANK. To squeal, as a child in pain. Dut., ***janken***.

'The wild gander leads his flock through the cool night;
Ya-honk, he says, and sounds it down to me like an invitation.'
Walt Whitman.

YANT. A gaiter. Fr., ***guante***; Su.-Goth., ***wante***; Isl., ***vante***; Dut., ***want***, mittens, gloves.

YARD. The garden belonging to a cottage or ordinary messuage. A.S., ***yrd***, Wel., ***gardd***, a little garden. Sc., ***garth***.

YARMOUTH CAPON. A red herring. In Scotland, a Glasgow magistrate.

YARMOUTH MITTENS. Bruised or chapped hands.

YARWHELP. *Scolopax Œgocephala, Lin.* The black-tailed Godwit.

'A ***yarwhelp***, so thought to be named from its note.' *Sir T. Browne.*

Common about Breydon, near Yarmouth, says *Morris, Brit. Birds, v. 4.* He adds, its note has been compared to the syllables, *grutto, grutto, grutto.*

YARY. Brisk. A.S., ***gearo***; Su.-Goth., ***yr***, vivacious.

YAUP, YARM, YAWM, YAWL, YAMMER. To shriek or yell. Isl., ***gola***; A.S., ***geomerian***; Ger., ***jammer***; Su.-Goth., ***jama***.

YELK, YULK. Clay kneaded with straw and stubble for wattle and dab, in Norf. In Suff., to level and ram down a clay floor or foundations.

A.S., ***hulc***, a den, cabin, cottage.

YELM. To lay straw in quantities and regular order to be used by a thatcher. The portion so laid down ready for the thatcher, or as much as can be conveniently carried under the arm for that purpose. A.S., ***haelm***, stubble; O. Fr. ***chaulme***; Isl., ***halmr***.

Also A.S., ***gylm***, a handful of reaped corn, a bundle, bottle of straw.

'And in his own chambre (the miller) hem made a bedde,
With shetes and with ***chalons*** faire yspredde.' *Chaucer's Norfolk Reve's Tale.*

YERK, JERK. To beat, switch soundly, a smart stroke. Isl., ***hreckia***; Su.-Goth., ***yereken***.

'That with his whyp his mares was wonte to ***yarke***.' *Skelton.*

'So a body having bequeathed it one degree of start or ***yerk***, in one now of time, and hitching thereupon one atome of room, may upon taking in ten or twenty degrees of the same, in the next, sturt to many atoms in length.' *Fairfax.*

YFE. The yew tree, Suff. 'V tree (***uv*** tre) taxus,' *Pr. Pv.* Fr., ***if.***

Wel., ***ywydd*** (th); Gael., ***iuthar***; Corn., ***hivin***; A.S., ***iv***; Sp., ***iva***; Ger., ***eibe***; O.H.G., ***iwa***.

YIP. To chirp like a new hatched chicken or young bird. In Exmoor Dial, to ***yeppy***.

'Yppyn as bryddys, pululo.' *Pr. Pv.*

YIPPER. Brisk, uppish. Su.-Goth., ***yppig***, superbus, vanus, ***ypper***; Isl., ***yppare***, distinguished, surpassing.

YOFERS, or **SPURSHERS**. Straight fir poles for scaffolding, &c.; Gael., ***giubhas*** (***bh*** pron. in Gaelic ***v***), ***giuthas***, fir trees.

Spurshers may der. from ***spar***; Su.-Goth., ***sparre*** and ***spärra***, a beam, prop; the root, O.G., ***sparjan***, to fasten. Possibly the term applies to scaffold poles used in ***spurging*** (which see), or plastering. L. Ger., ***spurgil***; Fr., ***espurger***.

YOLK. The dirty greasy state of wool after shearing and before it is washed.

The grease of wool, Northampt.; ***yokey***, tawney, ***yoky-wool***, unwashed, Devon. Wel., ***golc***, a washing, lye, urine; ***golci***, to cleanse, washed; ***in olchi***, unwashed.

YOPPEN. Barking, yelping. N. Ang., ***yauping***; Isl., ***yapa***; Fr., ***japer***; L. Ger., ***galpen***. Northants., ***yowking***.

Wappet, a yelping cur, E. Ang. '***Wappyn***, or baffyn, as howndys... do whan they folow here pray or that they wolde harme to.' *Pr. Pv.*

YULK. See ***Julk***.

Bibliography

Items in square brackets have not been traced

Ainsworth, Robert, *Thesaurus linguae Latinae Compendiarius*, 1736, ed. Morell, 1808.

Anderson, Robert, *Ballads in the Cumberland Dialect*, 1840.

Aphelen, Hans von, *French-Danish Lexicon*, 1814.

Ash, John, *The New and Complete Dictionary of the English Language*, 1775.

Bailey, Nathan, *An Universal Etymological English Dictionary*, 1721, 1735.

Bailey, Nathan, *Dictionarium Britannicum: or a more compleat Etymological English Dictionary*, 1730.

[Bailey, —, *Dict. of Cant Words*, 1776]

Baker, Anne. E., *Glossary of Northamptonshire Words and Phrases,* 1854.

Baldwin, William, see *Mirour for Magistrates.*

Bale, John, *The Actes of the Englysh Votaryes*, 1546-50.

Bale, John, *Kynge Johan: a Play*, c.1550 (Camden Soc. 1838).

Bale, John, *The Apology of J.B. agaynste a ranke papyst*, 1550.

Bamford, Samuel, *The Dialect of South Lancashire, or Tim Bobbin's Tummus and Meary, with his rhymes, with glossary*, 1854.

Barclay, Alexander, *Certayne Eclogues*, 1515 (1570).

Barlement, Noel van, *The English, Latine, French, Dutch schol-master...*, 1637 [*French school-master*, 1636].

Barnes, William, *A Grammar and Glossary of the Dorset Dialect*, 1863.

Bartlett, John R., *Dictionary of Americanisms*, 1848, 1859, 1860.

Batchelor, Thomas, *Orthoepical Analysis of the English Language*, 1809, [Beds. Dial.]

Bloomfield, Robert, *Works*, 1824.

Blount, Thomas, *Glossographia, or a dictionary interpreting such hard words...as are now used*, 1656.

Blundevil, Thomas, *The fower chiefyst offices belonging to horsemanshippe...* (1558), 1565-6.

Bosworth, Joseph, *An Anglo-Saxon Dictionary*, 1838.

Bosworth, Joseph, *A compendious dictionary of Anglo-Saxon*, 1848 etc.

Brockett, John T., *A glossary of North Country words*, 1825, 1829, 1846.

Brome, Richard, *English Moor*, c.1652.

Browne, Sir Thomas, *Works*, ed. Wilkin, S., 1835-6.

Browne, William, *Britannia's pastorals*, 1613.

Browne, William, *The Shepheard's Pipe*, 1614.

Brunne, Robert Manning of, *Langtoft's Chronicle* 1338, 1728, 1810.

Brunne, Robert Manning of, *Handlyng Synne*, 1303 (Roxburgh Club, 1862).

Burrill, Alexander, *A new law dictionary and glossary*, 1850.

Bury Wills (Camden Soc. 49, 1850-1).

Capgrave, John, *The Chronicle of England* 1460 (Rolls series 1858).

Carew, Richard, *The survey of Cornwall*, 1602.
Carr, William, *The dialect of Craven, in the West Riding of the County of York*, 1824.
Caxton, William, *The mirrour of the World*, 1481.
Clarke, C., *A glossary of provincial words used in the county of Essex*, 1851.
Coleridge, Herbert, *Glossarial Index to the printed English literature of the Thirteenth Century*, 1859.
Coleridge, Herbert, *A Dictionary of the first or oldest words in the English language from the semi-Saxon period of A.D. 1250 to 1300*, 1862. [Dict. of Old English Words].
Coleridge, H., [Dict. of Old Norse].
Coles, Elisha, *A dictionary English-Latin, and Latin-English*, 1677.
Cooper, William D., *A glossary of the provincialisms in use in the county of Sussex*, 1836 (1853).
Cotgrave, Randle, *A dictionarie of the French and English Tongues*, 1611; see Sherwood.
Creech, Thomas, *Miscellany Poems*, 1684 [Virgil].
Cullum, Sir John. *The history and antiquities of Hawstead and Hardwick in the County of Suffolk*, 1784 (1813).
Davies, J, 'Dialect of Lancashire' in *Philological Society's Transactions* 1855.
De Roche, —, *Neder Duytsch-Friesic Woordenboek*, 1835.
Dickinson, William, *A Glossary of words and phrases pertaining to the dialect of Cumberland* (E.D.S. 1878).
Diez, Friedrich Christian, *Grammatik der Romanische Sprachen*, 1838-42.
Discourse concerning the drayning of fennes and surrounded grounds...1629.
Drayton, Michael, *The barrons warres in the raigne of Edward the second*, 1603 (1619).
Drayton, Michael, *Poly-olbion, or a choragraphicall description of...Great Britain*, 1612, 1622.
Du Cange, Charles Dufresne, Sieur, *Glossarium mediae et infimae Latinitatis*, 1840-50.
Elwyn, Alfred L., *Glossary of supposed Americanisms* , 1859.
Elyot, Sir Thomas, *The Dictionary of Syr T. Eliot, knyght*, 1538, 1545 (Latin-English). Revised by Thomas Cooper in *Bibliotheca Eliotae*, 1550, 1552, 1559.
Evan, D. Silvan, *English-Welsh Dictionary*, 1852.
Fairfax, Nathaniel, *A Treatise of the Bulk and Selvedge of the World...*, 1674.
Ferrall, James Stephen, Repp, Thorleifr Gudmanson, and Rosing, Svend, *Danish and English Dictionary*, 1863.
Fletcher, Giles, *Christs victorie and triumph in heaven, and earth, over, and after death*, 1610.
Fletcher, Phineas, *The purple island, or the Isle of Man, together with piscatorie eclogs and other poeticall miscellanies*, 1633.
Flint, Timothy, *A condensed geography and history of the western states, or the Mississippi valley*, 1828.

Florio, John *A worlde of wordes, a most copious and exact dictionarie in Italian and English*, 1598. See also Torriano.
Foley, Daniel, *An English-Irish Dictionary*, 1855.
Flugel, Johann Gottfried, *Vollständiges Englisch-Deutsches und Deutsch-Englisches*, 1830, 1853.
Foxe, John, *Actes and monuments of these latter and perilous dayes*, 1563 etc.
Fraunce, Abraham, *The Countesse of Pembrokes Yuychurch, conteining the affectionate life and unfortunate death of Phillis and Amyntas...*, 1591.
French Schoolmaster, 1636, see Barlement, Noel van.
Forby, Robert, *The Vocabulary of East Anglia*, 1830, 1858.
Fuller, Thomas, *A Pisgah-sight of Palestine*, 1650.
Fuller, Thomas, *The history of the Worthies of England*, 1662.
Gage, John, *The history and antiquities of Suffolk, Thingoe Hundred*, 1838.
Garnet, Richard, *Philological Essays*, 1859.
Gascoigne, George, *The fruites of warre*, *c.*1572 (1831).
Gascoigne, George, *The steele glas, a satyre*, 1576.
Gaskell, William, *'Two Lectures on the Lancashire Dialect'*, 1844.
Gerard, John, *The herbal, or general historie of plants*, 1597, 1633.
Gifford, George, *A dialogue concerning witches and witchcrafts*, 1603 (Percy Society, 1842).
Gifford, William, *Works of Ben Jonson*, 1816.
Goodrich, Samuel Griswold, (Peter Parley), *Reminiscences of early New English Customs.*
Gosson, Stephen, *The schoole of abuse, containing a pleasant invective against poets, pipers, plaiers, iesters and such like caterpillers of a commonwelth*, 1579.
Gouldman, Francis, *A copious dictionary in three parts*, 1664.
Greene, Robert, *A Quip for and upstart courtier*, 1592.
Greene, Robert, *A disputation betweene a Hee Conny-catcher and a Shee Conny-catcher*, 1592;
edition of 1617 called *Theeves falling out, true men come by their goods.*
Greene, Robert, *Pandosto the triumph of time (The hystorie of Dorastus and Fawnia)*, 1588, (1607, 1843).
Greene, Robert, 'Radagon in Dianam' in *Works of Robert Greene*, ed. Alex. Dyce, 1831.
Greene, Robert, see Rich, Barnabe.
Grieb Adler, Georg J., *Dictionary of the German and English Languages*, 1861, 1864.
Grimoalde, Nicholas, 'Death of Cicero' in *Songs and Sonettes*, 1557.
Grimm, Jacob and Wilhelm, *Deutsches Wörterbuch*, 1858-64.
Grose, Francis, *A classical dictionary of the vulgar tongue*, 1785, 1796, 1823.
Grose, Francis, *A provincial glossary, with a collection of local proverbs etc.*, 1787. [Grose's Specimen of Suffolk Dialect]. See Pegge, S.
Gurney, Anna, 'Provincial words of Norfolk' in *Philological Society's Transactions*, 1855.

Gurney, D. ed. *Household and privy purse accounts of the Le Stranges of Hunstanton from A.D. 1519 to A.D. 1578*, (*Archaeologia* xxv, 1834).
Hacket, John, *Scrinia Reserata: a memorial offered to the great deservings of John Williams, D.D.*, 1693.
Hall, Joseph, 'Elegy on Dr. Whitaker' in collection of elegies on death of Dr. Whitaker, 1596.
Hall, Joseph, *Virgidemiarum, sixe bookes: first three bookes of toothless satyrs, 1597; the three last bookes, of byting satyres*, 1598.
Hall, Joseph, *A common apologie of the Church of England against the unjust challenges of the...Brownists*, 1610.
Hall, Joseph, *Contemplations upon the principal passages of the holie storie*, 1612-26.
Hall, Joseph, *Paraphrase of Hard Texts from Genesis to Revelation*, 1633.
Hall, Joseph, *Works*, ed. P. Wynter, 1863 [Of the Vainglorious].
Halliwell, James, *A dictionary of archaic and provincial words...from the fourteenth century*, 1847. See Topsell, Edward.
Hamilton, Richard Winter, 'Yorkshire Dialect' in *Nugae Literariae*, 1841.
Hartshorne, Charles H., *Salopia Antiqua...with a glossary of words used in the county of Salop*, 1841.
Harvey, Gabriel, *Foure Letters and certaine sonnets, especially touching R. Greene*, 1592.
Harvey, Gabriel, *Pierce's Supererogation, or a new prayse of the old asse*, 1593.
Harvey, Richard, see Nashe.
Hawes, Stephen, *The pastime of pleasure*, 1509, 1554 (Percy Soc. 1845).
Hayward, John, *A dialogue conteinyng the nomber in effect of all the prouerbs in the Englishe tongue*, 1546.
Heywood, Thomas, *A marriage triumphe*, 1613 (Percy Soc. 1842).
Higgens, John, translator, *The nomenclator, or remembrancer of Adrianus Junius*, 1585, and see *Mirour for Magistrates*.
Hingeston, F.C., glossary to Capgrave's *The Chronicle of England 1460*, (Rolls ser.1858)
Holland, Philemon, *Plutarch's Philosophie, commonlie called, the Morals*, 1603 (1657).
Hollyband, Claudius, *A dictionarie French and English*, 1593.
Holme, Randle, *The Academy of Armory, or a storehouse of Armoury and Blazon...*, 1688, 1701.
Howell, James, *Epistolae Ho-Elianae: familiar letters domestic and forren*, 1645; *a new volume of letters*, 1647 etc.
Ihre, Johan, *Glossarium Suio-Gothicum*, 1769.
Jamieson, John, *An etymological dictionary of the Scottish language*, 1808, 1825.
Jennings, James, *Observations on some of the dialects in the west of England, particularly Somersetshire*, 1825.
Johnson, Samuel, *A dictionary of the English Language*, 1755, 1773, 1818, 1866 etc.
Jonsson, Erik, *Old Nordisk Ordbog*, 1863.

Kelham, Robert, *A dictionary of the Norman or old French language*, 1779.
Kersey, John, *Dictionarium Anglo-Brittannicum or a general English dictionary*, 1708.
Kilian, —, *Etymologicum Teutonicae Linguae*, 1777.
Latham, Robert, *The English Language*, 1841.
Leeds, see Smith, John Russell.
Le Gonidec, Jean François Marie, *Dictionnaire Celto-Breton ou Breton Français*, 1821.
Leo, —, *Anglo-Saxon Nomenclature*, 1852.
L'Estrange Accounts see Gurney, D.
L'Estrange, Roger, *The vision of Don Francisco de Quevado Villegas...*, 1667.
L'Estrange, Roger, *Twenty select Colloquies of Erasmus Roterdamus...*, 1680.
L'Estrange, Roger, *The Fables of Æsop and other eminent mythologists, with moral reflections*, 1692.
Lewis, George Cornewall, *A glossary of provincial words used in Herefordshire and some of the adjoining counties*, 1839.
Linton, W.J., *The Lake Country*, 1864. [Linton, *Lake Scenery*].
Lydgate, John, *Of a mariage betwixt an olde man and a yonge wife*, before 1451.
Lydgate, John, 'Troy Book' written 1412-20, printed 1513; as *The auncient history and onely trewe and sincere Cronicles of the Warres betwixt the GreciansandTrojans...*1555.
[Lydgate, John, 'Prioress and her Lovers'].
Lyly, John, *Euphues, the anatomy of wit*, 1579.
Lyly, John, *Pappe with a hatchet*, 1589 [Nashe's Pap with a Hatchet].
Macleod, John, (ed.) *Dictionary of the Gaelic Language*, 1828.
Macleod, John, (ed.) *Gaelic Dictionary*, 1845.
Marshall, William, *The Rural Economy of Norfolk*, 1787.
Michel, Francisque, *Etudes de Philogie comparée sur L'Argot*, 1856.
Minsheu, Josef, *Çãåìùõ åβò ôÜò ãëþóóáò id est Ductor in lingua The Guide into Tongues etc*, 1617.
Mirrour for Magistrates, The, 1587, originally *A myrroure for magistrates*, ed. William Baldwin, 1559, 1563; the 1587 edition combined *The firste parte of the mirour*, ed. John Higgens, 1574, and *The laste parte of the mirrour*, ed. William Baldwin, 1571.
Molbech, Christian, *Danske Dialect Lexicon*, 1841.
Moor, Edward, *Suffolk words and phrases*, 1825.
More, Henry, *An antidote against Atheisme*, 1653.
Morris, Francis Orpen, *A History of British birds*, 1851-7.
Morriss, see *Pricke of Conscience.*
Nares, Robert, *A glossary; or, a collection of words, phrases...in English authors...*, 1822; new edition, 1859, 1888.
Nashe, Thomas, *Almond for a parrat or Cuthbert Curry-knaues Almes*, 1589.
Nashe, Thomas, *Pierce Penilesse his supplication to the divell*, 1592.
Nashe, Thomas, *Christ's Teares over Ierusalem*, 1593.